International Arbitration: Law and Practice

International Arbitration: Law and Practice

Zander Fleming

NY RESEARCH PRESS
New York

Published by NY Research Press
118-35 Queens Blvd., Suite 400,
Forest Hills, NY 11375, USA
www.nyresearchpress.com

International Arbitration: Law and Practice
Zander Fleming

International Standard Book Number: 978-1-64725-397-4 (Hardback)

Cataloging-in-Publication Data

International arbitration : law and practice / Zander Fleming.
p. cm.
Includes bibliographical references and index.
ISBN 978-1-64725-397-4
1. Arbitration (International law). 2. Arbitration and award. 3. Conflict of laws--Arbitration and award. 4. International commercial arbitration. I. Fleming, Zander.

KZ6115 .I58 2023
341.522--dc23

Contents

Preface

Every book is initially just a concept; it takes months of research and hard work to give it the final shape in which the readers receive it. In its early stages, this book also went through rigorous reviewing. The notable contributions made by experts from across the globe were first molded into patterned chapters and then arranged in a sensibly sequential manner to bring out the best results.

Arbitration refers to a method of resolving disputes in which both the parties engaged in the dispute agree to have their disputes resolved by one or more private individuals known as arbitrators, rather than by a court of law. International arbitration refers to the arbitration between individuals or companies belonging to different countries. For dispute resolution through arbitration, the agreement of the parties is essential. The consent of parties is obtained by including an arbitration clause in the agreement or contract. The parties can avoid going through local court procedures by using international arbitration. It follows different rules than domestic arbitration and has its own non-country specific standards of ethical conduct. This book presents the laws and practices associated with international arbitration in the most comprehensible and easy to understand language. It is appropriate for students seeking detailed information in this area as well as for experts.

It has been my immense pleasure to be a part of this project and to contribute my years of learning in such a meaningful form. I would like to take this opportunity to thank all the people who have been associated with the completion of this book at any step.

Zander Fleming

1

International Arbitration: An Introduction

§ 1 International Arbitration and its Limitations

International arbitration is truly a sphere of its own. Unlike in state court litigation, in arbitration the parties have almost unlimited discretion to tailor the proceedings to their needs–for example, to appoint the arbitrators, choose a neutral seat of arbitration, agree on procedural rules and determine the applicable substantive law.[1] Not only do the arbitral proceedings remain strictly confidential, but most often, the arbitral award can be challenged only on very limited grounds.[2] Besides, in order to facilitate the arbitral proceedings, the parties can choose from among numerous arbitration institutions seated all over the world. It is therefore unsurprising that, especially in the field of cross-border disputes, international arbitration remains the preferred dispute settlement mechanism.[3]

In light of these advantages, one could easily conclude that there is no reason *not* to choose arbitration as *the* alternative to state court litigation. However, since arbitration is mostly a purely private matter between the parties, the arbitral tribunal's power does not extend beyond this private realm. This issue becomes especially evident with regard to the taking of evidence. While the arbitral tribunal may request the parties to produce evidence, this does not apply to third parties outside the respective arbitration.[4] In such a scenario, assistance from state courts is essential. However, numerous procedural questions arise from this course of action, as illustrated by the following example.[5]

A French company commences an ICC arbitration seated in Geneva against its trading partner company located in the US. Most likely, the crucial evidence will be located not at the seat of the arbitral tribunal in Geneva, but rather in France, the US or elsewhere in the world. If the evidence in question

1 BORN, *Law and Practice*, ch. 1.03 n. 26; LEW, 490 et seqq.

2 SUTTON et al., n. 1-023 et seqq.

3 Queen Mary Survey (2018), 5; BLACKABY et al., n. 1.01; WAINCYMER, *Evidence*, 3.

4 DONDE, 269; DUPEYRON, 464; SCHAEFER, 529 et seq.

5 *See also* the example given by DONDE, 270.

is in the possession of third parties, the arbitral tribunal cannot force them to produce such evidence and court assistance becomes necessary. But which state court will render such assistance: the Swiss court in Geneva or the court where the evidence is located? Who is authorised to make a request for assistance and according to which law will the assistance be rendered? In what ways can the arbitral tribunal and the parties to the arbitration influence this procedure and how can third parties defend themselves?

§ 2 Importance of Court Assistance in Taking Evidence

These questions are indeed justified. After all, the purpose of arbitration is to submit a dispute to a non-governmental decision maker; thus, the court assistance that is the topic of this book could be variously described as either helpful aid or unwelcome intervention.[6] Ultimately, the issue at hand is positioned at the intersection between state courts and international arbitral tribunals; or, to put it in the words of ANDREWS[7]:

> "The marriage between courts and arbitration is at times tempestuous ..., at other times harmonious. But the relationship is always interesting. The marriage has not broken down: too many depend on its success."

This book will provide the reader with helpful insights concerning court assistance in the taking of evidence and its effect on efficient arbitral proceedings. However, court assistance in general, and in taking evidence in particular, has received little attention in the past. Although the possibility to seek state court assistance in the taking of evidence is foreseen in many arbitration rules, the UNCITRAL ML and various *leges arbitri*, the process has generally been considered too time consuming, burdensome and costly.[8] However, two important exceptions suggest that this is about to change.

First, since the US Supreme Court's *Intel* decision in 2004, a broad discourse has emerged around the availability of US discovery in aid of arbitral proceedings. To this day, US case law and legal doctrine remain inconsistent regarding this question, and as the latest decisions show, the discussion

6 *See* p. 91 et seqq. *infra*.

7 ANDREWS, n. 1.14.

8 DUPEYRON, 459; DASSER, *Schiedsgerichte*, 120; SCHAEFER, 522; Born, *Law and Practice*, ch. 9.02 n. 24; KNEISEL/LECKING, 153; *see also* Arts. 3 (9) and 4 (9) IBA Rules; Art. 27 UNCITRAL ML; Art. 184 (2) PILA CH; § 1050 CCP FR; S. 43 and 44 EAA 1996.

appears to be ongoing.[9] As a result, the topic of this book remains highly relevant–but not only as regards the situation in the US.

Second, in a recent study of more than 900 arbitration practitioners conducted at Queen Mary University of London, the lack of power in relation to third parties was rated as one of the three worst characteristics of international arbitration.[10] Indeed, at a time when international disputes have become more complex, in terms of multiple contracts, parties, jurisdictions and third parties, the mechanisms for obtaining assistance from state courts in the taking of evidence are more crucial than ever.[11] This also holds true in the light of big data and related requests for vast categories of electronic documents stored in the form of emails, chat histories and e-databases.[12]

All in all, the present contribution aims to provide a thorough analysis of the relationship between state courts and arbitral tribunals, concentrating on the taking of evidence. At the heart of this debate lies the question of whether, when and under what conditions a state court can assist in the taking of evidence in international arbitral proceedings. Furthermore, it remains to be seen whether this process can be subject to a subsequent appellate proceeding, either directly against the decision of the respective state court or by challenging the arbitral award itself, immediately or during the recognition and enforcement stage. Such an in-depth examination will not only contribute to a better common understanding of this problem, but will also provide arbitration practitioners with helpful advice for their next tactical moves.

§ 3 Method and Distinctions

Since the present question can hardly be answered in general, the focus will mainly be on the situation in Switzerland. Quite recently, the Swiss *lex arbitri* has undergone several amendments in order to facilitate arbitral proceedings, including in relation to court assistance in the taking of evidence.[13] Accordingly, it is intended that Swiss courts will now provide assistance in the taking of evidence to foreign arbitral tribunals with their seat outside Switzerland.[14] Such assistance may be provided in many ways, offering foreign

9 *See* p. 198 *and* p. 202 et seq. *infra*.

10 Queen Mary Survey (2018), 8.

11 *Ibid*.

12 *See* e.g. Art. 3 (3) (a) (ii) IBA Rules; MARGHITOLA, 35; DASSER, *Schiedsgerichte*, 120.

13 *See* p. 223 et seqq. *infra*.

14 Art. 185a (2) Draft-PILA CH.

arbitral tribunals a more efficient means of obtaining evidence than the cumbersome route of international court assistance through, for instance, the Hague Convention on the Taking of Evidence Abroad in Civil or Commercial Matters.[15]

By means of a comparative approach, this book presents an overview of how court assistance in the taking of evidence is provided in other important arbitration-friendly jurisdictions, such as England, France, the US and Germany. This comparison paves the way to assess the Swiss status quo and analyse it in depth. It will be shown that in Swiss case law as well as legal doctrine, the matter in question has not yet been sufficiently explored. This holds especially true as, in comparison to statutory law in Swiss domestic arbitration (CCP CH), its international counterpart (PILA CH) says very little about court assistance in the taking of evidence and thus leaves ample room for interpretation. As a consequence, the CCP CH will often provide helpful guidance and space for analogous application.

As the title of this book indicates, the focus primarily lies on the process of taking evidence itself, rather than the means through which evidence is taken (e.g., witnesses, document production, inspections). Other court assistance–for instance, as regards the constitution of the arbitral tribunal at the beginning of the arbitration or assistance during the enforcement stage–is only rarely discussed.[16] This also applies to interim measures, which are not examined extensively, even though admittedly they are closely related to the taking of evidence. Finally, although the emerging field of international investment arbitration affords considerable scope to examine interesting issues related to the present one, this would go beyond the main focus of this book.

§ 4 Structure of the Book

This book is divided into nine chapters. The next chapter provides a brief outline of how the different approaches to the taking of evidence in international arbitral proceedings with parties from common and civil law countries work in general. In the third chapter, the legal framework for the taking of evidence in international arbitration is set out. To this end, various *leges arbitri* as well as the arbitration agreement itself and (ad hoc and institutional) arbitration rules are compared, with a focus on the two examples of document production and witnesses. Since parties might not always comply with

15 *See* p. 118 et seqq. *infra*.

16 LEW, 496 et seqq.; DUPEYRON, 458.

evidentiary orders, the arbitral tribunal can impose various sanctions on non-compliant parties; this is the subject of the fourth chapter. To understand why sanctions might not always prove helpful and why there is thus an urgent practical need for court assistance, the fifth chapter outlines the limitations of the arbitral tribunal's powers in relation to the taking of evidence.

The sixth chapter goes on to analyse the different measures that national courts can offer in this regard and considers whether court assistance in the taking of evidence may be regarded as true assistance or rather an unwelcome intervention. One might further ask whether national courts might even be obliged to assist in international arbitral proceedings, based on Swiss constitutional and international public law; if this is in fact the case, the national courts' discretion as regards whether to assist will be very limited. Having answered this crucial question, the seventh chapter compares the German, French, English and US *leges arbitri*, in order to arrive at a clearer picture of how different jurisdictions deal with the issue at hand.

Based on this comparison, the eighth chapter sets out an exhaustive analysis of the Swiss approach to court assistance in the taking of evidence, examining it at every stage of the arbitral proceedings. Finally, the ninth chapter draws conclusions on all relevant outcomes and provides a short summary of possible future developments in this area.

2

Taking of Evidence: Multiple Methods

§ 1 Introduction

In state jurisdictions as well as in arbitration, it is widely acknowledged that success in a case largely hinges on the evidence that the winning party can gather to support its claims.[17] In fact, it is assumed that about 60% to 70% of all cases in international arbitration are decided based on the facts, rather than on the application of the relevant principles of law.[18] Hence, it is crucial to understand how the evidentiary rules work in this regard. Needless to say, the fact that every legal system has its own methodology of fact finding does not make this objective any easier.

Compared to domestic litigation, in arbitration the parties and the arbitral tribunal have broad discretion when it comes to the taking of evidence, and the parties can tailor the proceedings in accordance with their needs.[19] In most cases, therefore, subject to any party agreement or mandatory law, domestic rules of evidence are not applicable.[20] If the parties choose arbitration over litigation, they must decide whether they wish to proceed either in ad hoc arbitration or under an arbitration institution.[21] If the parties desire their own tailor-made arbitration rules, they are more likely to choose ad hoc

17 WAINCYMER, *Evidence*, 743.

18 BLACKABY et al., n. 6.75.

19 See the *numerus clausus* in many civil procedural rules such as Arts. 168 et seqq. CCP CH.

20 POUDRET/BESSON, n. 644. *See* e.g. Section 2 (1) of the Singapore Evidence Act which expressly excludes–with the exception of evidence in banking matters–arbitral proceedings from its scope of application. Theoretically, because of the parties' discretion in evidentiary matters, they could agree upon the application of national rules of evidence. This can be seen in domestic arbitration quite often, but it is not recommended in international arbitration where the parties come from different legal backgrounds and are thus not willing to agree upon 'foreign' rules of evidence; *see also* S. 34 (2) (f) EAA 1996, which provides an opt-in clause to apply any law of evidence.

21 BORN, *Law and Practice*, ch. 1.06 n. 35. Within the field of institutional arbitration, several institutions are now specialised in various matters such as sports, investment or IP/IT arbitration.

arbitration. However, one of the main disadvantages of this type of arbitration is the lack of a supporting institution; the effectiveness of the proceedings thus depends fully on the cooperation of the parties.[22] That is why in most cases, the applicable procedure rules are chosen by referring to the rules of an experienced arbitration institution.[23]

However, even where such a set of rules is referenced, it often says very little about the process of taking evidence.[24] In such cases, the normal reaction would be to seek inspiration from the national civil procedure rules of the country where one has been educated. Indeed, since there is no mandatory 'international arbitration law', a practitioner has many good reasons to look for help to the domestic legal system in which he or she was trained and educated.

As long as the parties come from the same country and are used to the same procedural rules, the chances of reaching agreement on the applicable evidentiary rules are quite high. However, if the parties are from countries with different legal backgrounds (e.g., common law versus civil law), the situation becomes more complex.[25] Quite often, parties from these backgrounds have almost opposing views as to how evidentiary matters should be handled–for instance, regarding whether document production is permissible or how witnesses are examined. Hence, from the arbitration practitioner's perspective, it is in many ways beneficial–if not crucial–to understand the most significant differences between common and civil law systems concerning the taking of evidence. Only with this insight can arbitrators govern the proceedings accurately and judiciously, and render a verdict that is truly international and not merely a replication of domestic procedural rules applied to international arbitration.[26] If the arbitral tribunal can balance the two legal cultures and their diversities, the parties will be more willing to commit to arbitration and more likely to accept the arbitral award.

22 BLACKABY *et. al.*, n. 1.145.

23 BÖCKSTIEGEL, Beweiserhebung, 4; *see* e.g. Art. 25 ICC Rules; Art. 24 Swiss Rules; Art. 34 AAA Rules.

24 E.g. Arts. 27-29 UNCITRAL Rules; Art. 22 HKIAC Rules; Art. 22.1 (vi) LCIA Rules.

25 HAY, n. 16; SLAPPER/KELLY, 4 et seq. Very broadly speaking, common law can be described as the law based on decisions, while civil law is based on statutes. In practice, however, both common law and civil law system are mostly mixed systems whit a greater or smaller part of case or statutory law.

26 BORN, *Law and Practice*, ch. 9.01 n. 16.

§ 2 Distinctions

The interplay in international arbitration between arbitrators and the parties and their counsel, all of whom may sometimes be from different legal backgrounds, is unique. This is especially true when it comes to the taking of evidence and the clash of views in cross-cultural arbitration is a much-debated topic.[27] As this book examines court assistance in the taking of evidence in common and civil law countries, the following remarks focus primarily on these two legal systems.[28] In this regard, two preliminary remarks must be made.

First, anyone who tries to combine the two systems in an attempt to arrive at 'the best of both worlds' must bear in mind that the goal is to find an optimal, tailor-made compromise, and never a perfect solution or a feeling of being 'at home' in a procedural sense, which would contradict the very nature of *international* arbitration.[29]

Second, the term 'common and civil law' is very broad and should not be overestimated or generalised.[30] As an example, a closer look at the rules of discovery/disclosure of two (mostly) common law countries, such as the US and England, reveals significant differences and variations.[31] The same applies, of course, to civil law countries: again, there are significant differences between the Roman and German families of civil law.[32] Nonetheless, and despite these divergences, there seems to be enough uniformity in evidentiary matters to justify the classification of common and civil law countries.[33]

27 WAINCYMER, *Evidence*, 746 et seqq.; BORN, *Law and Practice*, ch. 9 n. 16; BLACKABY et al., n. 6.77 et seq.

28 For an in-depth analysis in comparative law of other legal families *see* ZWEIGERT/KÖTZ, 62 et seqq.

29 REYMOND, 367; WAINCYMER, *Evidence*, 41.

30 BLACKABY et al., n. 6.77 et seqq.; BORN, *Law and Practice*, ch. 9 n. 16; BORN, *Int. Comm. Arb.*, 2206; MARGHITOLA, 12. REYMOND even argues that there is no 'Civil Law Procedure' in civil and commercial litigation because of the lacking common origin. He reasons therefore that there are as many civil procedures as countries in Europe (358).

31 For example, in obtaining evidence, US-style discovery is much broader than the disclosure procedure in England; BETTINGER, 30 et seqq. and 125 et seqq.

32 ZWEIGERT/KÖTZ, 73 et seqq., 130 et seqq.

33 BLACKABY et al., n. 6.77, n. 6.80.

§ 3 Common Law Approach

The common law has its origins primarily in England and its former colonies, including the US, Canada, Australia, New Zealand and many more.[34] Despite the technical differences concerning evidentiary rules in many common law countries, some common principles can be identified in order to distinguish the common law approach to the taking of evidence from its civil law counterpart.[35]

First, the common law system is in many ways adversarial, with the rivalry of the parties at its centre.[36] This is true even, for instance, of English law, where the adversarial approach has been maintained despite the revision of civil procedure and its partial adaption to civil law countries.[37] For the sake of simplicity, the following remarks will therefore focus on the US approach according to the FRCP USA, where the adversarial method is best illustrated.[38]

The common law civil procedure for the taking of evidence can be divided into five stages: (1) filing the complaint, followed by (2) the pre-trial stage, during which the parties gather the relevant evidence for (3) the trial stage, when it is presented to the court, after which (4) the judge (as the case may be, together with a jury) renders his or her verdict;[39] (5) an appeal may follow if one of the parties wants to challenge the decision.

Compared to civil law proceedings, the complaint in common law proceedings is not as detailed and only defines the scope and nature of the action[40]–or, in the words of the US Supreme Court, 'enough facts to state a claim to relief that is plausible on its face'.[41] Next, as opposed to civil law proceedings, where evidence is gathered through the exchange of written submissions and in the court proceedings, the pre-trial stage serves to obtain a wide range of evidence from the adverse party prior to any court proceeding.[42] In

34 SLAPPER/KELLY, 4; HAY, n. 1 et seqq.; KIDANE, 181; BETTINGER, 30 et seq.

35 HAY, n. 15; DENNIS, n. 1.015; MARGHITOLA, 12.

36 CRAIG, 12.

37 BETTINGER, 49 and 135 et seq.; *see also* the remarks about the trend to alternative dispute resolution under the CPR 1998 (*Ibid.*, 119 et seq.).

38 For the approach under English law, *see* e.g. BETTINGER, 125 et seqq.

39 WIRTH, 10; DFT 4A_315/2017 of 17 Jan. 2018, cons. 5.3.1; DFT 132 III 291, cons. 2.1; HAY, n. 150 et seqq.

40 Rule 8 (a) (2) FRCP USA: 'a short and plain statement of the claim showing that the pleader is entitled to relief ...'; HANOTIAU, 361; BETTINGER, 41 et seq.; DFT 132 III 291, cons. 2.1.

41 *Bell Atl. Corp. v. Twombly*, 550 U.S. 544, 570 (2007); *Ashcroft v. Iqbal*, 556 U.S. 662, 678 (2009); BETTINGER, 43.

42 *See* p. 206 et seqq. *infra*.

this critical stage, the parties try to collect evidence in the form of depositions, interrogatories, production of documents and even inspections.[43] If the evidence in question is protected by privilege, the court can impose a protective order.[44]

In contrast, if a party fails to produce evidence without a valid reason, it can be forced to pay any expenses resulting from its failure to produce evidence, or the misconduct may be treated as contempt of court.[45] Aside from this, however, the role of the court is rather passive.[46] To summarise, during the pre-trial stage, the parties weigh up their chances of success and are encouraged to reach a settlement before the trial begins.[47]

In the trial stage, the judge takes a mostly passive role and does not participate in the gathering of evidence, but rather acts as referee by determining whether the evidence offered by the parties (gathered in the pre-trial discovery) is admissible and choosing between the two options presented by the parties.[48] The idea here is that the best way to reveal the truth is to leave it solely to the parties to prepare and present their cases, in order to convince the court.[49] This should ensure a fair and just trial, since the judge remains receptive to the arguments of both parties until he or she finally renders a verdict.[50]

Although a strict application of the adversarial method makes sense from a theoretical point of view, in most common law systems, no such strict model exists.[51] In the interests of clarification, the judge is free to ask questions directly to witnesses, or to interrupt their examination if there is no need for further evidence on either a certain point or the entire case. Nevertheless, the judge must be very cautious on this point, to avoid a possible violation of the right to be heard.[52]

43 *See* e.g. Rules 26 (a) (1) (A) (ii) *and* (3) (A) (ii) FRCP USA; BETTINGER, 44.

44 Rules 26 (c) (1) (g) *and* 45 (d) (3) (iii) FRCP USA.

45 Rule 37 (b) (2) (B) FRCP USA; BETTINGER, 45.

46 As an exception, *see* the possibility of a pre-trial conference, for instance, to facilitate an early settlement or discourage 'wasteful pre-trial activities' (Rule 16 (a) FRCP USA).

47 DFT 132 III 291, cons. 2.1; HAY, n. 184 et seqq.

48 DENNIS, n. 1.015; Blackaby et al., n. 6.77; SUTCLIFFE/WIRTH, 34; KIDANE, 182.

49 ZWEIGERT/KÖTZ, 268; SUTCLIFFE/WIRTH, 34; RAESCHKE-KESSLER, *Discovery*, 45; BETTINGER, 46.

50 STAUGHTON, 353.

51 *Ibid.*, 353 et seqq.

52 *Ibid.*, 355. In addition, a constant excessive intervention by the judge is considered 'entirely at odds with the adversarial system' (*Lord Borough of Southwark v. Kofi-Adu* [2006] EWCA, Civ. 281, n. 148).

Second, a great deal of common law evidentiary rules become comprehensible when considered in light of the jury trial.[53] Its underlying principle is that a person can be judged fairly only by a group of ordinary people (the jury).[54] The task of the jury is to determine the facts; the judge has exclusive authority over the application of law.[55] Traditionally, in civil and criminal cases, the arguments are presented to the court orally by the parties and their counsel in such a way that the jurors–who mostly have no legal education–can understand the relevant facts and arguments in order to render a verdict.[56]

The principle of orality has its historical foundation in the idea that the most direct way to reveal the truth is by examining and cross-examining witnesses.[57] In this way, parties can confront their accusers and even disprove certain facts or the claim as a whole.[58] Because of the mandatory attendance of the jury, trials can last for hours, if not days; thus, court proceedings reach their climax in a single trial.[59] Consequently, lawyers must obtain relevant evidence before trial in order to present it to the judge.[60] While the role of the jury has weakened in recent times, its tradition and the important role of lawyers in convincing the jury have persisted.[61] The fact that there are also lay judges in the judiciary, and that juries consist of individuals without any legal education, has necessitated complex laws of evidence relating to how evidence is obtained, adduced and evaluated at trial.[62] Otherwise, misleading evidence could impress a jury and unduly influence their verdict.[63] While these laws of evidence are not binding on arbitrators, they may serve as inspiration in conducting the arbitral proceedings.[64]

With these two differences in mind, it makes sense that a discovery procedure exists in common law countries, whereby all relevant–and even unfavourable–documents must be disclosed to the other party.[65] If the court

53 CRAIG, 11; ZWEIGERT/KÖTZ, 266.

54 CRAIG, 11.

55 *Ibid.*, 12.

56 *Ibid.*, 11.

57 DENNIS, n. 1.015.

58 *Ibid.*

59 ZWEIGERT/KÖTZ, S. 266 et seqq.

60 CRAIG, 14.

61 *Ibid.*, 11.

62 DENNIS, n. 1.001, 1.015; ZWEIGERT/KÖTZ, 270.

63 CRAIG, 12.

64 BORN, *Law and Practice*, ch. 8.08 n. 51; *see* e.g. S. 34 (2) (f) EAA 1996; Civil Evidence Act 1995.

65 KÜHN, 3.

has not had all available relevant information, it cannot render a just verdict.[66] Notably, US discovery under the FRCP USA is very wide ranging,[67] while so-called 'disclosure' under the CPR 1998 is much more restrictive.[68] As will be discussed in detail, 'discovery' in international arbitration is less extensive than in domestic litigation, but nonetheless plays a vital role.[69]

To sum up, one must bear in mind that the aim in common law systems is to reveal the 'whole truth'.[70] This is possible only if the means of gathering evidence are very wide ranging.

§ 4 Civil Law Approach

Compared to the common law approach, with its search for truth through the adversarial method and the climax in a single trial, the civil law method is different in many ways. It has its origins in many European countries. In fact, depending on how one classifies civil law, there are at least three legal families: Roman, German and Nordic.[71] Therefore, their origins extend from France through Spain and Italy, across Germany, Austria and Switzerland and north to Scandinavia. Here again, while there are various procedural differences within the civil law system, some commonalities in the approach to evidence can be identified that distinguish it from its common law counterpart.

While common law proceedings are mainly adversarial (party-led), civil law proceedings are in many ways inquisitorial (judge-led).[72] They are informed more by the Roman law principle of '*Quod non est in actis non est in mundo*' ('What is not kept in the records does not exist') than by the search for the whole truth.[73] Accordingly, the gathering of evidence is largely controlled by the judge and the parties have no wide-ranging discovery rights.[74] In light of this, a common law lawyer would claim that it is quite unfair for the adverse party to withhold documents which the other side does not know

66 *Davies v. Eli Lilly & Co.*, [1987] 1 WLR 428, 431.

67 *See* Rule 26 et seqq. FRCP USA.

68 *See* Pt. 31 et seqq. CPR 1998.

69 BORN, *Law and Practice*, ch. 9 n. 36; *see* p. 194 et seqq. *infra*.

70 TRITTMANN, 20; Wagner, 463.

71 ZWEIGERT/KÖTZ, 73; KIDANE, 195.

72 WAINCYMER, *Evidence*, 746; BORN, *Int. Comm. Arb.*, 2344 et. seqq.; RISSE/HALLER, n. 8.

73 DASSER, *Schiedsgerichte*, 120; *see also* p. 12 et seq. *supra*.

74 BORN, *Int. Comm. Arb.*, 2345.

about. In contrast, the civil law lawyer would respond that broad discovery rights are a severe invasion of privacy, admissible only in criminal cases;[75] and further that it would be quite odd to file a complaint first and only then search for evidence to support the complaint.[76]

The inquisitorial approach is mirrored in the different stages of civil law proceedings, which can, broadly speaking, be divided into five stages: (1) filing of the complaint, (2) exchange of written submissions, (3) the court proceeding, (4) the decision stage and (5) a possible appellate procedure.[77] In the first stage, the parties file a detailed complaint in which they set out the claimed facts and the law on which the complaint is based.[78] Furthermore, all relevant documents to the complaint and/or an exact explanation of which further evidence should be obtained must be attached.[79] Unlike in common law, where the initial complaint is more a summary of the facts and the legal bases of the claim, the complaint in civil law is much more detailed and conclusive.[80]

The second stage is a sort of 'interim stage', in which the adverse party has time to respond to the complaint and the judge can intervene by holding an instruction hearing in preparation for the main hearing.[81] At the instruction hearing, the matter in dispute can be discussed informally and the facts can be completed–for instance, by means of a precautionary taking of evidence.[82] Finally, the instruction hearing gives the parties a first chance to reach agreement before the main hearing begins. All in all, in the interest of procedural economy, the second stage tries to balance out the level of information of the parties and ensure that in the subsequent main hearing, only matters which have not been subject to the second stage will be discussed.[83]

The third stage involves the pleadings of the parties and the taking of evidence under the control of the judge.[84] During this stage, the role of the judge is very active–not only in the conduct of the proceedings, but also in the gathering of evidence (e.g., by examining witnesses and allowing or denying evi-

75 REYMOND, 360; HAZARD, 1022.

76 TERCIER/BERSHEDA, 80.

77 WILLISEGGER, 321; BETTINGER, 69 et seqq.

78 ELSING/TOWNSEND, 60.

79 WIRTH, 10.

80 ELSING/TOWNSEND, 59 et seqq.; HANOTIAU, 361.

81 Art. 226 CCP CH.

82 Art. 158 CCP CH.

83 BETTINGER, 70 et seq.

84 *See* e.g. Arts. 228 et seqq. CCP CH.

dence requests).[85] The judge is obliged to identify the legal issues and deal with them accordingly in the fourth stage.[86] When the judge comes to render a verdict, he or she is usually bound by what the parties have demanded and will not go beyond what they have requested (*non ultra petita*).[87] In doing so, the judge may freely choose the applicable rule of law and assess the facts presented.[88]

Because there is no jury, civil law proceedings take place in a succession of hearings, which ends with pronouncement of the verdict.[89] Compared to common law proceedings, the principle of orality does not play such a vital role and consequently the weight lies mainly on documentary evidence.[90] Therefore, witnesses are rarely cross-examined.[91] Likewise, in many civil law jurisdictions, contact between lawyers and witnesses in order to interview or prepare them for trial is prohibited.[92] Although there are some rules of evidence in various civil law rules of procedure,[93] they are not as detailed as their common law counterparts.[94]

To sum up, it may be said that the aim in civil law systems is to find the 'relative truth'. 'Relative' in this sense means that the truth is revealed based on what the parties present to the court, rather than what they are obliged to disclose through discovery.

§ 5 Conclusion

From this short outline of the different approaches to gathering evidence in common and civil law, it is evident that each system has its own advantages and disadvantages. While the common law procedure is more adversarial and party-led, the civil law system is largely inquisitorial and judge-led. The

85 WAINCYMER, *Evidence*, 746; BORN, *Int. Comm. Arb.*, 2345; BLACKABY et al., n. 6.77; KIDANE, 201.

86 HAZARD, 1021.

87 *See* e.g. Art. 58 (1) CCP CH.

88 REYMOND, 366. This principle goes back to the Latin maxim of *iura novit curia* (the court knows the law); KIDANE, 199.

89 REYMOND, 359.

90 HANOTIAU, 360.

91 VAN HOUTTE, 458.

92 For Switzerland *see* e.g. DFT 2C_8/2010 of 4 Oct. 2010, cons. 3.2.2; for France *see* Paris Court of Cassation, 10 Sept. 2014, 13-22400, cons. 1; VAN HOUTTE, 461.

93 E.g. Arts. 150 et seqq. CCP CH; Arts. 132 et seqq. CCP FR.

94 E.g. the FRCP USA.

latter method is clearly apparent once the judge takes control of the whole case,[95] which occurs at a much earlier point in the civil law system. On the other hand, there is almost no court interference in the pre-trial procedure in the common law system, and it is almost fully incumbent on the parties to gather evidence and prepare it for trial.

These systemic differences may influence the dynamic in international arbitration–which suggests that the task of finding a compromise in the approach to taking evidence could be quite challenging. It is, to say the least. However, despite this clash of cultures, the parties have the main advantage of being able to choose the procedure *à la carte*.[96] Thus, for all participating parties, an understanding of the legal backgrounds at play is crucial in figuring out how evidentiary matters should be addressed. However, understanding the differences is just the first step. The next step is to decide where and when to agree to evidentiary rules, which leads to the legal framework for the taking of evidence in international arbitration.

95 REYMOND, 367.

96 HANOTIAU, 362.

3

Taking of Evidence: A Glance at the Legal Configuration

§ 1 Introduction

At the time the parties to a contractual relationship agree on an arbitration clause, evidentiary issues seem to be of little importance. The parties rather hope that no dispute will arise in the first place, but nevertheless agree that should this come to pass, the dispute will be resolved by an arbitral tribunal.[97] However, evidentiary rules must be addressed once a dispute arises, so it is crucial to understand where, when, how and by whom this is done. This gives rise to many questions about which procedural framework is applicable to the arbitral proceedings. Because of the parties' broad discretion in determining the procedural framework in arbitration, the range of legal sources can be (and often is) quite vast. Thus, it is paramount for the parties and arbitrators to know and define which laws and procedural rules will shape the taking of evidence.

In this respect, national arbitration laws (henceforth '*leges arbitri*') act as a kind of minimal standard,[98] and set the scene for the arbitral proceedings to take place within the boundaries of the parties' agreement and (in the vast majority of cases) institutional arbitration rules. One may think of the legal framework in international arbitration as a temple built on these three pillars. In this chapter, the three pillars will be examined, with a focus on how the taking of evidence may be conducted by the parties and the arbitral tribunal.

§ 2 Leges Arbitri

A. Introduction

As the first pillar, the *leges arbitri* play a key role by determining not only 'external' procedural issues (i.e. the relationship between the arbitral tribunal and the national courts–for example, in relation to the possible annulment

97 BLACKABY et al., n. 1.41.

98 GÖKSU, n. 181.

of the arbitral award), but also 'internal' matters (e.g. the appointment, removal and replacement of arbitrators and the taking of evidence).[99] Before comparing various *leges arbitri* and their approach to the taking of evidence, a few remarks are necessary to distinguish this term from other concepts.

First, the *leges arbitri* should not be confused with the substantive law governing matters in dispute such as the interpretation and validity of the contract or the rights and obligations of the parties.[100] This law, also called the 'applicable law' or the 'governing law', is usually stated in a choice of law clause within the arbitration agreement.[101] Even though the substantive law usually does not address evidentiary procedural issues, it is contentious if, for example, the burden of proof–which is clearly an evidentiary issue–falls under the regime of either substantive or procedural law.[102] That is why the arbitral tribunal, when determining the applicable procedure for the taking of evidence, may also have to consider the substantive law.[103]

Second, the term 'procedural rules' must be distinguished from the *leges arbitri*. While the *leges arbitri* serve as some sort of general legal framework, the procedural rules are found in more detailed institutional arbitration rules.[104] As will be discussed shortly *(see* p. 26 et seqq. *infra),* even these institutional arbitration rules are often insufficiently specific as regards the taking of evidence.

Third, although the national civil procedure laws at the seat of the *lex arbitri* can influence certain aspects of the arbitral proceedings, they do not apply in general.[105] Instead, it is the respective *lex arbitri* which establishes the general legislative (procedural) framework. The term 'procedural law of arbitration' is therefore nowadays understood as the *lex arbitri* of the selected state and not the respective national civil procedure law.[106] Luckily, the outmoded doctrine of automatically applying domestic civil procedure rules to international arbitral proceedings has long been rejected by nearly every jurisdiction.[107] Notwithstanding that in some cases (especially in domestic

99 BORN, *Law and Practice*, ch. 6.01 n. 6.

100 BLACKABY et al., n. 3.37. While the substantive law of the arbitration agreement and the law of the underlying contract can differ, they are most often the same law.

101 *Ibid.*, n. 3.107. Which substantive law is chosen depends on the parties' choice of which law they consider suitable to govern the contractual relationship (*see ibid.*, n. 3.114 et seqq.).

102 BORN, *Int. Comm. Arb.*, 2315; WAINCYMER, *Evidence*, 746 et seqq.; EMANUELE et al., vii.

103 For the situation in Germany, *see* TRITTMANN, 21.

104 BLACKABY et al., n. 3.51.

105 O'MALLEY, n. 1.18; RADICATI DI BROZOLO, 52 et seqq.

106 BORN, *Int. Comm. Arb.*, 1624.

107 BORN, *Law and Practice*, ch. 6.02 n. 14.

arbitration) it can make sense to apply national civil procedure rules, this is not generally recommended in international arbitration, where far more procedural flexibility is needed.[108]

With these distinctions in mind, the question arises of which of the many *leges arbitri* to apply in international arbitral proceedings. Since the parties are free to agree on almost any procedural aspect of the proceedings, this should also apply to the choice of the *lex arbitri*.

B. Seat of Arbitration

According to the well-established 'seat theory', the applicable *lex arbitri* is always that at the seat of arbitration.[109] Not only the UNCITRAL ML, but also the NYC and several *leges arbitri* provide that the *lex arbitri* at the seat of arbitration governs the most important issues of the arbitral proceedings.[110] Thus, the seat of arbitration is not merely a geographical matter, but defines the place where the arbitration is held and which *lex arbitri* will be applied. The parties should therefore choose a seat in a jurisdiction which provides a certain degree of autonomy for arbitral proceedings and at the same time grants the necessary support.[111] Although the seat of arbitration is essential, this does not mean that the hearings must actually be held there (i.e. at a specific geographical location). In fact, the flexibility of international arbitral proceedings and practical reasons–such as the domicile of the parties and thus potentially high travel costs–mean that the hearings may need to be held elsewhere.[112] Although it is theoretically possible to change the seat of arbitration during the course of the proceedings, this is not recommended due to various procedural difficulties, such as the competence of different jurisdictions.[113]

The *lex arbitri* as the law which governs the basic principles of the arbitral proceedings is not necessarily the *lex arbitri* at the seat of arbitration. Hence, parties which have chosen the seat of arbitration in State A can agree on a foreign *lex arbitri* of State B. The Swiss *lex arbitri*, for instance, allows the

108 GIRSBERGER/VOSER, n. 894; *see also* Art. 176 (2) PILA CH which provides an opt-out clause for the domestic arbitration rules as stated in the CCP CH (Arts. 353 et seqq. CCP CH).

109 BORN, *Law and Practice*, ch. 6.02 n. 16; RADICATI DI BROZOLO, 49 et seqq.

110 Art. 1 (2) UNCITRAL ML; Art. V (1) (a) (d) NYC; Art. 176 PILA CH; S. 2 and 3 EAA 1996.

111 RADICATI DI BROZOLO, 57.

112 BLACKABY et al., n. 3.57; WAINCYMER, *Evidence*, 172 et seqq.; BORN, *Law and Practice*, ch. 6 n. 4; Art. 20 (2) UNCITRAL ML.

113 WAINCYMER, *Evidence*, 172.

parties to proceed in this way.[114] While the parties are free to do so, the arbitral tribunal must be aware that equal treatment of the parties and the right to be heard must be guaranteed at all times.[115] This scenario gives rise to numerous practical questions. For example, in which jurisdiction can a party challenge the arbitral award–at the seat of arbitration or before the court in the country of the foreign *lex arbitri*? Are there any differences as to how the courts approach procedural and substantive matters? In light of these procedural complexities, it becomes obvious why in the vast majority of cases the parties choose the same *lex arbitri* as that at the seat of arbitration.[116]

C. Broad Discretion of Leges Arbitri

The *leges arbitri* take various approaches in defining the parameters of the arbitral proceedings. However, most often, the arbitral tribunal, subject to the parties' agreement, has broad discretion in conducting the arbitral proceedings, including as regards the taking of evidence. With the aim of harmonising the various *leges arbitri* of common law and civil law countries, and thus harmonising international arbitral proceedings, the UNCITRAL ML of 1985 states that the parties are free to agree on the rules of procedure:[117]

> "(1) Subject to the provisions of this Law, the parties are free to agree on the procedure to be followed by the arbitral tribunal in conduction the proceedings."
>
> "(2) Failing such agreement, the arbitral tribunal may, subject to the provisions of Law, conduct the arbitration in such manner as it considers appropriate. The power conferred upon the arbitral tribunal includes the power to determine the admissibility, relevance, materiality and weight of any evidence."

In the absence of such agreement, the arbitral tribunal can conduct the proceedings in an appropriate manner.[118] This also includes the power to determine the admissibility, relevance, materiality and weight of any evidence

114 Art. 182 (1) PILA CH.

115 Art. 182 (3) PILA CH.

116 BORN, *Int. Comm. Arb.*, 212. In contrast, the Swiss approach is very liberal and thus allows the parties to choose a foreign *lex arbitri* (Art. 182 (1) PILA CH).

117 *See* Art. 19 UNCITRAL ML. So far, 80 of a total of 111 jurisdictions have based their *lex arbitri* on the UNCITRAL ML. For a detailed list, *see* the current status.

118 Art. 19 (2) UNCITRAL ML; Art. 182 (3) PILA CH; § 1042 (1) CCP DE; Art. 1510 CCP FR; S. 33 (1) (a) EAA 1996.

presented to the arbitral tribunal.[119] It is important to note that S. 34 (1) (f) of the EAA 1996 gives the arbitral tribunal, subject to the parties' agreement, the power to apply strict rules of evidence. It refers to the laws of evidence which have already been mentioned *(see* p. 12 *supra)*. Even though the EAA 1996 provides such an opt-in clause, arbitrators will not usually impose restrictions according to laws of evidence.[120] At this point, much could be said about the assessment of evidence and the burden of proof in different legal traditions, let alone in institutional arbitration rules. Nonetheless, it should suffice to state that when it comes to the conduct of the proceedings, the arbitral tribunal and the parties enjoy the widest discretion.

D. Limits to the Broad Discretion

In addition to the parties' agreement, the broad discretion of the arbitral tribunal is limited by the principle of due process, which includes the right to equal treatment and the opportunity to present a case.[121] Art. 18 UNCITRAL ML reads as follows:

> "The parties shall be treated with equality and each party shall be given a full opportunity of presenting his case."

Equality requires, for instance, that both parties be subject to the same time limits or be allowed to present the same number of expert witnesses.[122] The opportunity to present a case entitles each party to give its opinion on the relevant facts, to present the legal arguments and the supportive evidence, to comment on the arguments of the opponent and its presented evidence, and finally to present new evidence in reply.[123] S. 33 (1) (a) of the EAA 1996 recognises the right to present a case as one aspect of the principle of fair and impartial treatment, stating:

> "The tribunal shall act fairly and impartially as between the parties, giving each party a reasonable opportunity of putting his case and dealing with that of his opponent … ."

119 Art. 19 (2) UNCITRAL ML; *see also*, for example, Art. 184 (2) PILA, § 1042 (4) CCP DE, Art. 1509 CCP FR, S. 34 (1) (f) EAA 1996 and S. 12 (3) IAA SG.

120 SHEPPARD, S. 34 EAA 1996 n. 8.

121 O'MALLEY, n. 1.12; for examples in *Leges arbitri, see* e.g. Art. 18 UNCITRAL ML; Art. 182 (3) PILA CH; § 1042 (1) CCP DE; Art. 1510 CCP FR. Of course, there are other legal principles which must also be considered, such as attorney-client privilege or commercial or technical confidentiality. However, the main focus in this chapter remains due process.

122 Schütze-PATOCCHI/NIEDERMAIER, n. 339.

123 DFT 117 II 346, cons. 1; Schütze-PATOCCHI/NIEDERMAIER, n. 340.

While the UNCITRAL ML refers to the 'full' opportunity to present a case, the EAA 1996 gives each party only a 'reasonable' opportunity to present its case. This English approach does not seek to limit the parties' right to present their case, but rather aims to set boundaries to prevent the potential misuse of this right.[124] Accordingly, the parties have no right to present as many witnesses as they like or to ignore procedural deadlines on the grounds of due process.

The arbitral tribunal's obligation to ensure due process can be quite demanding, especially in an international context in which the parties all have different ideas of this concept. In this regard, the situation may arise where one party from a common law country believes that broad discovery rights are a crucial part of due process, while the adverse party from a civil law background believes quite the contrary. Therefore, the parties must agree on rules which address the principle of due process more specifically. In this regard, it will be demonstrated that the IBA Rules on the Taking of Evidence in International Arbitration (IBA Rules) serve as the authoritative body and best practice when it comes to rules of evidence in international arbitration.[125]

E. Summary

The foregoing has shown that in order to define the term '*leges arbitri*', a distinction must be made between the substantive law which governs the arbitration agreement and not only that which governs the underlying contract, but also the procedural rules–that is, the (institutional) arbitration rules and the national civil procedural rules at the seat of arbitration. According to the widely accepted seat theory, the *lex arbitri* at the seat of arbitration is applicable to the respective arbitral proceedings. Although this is not recommended, the parties can choose a different *lex arbitri* from that at the seat of arbitration. In such case they should be aware that they will still be bound by certain mandatory rules of the *lex arbitri* at the seat of arbitration and will also face numerous other procedural difficulties and uncertainties.

It is apparent from an outline of various *leges arbitri* that the arbitral tribunal has broad discretion–subject to the parties' agreement–to tailor the arbitral proceedings. This discretion is limited by the principle of due process, which encompasses the right to be heard and the opportunity to present a case. Because there is no uniform consensus about this principle, it must be addressed in a more specific set of rules. The earliest possible way to agree on such rules is in the arbitration agreement.

124 HARRIS et al., S. 33 EAA 1996 n. 33D; WAINCYMER, *Evidence*, 185.

125 O'MALLEY, n. 1.16; *see* p. 31 et seqq. *infra*.

§ 3 Arbitration Agreement

A. Introduction

The importance of the arbitration agreement as the second pillar cannot be stressed enough, since it is the basic condition for the arbitral proceedings to take place. According to the NYC, if there is no (valid) arbitration agreement, the arbitration itself is invalid and, as a consequence, there is no enforceable arbitral award.[126] When considering the process of taking evidence, the question arises as to whether the arbitration agreement mentions evidentiary issues by means of either direct or indirect reference. Furthermore, a few remarks about the features of a valid arbitration agreement highlight its importance.

B. Content of the Arbitration Agreement

In the overwhelming majority of cases, the arbitration agreement will have been included in a commercial contract between the parties *before* the dispute arises.[127] If that is not the case and the parties nevertheless wish to commit to arbitration, they can still draft a separate agreement to this effect–a so-called 'submission agreement' or 'compromise'.[128] This seldom happens, however, as the parties may have already developed their litigation tactics by this stage and are therefore unlikely to agree to settle the dispute through arbitration.[129]

As regards content, the parties are largely free in drafting the arbitration agreement.[130] That is why the extent of arbitration agreements varies so widely. For instance, an arbitration clause which says simply that 'any dispute is to be settled by arbitration in Geneva' is considered to be valid.[131] Nonetheless, it is highly recommended that the arbitration agreement at least includes key elements such as the agreement to arbitrate, the scope of the disputes to be submitted to arbitration, the institutional arbitration rules, the

126 *See* Arts. II (1) and V NYC.

127 Art. 7 (1) UNCITRAL ML; BLACKABY et al., n. 1.40; BORN, *Law and Practice,* ch. 1.07 n. 52; WAINCYMER, *Evidence,* 130.

128 BORN, *Law and Practice,* ch. 1.07 n. 52; WAINCYMER, *Evidence,* 131.

129 BORN, *Law and Practice,* ch. 1.07 n. 52; WAINCYMER, *Evidence,* 131.

130 BORN, *Int. Comm. Arb.,* 204.

131 BLACKABY et al., n. 1.49; Art. 179 (2) Draft-PILA CH.

arbitral seat, the language of arbitration and a choice of law clause.[132] The parties can also agree *directly* to certain evidentiary rules, although this rarely seems to happen.[133] This view is also confirmed in light of various standard arbitration clauses: no such clause–whether under the AAA[134], DIS[135], HKIAC[136], ICC[137] or LCIA[138] Rules–refers directly to evidentiary issues. In this regard, the standard clause of the Swiss Rules[139] is an exception by proposing wording which allows an arbitral award based only on documentary evidence. Usually, however, parties handle evidentiary issues *indirectly* by referring to an institutional arbitration clause, in which these are addressed more specifically. In addition to institutional arbitration rules, it is possible to refer to international guidelines for the taking of evidence, such as the IBA Rules, which are analysed below (*see* p. 31 et seqq. *infra*).

C. Separability

In discussing the arbitration agreement, the concept of separability must inevitably be addressed. The existence of a valid arbitration agreement is crucial in order to decide whether the parties are willing to submit the dispute to an arbitral tribunal or a state court. In this respect, the principle of separability, which is enshrined in almost all *leges arbitri*, comes into play.[140] This means that the arbitration agreement, which is usually included within a contract, is to be considered separate from that contract.[141] If the arbitral tribunal concludes that the contract in dispute is invalid, this would logically encompass the arbitration agreement too. Accordingly, in order to uphold the parties' commitment to arbitrate, separability ensures that the arbitration agreement can exist on its own, separate from the (perhaps invalid) contract.

132 For a detailed checklist of elements in international arbitration agreements *see* BORN, *Law and Practice*, ch. 1.07 n. 53 *et seqq.*

133 CRAIG, 21. He points out that Amercian parties occasionally draft arbitration clauses which refer to some provisions of the FRCP USA regarding discovery; WAINCYMER, *Evidence*, 754.

134 Standard AAA-ICDR arbitration clause.

135 Standard DIS arbitration clause.

136 Standard HKIAC arbitration clause.

137 Standard ICC arbitration clause.

138 Standard LCIA arbitration clause.

139 Standard Swiss Rules arbitration clause.

140 *See* e.g. Art. 16 (1) UNCITRAL ML; Art. 178 (3) PILA CH; Art. 1506 i.c.w. Art. 1447 CCP FR; S. 7 EAA 1996.

141 BLACKABY et al., n. 2.101. Of course, the problem is less obvious when there is a submission agreement, which is indeed separate from the contract from the outset of the dispute.

Because of this principle of separability, the aforementioned choice of law clause may address not only the applicable law applying to the underlying contract (i.e. the substantive law), but also a different law which may apply to disputes in relation to the arbitration agreement itself.[142] In most cases, however, the applicable law governing the arbitration agreement is not specifically addressed, and in case of a dispute it is anything but clear which law must be applied.[143]

This issue, called the 'conflict of laws', is the subject of heated debate in legal doctrine, which shall not be explored further at this point.[144] Rather, it is sufficient to summarise that in such cases, the doctrine considers the applicable law to be either the law chosen by the parties, the law of the underlying contract or the *lex arbitri* at the seat of arbitration.[145] Apart from that, there are two less popular positions that are nonetheless noteworthy. First, the Swiss approach represents a so-called 'validation principle', whereby the arbitration agreement is valid under either the law chosen by the parties, the law of the contract or Swiss law.[146] Second, the French position, tailored by numerous decisions of the Paris Court of Appeal, has the parties' intention at its centre and thus is not bound to national laws.[147] Accordingly, the arbitration agreement remains independent and there is no conflict of laws to be settled at all.[148]

This short outline of the different laws which might possibly be applied to an arbitration agreement reveals that the complexity of the conflict of laws can be very challenging if the parties have not addressed this issue in advance. Therefore, it is highly recommended to determine the law applicable to the arbitration agreement, as well as that applicable to the matter in dispute, when drafting the arbitration agreement.[149]

142 *See* p. 23 *supra;* BORN, *Int. Comm. Arb.*, 209.

143 BORN, *Law and Practice,* ch. 2.06 n. 32.

144 For an overview of how this problem is treated by various authors and jurisdictions, *see* WAINCYMER, *Evidence*, 136 et seq.; BLESSING, *Applicable Law,* 169 et seqq.

145 WAINCYMER, *Evidence*, 135; BLACKABY et al., n. 3.11; BORN, *Law and Practice,* ch. 2.06 n. 30 et seq.

146 *See* Art. 178 (2) PILA CH.

147 *Société d'étude et représentations navales et industrielles (SOERNI) et autres. v. Société Air Sea Broker limited (ASB)*, Paris Court of Appeal, Cass., 1st Civil Chamber, 8 Jul. 2009, 08-16.025.

148 BLACKABY et al., n. 3.33.

149 *Ibid.*, n. 3.10. For conflict of law clauses regarding the substantive law, *see* e.g. Art. 187 (1) PILA CH and Art. 24.1 DIS Rules.

D. Summary

The principle of separability ensures that the arbitration agreement survives even if the arbitral tribunal concludes that the underlying contract is invalid. Precisely because of this separation, the law applicable to the agreement can differ from that governing the underlying contract. Because the parties can choose from a multitude of laws which could be applicable to the arbitration agreement, they would be well advised to agree explicitly on the law which governs any dispute in relation to the agreement in order to avoid a conflict of laws.

As the drafting of the arbitration agreement is completely in the hands of the parties, evidentiary issues can be addressed as part of this process. The parties can thus agree directly on certain matters, such as the extent of discovery or proceedings based solely on documentary evidence. In practice, however, this seldom seems to happen, as a short summary of different standard arbitration clauses reveals. It seems that these clauses are drafted rather briefly and generally, simply stating the intention to settle disputes through arbitration and designating the applicable laws and rules to the arbitration. Hence, evidentiary issues are referred to indirectly through the choice of applicable institutional arbitration rules. These rules address evidentiary matters in far more detail than the *leges arbitri* and the arbitration agreement.

§ 4 Arbitration Rules

A. Introduction

Where the *lex arbitri* does not provide for adequate procedural measures, the parties themselves can draft rules which are tailored to their specific needs (ad hoc arbitration rules). In practice, however, this seldom tends to happen; the parties normally choose institutional arbitration rules to govern the arbitral proceedings. This third pillar is examined next.

The popularity of these rules is due to the fact that the arbitral proceedings are conducted under a standard set of rules, managed by professional staff and held almost anywhere in the world–that is, not only at the seat of the institution.[150] Furthermore, today more than ever, arbitration institutions

150 BORN, *Law and Practice*, ch. 1.06 n. 38.

provide a fast and efficient way to settle disputes.[151] Their rules offer a comprehensive procedural framework, addressing the composition of the arbitral tribunal, the arbitral proceedings, the award and the costs. In this way, the proceedings become more predictable and therefore more likely acceptable by the parties than the sometimes very general default provisions of the *leges arbitri*.[152]

There follows an examination of various approaches to the taking of evidence under several of the most popular institutional arbitration rules from common law and civil law countries. It begins by looking at the general power of the arbitral tribunal to conduct the proceedings in taking evidence. Next, in order to understand how the arbitral tribunal and the parties must find a compromise in this respect, a few observations are made about the initial evidentiary issues to be addressed. The process of taking evidence is very broad; this is illustrated by considering two types of evidence as examples–document production and witnesses. It is beyond the scope of this book to analyse all evidence extensively (e.g. documentary evidence, witnesses, party and tribunal-appointed experts, inspections); it should rather be sufficient to focus on these two examples, which play prominent roles in international arbitral proceedings.

As will be seen, there are significant differences between the approaches of common and civil law institutional arbitration rules–sometimes quite contrary to what one might have expected. Thus, the arbitral tribunal must do its best to find a compromise in this regard. In this respect, the IBA Rules offer a well-established tool to harmonise and simplify the taking of evidence in international arbitration by combining common law and civil law approaches. These rules will be considered in showing how document production and witnesses are treated in international arbitration.

B. General Provisions

Although all institutional arbitration rules provide that the arbitral tribunal shall conduct the arbitral proceedings with broad discretion, there are noteworthy differences in the exact wording in which they do so. In this regard, and although UNCITRAL is not an institutional arbitration organisation, its rules have played an important role in inspiring the wording of institutional

151 *See* the recent developments in relation to expedited arbitration rules, which apply either automatically or by means of an opt-in clause; Art. 30 ICC Rules; Art. 42 Swiss Rules; Rule 5 SIAC Rules; Art. 1 (4) ICDR Rules.

152 UNCITRAL Notes, n. 7.

arbitration rules.[153] Like their counterpart, the UNCITRAL ML, their goal is to harmonise arbitral proceedings and to avoid discrepancies.[154] Art. 17 (1) UNCITRAL Rules reads as follows:[155]

> "Subject to these Rules, the arbitral tribunal may conduct the arbitration in such manner as it considers appropriate, provided that the parties are treated with equality and that at an appropriate stage of the proceedings each party is given a reasonable opportunity of presenting its case. The arbitral tribunal, in exercising its discretion, shall conduct the proceedings so as to avoid unnecessary delay and expense and to provide a fair and efficient process for resolving the parties' dispute."

Similar provisions can be found in the Swiss, ICDR, ICC and LCIA Rules, with only small linguistic differences.[156] The DIS Rules even emphasise procedural efficiency by stating: 'The arbitral tribunal and the parties shall conduct the proceedings in a time- and cost-efficient manner, taking into account the complexity and economic importance of the dispute.'[157] The SIAC Rules put it slightly differently, stating that the arbitral tribunal must ensure a 'fair, expeditious, economical and final resolution'.[158] The first sentence of Art. 17 UNCITRAL Rules is a clear reminder of the provisions of the various *leges arbitri* previously mentioned *(see* p. 20 et seqq. *supra).* As in the *leges arbitri*, the institutional arbitration rules equip the arbitral tribunal, subject to the parties' agreement, with broad discretion in governing the proceedings. The limits are again found in the principle of due process and therefore reference can be made to what has already been said in this respect.[159]

Compared to the *leges arbitri*, the UNCITRAL Rules provide for the case to be presented at an 'appropriate stage of the proceedings', which refers to the provisions set out in the procedural timetable, as will be discussed shortly.[160] The second phrase of Art. 17 (1) UNCITRAL Rules obliges the arbitral tribunal to act as a diligent case manager, and therefore to avoid delay and

153 Schütze-PATOCCHI/NIEDERMAIER, n. 1, 6, 13.

154 UNCITRAL YB (1968-1970), 261, n. 1.

155 *See* Art. 17 (1) UNCITRAL Rules; While Art. 18 UNCITRAL ML speaks of the 'full opportunity' to present the case, the UNCITRAL Rules, under the same reasoning as the EAA 1996, mention only a 'reasonable opportunity' *(see* p. 21 *supra).*

156 Art. 15 (1) Swiss Rules; Art. 20 (1) ICDR Rules; Art. 22 (4) ICC Rules; Art. 14.4 (i) LCIA Rules.

157 Art. 27.1 DIS Rules; SCHARDT, 29.

158 *See* Rule 19 (1) SIAC Rules and the similar provision in Art. 14 (5) LCIA Rules, but from the point of view of the parties.

159 *See* p. 23 et seqq. *supra.*

160 Schütze-PATOCCHI/NIEDERMAIER, n. 343; *see* p. 29 et seqq. *infra.*

expenses and ensure a fair and efficient process.[161] To avoid delay, therefore, the preliminary meeting may take place by telephone conference instead of waiting to find a convenient date when all the parties can meet in person.[162] To avoid unnecessary expense, in lieu of granting a party's request for the appearance of eight witnesses, the arbitral tribunal may limit this number to two significant witnesses.[163] Thus, the question of whether it is appropriate to present the case at any stage of the proceedings depends on whether this accords with the schedule as set out in the procedural timetable.

C. Case Management Conference

At the outset of the proceedings, many institutional arbitration rules include a preliminary meeting (also called a 'case management conference'),[164] at which the arbitral tribunal will consult the parties on procedural issues and establish a timetable which sets out the time limits for each step of the proceedings.[165] The content of this conference depends in large part on the institutional arbitration rules and–as always–on the will of the parties. Thus, the arbitral tribunal must find a proper balance between the intentions of the parties and the arbitral tribunal's duty to ensure fair and efficient proceedings, avoiding unnecessary delay and expenses.[166]

The case management conference usually includes a timetable for the initial pleadings, claims and counterclaims, and the timeframe within which the arbitral award must be rendered.[167] As regards evidentiary matters, an overview of issues that must be dealt with gives an idea of how complex the case management conference can be:[168]

— Document production: timeframe for submission and request of discovery/disclosure, consequences of failure to submit documents, presentation of documentary evidence;

161 *See also* Art. 14.4 (ii) LCIA Rules; Rule 19 (1) SIAC Rules; Schütze-PATOCCHI/NIEDERMAIER, n. 345.

162 It has become common practice to hold the preliminary meeting via telephone or videoconference (BLACKABY et al., n. 6.41); *see* e.g. Art. 24 (4) ICC Rules; Rule 19 (3) SIAC Rules.

163 Schütze-PATOCCHI/NIEDERMAIER, n. 346.

164 *See* e.g. Art. 24 ICC Rules; Art. 27.2 DIS Rules.

165 *See* e.g. Art. 17 (2) UNCITRAL Rules; Rule 19 (3) SIAC Rules; Art. 20 (2) ICDR Rules; Art. 27.2 DIS Rules.

166 Art. 17 (1), 2nd sentence *in fine* UNCITRAL Rules; BORN, *Law and Practice,* ch. 8.07 n. 31.

167 *Ibid.*; as regards an expedited procedure whereby an arbitral award must be rendered within six months of the case management conference, *see* Art. 30 ICC Rules.

168 This short overview is inspired by Art. 2 IBA Rules and Arts. 13-17 UNCITRAL Notes; *see also* ICC, Effective Management of Arbitration; DIS Rules annex 3; SCHARDT, 30 et seqq.

— Hearings: decision on whether to hold hearings, schedule of hearings, admission of cross-examination;
— Witnesses: permitted number of witnesses, their preparation and the timing of submission of witness statements;
— Party and tribunal-appointed experts: permitted number of experts and timing of submission of expert reports;
— Inspections: measures of safekeeping physical evidence and organisation of inspection of site, property or goods; and
— Confidentiality: rules applicable to commercial or technical confidentiality.

The approaches taken to these issues under various institutional arbitration rules vary significantly, as will be demonstrated below (*see* p. 34 et seqq. *infra*). Moreover, the parties often have divergent opinions–for example, on whether cross-examination of witnesses and experts should take place or whether the parties can make disclosure requests. The arbitrators, in establishing the procedural measures, should consider all different points of view in order to ensure fair and equal proceedings. To facilitate and harmonise the taking of evidence in international arbitration, several organisations have provided helpful guidelines.

D. Harmonisation Initiatives

One could argue that since every international arbitration has its own difficulties and challenges, there is no need to harmonise such proceedings through international guidelines. On the one hand, it is true that every case should be treated differently by considering its peculiarities. On the other hand, however, if the parties come from different legal backgrounds, the guidelines offer a well-established compromise between different views of how evidence might be taken in international arbitration. Moreover, where such guidelines are used, the proceedings become more predictable and transparent, while the arbitrators retain the right to adapt them in order to meet the special needs of the respective arbitration.[169]

169 BORN, *Law and Practice*, ch. 1.08 n. 65.

In this respect, there is one main source, among others,[170] which serves as a guideline for the taking of evidence and can be used in conjunction with institutional arbitration rules: the IBA Rules. These guidelines are not institutional arbitration rules, but rather a code of best practice.[171] The term 'rules' can therefore be misleading, especially if they are used purely as guidelines. The IBA Rules and another (less important) harmonisation initiative are addressed briefly below, before considering how institutional arbitration rules and such guidelines can work together.

1. IBA Rules

a. Content

The IBA Rules have become the preferred guidelines and best practice in harmonising the process of taking evidence in international arbitration.[172] First published in 1983 as the 'IBA Supplementary Rules Governing the Presentation and Reception of Evidence in International Commercial Arbitration', they were first revised in 1999, when their name was changed to the IBA Rules on the Taking of Evidence in International Arbitration. The IBA Rules were last revised in 2010. Their success depends significantly on the fact that they offer a broadly accepted combination of evidentiary rules from common law and civil law countries.[173] They include not only provisions on document production, witnesses, experts and inspections, but also detailed technical norms relating to the evidentiary hearing and the admissibility and assessment of evidence. In this way, where neither the *leges arbitri* nor the institutional arbitration rules provide enough guidance, the IBA Rules can fill this vacuum.[174]

b. Application

Although the IBA Rules are not institutional or ad hoc arbitration rules, they are intended to work in conjunction with them as supplementary guidance.[175]

170 *See* e.g. the CIArb Guidelines on Party-appointed and Tribunal-appointed Expert Witnesses in International Arbitration; CIArb Guidline on Documents Only Arbitration Procedures; ICC Commission Report on Controlling Time and Cots in Arbitration; ALI/UNIDROIT Principles of Transnational Civil Procedure.

171 BORN, *Int. Comm. Arb.*, 199.

172 WAINCMYER, 752; RISSE/HALLER, n. 6; EMANUELE et al., n. 58; BLACKABY et al., n. 6.95; O'MALLEY, n. 1.05; LAU, 563 et seqq.; IBA Report (2016), 1, 8 ff. According to this study, out of 845 respondents, 48% frequently refer to the IBA Rules. It is noteworthy that in certain key jurisdictions, the use of the IBA Rules varies significantly, *see ibid.*, 15; *see also* Queen Mary Survey (2015), 36. This survey involved more than 700 practitioners and shows that the IBA Rules are used in more than 60% of arbitrations.

173 Born, *Law and Practice*, ch. 9.01 n. 18; IBA Report (2016), 9.

174 RISSE/HALLER, n. 2.

175 IBA Rules, Preamble, n. 1.

As well as applying them in their entirety, it is possible to apply only parts thereof or to adapt them to particular circumstances.[176] Their binding application can be achieved in two ways: either by agreement of the parties or by direct order of the arbitral tribunal.[177] As an alternative, the IBA Rules can also be used as non-binding guidelines.[178]

Implementation by party agreement can take place by inclusion in the arbitration agreement, although this seldom seems to happen *(see* p. 23 *supra).*[179] More often, the parties will agree on their application at the case management conference upon the suggestion of the arbitral tribunal.[180] If the parties are silent as to the application of the IBA Rules, the arbitral tribunal can decide at its discretion whether and how to apply them. Usually, however, the IBA Rules are used as non-binding guidelines in the form of soft law.[181] This is confirmed by a recent survey, which revealed that of the 60% of respondents who applied the IBA Rules, 53% adopted them as guidelines and only 7% as binding rules.[182] In this way, the arbitral tribunal has maximum flexibility in taking evidence.[183] Consequently, the parties must be aware that they have no right to enforce the IBA Rules.[184]

Another advantage of using the IBA Rules as pure guidelines is that it strengthens the finality of the arbitral award. Several *leges arbitri* state that an arbitral award can be set aside if the arbitral tribunal did not consider the parties' agreement in conducting the proceedings.[185] Thus, in using the IBA Rules as non-binding guidelines, the risk of the arbitral award being set aside because of mistakes in the taking of evidence can be avoided or at least significantly reduced.[186]

176 *Ibid.*, n. 2.

177 RISSE/HALLER, n. 22 et seqq.

178 IBA Rules, Preamble, n. 2.

179 RISSE/HALLER, n. 23.

180 IBA Rules, Foreword, 3; RISSE/HALLER, n. 24.

181 Queen Mary Survey (2015), 36; Queen Mary Survey (2012), 11.

182 *See also* IBA Report (2016), 9, 16 et seqq. Accordingly, approximately 80% of respondents declared the IBA Rules as non-binding.

183 Queen Mary Survey (2012), 11; RISSE/HALLER, n. 27; EMANUELE et al., n. 59.

184 RISSE/HALLER, n. 27.

185 Art. V (1) (d) NYC; Art. 34 (2) (a) (iv) UNCITRAL ML; § 1059 (2) (1.) (d) CCP DE; S. 68 (2) (c) EAA 1996; conversely, *see* the Swiss perspective *(see* p. 270 *infra)*; ASA Bull. 2004, 779; DFT 117 II 346, cons. 1b.

186 EMANUELE et al., n. 59.

c. Scope of Application

Reading the previous remarks, one might easily conclude that there seem to be only advantages to using the IBA Rules as guidelines in an international arbitration. However, although the IBA Rules are a very effective and tested tool to be utilised in the taking of evidence, both parties and arbitrators must consider carefully whether to use them in their arbitration.

In this respect, two remarks are noteworthy. First, the IBA rules are designed to be used in international arbitration.[187] Where the arbitration is purely domestic, even though the rules could be applied, the parties should refrain from doing so and should choose familiar evidentiary rules, instead of international guidelines. Second, although the IBA Rules represent a well-accepted compromise between common law and civil law, they remain a compromise between 'different legal traditions'.[188] If the parties are both from either the common law or civil law tradition, the application of the IBA Rules can present unnecessary difficulties. This becomes evident in the context of an international arbitration where the parties are both from civil law countries. To implement document production according to the IBA Rules, which contain several common law elements, would not meet the parties' expectations; nor would it have any other justification from an objective point of view.[189]

d. Result

When the parties must agree on evidentiary matters in international arbitration, the IBA Rules are the most commonly used tool, as they cleverly combine common law and civil law elements. They fill the gap if neither the *lex arbitri* nor the institutional arbitration rules are of help regarding evidentiary issues. Therefore, they are meant to be used in conjunction with (institutional or ad hoc) arbitration rules. Not only can the parties agree on their application; in the absence of such an agreement, the arbitral tribunal can declare them applicable and binding, either in whole or in part. However, they are most commonly applied in a non-binding way–that is, as pure guidelines. This strengthens the finality of the arbitral award, while at the same time supporting the arbitral tribunal in its procedural flexibility. However, application of the IBA Rules makes sense only if the arbitral proceedings are international and the parties are from different legal traditions. Otherwise, there is no logical reason for implementing rules with which the parties and their lawyers are unfamiliar.

187 IBA Rules, Preamble, n. 1.

188 *Ibid.*, n. 1; RISSE/HALLER, n. 33.

189 *Ibid.*

2. UNCITRAL Notes

In addition to this preferred evidentiary tool, another harmonisation initiative should be mentioned. Although not comparable in importance to the IBA Rules, the UNCITRAL Notes on Organizing Arbitral Proceedings provide helpful inspiration in shaping international arbitral proceedings.[190] First established in 1996 and revised in 2016, they can be used in conjunction with ad hoc or institutional arbitration rules. The notes–as compared to the IBA Rules–are not intended to serve as a code of best practice; their *raison d'être* is rather to be used as a sort of general checklist.[191] Since the UNCITRAL Notes are not binding and serve only as guidelines, the parties can use them or refer to them at their full discretion.[192] Regarding evidentiary issues in particular, the UNCITRAL Notes contain recommendations about document production, witnesses, experts, inspections and hearings. Hence, it might be helpful for arbitrators and the parties to consult the UNCITRAL Notes at the beginning of arbitration to check whether the most import (evidentiary) issues have been addressed.

E. Examples of Evidence in International Arbitration

In the following, two examples of evidence will be examined in order to show the differences in their treatment under different sets of institutional arbitration rules. In particular, it shall be demonstrated to what extent institutional arbitration rules mirror the legal domestic regime at their headquarters (e.g. the ICC in Paris, France). In doing so, one should remember that how institutional arbitration rules are applied in practice always depends on the parties and arbitrators. An ICC arbitration with parties from Austria and Switzerland and a German arbitrator will therefore be conducted differently from an arbitration under the same rules but with parties from England and the US and an Australian arbitrator.

In order to bridge the gaps between different legal traditions, and where institutional arbitration rules might not provide an answer, the aforementioned IBA Rules can provide helpful guidance in order to find a compromise regarding evidentiary issues. The two examples that will be examined have not been chosen randomly. The way that document production and witnesses

190 Queen Mary Survey (2015), 35, 36. Even though the UNCITRAL Notes 1996 seem to be known in international arbitration, they are not yet used frequently.

191 UNCITRAL Notes, n. 1-2.

192 *Ibid.*, n. 3.

of fact are treated in international arbitration serves as a perfect illustration of its flexibility and facility to settle disputes in a fast and efficient manner. Furthermore, as has been shown, the oral and written parts of arbitral proceedings differ significantly between the civil law and common law traditions.

1. Document Production

a. Introduction

As a rule, of all types of evidence in international arbitration, documentary evidence enjoys the greatest credibility.[193] This is especially true in commercial disputes, where documentary evidence provides a record of what the parties have undertaken and agreed upon (e.g. in the minutes of the board of directors or balance sheets).[194] In addition, it is often far less time consuming and costly to present documentary evidence than to examine witnesses, who might have to be prepared to give testimony on an event that happened years ago.[195] As mentioned above (*see* p. 12 *supra*), the weight in common law countries still lies heavily on oral testimony, while in civil law countries documentary evidence is paramount.[196] Anyone who might conclude that international arbitration is primarily influenced by civil law should bear in mind that 'documentary evidence' is not the same as 'document production'. While the former is a form of evidence, the latter relates to how documentary evidence is made available for the parties and the arbitral tribunal.

A quick look at a selection of international arbitration rules reveals that the arbitral tribunal has broad discretion to order document production, which has its origins in the common law tradition. Therefore, document production as a means of requesting a party to disclose documents which it has not voluntarily delivered itself is widely accepted in international arbitration.[197]

Nonetheless, there are some differences between the institutional arbitration rules in this regard. It would be logical to conclude that although arbitration institutions in civil law countries accept document production, their provisions are more moderate, given that in the courts in civil law countries are very reluctant to order broad document production (*see* p. 13 *supra*). In contrast, common law arbitration institutions would be assumed to have more extensive provisions in this regard. Before examining whether this

193 BORN, *Law and Practice*, ch. 8.07 n. 38; WAINCYMER, *Evidence*, 826; KARRER, 54.

194 WAINCYMER, *Evidence*, 826.

195 BLACKABY et al., n. 6.90.

196 WAINCYMER, *Evidence*, 827; O'MALLEY, n. 3.02.

197 O'MALLEY, n. 3.03.

assertion holds true, the IBA Rules on document production will be quickly examined in order to outline why they are such a widely accepted compromise between the common law and civil law traditions.

b. Document Production in the IBA Rules

Art. 3 IBA Rules deals with three groups of documents: (1) documents on which the parties base their claim and defence; (2) documents on which one party wants to rely but cannot produce it on its own; and (3) and documents held by third parties. As document production plays a vital role in international arbitration, Art. 3 is one of the provisions most commonly referred to.[198] Although extensive US or English-style discovery/disclosure is not available in international arbitration, there is a consensus that document production is appropriate to a certain degree.[199] Thus, various institutional arbitration rules state that the arbitral tribunal must establish the facts 'by all appropriate means'.[200] Hence, the question is not whether, but rather to what extent, there should be document production.[201]

Art. 3 (3) IBA Rules limits document production in various ways:

- lit. a: Each requested document must be identified sufficiently (author, date and content);[202]
- lit. b: The requesting party must provide a statement as to how the document is relevant to the case and material to its outcome; and
- lit. c: A further statement is necessary, confirming that the requested document is not in the possession of the requesting party, and stating why it would be unreasonably burdensome to produce the document on its own and why the party assumes that the requested document is in possession of the adverse party.

Following the document request, the arbitral tribunal will set a time limit within which the party to which the request is addressed must either produce the document or raise an objection (e.g. attorney-client privilege or commercial or technical confidentiality).[203] In case of an objection, the arbitral tribunal will consult the parties in order to reach agreement.[204] If no

198 IBA Report (2016), 15 et seq.

199 IBA Review Subcommittee (2010), 7.

200 *See* e.g. Art. 25 (1) ICC Rules; Art. 22.1 (iii) LCIA Rules.

201 ZUBERBÜHLER et al., Art. 3 IBA Rules n. 34.

202 *Ibid.*, n. 109 et seqq.

203 Art. 3 (4), (5) IBA Rules; Art. 9 (2) IBA Rules.

204 Art. 3 (6) IBA Rules.

agreement is reached, the arbitral tribunal will finally decide whether to order document production.[205]

This rather narrow extent of document production combines the different common law and civil law approaches quite thoughtfully. On the one hand, parties from civil law countries consider these provisions helpful, since they limit document production to a degree where the requested documents must be sufficiently specified and fishing expeditions are thus avoided, or even impossible.[206] Furthermore, the high costs of document production in state court litigation can be bypassed by focusing on those documents that are claimed to be relevant to the case. On the other hand, parties from common law countries who are used to discovery/disclosure rights in state court litigation can still seek access to internal documents form the adverse party.[207] With Art. 3 IBA Rules in mind, the focus will now shift to the provisions of document production under common law and civil law institutional arbitration rules.

c. Civil Law Institutional Arbitration Rules

To begin with, Art. 24 (3) Swiss Rules reads as follows:

> "At any time during the arbitral proceedings the arbitral tribunal may require the parties to produce documents, exhibits or other evidence within such a period of time as the tribunal shall determine."

This provision, as an exact copy of Art. 27 (3) UNCITRAL Rules, affords the arbitral tribunal broad discretion to order document production. The term 'other evidence' refers to inspections of sites or even witness examination.[208] Similar provisions are found in Art. 25 (5) ICC Rules and Art. 28 (2) DIS Rules. None of these rules seems to limit the discretion of the arbitral tribunal to order document production beyond the general limits of due process. Accordingly, the extent of document production here is even wider than under the IBA Rules, Nonetheless, various commentators point out that although the abovementioned rules do not explicitly impose any restrictions on document production, they are not intended to pave the way for wide-ranging discovery/disclosure rights.[209] Rather, the arbitral tribunal is bound by the principle of due process and must thus conduct the proceedings accordingly (i.e. also meeting the expectations of the parties).

205 Art. 3 (7) IBA Rules.

206 ZUBERBÜHLER et al., Art. 3 IBA Rules n. 108; IBA Review Subcommittee (2010), 8.

207 *Ibid.*

208 Zuberbühler et al.-NATER-BASS/ROUVINEZ, Art. 24 Swiss Rules n. 30.

209 GIRSBERGER/VOSER, n. 994; Schütze-REINER/ASCHAUER, n. 552.

d. Common Law Institutional Arbitration Rules

Unlike institutional arbitration rules from civil law countries, those from common law origins are less uniform. This shall be demonstrated by means of two examples.

According to Art. 22.1 (v) LCIA Rules, the arbitral tribunal has the following power:

> "To order any party to produce to the Arbitral Tribunal and to other parties documents or copies of documents in their possession, custody or power which the Arbitral Tribunal decides to be relevant."

This provision specifies that only documents in the parties' 'possession, custody or power' can be subject to document production. Moreover, the documents must be 'relevant'. These limitations have been drafted bearing in mind that the arbitration might be held in a civil law country with very restricted (or even no) discovery or disclosure rights.[210] Art. 22.1 (v) LCIA Rules is therefore quite similar to Art. 3 (3) IBA Rules, since it limits the scope of document production and therefore takes into account that the provisions will be potentially used in an international context between parties from different legal traditions.

Another example is Art. 21 (4) ICDR Rules, which reads as follows:

> "The tribunal may, upon application, require a party to make available to another party documents in that party's possession not otherwise available to the party seeking the documents, that are reasonably believed to exist and to be relevant and material to the outcome of the case. Requests for documents shall contain a description of specific documents or classes of documents, along with an explanation of their relevance and materiality to the outcome of the case."

In general, Art. 20 (4) ICDR Rules provides that the tribunal can order document production which it finds necessary or appropriate. Unless the parties agree otherwise, this article shall be applicable. At first glance, there seem to be no differences at all compared to Art. 3 (3) IBA Rules: The requested documents have to be specified, relevant and material to the outcome of the case. Furthermore, they need to be not otherwise available to the requesting party.

---

210 SCHERER et al., Art. 22 LCIA Rules n. 28.

Despite the resemblance to the IBA Rules, two differences should be pointed out. The first one concerns categories of documents. While the IBA Rules speak of 'narrow and specific requested category of documents'[211], Art. 21 (4) ICDR Rules requires only 'specific documents or classes of documents'. The fact that the parties can ask for a whole category of documents has led to much discussion.[212] Behind the 'narrow and specific' standard lies the argument that there might be a relevant document that cannot be identified sufficiently specifically.[213] This is the case, for instance, if a party knows that the adverse party has made a decision–for example, about the termination of a contract–which should have been recorded in the minutes of the meeting of the board of directors.[214] The party may be unable to specify the author, date and exact content of such a document, but may nonetheless be able to describe the requested document in a narrow and specific way.

The ICDR Rules do not seem to have adopted this standard and therefore they do not limit document production to narrow categories of documents.[215] Consequently, they provide for even wider document production than under the IBA Rules. One would be mistaken in assuming that this broad document production under the ICDR Rules is due to the wide-ranging discovery rights in US state court litigation. Art. 21 (10) ICDR Rules explicitly states that certain measures of US-style discovery are not applicable in arbitration under the ICDR Rules.

The second difference concerns control over the requested documents. According to Art. 21 (4) ICDR Rules, the arbitral tribunal can require a party to present only documents that are in its possession. By contrast, Art. 3 (3) (c) (ii) IBA Rules obliges the requesting party to provide a statement of the reasons why it assumes that the documents requested are in the possession, custody or control of another party. This difference can be explained by the fact that US law grants arbitral tribunals the power, under certain conditions, to order

211 Art. 3 (3) (a) (ii) IBA Rules.

212 O'MALLEY, n. 3.35 et seq.; IBA Review Subcommittee (2010), 9; ZUBERBÜHLER, Art. 3 Swiss Rules n. 114.

213 IBA Review Subcommittee (2010), 9.

214 *Ibid.*

215 MARGHITOLA, 29; *see also* Art. 21 (6) ICDR Rules, which states that requests for document production regarding e-documents must be 'narrowly focused'. Therefore, the extent of document production for e-documents is more limited than that for physical documents. However, this provision only complements the general rule about physical document production in Art. 21 (4) ICDR Rules and does not adopt the 'narrow and specific' standard (GUSY/ILLMER, 289).

documents from third parties which are not part of the arbitration.[216] Therefore, Art. 21 (4) ICDR Rules refers only to documents in the possession of the requested party and does not mention third parties.[217]

e. Result

The previous remarks on document production in international arbitration have revealed different controversies. Although virtually all institutional arbitration rules provide for document production, there are significant differences. The thesis was proposed that since civil law countries tend not to provide for broad document production, institutional arbitration rules from these countries would mirror this in their provisions by limiting document production; and vice versa for institutional arbitration rules from common law countries. This thesis has been disproved, at least partially.

Institutional arbitration rules from civil law countries grant broad discretion when it comes to document production, subject only to the general principle of due process and other legal principles such as attorney-client privilege and commercial and technical confidentiality. However, this broad discretion does not form the basis for far-reaching discovery/disclosure rights. Still, compared to the IBA Rules, the Swiss, ICC and DIS Rules take a very liberal, arbitration-friendly approach. The institutional arbitration rules from common law countries show a different picture. The LCIA Rules are quite similar to the IBA Rules. Anticipating that they may also be used in international arbitral proceedings with parties from different legal traditions, they narrow document production accordingly. At the other end of the scale are the ICDR Rules, which, despite many similarities to the IBA Rules, do not adopt the 'narrow and specific' standard with regard to requests for categories of documents. Therefore, the ICDR Rules allow for broader document production than the IBA Rules.

What consequences can be drawn from this brief examination? The fact that common law institutional arbitration rules contain detailed provisions on document production is because this procedure is also well known in state court litigation in those countries. On the other hand, arbitration institutions from civil law countries, which are unfamiliar with document production, content themselves with affording the arbitral tribunal broad discretion. At the end of the day, however, institutional arbitration rules should leave enough space for the parties and the arbitral tribunal to reach agreement on the degree of document production that is permissible.

216 MARGHITOLA, 30; S. 7 FAA USA; *see* p. 183 *infra*.

217 MARGHITOLA, 30.

2. Witnesses

a. Introduction

Despite the preference in international arbitration to rely mainly on documentary evidence, the practical significance of fact witnesses is considerable.[218] The main advantage of examining witnesses is that questions can be asked directly by all parties. Even though the arbitral tribunal governs the hearings, it has become standard practice in international arbitral proceedings that the parties themselves (i.e. their lawyers) can question not only their own witnesses, but also those of the adverse party. The drawbacks to this are the significant expenses and often time-consuming examinations involved.[219] Nonetheless, the significance of fact witnesses should not be underestimated. This is especially true given that documentary evidence and the examination of fact witnesses are regularly linked. Witnesses are often indispensable to explain the background and nature of documentary evidence.[220] Many institutional arbitration rules therefore include detailed provisions on the hearing and the examination of witnesses.[221]

The differences in the approach to witnesses in common law and civil law countries are quite astonishing.[222] As previously mentioned (*see* p. 12 *supra*), compared to civil law countries, orality plays a much more important role in state court litigation in common law countries. The two legal traditions differ with regard not only to who can be a witness, but also to how witnesses can be prepared for examination and how the examination itself works.[223] Even though the institutional arbitration rules examined below are designed for an international setting and the differences between legal traditions seem to be diminishing, it would be unsurprising if there were certain provisions that can be explained only within the context of their legal background. Whether this is in fact true shall now be analysed. To this end, the provisions on witnesses in the IBA Rules shall be quickly addressed before turning to institutional arbitration rules.

---

218 O'MALLEY, n. 4.01; BLACKABY *et. al.*, n. 6.120: WAINCYMER, *Evidence*, 885; MOLITORIS, n. 1.

219 WAINCYMER, *Evidence*, 885.

220 BLACKABY et al., n. 6.120.

221 *See* e.g. Arts. 17 (3), 27 (2), 28 and 31 UNCITRAL Rules; Arts. 15 (2), 25, 29 (2) Swiss Rules; Arts. 25 (3), 26 ICC Rules.

222 ZUBERBÜHLER et al., Art. 3 IBA Rules n. 4.

223 IBA Review Subcommittee (2010), 14.

b. Witnesses in the IBA Rules

With regard to witness examination, the IBA Rules have adopted many common law elements. This applies in relation not only to the identity of witnesses, but also to the degree of interaction between parties and witnesses. The examination also includes cross-examination, with which civil law lawyers will usually be unfamiliar.[224] Despite this common law approach, the IBA Rules also state that the arbitral tribunal shall have full power over the hearing at all times, which clearly refers to the judge-led civil law approach *(see* p. 13 et seqq. *supra).*

Art. 4 IBA Rules addresses numerous issues in regard to witnesses of fact. Thus, only those on which the common law and civil law traditions diverge most significantly are discussed here, which are as follows:

— Who can be a witness?
— How can parties interact with witnesses?
— How and by whom are witnesses examined?

I. *Identity of Witnesses*

The first issue concerns the identity of witnesses. Art. 4 (2) IBA Rules makes it quite clear that 'any person' may be a witness and present evidence, including the parties, their officers, lawyers, employees and other representatives. For a civil law practitioner, this may come as a surprise, as civil law systems often exclude parties from acting as witnesses; in common law systems, by contrast, the term 'witness' is interpreted broadly.[225] The exclusion of parties as witnesses in civil law countries is mostly due to the fact that as the parties have a special interest in the outcome of the proceedings, their statements are considered less valuable.[226] In international arbitration, however, the view has been established that anyone who is capable of commenting on the facts based on his or her own experience can be a witness.[227] While the parties and related persons can therefore testify as witnesses, their credibility can be tested according to their identity and relation with the parties.[228]

224 ZUBERBÜHLER et al., Art. 8 IBA Rules n. 19.

225 *See* e.g. for civil law: Art. 169 CCP CH; § 402 CCP DE (*see also* exceptions for minors according to § 455 (2) CCP DE); Art. 204 CCP FR; ZUBERBÜHLER et al., Art. 4 IBA Rules n. 8 et seqq; for common law *see* e.g. Rule 30 (a) (1) FRCP USA; Rule 34.1 (1) (b) CPR 1998.

226 WAGNER, 485 et seqq.; O'MALLEY, n. 4.08; BLACKABY et al., n. 6.125 et seqq.

227 BORN, *Law and Practice,* ch. 8.07 n. 43; BORN, *Int. Comm. Arb.,* 2276 et seq.; WAINCYMER, *Evidence,* 896 et seq.; O'MALLEY, n. 4.08; UNCITRAL Notes, n. 89.

228 WAINCYMER, *Evidence,* 897; BLACKABY et al., n. 6.129.

Consequently, the arbitral tribunal might weigh the statement of a party's officer differently from that of a more independent witness.[229]

II. Interaction Between Parties and Witnesses

The second question concerns the degree of interaction between the parties and witnesses. Art. 4 (3) IBA Rules states:

> "It shall not be improper for a Party, its officers, employees, legal advisors or other representatives to interview its witnesses or potential witnesses and to discuss their prospective testimony with them."

Again, the approaches in common and civil law systems differ significantly. The fact that in civil law countries, it is the judge (and not the parties' lawyers) who examines witnesses explains why contact between lawyers and (potential) witnesses prior to the hearing is considered unethical in some countries.[230] In contrast, because the proceedings are more party-led in common law countries, lawyers may discuss and prepare the statements with and of their own witnesses.[231] Despite these differences, in international arbitration the view has been adopted that lawyers are generally permitted to contact their[232] witnesses prior to the hearing in order to prepare and discuss their statements.[233]

While the degree of preparation may vary from a general discussion of the issues of the case to an intensive rehearsal of witness examination, there are certain limits.[234] It would be unethical and under some laws even criminal to encourage a witness to lie in court or to give misleading statements.[235] Therefore, lawyers would be well advised not to 'over-prepare' their witnesses, for

229 Art. 9 (1) IBA Rules; IBA Review Subcommittee (2010), 15.

230 IBA Working Party, 27; ZUBERBÜHLER et al., Art. 4 IBA Rules n. 12 et seqq.; O'MALLEY, n. 4.15; SINCLAIR, 29 et seqq.; *see* e.g. also the Swiss Federal Act of the Free Movement of Lawyers (SR 935.61), Art. 12a; Swiss National Rules of Professional Conduct, Art. 7; DFT 2C_8/2010 of 4 Oct. 2010, cons. 3.2.1.

231 IBA Working Part, 27; SINCLAIR, 36 et seq.

232 Art. 4 (3) IBA Rules. The IBA Rules are thus quite clear that to contact a party's own witness is permissible by speaking of 'its' witness–that is, the witness a party intends to present. As regards contacting adverse witnesses, the ICSID developed certain conditions under which this is allowed (*Azinian et al. v. United Mexican States*, ICSID, ARB (AF)/92/2), 1 Nov. 1999, n. 56); concerning contacting adverse witnesses in general *see* O'MALLEY, n. 4.19 et seqq).

233 IBA Review Subcommittee (2010), 16; BLACKABY et al., n. 6.123 et seqq; VON SEGESSER, *Witness Preparation*, 224; O'MALLEY, n. 4.15; WAINCYMER, *Evidence*, 898; *see also* IBA Guidelines 24.

234 VON SEGESSER, *Witness Preparation*, 225.

235 ZUBERBÜHLER et al., Art. 4 IBA Rules n. 15; BLACKABY et al., n. 6.124; VON SEGESSER, *Witness Preparation*, 225; HOFFMANN/SHETTY, 211; *see also* IBA Guidelines 23.

fear of losing credibility.[236] This also applies to witness statements that contain testimony on the facts experienced by a witness.[237] These statements not only help the parties to prepare for the hearing, but also help the arbitral tribunal to conduct the proceedings time and cost efficiently.[238] Nonetheless, the arbitral tribunal should consider carefully whether such statements are in fact necessary. This is especially true if the arbitral tribunal intends to rely solely on a witness statement and does not request direct examination of the witness. Thus, a well-prepared witness statement can be time consuming and costly for the parties.[239]

III. Examination of Witnesses

The third and last point concerns how and by whom witnesses are examined in the hearing. As already mentioned, one of the significant differences between common law and civil law proceedings is the fact that in common law countries, the proceedings are more party led and therefore witnesses are mostly examined by the parties; while in civil law countries, witnesses are usually questioned by the judge (*see* p. 14 *supra*). Notwithstanding this fact, it is common practice in international arbitration that a witness who has delivered a witness statement must appear in person at the hearing for examination and cross-examination if his or her attendance is requested by either the parties or the arbitral tribunal.[240] Cross-examination as a main feature of adversarial (common law) proceedings has become widely accepted in international arbitral proceedings.[241] Even civil law lawyers today appreciate it, because it allows them not only to elicit facts that were not mentioned in the witness statement, but also to reveal contradictions and to undermine the reliability and credibility of a witness.[242]

According to Art. 4 (7) IBA Rules, the arbitral tribunal will usually disregard the witness statement if a witness whose attendance has been requested fails to appear without any valid reason. According to Art. 8 IBA Rules, the arbitral tribunal shall have full control over the hearings and shall therefore conduct and govern it appropriately–a provision which calls to mind judge-led

236 ZUBERBÜHLER *et al*, Art. 4 IBA Rules n. 16; VON SEGESSER, *Witness Preparation*, 225; SINCLAIR, 31; *see also* IBA Guidelines 21.

237 Arts. 4 (4)-(6) IBA Rules; ZUBERBÜHLER et al., Art. 4 IBA Rules n. 22 et seqq.; SINCLAIR, 29 et seqq.

238 IBA Review Subcommittee (2010), 16; OETIKER, *Witnesses*, 254; O'MALLEY, n. 4.23.

239 ZUBERBÜHLER et al., Art. 4 IBA Rules n. 25; OETIKER, *Witnesses*, 255.

240 Art. 8(1) IBA Rules; IBA Review Subcommittee (2010), 17.

241 SINCLAIR, 41; VAN HOUTTE, 459 et seq.

242 SINCLAIR, 41; MEKAT, 121; NEWMAN, 408 et seqq.

civil law proceedings.[243] Furthermore, Art. 8 (3) IBA Rules recommends the order in which the examination should be carried out: starting with the claimant's witnesses, followed by the respondent's witnesses and experts. After the direct examination of each witness, there is the possibility for cross-examination by the adverse party and in some cases even for re-examination.[244] Since the IBA Rules aim to provide for flexible proceedings, the arbitral tribunal can change the suggested order of examination as it considers appropriate.[245]

c. Civil Law Institutional Arbitration Rules

When it comes to witnesses, institutional arbitration rules based in civil law countries differ in their level of detail. While the Swiss Rules govern witness examination quite specifically, the DIS and ICC Rules content themselves with a few general provisions. Art. 25 (1) ICC Rules merely states:

> "The arbitral tribunal shall proceed within as short a time as possible to establish the facts of the case by all appropriate means."

Although this wording is a clear reminder of the inquisitorial civil law approach, the tendency in international arbitration is that responsibility for producing and presenting the evidence falls first and foremost on the parties.[246] At the same time, the arbitral tribunal has maximum flexibility, since it must establish the facts of the case 'by all appropriate means'. This allows the arbitral tribunal to consider the different legal backgrounds of the parties and to tailor the proceedings accordingly. Concerning witnesses, the ICC Rules provide a general procedural framework only, and refrain from establishing specific and detailed rules.[247] Consequently, this leaves plenty of space to handle every case individually and specifically. Apart from these general remarks, Art. 26 (3) ICC Rules says that the arbitral tribunal, subject to the parties' agreement, shall be in full charge of the hearings, which underlines the arbitral tribunal's broad discretion in tailoring the arbitral proceedings.[248] This means, for instance, that the arbitral tribunal may hear witnesses on its own initiative.[249]

243 *See* p. 13 *supra;* Art. 8(2) IBA Rules; IBA Review Subcommittee (201), 23. The arbitral tribunal is therefore entitled not only to question witnesses at any time, but also to limit or exclude questions and answers if it considers them unnecessary (Arts. 8(2) and 8 (3) (g) IBA Rules).

244 Art. 8 (3) (a) IBA Rules; IBA Review Subcommitte (2010), 23.

245 Art. 8 (3) (f) IBA Rules; IBA Review Subcommitte (2010), 24.

246 VERBIST/SCHÄFER/IMHOOS, 140.

247 Mistelis-BOND/PARALIKA/SECOMB, Art. 25 ICC Rules n. 1 and 2.

248 *Ibid.*, Art. 26 ICC Rules n. 2; VERBIST/SCHÄFER/IMHOOS, 150.

249 Arts. 25 (2) and (3) ICC Rules.

A typical civil law approach is pursued by the DIS Rules, Art. 28.2 of which states the following:

> "For this purpose, the arbitral tribunal may, inter alia, on its own initiative, appoint experts, examine fact witnesses other than those called by the parties, and order any party to produce or make available any documents or electronically stored data. The arbitral tribunal shall not be limited to admit only evidence offered by the parties."

The arbitral tribunal has full discretion in hearing witnesses on its own initiative and is not bound by the parties' offer of evidence. Here, the inquisitorial civil law approach is mirrored by defining the arbitral tribunal as an active case manager.[250] This is confirmed by the new Art. 27.2 DIS Rules, as amended in 2018, which obliges the arbitral tribunal to hold a case management conference as soon as possible after its constitution.[251] The fact that the DIS Rules emphasise the active role of the arbitrator does not mean that he or she must act purely inquisitorially, as judges do in some state court litigation proceedings.[252] Rather, Art. 28.2 is modelled as a 'may' provision, leaving the arbitral tribunal with broad discretion.[253]

According to a practitioner of the DIS Rules, most DIS arbitral tribunals seem to avoid being too proactive in conducting the proceedings, but rather leave it to the parties to present the relevant evidence or to file requests to produce evidence.[254] However, this may change following the amendment of the DIS Rules in 2018 and the introduction of the mandatory case management conference.[255] Annex 3 of the DIS Rules sets out a list of measures to increase procedural efficiency. Accordingly, the arbitral tribunal can discuss with the parties, for example, whether to limit the length or number of submissions of any written fact witness statements or expert reports.[256] Further suggestions are made–for example, to hold only one oral hearing, including any taking of evidence, or to limit requests regarding document production.[257]

250 BESCH/KREUZEDER, 266; Böckstiegel et al.-RISSE, S. 27 DIS Rules n. 2.

251 *See also* DIS Rules annex 3; BESCH/KREUZEDER, 257 et seq.; SCHARDT, 29; BOOG/WIMALASENA, 25 et seq.

252 Böckstiegel et al.-RISSE, S. 27 DIS Rules n. 2. In this regard *see*, for example, § 139 CCP DE, stating that in order to establish the relevant facts of each case, state courts must question the parties.

253 BESCH/KREUZEDER, 256.

254 Böckstiegel et al.-RISSE, S. 27 DIS Rules n. 6.

255 Art. 27.2 DIS Rules.

256 DIS Rules Annex 3, A.

257 DIS Rules Annex 3, B and E.

On the other hand, the Swiss Rules contain detailed provisions on witnesses. In many ways inspired by the UNCITRAL Rules, they cover not only who can be a witness, but also interaction with and examination of witnesses.[258] Art. 25 (2) Swiss Rules says:

> "Any person may be a witness or an expert witness in the arbitration. It is not improper for a party, its officers, employees, legal advisors, or counsel to interview witnesses, potential witnesses, or expert witnesses."

Regarding the identity of witnesses, the Swiss Rules are in line with international standard practice, as in Art. 4 (2) IBA Rules, by confirming that 'any person may be a witness'. As compared to the UNCITRAL Rules, they take a more liberal approach by declaring that interaction with (potential) witnesses is not improper.[259] Since such contact is allowed, it is standard practice for the evidence of witnesses to be presented in the form of witness statements.[260] As compared to Art. 4 (3) IBA Rules, the Swiss Rules do not limit contact with witnesses that a party has requested to present, although they do distinguish between potential witnesses and named witnesses. Since a potential witness does not belong to either party, it is theoretically not improper to interview witnesses of the opposing party.[261] To avoid any uncertainty in this regard, the parties should discuss this issue early in the proceedings. They could, of course, exclude any contact with witnesses of the opposing party by applying Art. 4 (3) IBA Rules.

As regards the way in which witnesses are examined, Art. 25 (4) Swiss Rules provides:

> "At the hearing, witnesses and expert witnesses may be heard and examined in the manner set by the arbitral tribunal."

No suggestions are made about the manner and order in which witnesses should be examined. Thus, the arbitral tribunal, in accordance with the

258 *See* Art. 27 (1) UNCITRAL Rules; Zuberbühler et al.-BESSON/THOMMESEN, Introduction Swiss Rules n. 6 et seqq.; Zuberbühler et al.-NATER-BASS/ROUVINEZ, Art. 25 Swiss Rules n. 3, 4.

259 Zuberbühler et al.-NATER-BASS/ROUVINEZ, Art. 25 Swiss Rules n. 11. Even though the UNCITRAL Rules do not expressly allow contact with witnesses, they seem to accept this, given that witness statements are foreseen in Art. 27 (2) UNCITRAL Rules. The UNCITRAL Rules, as compared to other institutional arbitration rules, say little about the conduct of hearings to avoid over-regulating arbitral proceedings (UNCITRAL, A/CN.9/669 (2009), n. 69).

260 Art. 25 (3) Swiss Rules.

261 Zuberbühler et al.-NATER-BASS/ROUVINEZ, Art. 25 Swiss Rules, n. 13; BLESSING, *Witnesses*, 46; OETIKER, *Witnesses*, 264 et seq.

parties, must choose the appropriate way to do so. Depending on the arbitration, arbitrators often choose the common law practice of examining, cross-examining and re-examining witnesses.[262] Furthermore, the arbitral tribunal is free to order 'witness conferencing', where various witnesses are examined at the same time on specific issues.[263]

d. Common Law Institutional Arbitration Rules

As is the case with document production, the institutional arbitration rules diverge considerably in their provisions about witnesses. The LCIA Rules, which are some of the most detailed institutional arbitration rules, provide in Art. 19 (2):

> "The Arbitral Tribunal shall have the fullest authority under the Arbitration Agreement to establish the conduct of a hearing, including its date, form, content, procedure, time-limits and geographical place."

As a general statement, this passage makes it crystal clear that the arbitral tribunal enjoys the widest discretion in conducting the hearings. Not surprisingly, Art. 20.6 LCIA Rules declares that even a party itself can testify as a witness:

> "Subject to any order by the Arbitral Tribunal otherwise, any individual intending to testify to the Arbitral Tribunal may be treated as a witness notwithstanding that the individual is a party to the arbitration or was, remains or has become an officer, employee, owner or shareholder of any party or is otherwise identified with any party."

The word 'may' indicates that the drafters of the LCIA Rules were aware that the parties cannot be considered as witnesses in all countries, and therefore they allow exceptions.[264] Also, like the Swiss Rules, Art. 20.5 LCIA Rules allows contact with potential witnesses:

> "Subject to the mandatory provisions of any applicable law, rules of law and any order of the Arbitral Tribunal otherwise, it shall not be improper for any party or its legal representatives to interview any potential witness for the purpose of presenting his or her testimony in written form to the Arbitral Tribunal or producing such person as an oral witness at any hearing."

262 WIRTH, 14; GIRSBERGER/VOSER, n. 1009; ZUBERBÜHLER et al., Art. 25 IBA Rules n. 19.

263 Zuberbühler et al.-NATER-BASS/ROUVINEZ, Art. 25 Swiss Rules, n. 30; HANOTIAU, 376 et seq.; MCILWRATH/SAVAGE, n. 5-243; PETER, 47 et seqq.; RAESCHKE-KESSLER, *Witness Conferencing*, 415 et seqq.

264 SCHERER et al., Art. 20 LCIA Rules n. 37. While the LCIA version of 1998 used to contain the word 'shall', under the revised version of 2014 it is now possible to treat parties differently from witnesses.

Here again, it is acknowledged that in some jurisdictions, witness contact might not be permissible and therefore the arbitral tribunal will be bound by such restrictions. The ability of the arbitral tribunal to forbid any pre-hearing contact with witnesses serves to level out the imbalance where one party might not be allowed to make such contact due to national laws or professional standards.[265] Reading this passage in its strict wording, one might recognise that it speaks only of 'potential witnesses', and not of all witnesses. Compared to Art. 4 (3) IBA Rules, which allows contact with all witnesses, the LCIA Rules are therefore more restrictive. However, since Art. 20.5 LCIA addresses only interviewing witnesses, *preparing* witnesses is considered permissible.[266]

When the hearing finally takes place, Art. 20.8 LCIA Rules provides for different possibilities:

> "Any witness who gives oral testimony at a hearing before the Arbitral Tribunal may be questioned by each of the parties under the control of the Arbitral Tribunal. The Arbitral Tribunal may put questions at any stage of such testimony."

While the parties are often limited in the time given for their examination and cross-examination, the arbitral tribunal may put questions to the witnesses at any given time. Like judge-led examination, this supports a fast and efficient hearing, without too much time lost to exhaustive examinations. Although Art. 20.8 LCIA Rules is not as detailed as Art. 8 (2) IBA Rules *(see* p. 44 *supra)*, it puts the arbitral tribunal in full control of the hearing. However, the arbitral tribunal must consult the parties about the manner in which the examination should take place–for example, by proposing time limits for examination and cross-examination.

As compared to the LCIA Rules, the ICDR Rules mention witnesses and their examination just briefly in Art. 23 (4):

> "The tribunal shall determine the manner in which witnesses are examined and who shall be present during witness examination."

Like the respective provisions in the UNCITRAL Rules and the Swiss Rules, Art. 23 (4) ICDR Rules reminds the arbitral tribunal to choose a method of examination which is appropriate to the case.[267] Apart from that, there are no other provisions on the identity of witnesses, let alone about contact with

265 SCHERER et al., Art. 20 LCIA Rules n. 34.

266 *Ibid.*, Art. 20 LCIA Rules n. 35.

267 Art. 28 (2) UNCITRAL Rules; Art 25 (4) Swiss Rules; GUSY/HOSKING, Art. 23 ICDR n. 23.10.

witnesses or the examination of witnesses. Art. 23 (4) ICDR Rules gives a hint in this regard by saying:

> "Unless otherwise agreed by the parties or directed by the tribunal, evidence of witnesses may be presented in the form of written statements signed by them. In accordance with a schedule set by the tribunal, each party shall notify the tribunal and the other parties of the names of any witnesses who have presented a witness statement whom it requests to examine. The tribunal may require any witness to appear at a hearing."

As a default, the ICDR Rules follow the IBA Rules by suggesting that unless a party asks to examine a witness who has submitted his or her statement, there is no need for direct examination.[268] It seems to be common practice in ICDR proceedings to draft witness statements together with the witnesses and, if necessary, to prepare them for the hearing where they will be (cross-) examined.[269] As always, the parties and/or the arbitral tribunal can depart from this default procedure. Although in many cases witness statements contribute to efficient and less expensive proceedings, they should not be allowed without careful consideration, given the time and effort needed to produce well-prepared witness statements.[270] This is especially true if there are just a few witnesses and the issues at stake are limited.[271]

e. Result

The thesis that various provisions concerning witnesses in institutional arbitration rules make sense only when considered in the context of their legal background has only partially been affirmed. One might have expected that since the principle of orality is paramount in common law proceedings, institutional arbitration rules from common law countries would include detailed and extensive provisions on witnesses and the hearing itself. On the other hand, because the main emphasis in civil law proceedings is on documentary evidence, the rules of arbitration institutions based in civil law countries might be thought more likely to limit the oral part of the proceedings (i.e. the presentation and examination of witnesses). As the previous examples have demonstrated, however, institutional arbitration rules from civil and common law countries do not result in a uniform picture, either as a whole or within each system.

268 Arts. 4 (4)-(8) IBA Rules.

269 Mistelis-FELLAS/MOSQUERA, Art. 23 ICDR Rules n. 2.

270 OETIKER, *Witness Statements*, 30; OETIKER, *Witnesses*, 255.

271 *Ibid.*

Compared to the Swiss and IBA Rules, the ICC Rules say very little about how to treat witnesses. That the silence of the ICC Rules on typical witness issues, such as their identity, interaction and examination, is due to their civil law background seems unlikely. Rather, to grant maximum flexibility, the ICC Rules provide the arbitral tribunal with broad discretion when it comes to witnesses. The DIS Rules in turn allow for the arbitral tribunal to act in a quasi-inquisitorial (civil law) way. While this might be suitable for German domestic arbitration, the practice in international DIS arbitration places the responsibility for presenting evidence largely on the parties. At the other end of the spectrum, the Swiss Rules include more specific provisions about witnesses. As previously discussed, they adopt the common law approach not only by allowing anyone to be a witness, but also by allowing for the parties to interact with witnesses quite freely. Therefore, they represent a very liberal, up-to-date set of rules that mirror modern practice in international arbitration, quite similar to, but not as detailed as, the IBA Rules.

The provisions on witnesses in the LCIA Rules are almost as detailed as those in the IBA Rules. In terms of content, the LCIA Rules not only allow the parties to serve as witnesses, but also consider contact with witnesses as permissible and cross-examination as standard procedure. Furthermore, as the arbitral tribunal is in full control of the hearings, the arbitrators can put questions to witnesses at any given time. Thus, the LCIA Rules combine common and civil law elements regarding the treatment of witnesses. In contrast, the ICDR Rules say very little about witnesses. Much less detailed than the LCIA Rules, they leave it almost entirely to the arbitral tribunal to decide how witnesses should be treated. The provisions on witness statements, which are quite similar to the IBA Rules, are therefore exceptional.

To sum up, it has been shown that, regarding witnesses, institutional arbitration rules, regardless of their legal background, are either very detailed or just briefly mention the issue. In only a few cases are the provisions explicable solely due to their legal background (e.g. the DIS Rules, *see* p. 46 et seqq. *supra*). Hence, traces of domestic civil court litigation in institutional arbitration rules are increasingly seeming to disappear.[272] The overwhelming majority of rules provide the arbitral tribunal with broad discretion to conduct the proceedings in regard to witnesses. This could include applying the IBA Rules as a whole or at least partly, especially in cases where institutional arbitration rules say almost nothing about witnesses (*see e.g. the ICC and DIS Rules*, p. 45 et seqq. *supra*).

272 SINCLAIR, 47 et seq.

F. Summary

This part of the chapter has highlighted the effectiveness and flexibility of institutional arbitration rules. Their general provisions grant the arbitral tribunal broad discretion in conducting the proceedings, which finds its limits mainly in the principle of due process. Regarding evidence, it has been demonstrated that to ensure the proceedings run smoothly, all sorts of evidentiary issues should be addressed in the case management conference. Here, parties may have very different views–for example, concerning document production or the conduct of hearings. The IBA Rules provide solid guidelines to bridge the gap between opposing opinions. In most cases, they are used not as binding rules, but as guidelines, which strengthens the flexibility of the fact finding and the finality of the arbitral award. Despite these advantages, their application should not be ordered or agreed upon without due consideration. Since they are made to work between parties from different legal traditions, their application in domestic arbitration is often against the parties' intentions.

In a further step, an examination of the treatment of document production and witnesses under institutional arbitration rules and the IBA Rules has revealed the following findings. Regarding document production, the difference between common and civil law countries is evident in either detailed provisions (common law approach) or provisions which afford the arbitral tribunal broad discretion to decide to what extent document production is permissible (civil law approach). This difference might be due to the fact that in civil law state court litigation, document production is almost unknown. Under both approaches, however, there is enough space for the arbitral tribunal, in accordance with the parties and the guidance of the IBA Rules, to find a suitable solution for each case. The situation regarding witnesses is more complex. The rules are either general remarks or rather detailed provisions, with no commonalities evident among common and/or civil law institutional arbitration rules. Compared to document production, the traces of the legal traditions within which the specific institutions are based seem to have disappeared over time. Here too, the IBA Rules offer useful solutions and a balanced compromise between the common law and civil law traditions in handling witnesses.

Summing up, with regard to the taking evidence, institutional arbitra tion rules in themselves provide barely enough guidance. In conjunction with the IBA Rules, however, the process of taking evidence becomes more tangible and effective for both the parties and the arbitral tribunal.

§ 5 Conclusion

After examining the three pillars of the legal framework of international arbitration–namely the *leges arbitri,* the arbitration agreement and the institutional arbitration rules–several conclusions can be drawn.

The *leges arbitri* contain the general legislative framework by determining external issues such as the relation between state courts and the arbitral tribunal, as well as internal matters such as the taking of evidence. It has been shown that the parties should choose as the seat of arbitration an arbitration-friendly country where state courts will not interfere in the arbitral proceedings without good reason, and will also grant support (e.g. assistance in taking evidence or enforcement of the arbitral award). Unsurprisingly, the *leges arbitri* examined in this chapter are all very arbitration friendly, granting the arbitral tribunal wide discretion to govern the arbitral proceedings as long as due process is respected. Even though the *leges arbitri* provide a general procedural framework, the taking of evidence is in most cases only briefly mentioned. Thus, the question is where the parties should agree more specifically on evidentiary matters.

The arbitration agreement is crucial, since the validity of the arbitration itself–let alone that of the arbitral award–hinges on its validity. Because of the principle of separability, parties would be well advised to agree on the law governing the arbitration agreement and the underlying contract. In the arbitration agreement itself, the parties usually refer to evidentiary matters indirectly by agreeing on the application of institutional arbitration rules, in which all sorts of evidentiary issues are addressed in more detail. Although the parties can directly agree on the application of, for instance, the IBA Rules in the arbitration agreement, this seldom happens in practice.

An examination of the institutional arbitration rules reveals that, as in the *leges arbitri,* the arbitral tribunal has vast discretion to choose the procedural rules *à la carte.* In consultation with the parties, the arbitral tribunal should address matters of evidence at the outset of the proceedings (i.e. at the case management conference). By means of two examples, it has been demonstrated how views on these matters differ among institutional arbitration rules from common law and civil law systems. In this regard, the IBA Rules combine different elements from common law and civil law, and therefore represent an excellent compromise that works well in conjunction with institutional arbitration rules.

From this study of the legal framework, one thing is clear: in arbitration, as perhaps nowhere else, party autonomy is paramount.[273] This is evident in all three pillars of the arbitral procedural framework. Applied to the taking of evidence, the parties are at liberty, according to their intentions, to choose the seat of arbitration, draft the arbitration agreement and agree therein on a suitable set of institutional arbitration rules. In addition, those arbitration rules can be tailored to a high degree to the special needs of the respective case. Thus, compared to state court litigation, the taking of evidence in international arbitration seems to be almost limitless.

Obviously, however, this is true only as long as the parties play by the rules. So what happens if the parties do not comply with evidentiary orders? How can the arbitral tribunal respond? Can it sanction the disobedient party and if so, by what means? The next chapter will focus on the various possibilities the arbitral tribunal has at its disposal in this regard.

---

273 RADICATI DI BROZOLO, 40.

4

Arbitral Tribunal and the Sanctions it can Impose

§ 1 Introduction

The previous chapter has shown the arbitral tribunal's broad discretion to order document production and to summon witnesses as it deems appropriate. However, because the tribunal has no coercive power, the effectiveness of such orders depends largely on the parties' compliance. In this regard, there are several good reasons for parties to comply with evidentiary orders. First, they have an interest in the smooth functioning of the proceedings, in order to obtain an arbitral award within a reasonable timeframe. Second, since it is the arbitral tribunal that will eventually decide on the merits of the case, the parties are usually inclined to follow its procedural orders to keep the arbitral tribunal onside.[274] Third, despite the arbitral tribunal's lack of coercive power, it has some very effective sanctions at hand, which the parties should try their best to avoid.

Inevitably, however, in certain situations it may be impossible to present evidence, due to *force majeure* or other unforeseen circumstances.[275] In addition, the parties might have the right to refuse to comply with evidentiary orders due to (among other things) attorney-client privilege, technical and/or commercial confidentiality, or loss or destruction of a document.[276] However, the arbitral tribunal has various sanctions at its disposal if a party is unable to explain sufficiently why evidence has not been produced or if other obstructionist behaviour is revealed. Otherwise, parties might be able to unduly influence the proceedings by destroying or forging documents,[277] by providing false testimony or by improperly influencing witnesses and their statements.[278] This chapter outlines several sanctions that the arbitral tribunal

274 SACHS/NIEDERMAIER, n. 4.

275 HOSANG, *Obstructionist Behaviour*, 81.

276 Art. 9 (2) IBA Rules.

277 HOSANG, *Obstructionist Behaviour*, 110 et seq.

278 *Ibid.*, 112 et seqq.

can impose and considers whether they are in fact helpful to effectively gather evidence.[279] The focus is on the main sanction–so-called 'adverse inference'–although cost sanctions, sanctions against party representatives and monetary penalties are also addressed.

§ 2 Adverse Inference

A. Introduction

The previous chapter has demonstrated the paramount significance that evidence plays in arbitral proceedings. As pointed out in the introduction to this chapter, the parties' compliance with evidentiary orders is crucial for the arbitral proceedings to function smoothly. In order to facilitate the parties' right to present their case and to render an award based on a broad evaluation of the facts, a certain degree of disclosure is necessary.[280]

In contrast, if a party fails to produce a document without sufficient reason, the arbitral tribunal can draw an adverse inference under certain circumstances–that is, conclude that the document is adverse to the interests of the reluctant party. Or, to put it differently, the arbitral tribunal may consider a fact as proven despite the absence of the evidence in question.[281] This principle is widely accepted in international arbitration.[282] Its origin is found in English common law rules of evidence, but it has also become popular in civil law jurisdictions as a tool to sanction non-compliant parties.[283] Its *raison d'être* lies in the tension between parties' reluctance to present evidence that is harmful to their case and the arbitral tribunal's lack of coercive power to order the parties to present such evidence.[284] By contrast, any party which has evidence that is advantageous to its case in its possession would present this to the arbitral tribunal. International arbitration resolves this situation by letting the arbitral tribunal draw an adverse inference from any failure to

279 In the Queen Mary Survey of 2015, 46% of all respondents cited the 'lack of effective sanctions during the arbitral process' as one of the main disadvantages of international arbitration (7).

280 SHARPE, 550.

281 SOURGENS et al., n. 8.01.

282 WAINCYMER, *Evidence*, 775; O'MALLEY, n. 7.37; GREENBERG/LAUTENSCHLAGER, 181; BORN, *Int. Comm. Arb.*, 2391; for investment arbitration *see also* SOURGENS et al., n. 8.03.

283 LUTTRELL, 283 et seq., 285; O'MALLEY, n. 7.03; DFT 4A_2/2007 of 28 Mar. 2007, cons. 4. *see also* Art. 10 and 11 CCP FR i.c.w. Art. 1464 CCP FR, according to which an arbitrator may draw an adverse inference in case of non-compliance with evidentiary orders.

284 SHARPE, 549; GREENBERG/LAUTENSCHLAGER, 180; LUTTRELL, 281.

present evidence by concluding that the reluctant party has something to hide and such evidence is adverse to its interest.[285] Another advantage of this sanction is the fact that it need not be enforced separately in state courts.[286]

In terms of proportionality, the arbitral tribunal should always consider whether the other evidence in the case is already sufficiently strong that drawing an adverse inference becomes superfluous.[287] Since this sanction can have a significant influence on both the arbitral proceedings and the award, its application is subject to certain conditions, which are examined below.

B. Sources of Adverse Inference in International Arbitration

1. Leges Arbitri and Institutional Arbitration Rules

Today, the power of the arbitral tribunal to draw an adverse inference is broadly accepted in international arbitration.[288] That said, there are very few provisions regarding this issue in *leges arbitri* and institutional arbitration rules. Although several 'default clauses'[289] are included in some *leges arbitri* and institutional arbitration rules, they should not be confused with the right to draw an adverse inference. These clauses provide only that the arbitral tribunal may continue the proceedings if a party fails to participate and produce evidence. Consequently, the arbitral tribunal can render an award based on the evidence at hand. Still, it must take care not to violate the right of the parties to present their case.[290] This is why it is common practice to keep a passive party updated about every step of the proceedings and why there is no automatic award in favour of the other (more active) party.[291]

Most *leges arbitri*, however, contain no provisions concerning adverse inference. S. 41 (7) (b) EAA 1996 is therefore exceptional by allowing the arbitral tribunal to draw an adverse inference 'from the act of non-compliance as the circumstances justify' within the scope of a peremptory order. Under English law, peremptory orders go one step further than normal procedural orders by setting a timeframe for compliance for the production of docu-

285 HOSANG, *Obstructionist Behaviour*, 147 et seq.

286 HOSANG, *Adverse Inferences*, 803.

287 GREENBERG/LAUTENSCHLAGER, 204.

288 WAINCYMER, *Evidence*, 775; SHARPE, 549 et seq.; GREENBERG/LAUTENSCHLAGER, 181; SACHS/NIEDERMAIER, n. 3.

289 *See* e.g. Art. 25 (c) UNCITRAL ML; Art. 30 (3) UNCITRAL Rules; Art. 28 (3) Swiss Rules; Art. 30 DIS Rules; Art. 26 (3) ICDR Rules.

290 Mistelis-BREKOULAKIS et al., Art. 25 UNCITRAL ML, 887.

291 BUTCHERS/KIMBROUGH, 236.

ments, for example.[292] If a party fails to produce the document, the arbitral tribunal can draw an adverse inference, among other measures.[293] The EAA 1996 thus sees adverse inference not as an automatic sanction, but merely as one possibility among others.[294] According to other *leges arbitri*–for instance, those of Germany and Switzerland–even though it is not mentioned explicitly, adverse inference is considered to be inherent in the powers of the tribunal to conduct the taking of evidence.[295]

Institutional arbitration rules present a similar picture. Of the examined institutional arbitration rules, only the ICDR Rules explicitly allow the arbitral tribunal to draw an adverse inference.[296] However, many other rules equip the arbitral tribunal with the power to assess the evidence by determining its admissibility, relevance, materiality and weight.[297] In drawing an adverse inference, the arbitral tribunal is in fact assessing the evidence by deciding how to weigh the fact that certain evidence has not been presented as requested.[298] Over the years, arbitral practice has developed various criteria under which it is possible to draw an adverse inference. Although these conditions should not be understood as strict rules, they ensure that this part of the assessment of evidence is more rational, predictable and equitable.[299]

2. IBA Rules

Art. 9 (5) and (6) IBA Rules expressly allow the arbitral tribunal to draw an adverse inference:

> "If a Party fails without satisfactory explanation to produce any Document requested in a Request to Produce to which it has not objected in due time or fails to produce any Document ordered to be produced by the Arbitral Tribunal, the Arbitral Tribunal may infer that such document would be adverse to the interests of that Party."
>
> "If a Party fails without satisfactory explanation to make available any other relevant evidence, including testimony, ... the Arbitral Tribunal may infer that such evidence would be adverse to the interests of that Party."

292 S. 41 (5) EAA 1996.

293 S. 41 (7) (b) EAA 1996; SHEPPARD, S. 41 EAA 1996 n. 4; HARRIS et al., S. 41 EAA 1996 n. 41E.

294 VAN HOUTTE, 200; HARRIS et al., S. 41 EAA 1996 n. 41E.

295 BSK-SCHNEIDER/SCHERER, Art. 184 PILA CH n. 21; Stein/Jonas-SCHLOSSER, § 1042 CCP DE n. 65.

296 Arts. 20 (7) and 21 (9) ICDR Rules.

297 *See* e.g. Art. 27 (4) UNCITRAL Rules; Art. 24 (2) Swiss Rules; Art. 22.1 (vi) LCIA Rules.

298 SHARPE, 550 et seqq; VAN HOUTTE, 198; GREENBERG/LAUTENSCHLAGER, 183.

299 SHARPE, 571.

Although in practice the main reason for which an adverse inference is sought is due to non-production of documents, the IBA Rules also allow this where 'other evidence' (e.g. examination of witnesses) is not presented.[300] That is why Art. 9 (5) and (6) IBA Rules must be understood in conjunction with Art. 3 (3) and 4 (9), which list the conditions under which document production and the examination of witnesses can be requested. Under Art. 9 (5) and (6), an adverse inference may be drawn if a party fails to produce evidence (which it has not objected to) without satisfactory explanation, or if the arbitral tribunal has ordered either document production or production of other evidence (e.g. examination of a witness). Therefore, the arbitral tribunal has discretion to draw an adverse inference either by request of a party or on its own motion.

VAN HOUTTE points out that since it is the arbitral tribunal that ultimately decides on requests according to Art. 3 (3) and 4 (9) IBA Rules, Art. 9 (5) and (6) IBA Rules could be interpreted that no adverse inference can be drawn unless a direct order of the arbitral tribunal has been disregarded.[301] Consequently, if a party fails to produce evidence upon request of the other party and the arbitral tribunal has not confirmed this request, no adverse inference can be drawn. GREENBERG/LAUTENSCHLAGER, on the other hand, argue that if a party that has been requested to produce evidence fails to object to this request, it is considered to have accepted the request.[302] As a result, they suggest that in this case, an express order to produce evidence seems superfluous, and if the requested party nonetheless fails to produce evidence, it is appropriate to draw an adverse inference. In addition, they hold that the procedural timetable is itself an indirect order of the arbitral tribunal.

However, along with GREENBERG/LAUTENSCHLAGER, the view taken here is that in such a situation, the party should nonetheless be made aware that an adverse inference may be drawn.[303] This gives that party one last chance to explain why the relevant evidence has not been produced. Although this warning should not be considered as a legal gateway to draw an adverse inference, it will certainly strengthen the evidentiary weight of that inference.[304]

300 GREENBERG/LAUTENSCHALGER, 191 et seq.

301 VAN HOUTTE, 202.

302 GREENBERG/LAUTENSCHLAGER, 189.

303 *Ibid.*; VAN HOUTTE, 202; SACHS/NIEDERMAIER, n. 73.

304 WAINCYMER, *Evidence*, 777.

The previous remarks have shown that the IBA Rules provide little guidance, but rather minimal standards regarding the circumstances in which an adverse inference may be drawn. A more extensive source of guidance in this respect is the vast case law of the Iran-United States Claims Tribunal.

3. Iran-United States Claims Tribunal

This tribunal has had to address a lack of evidence several times, due to the revolutionary turmoil in Iran.[305] In order to shed some light on the matter of adverse inference, SHARPE has highlighted the following conditions from these cases:[306]

> "(1) The party seeking the adverse inference must produce all available evidence corroborating the inference sought;
> (2) the requested evidence must be accessible to the inference opponent;
> (3) the inference sought must be reasonable, consistent with facts in the record and logically related to the likely nature of the evidence withheld;
> (4) the party seeking the adverse inference must produce prima facie evidence; and
> (5) the inference opponent must know, or have reason to know, of its obligation to produce evidence rebutting the adverse inference sought."

Several of these conditions are included to some extent in the IBA Rules. The first,[307] however, is just partially covered by them. While Art. 3 (3) (c) (i) IBA Rules expressly provides that the requesting party must state that the requested document is not in its possession, custody or control, Art. 4 (9) IBA Rules does not contain an equivalent provision regarding other evidence, such as witnesses. Nevertheless, the arbitral tribunal should also apply this criterion in regard to witnesses and other evidence.

The second condition[308] is quite similar to Art. 3 (3) (c) (ii) IBA Rules, as it obliges the requesting party to explain why it assumes that the requested documents are in the custody or control of the other party. This is unsurprising, since the arbitral tribunal has no reason to draw an adverse inference if it has not been shown that the other party is in fact in possession of certain evidence.[309] Here again, no similar provision exists that would apply to other evidence except documents. Therefore, under the same reasoning as before, the second condition should also apply to other evidence.

305 SHARPE, 551.

306 SHARPE, 551.

307 *Ibid.*, 554 et seqq.; VAN HOUTTE, 203 et seq.; GREENBERG/LAUTENSCHLAGER, 197.

308 SHARPE, 557 et seq; VAN HOUTTE, 204; GREENBERG/LAUTENSCHLAGER, 197 et seq.

309 *Ibid.*

The third condition[310] is divided into three parts. The first part–that the inference sought be reasonable–might seem superfluous. What is meant here is that the arbitral tribunal can draw an adverse inference only if there is no substantial suspicion that drawing it would be inconsistent with the commercial reality.[311] Parties can hence expect that the arbitral tribunal will be familiar with common business practices and will draw an adverse inference only where this makes sense within the broader picture (i.e. given the *external* facts).[312] This could mean, for instance, that in the absence of any contemporaneous objection, invoices or payment documents presented during the course of a contract are considered to be correct.[313] The second part mirrors the first in providing that an adverse inference should also be consistent with the *internal* facts–that is, the facts of the record.[314] By requiring consistency with both external and internal facts, these two parts go beyond the IBA Rules. The third part presupposes that there must be a logical connection between the nature of the documents withheld and the inference derived therefrom.

In the illustrative *Riahi* case, the respondent failed twice to prove its ownership of a certain amount of bearer shares.[315] However, the arbitral tribunal refused to draw an adverse inference, based on the fact that according to Iranian law, there is no obligation to register bearer shares in a company's share register. Consequently, because the arbitral tribunal was not convinced that there was any connection, it did not draw an adverse inference.[316] This third part goes in the same direction as Art. 9 (5) IBA Rules by stating that the adverse inference cannot go further than the withheld document.[317]

The fourth condition[318] requires that the requesting party have a factual basis for the allegation according to which it seeks adverse inference.[319]

310 SHARPE, 558 et seq; VAN HOUTTE, 204 et seq.; GREENBERG/LAUTENSCHLAGER, 199 et seq.

311 SHARPE, 559; HOSANG, *Obstructionist Behaviour,* 154; LUTTRELL, 287 et seq.; SOURGENS et al., n. 8.12 et seqq.

312 HOSANG, *Obstructionist Behaviour,* 154.

313 *See* e.g. *Houston Contracting Co. v. National Iranion Oil Co.,* IUSCT, 22 Jul. 1988, 378-173-3.

314 *See* e.g. *Methanex Corporation v. Government of the United States of America,* ICSID, 3 Aug. 2005, pt. II, ch. G, n. 25.

315 *Frederica Lincoln Riahi v. Government of the Islamic Republic of Iran,* IUSCT, 27 Feb. 2003, 600-485-1; *see also* the dissenting opinion of Judge BROWER, pointing out that the arbitral tribunal should not have rewarded the respondent for 'stonewalling' by refusing to draw an adverse inference (Y.B. Comm. Arb. 2003, n. 533 et seqq.).

316 VAN HOUTTE, 207; *see also* the illustrative example in LUTTRELL, 287 et seq.

317 MARGHITOLA, 176; VAN HOUTTE, 207; SACHS/NIEDERMAIER, n. 39.

318 SHARPE, 564 et seqq.; VAN HOUTTE, 205 et seq.; GREENBERG/LAUTENSCHLAGER, 200 et seq.

319 O'MALLEY, n. 7.41.

More specifically, this prima facie evidence ought to be consistent, complete and detailed, which is not always easy to demonstrate.[320] Compared to the IBA Rules, this condition limits the possibility to draw an adverse inference even further.

The fifth condition[321] relates directly to the principle of due process[322] and requires the arbitral tribunal to inform a party that fails to produce evidence without sufficient reason that an adverse inference might be drawn.[323] If the arbitral tribunal fails to do so, not only do the proceedings become less efficient and fair, but the arbitral award might ultimately be unenforceable.[324]

The IBA Rules do not mention this fifth condition. Of course, it could be argued that since the arbitral tribunal normally addresses the possibility of adverse inference in the case management conference, it is not necessary to repeat this warning if a party fails to produce evidence. This view was taken in a recent ICC case and later confirmed by the Paris Court of Appeal.[325] What was particularly interesting here was that a party requested that certain documents be produced by the adverse party, which never responded. Neither the requesting party nor the arbitral tribunal commented on this failure to produce evidence. Eventually, the arbitral tribunal drew an adverse inference by its own motion without first consulting with the parties. Before the Paris Court of Appeal, the claimant stated that because the arbitral tribunal had not informed the parties of its intention to draw an adverse inference in advance, it had violated due process. However, the Paris Court of Appeal held that since the parties had agreed in the case management conference on the application of the IBA Rules, the arbitral tribunal, in applying those rules, was authorised to draw an adverse inference without first consulting the parties.[326] Moreover, it held that the parties had had sufficient opportunity

320 SHARPE, 564 et seqq.; MARGHITOLA, 176.

321 SHARPE, 568 et seqq; VAN HOUTTE, 205 et seq.; GREENBERG/LAUTENSCHLAGER, 201 et seq.

322 VAN HOUTTE, 208; GREENBERG/LAUTENSCHLAGER, 201.

323 SHARPE, 568 et seq.

324 SHARPE, 570; GREENBERG/LAUTENSCHLAGER, 202 et seq.; *Dongwoo Mann + Hummel Co. Ltd. v. Mann + Hummel GmbH* [2008] SGHC 67; MARGHITOLA points out that not every unjustified adverse inference leads to the annulment of the arbitral award based on the grounds of a violation of the right to be heard. Rather, he argues that parties against whom an adverse inference is sought should be warned first. Thus, due process is upheld if parties are made aware in the case management conference of the possibility that the arbitral tribunal may draw an adverse inference under certain conditions (MARGHITOLA, 214 et seq.).

325 *Société Dresser-Rand Group Inc. v. Société Diana Capital I F.C.R.*, Paris Court of Appeal, 28 Feb. 2017, First Civil Chamber, 15/06036.

326 *Ibid.*, n. 292.

during the proceedings to explain why the relevant documents were not presented. Thus, the Court of Appeal reasoned that due process had been upheld at all times.

This decision certainly promotes the use of adverse inference.[327] Parties should therefore think carefully before deliberately refusing to produce evidence, pursuant either to a direct order of the arbitral tribunal or to a request of another party. Moreover, the decision affirms that as long as the parties are given an opportunity to comment on the non-production of evidence, due process is sufficiently upheld.[328] Despite this very straightforward and generally welcome decision, arbitral tribunals would be well advised to give the party a final opportunity to restate its reasons for non-production of evidence[329]–if only because often the mere threat of adverse inference can be enough to persuade a party to comply with evidentiary orders.[330]

C. Anticipated Assessment of Evidence

As stated above *(see* p. 60 et seqq. *supra)*, the conditions under which an adverse inference can be drawn should not be understood as mandatory.[331] This is rather a question of how the arbitral tribunal freely assesses the evidence (both presented and missing) and acts according to its 'inner conviction'.[332] Consequently, a party that requests the arbitral tribunal to draw an adverse inference has no right to the grant of its request.[333] In Switzerland, the SFT has emphasised several times that an arbitral tribunal's refusal to draw an adverse inference does not violate the right to be heard, but rather falls within the scope of its free assessment of evidence.[334] In this respect, the SFT also refers to the 'anticipated assessment of evidence', which will be subject to closer scrutiny *(see* p. 272 et seqq. *infra)*.[335] Simply put, this concept allows the arbitral tribunal, for example, to refuse to examine further

327 DE WESTGAVER/ZINATULLINA, Will Adverse Inferences Help Make Document Production in International Arbitration More Efficient?.

328 *Ibid.*

329 SHARPE, 570; VAN HOUTTE, 209; WAINCYMER, *Evidence*, 777.

330 SHARPE, 550.

331 GREENBERG/LAUTENSCHLAGER, 188.

332 O'MALLEY, 7.39; VAN HOUTTE, 198.

333 SACHS/NIEDERMAIER, n. 66.

334 DFT 4A_450/2007 of 9 Jan. 2008, cons. 4.2.2; DFT 4A_2/2007 of 28 Mar. 2007, cons. 4; DFT 4P.22/1996 of 25 Jul. 1997, cons. 3c, in: ASA Bull. 2000, 103.

335 Art. 157 CCP CH; FCDisp CCP CH (2006), 7312.

evidence as it considers the fact already proven.[336] Accordingly, this assessment of evidence can be examined only under the very limited scope of a violation of public policy.[337]

As a consequence, the arbitral tribunal can–but need not–draw an adverse inference if a party refuses to produce evidence.[338] The same applies in civil state court proceedings: pursuant to Art. 164 CCP CH, if a party refuses to cooperate without valid reasons, the court shall take this into account when appraising the evidence. The SFT has held that this provision does not instruct the court to automatically draw an adverse inference, but rather leaves the respective consequences to the court's free assessment of evidence.[339] It has further stated that although this fact must be assessed to the detriment of the non-compliant party, a *de facto* reversal of the burden of proof would go too far.[340]

D. Drawing of an Adverse Inference in Practice

In practice, however, arbitral tribunals are often hesitant to draw an adverse inference because of a potential violation of due process.[341] Although the arbitral tribunal's exercise of its discretion must always be balanced with the principle of due process, the fear of annulment or non-enforcement of the arbitral award is often unfounded.[342] As previously pointed out *(see p. 59, 63 supra)*, state courts are less likely to set aside an arbitral award if the parties had sufficient opportunity to argue on the point of whether an adverse inference is appropriate. This is true even where it turns out that the adverse inference was in fact unjustified.[343] Moreover, one should bear in

336 *See* e.g. DFT 4A_427/2017 of 22 Jan. 2018, cons. 5.1.1; DFT 4A_277/2017 of 28 Aug. 2017, cons. 3.1.

337 Art. 190 (2) (e) PILA CH; DFT 142 III 360, cons. 4.1.1.

338 BSK-SCHNEIDER/SCHERER, Art. 184 PILA CH n. 21; BERGER/KELLERHALS, n. 1358. In this respect, arbitrators should bear in mind that if they allow an adverse inference only under very severe conditions, parties have no more incentives to comply with evidentiary orders (MARGHITOLA, 177).

339 DFT 140 III 264, cons. 2.3.

340 *Ibid.*; BK-RÜETSCHI, Art. 164 CCP CH n. 7; BSK-SCHMID, Art. 164 CCP CH n. 2; Sutter-Somm et al.-HASENBÖHLER, Art. 164 CCP CH n. 6.

341 Queen Mary Survey (2012), 21; GREENBERG/LAUTENSCHLAGER, 180, 202; BORN, *Int. Comm. Arb.*, 2393; LUTTRELL, 293 et seqq.; SOURGENS et al., n. 8.46.

342 VAN HOUTTE, 214.

343 MARGHITOLA, 214 et seq. He argues that an unjustified adverse inference is not a violation of equal treatment of the parties, and that this principle should not be misused to examine whether the arbitral tribunal's discretion has been proportionate in regard to evidentiary measures.

mind the (even worse) alternative: allowing a party to deliberately disregard an evidentiary order of the arbitral tribunal. Both common sense and a basic understanding of justice require that a non-compliant party be sanctioned in such a case (*'venire contra factum proprium'*–that is, 'no one may set himself in contradiction to his own previous conduct').[344] Faced with a hesitant tribunal, a party would be well advised to substantiate the consequences of *not* drawing an adverse inference and its possible influence on the arbitral award.[345] In addition, since common law is more familiar with the concept of adverse inference, the legal background of an arbitrator should be considered.[346] All in all, where a party fails to produce evidence without substantial reasons, the arbitral tribunal should not be too reluctant to use this powerful tool.[347]

E. Summary

As stated previously, adverse inference is the sanction most commonly imposed where a party fails to produce evidence without satisfactory reason in international arbitration (*see* p. 56 et seqq. *supra*). Although it is mentioned in very few institutional arbitration rules, it is common sense that the right to draw an adverse inference derives from the arbitral tribunal's duty and right to freely assess the evidence. In contrast, although they say very little about the 'how' and 'when', the IBA Rules empower the arbitral tribunal to draw an adverse inference under certain conditions. Therefore, the conditions carved out by SHARPE provide arbitrators with helpful guidance on the circumstances under which this sanction should be imposed. These requirements are not engraved in stone, but should rather be applied on a case-by-case basis. In doing so, the arbitral tribunal must pay particular attention to ensure that the threshold of prima facie evidence is not too high for the requesting party. In addition, it has been shown that the decision on whether to draw an adverse inference always involves a balancing act between freely assessing the evidence and observing due process. In this regard it seems fair–albeit perhaps not strictly necessary–to grant the reluctant party a final chance to comply with the evidentiary order. Furthermore, the mere threat of drawing an adverse inference can often induce parties to produce the evidence in question.

344 BORN, *Int. Comm. Arb.*, 2393.

345 LUTTRELL, 294 et seq.

346 *Ibid.*, 295.

347 HOSANG, *Adverse Inferences*, 804.

Despite the broad acceptance of this measure, arbitral tribunals seem to be rather reluctant to draw adverse inferences in practice. Concerns regarding the possible annulment or non-enforcement of an arbitral award because of an (even unjustified) adverse inference have been disproved. It is thus hoped that arbitral tribunals and state courts will take brave steps forward by applying this concept more often. This is especially true given that adverse inference is by far the most effective tool to sanction a party that refuses to produce evidence. However, whether other state courts will commit to adverse inference based on the far-reaching model of the Paris Court of Appeal remains to be seen.

§ 3 Cost Sanctions

A. Introduction

In addition to drawing an adverse inference, the arbitral tribunal can sanction non-compliant parties through the allocation of costs. The most important monetary sanctions with regard to evidence are addressed below. The question to be answered here is whether these cost sanctions are worthy alternatives to an adverse inference.

B. Allocating the Costs

The most common way to sanction a non-compliant party is through the allocation of costs in the arbitral award. This principle is widely accepted in international arbitration.[348] In this case, the arbitral tribunal deviates from the common principle that costs 'follow the event'–that is, the costs reflect the parties' relative success and failure.[349] Consequently, a prevailing party may nonetheless be sanctioned to bear the costs of arbitration (partially or in full) due to non-compliance.[350] Therefore, in the absence of agreement between the parties, several *leges arbitri* and institutional arbitration rules allow the arbitral tribunal, in allocating costs, to consider the respective circumstances of the case, such as the conduct of a party during the proceedings.[351] Art. 28.4 LCIA Rules, as one of the most explicit provisions in this regard, states:

348 O'MALLEY, n. 7.43; BLACKABY et al., n. 9.96; ROSELL, 117 et seq.

349 S. 61 (2) EAA 1996; Art 28.4 1st sentence LCIA Rules; ROSELL, 116.

350 HOSANG, *Obstructionist Behaviour*, 213.

351 Arbitration Rules: *see* e.g. Art. 42 (1) UNCITRAL Rules; Art. 37 (5) ICC Rules; Art. 34 ICDR Rules; Art. 33.3 DIS Rules; *Leges arbitri*: *see* e.g. § 1057 (1) CCP DE; Art. 1467 CCP FR; S. 61 (2) EAA 1996.

> "The Arbitral Tribunal may also take into account the parties' conduct in the arbitration, including any co-operation in facilitating the proceedings as to time and cost and any non-co-operation resulting in undue delay and unnecessary expense. Any decision on costs by the Arbitral Tribunal shall be made with reasons in the award containing such decision."

Similarly, Art. 33.3 DIS Rules reads as follows:

> "The arbitral tribunal shall make decisions concerning the costs of the arbitration in its discretion. In so doing, it shall take into account all circumstances that it considers to be relevant. Such circumstances may include the outcome of the arbitration and the extent to which the parties have conducted the arbitration efficiently."[352]

As it is the case with adverse inference, a party on whom a monetary sanction might be imposed should be warned first in order to observe due process.[353]

Focusing specifically on the process of taking evidence, Art. 9 (7) IBA Rules reads as follows:

> "If the Arbitral Tribunal determines that a Party has failed to conduct itself in good faith in the taking of evidence, the Arbitral Tribunal may, in addition to any other measures available under these Rules, take such failure into account in its assignment of the costs of the arbitration, including costs arising out of or in connection with the taking of evidence."

Unsurprisingly, the concept of 'good faith' is understood very differently among various legal cultures. As previously discussed, in one legal system, interaction between lawyers and potential witnesses prior to the hearing is considered standard procedure; while in another, it is considered unethical (*see* p. 43 et seqq. *supra*). That is why the concept of 'good faith' should not be culturally motivated, but should rather represent an objective standard.[354] Therefore, to act in good faith means first and foremost to cooperate in the taking of evidence by presenting the requested evidence in accordance with the procedural timetable.[355] Furthermore, it includes refraining from actions that would threaten or hinder another party's access to evidence.[356]

352 *See also* SCHARDT, 35.

353 REED, 100 et seq; ROSELL, 118.

354 O'MALLEY, n. 7.44.

355 *Ibid.*, n. 7.46 et seqq.

356 *Ibid.*, n. 7.52.

Although the possibility to sanction an obstructionist party in allocating the costs in the arbitral award is widely accepted, this rarely happens in practice.[357] This is all the more astonishing given that practitioners seem to embrace the fact that improper conduct by a party will be reflected in the allocation of costs.[358] One explanation for the reluctance of arbitral tribunals to allocate costs other than by following the event is that the actual costs caused by the party's non-compliance must be shown, which can be hard to prove at times.[359] Still, in a number of ICC cases, the arbitral tribunal allocated the costs at the expense of parties that manipulated and unnecessarily delayed the arbitral proceeding.[360]

C. Sanctions Against Party Representatives

1. Introduction

In addition to the possibility to sanction non-compliant parties through the allocation of costs, recent discussions have highlighted the consequences of misconduct by party representatives and the issue of counsel ethics in general.[361] As 'guerrilla tactics', party representatives might make deliberately false statements, suppress and conceal documents or influence parties and/or witnesses to do so. In such cases, it is unclear whether the arbitral tribunal is authorised to sanction the party representative directly. To curb such misbehaviour and level the playing field between conflicting professional ethical rules, at least two institutions have produced ethical guidelines and rules thus far.[362] A general examination of the usefulness of guidelines and rules regarding the conduct of party representatives is beyond the scope of this book, which rather explores whether these could be helpful as sanctions in the taking of evidence.[363]

357 REED, 100.

358 Queen Mary Survey (2012), 41.

359 HOSANG, *Obstructionist Behaviour*, 213.

360 *Manufacturer v. Buyer*, ICC Case No. 8486 (1996), n. 26, in: Y.B. Comm. Arb. 1999, 172 et seq.; *Agent v. Principal and Managing director of principal*, ICC Case No. 7453 (1994), n. 44, in: Y.B. Comm. Arb. 1997, 124; *Buyer Y v. Seller A and others*, ICC Case No. 7661 (1996), n. 52 et seq., in: Y.B. Comm. Arb. 1997, 163.

361 *See* e.g. PARK, 409 et seqq.; SUSSMAN, 239 et seqq.; GEISINGER, 17 et seqq.; HWANG/HON, 658 et seqq.; LAU, 559 et seqq.; HODGES, 599 et seqq.; DASSER, *Guidelines*, 634 et seqq.

362 GEISINGER et al., 5. HODGES, 616; SUSSMAN, 251; DASSER, *Guidelines*, 641 et seq. DASSER argues that in terms of equality of arms, 'leveling the playing field' should take place in each individual arbitral proceeding, rather than according to an international guideline ('We do not need to level the world if we can level the hearing room.', 641).

363 For an introduction to guidelines, rules and other para-regulatory texts in international arbitration, *see* ASA Special Series no. 37.

2. IBA Guidelines

The relatively new IBA Guidelines on Party Representation in International Arbitration (henceforth 'IBA Guidelines') from 2013 may serve as a first example. These detailed guidelines address various issues, such as counsel misconduct with regard to submissions to the tribunal, document disclosure and the handling of witnesses and experts.[364] According to the IBA Guidelines, 'misconduct' is defined very broadly as 'a breach of the present Guidelines or any other conduct that the Arbitral Tribunal determines to be contrary to the duties of a Party Representative'.[365] The main feature of the IBA Guidelines is found in Guideline 26, which states that the arbitral tribunal is empowered to impose sanctions in case of misconduct by a party representative. Accordingly, it can thus (a) admonish the party representative, (b) draw an adverse inference, (c) apportion costs appropriately, and (d) take any other appropriate measures in order to preserve the fairness and integrity of the proceedings.

In stark contrast to the IBA Rules, the IBA Guidelines have been subject to harsh criticism since their introduction.[366] The main concern relates to the ability of the arbitrators, as the competent body, to decide the matter in dispute and to sanction a party representative at the same time. As a result, the arbitral tribunal might easily be tempted to show bias against parties and their representatives.[367] This potentially endangers not only the arbitral tribunal's impartiality, but also the relationship between parties and their representatives.[368] In other words, this double role not only distracts the arbitral tribunal from its main purpose of deciding on the merits of the case, but also creates an unhealthy tension between the tribunal and the party representatives, who will be much more likely to challenge the members of the arbitral tribunal because of possible bias against them.[369]

364 For an extended overview of the IBA Guidelines, *see* WAINCYMER, *Regulatory Developments*, 534 et seqq.; SUSSMAN, 252 et seqq.; ROGERS, n. 3.89 et seqq.

365 IBA Guidelines, 3; WAINCYMER, *Regulatory Developments*, 544.

366 SCHNEIDER, *IBA Guidelines*, 497 et seq.; DASSER, *Guidelines*, 637 et seq.; HODGES, 613 et seq.; LAU, 577 et seq.; BORN, *Int. Comm. Arb.*, 2854 et seq.; HWANG/HON, 658 et seq.; for the official ASA position, *see* GEISINGER et al., 1 et seq.; for a mediating position *see* WAINCYMER, *Regulatory Developments*, 550 et seq.

367 ASHFORD, Art. 26-27-18.

368 GEISINGER et al., 2; DASSER, *Guidelines*, 655, 660. He points out that parties would be unwilling to be interrupted by an investigation of counsel conduct which (in most countries) would fall under the competence of professional bodies such as the bar council or other supervisory authorities; for a different view, *see* LAU, 582 et seq.

369 HWANG/HON, 659; HODGES, 616; ASHFORD, 27-27-12 et seqq. After all, although not mentioned expressly in the IBA Guidelines, the official commentary states that before imposing any sanctions, the arbitral tribunal ought to hear the parties and the impugned representative (IBA Guidelines, 17).

As regards the effectiveness of the sanctions mentioned in the IBA Guidelines, several concerns are noteworthy. Of the four sanctions stated in Guideline 26, only sanction (a), which provides for the admonishment of a party representative, is a real sanction against counsel.[370] Sanctions (b) and (c), which involve drawing an adverse inference or apportioning the costs, already lie within the remit of the arbitral tribunal.[371] Finally, sanction (d) allows the arbitral tribunal to take appropriate measures to ensure the fairness and integrity of the proceedings. This provision has been drafted extremely broadly and is thus highly dubious, if not dangerous, in terms of the principle of legality.[372] Thus, the IBA Guidelines largely provide 'sanctions' which are already available to the arbitral tribunal. In addition, because sanctions (a) and (d) are drafted so broadly, there is always the danger of a party abusing the guidelines by making false and unfounded accusations of unethical behaviour of the adverse party's representative.[373]

Because of the numerous shortcomings of the IBA Guidelines, their adoption by parties, counsel and arbitral tribunals remains lacklustre.[374] The Queen Mary survey (2015) showed that the IBA Guidelines lack support among international arbitration practitioners; fewer than half of the survey respondents agreed that the conduct of party representatives should not be further regulated, but that tribunals should instead use the currently available sanctions.[375] Notwithstanding the various issues relating to the IBA Guidelines, they seem to be at least partially used as guidelines (but not as binding rules).[376]

370 DASSER, *Guidelines*, 649.

371 *Ibid.*, 649 et seq.; *see also* WAINCYMER, *Regulatory Developments*, 520, 545. He states that sanctioning an innocent party with costs for the behaviour of its representative is problematic, since the representative is not part of the arbitration agreement and is therefore acting as a third party. Thus, the IBA Guidelines 26 (c) do not constitute a basis to burden a party representative personally with such costs; for a different view, *see* ASHFORD, n. 1-3-24 et seqq., 26-27-9 et seqq. He argues for direct jurisdiction over party representatives and therefore the possibility to sanction them in cases of misconduct even if those representatives are not part of the arbitration agreement.

372 WAINCMYER, *Regulatory Developments*, 544 et seq.; DASSER, *Guidelines*, 651; ASHFORD, n. 26-27-36.

373 HWANG/HON, 659; SCHNEIDER, *IBA Guidelines*, 500; GEISINGER et al., 2; DASSER, *Guidelines*, 651 et seq.; ASHFORD, 26-27-15.

374 For a different view, *see* ROGERS, n. 3.100 et seq. In her opinion, international arbitration is in desperate need of clarity on the proper conduct of party representatives: 'Attorneys need more guidance about what constitutes proper conduct. Parties need to understand better how to plan their legal representation and related case strategy. Arbitrators need more clear guidance and support in making rulings on ethical issues. And ... national bar associations ... need assurance that there is a reliable regime in place to protect client and societal interests implicated in attorney conducts' (n. 3.98).

375 Queen Mary Survey (2015), 41. This view is confirmed in the more recent study by LAU, 571.

376 *Ibid.*, 565; IBA Report (2016), 74 et seqq.

3. LCIA Guidelines

The second example is the LCIA Rules, which are thus far the first and only rules to include provisions regulating the conduct of party representatives to 'promote the good and equal conduct of the parties' legal representative'.[377] To some degree inspired by the IBA Guidelines, the LCIA Rules, which were revised in 2014, now contain an annex with general guidelines concerning party representatives (henceforth the 'LCIA Guidelines').[378] Since according to the LCIA Rules, party representatives can act as such only after agreeing on the provisions set forth in the annex, the LCIA Guidelines apply automatically and there is no opt-out clause.[379]

Unlike the IBA Guidelines, the LCIA Rules do not define the term 'misconduct', but refer more generally to violation of the LCIA Guidelines.[380] The annex itself lists the possible types of misconduct of party representatives, such as making false statements, procuring or assisting in the preparation of false evidence and knowingly concealing documents. According to Art. 18.6 LCIA Rules, the arbitral tribunal, after consulting the parties and letting the parties' representatives explain themselves, may impose cascading sanctions as follows: (i) a written reprimand, (ii) a written caution as to future conduct in the arbitration, and (iii) finally, any other measure necessary to fulfil the general duties set forth in Art. 14.4 LCIA Rules. While the first two sanctions might already be sufficient to induce a party representative to comply with the LCIA Guidelines, the third requires a higher standard.[381] 'Any other measure necessary' can be imposed if this meets the requirements of due process under Art. 14.4 LCIA Rules. This could mean to report the misconduct to a local professional authority or even exclude the party representative from the arbitration.[382]

Needless to say, such severe sanctions should be imposed only in extreme situations and after due consideration. Unlike under the IBA Guidelines, and because the sanctions in Art. 18.6 LCIA Rules are meant to be

377 LCIA Guidelines n. 1; Mistelis-NESBITT/DAROWSKI, Art. 18 LCIA Rules n. 5.

378 Because the Annex applies to every arbitration under the revised LCIA Rules, the name of the guidelines, as compared to 'rules' or 'codes', is misleading. Nonetheless, the Annex is not intended to derogate from mandatory laws or professional codes of conduct which apply to party representatives in the arbitration (LCIA Guidelines, n. 1; SCHERER et al., Art. 18 LCIA Rules n. 21).

379 Art. 18.5 LCIA Rules; SCHERER et al., Art. 18 LCIA Rules n. 22.

380 Art 18.6 LCIA Rules.

381 SCHERER et al., Art. 18 LCIA Rules n. 63.

382 SCHERER et al., Art. 18 LCIA Rules n. 63 et seqq.

imposed directly against a party representative and not against the party itself, adverse inference and allocation of costs are not sanctions available under the LCIA Rules.[383]

There are plausible reasons to believe that the revised LCIA Rules will be of much greater significance and relevance than the IBA Guidelines. First, they enjoy greater legitimacy, since the parties agree indirectly to apply them by choosing the LCIA Rules in their arbitration agreement as the applicable procedural rules.[384] Because the party representatives must agree to comply with these rules, the arbitral tribunal is authorised to impose sanctions on them directly.[385] Second, compared to the IBA Guidelines, the LCIA Guidelines provide rather weak sanctions, but include strict requirements. As previously mentioned, the IBA Guidelines contain some sanctions which are already within the arbitral tribunal's remit to impose (*see* p. 70 *supra*). The LCIA Guidelines, on the other hand, contain more effective measures to control the behaviour of party representatives. In addition, the sanction of taking 'other measures' is narrowly drafted and requires that high standards be met. Third, according to recent data, practitioners suggest that if there is to be tighter regulation of party representatives, this should be done through institutional arbitration rules such as the LCIA Guidelines, rather than through the IBA Guidelines.[386] However, the extent to which the LCIA Guidelines help to control the conduct of party representatives remains to be seen.

4. Result

The previous remarks have sketched out the current debate on the regulation of party representatives' conduct in international arbitration. While some of these sanctions may be helpful in the taking of evidence, the arbitral tribunal should not be the competent body to impose them. While it is crucial that counsel misconduct is addressed and sanctioned, the arbitral tribunal should not have to play a double role of deciding on the merits of the case and sanctioning non-compliant party representatives. As explained, this role creates a risk of an impartial arbitral tribunal, making the arbitral award more vulnerable to challenge on the grounds of violation of due process or arbitrator

383 *Ibid.*, Art. 18 LCIA Rules n. 65; ASHFORD, Art. 26-27-32; for a different view, *see* MISTELIS-NESBITT/DAROWSKI, Art. 18 LCIA Rules n. 7. They argue that the behaviour of party representatives should be considered when allocating the costs (Art. 28.4 LCIA Rules).

384 PARK, 419; SCHERER et al., Art. 18 LCIA Rules n. 22 et seqq.

385 Art. 18.5 LCIA Rules; SCHERER et al., Art. 18 LCIA Rules n. 51 et seqq.; DASSER, *Guidelines*, 659.

386 Queen Mary Survey (2015), 41.

bias against party representatives. Only time will tell whether the competence to sanction non-compliant and/or obstructionist party representatives will be left to national bar councils or even, as suggested by the ASA, a global arbitration ethics council.[387]

D. Monetary Penalties

1. Introduction

Instead of assessing the costs to the detriment of the non-compliant party, in some jurisdictions arbitral tribunals are authorised to impose monetary penalties. Even the mere threat of such penalties often induces a party to comply with evidentiary orders.[388] The penalties are imposed either as a single lump sum or as a certain amount of money multiplied by the period of time for which the party is non-compliant.[389] In most jurisdictions, these penalties are of a private nature and the amount, which is fixed by the arbitral tribunal, must be paid to the opposing party, rather than to the arbitral tribunal or a state court.[390] The main purpose is therefore not to compensate a loss, but to punish a party for its misbehaviour.[391]

2. Legal Basis

France, among other jurisdictions, is familiar with the concept of monetary penalties (so-called '*astreintes*').[392] Art. 1467 (3) CCP FR reads as follows:[393]

> "If a party is in possession of an item of evidence, the arbitral tribunal may order that party to submit such evidence according to the terms and conditions the tribunal decides and, as need be, under penalty."

The Dutch and Belgian *leges arbitri* include similar provisions; but *astreintes* are not permissible under Swedish law.[394] In other countries, however, no

387 GEISINGER, 26 et seqq.; the work of the ASA-Working group in building a global arbitration ethics council is on hold, at least for the moment.

388 LANDROVE/GREUTER, 527 et seq.

389 MOURRE, *Judicial Penalties*, 355; HOSANG, *Obstructionist Behaviour*, 220; Vogenauer-SCHELHAAS, Art. 7.2.4 PICC n. 5.

390 LEVY, 26; LANDROVE/GREUTER, 529.

391 MOURRE, *Judicial Penalties*, 356.

392 For a brief historical overview of *astreintes* in France, *see* LANDROVE/GREUTER, 526 et seq.

393 According to Art. 1506 (3) CCP FR, Art. 1467 CCP FR applies not only to domestic arbitration, but also to international arbitration, unless the parties agree otherwise; *see also* Art. 1468 CCP FR in regard to *astreintes* concerning interim measures.

394 Art. 1056 CCP NL; Art. 1700 (4) JC BE; S. 25 (3) SAA SE.

such provisions can be found.[395] Moreover, the examined institutional arbitration rules do not allow for the possibility to impose *astreintes*–at least, not expressly.[396] Regarding the *lex mercatoria*, only Art. 7.2.4 of the UNIDROIT Principles of International Commercial Contracts (PICC) clearly empowers the arbitral tribunal to order *astreintes*. Still, as SCHELHAAS points out, this provision is largely inspired by French law and thus does not reflect a general principle of law.[397] Finally, in the absence of any agreement between the parties, arbitral tribunals seem reluctant to impose monetary penalties. Even in France, the homeland of *astreintes*, they are imposed only rarely.[398]

Hence, in the absence of any tangible legal basis, the question arises as to whether the arbitral tribunal can nonetheless order an *astreinte*. Since this question must be answered individually for each country, the focus below is on the situation in Switzerland. This issue must be separated from the problem of enforcing an *astreinte*, which is not within the scope of this book.

3. Astreintes in Switzerland

The Swiss *lex arbitri* is silent with regard to *astreintes*: it neither recognises nor denies them, but leaves this to the parties to agree in the arbitral proceedings.[399] While several authors recommend their application in both Swiss domestic and international arbitration, there is no consensus as to the conditions under which this should actually be possible. The 'inherent power theory' could serve as inspiration here. Accordingly, the arbitral tribunal, in fulfilling its jurisdictional power, has certain (inherent) powers and can consequently order *astreintes*.[400] Prior to the introduction of *astreintes* into French law, the Paris Court of Appeal reasoned that the power of the arbitral tribunal to impose monetary penalties is a necessary extension of its power.[401]

395 For a brief overview, *see* MOURRE, *Judicial Penalties*, 361.

396 HOSANG, *Obstructionist Behaviour*, 222 et seq.; MOSIMANN, 136.

397 Vogenauer-SCHELHAAS, Art. 7.2.4 PICC n. 1 et seq.; LANDROVE/GREUTER, 544.

398 HOSANG, *Obstructionist Behaviour*, 227 et seq.; *see* e.g. ICC Case No. 13490 (2007), where the respondent failed to produce certain documents. In the award, the arbitral tribunal repeated its order of document production paired with a daily fine (*astreinte*) of EUR 3,000, beginning one month after notification of the award until the respondent complied with the document production order.

399 Art. 182 (1) PILA CH.

400 LANDROVE/GREUTER, 544 et seq.; MOURRE, *Judicial Penalties*, 362 et seq.; MOSIMANN, 137; HOSANG, *Obstructionist Behaviour*, 225 et seq.

401 *Société Otor Participations et autres v. Carlyle Holdings 1 et autre*, Paris Court of Appeal, 7 Oct. 2004, in: Rev. Arb. 2005, 740. It is noteworthy that this decision was made prior to the implementation of *astreintes* as a mean of monetary penalty in the French *lex arbitri*.

This book does not support this view. First, besides the fact that Swiss law contains no explicit legal basis to impose *astreintes* in arbitration, the inherent power theory is a very vague foundation. This is one reason why *astreintes* were subsequently expressly included in the French *lex arbitri*. Second, this theory obviously lacks foreseeability–in particular for foreign parties, which could not anticipate the application of such a construct if it is stated in neither the *lex arbitri* nor the parties' agreement.[402]

Other authors propose–quite similar to the aforementioned theory of inherent powers–that the arbitration agreement be interpreted to determine whether the parties have (even tacitly) empowered the arbitral tribunal to impose monetary penalties ('implicit consent theory').[403] But here again, this book does not support this view. Since this reasoning served to support the arbitral tribunal's power to order interim measures *before* it was enshrined in almost all *leges arbitri* and institutional arbitration rules, it would go too far to use this theory to support such a drastic sanction as monetary penalties.[404] In addition, as is the case for evidentiary matters more broadly, at the time of agreeing to arbitrate, the parties will not usually consider the question of whether monetary penalties should be imposed in case of non-compliance.[405] To conclude, therefore, that the parties have nonetheless agreed upon the application of *astreintes* would appear to be mere speculation.[406] Based on the previous remarks, this book supports the prevailing view in Switzerland that no *astreintes* can be ordered in the absence of explicit agreement between the parties, unless the respective *lex arbitri* contains an explicit provision in this regard.[407] Still, although rarely seen in practice, the parties can empower the arbitral tribunal to order *astreintes* or choose a *lex arbitri* which is familiar with this concept.[408]

402 HOSANG, *Obstructionist Behaviour*, 225 et seqq.; MARGHITOLA, 180.

403 Art. 182 (2) PILA CH; GAILLARD/SAVAGE, n. 1274; LEVY, 29; MOURRE, *Judicial Penalties*, 362 et seq.; concerning interim measures, *see* BOOG, n. 156 et seq.; GIRSBERGER/VOSER point out that the arbitral tribunal's power to order an *astreinte* is justified only if it is enforceable. Therefore, they suggest that the arbitral tribunal can impose it and then confirm it in a partial award (n. 1110).

404 HOSANG, *Obstructionist Behaviour*, 226.

405 MOURRE, *Judicial Penalties*, 364; HOSANG, *Obstructionist Behaviour*, 226.

406 MOSIMANN, 138. In regard to *astreintes* in connection with interim measures, BOOG argues that as long as the parties do not expressly agree otherwise, they have implicitly empowered the arbitral tribunal to order *astreintes* to ensure a maximum of legal protection (n. 156 et seq.).

407 BERGER/KELLERHALS, n. 1263; MOSIMANN, 138; HOSANG, *Obstructionist Behaviour*, 227; MARHGITOLA, 180; GÖKSU, n. 302.

408 MARGHITOLA, 180.

4. Result

Astreintes as monetary penalties in international arbitration are used to punish a party for non-compliance. They can thus be a very powerful tool, forcing the reluctant party to comply with procedural orders and reinforcing the position of the arbitral tribunal.[409] Still, very few jurisdictions acknowledge this legal concept. In Switzerland, for instance, there is no legal basis for issuing a*streintes*, even though several authors have suggested their application. Although this is seldom done in practice, parties could voluntarily empower the arbitral tribunal to impose monetary penalties in case of non-compliance. Even where the parties or the respective *lex arbitri* allows the arbitral tribunal to apply such sanctions, this should be done only after due consideration, given that *astreintes* are drastic sanctions. To sum up, this book considers that an arbitral tribunal should order *astreintes* only if the parties have explicitly agreed on this or if this is enshrined in the respective *lex arbitri*.

E. Summary

The goal of this chapter was to examine whether cost sanctions are a worthy alternative to the drawing of an adverse inference. This question must be answered separately for each type of cost sanction. As discussed, the allocation of costs in the arbitral award is the most common way to sanction parties through costs, even though this is seldom done in practice. The fact that many institutional arbitration rules allow the arbitrators to take the parties' behaviour into account in allocating the costs should encourage arbitral tribunals to make use of this right. This applies all the more since the mere threat of allocating costs to the disadvantage of a non-compliant party can induce it to play by the rules. Thus, compared to the drawing of an adverse inference, allocating the costs accordingly is a viable–albeit less important–alternative.

With regard to the sanctioning of party representatives, the relatively new guidelines and rules reveal many shortcomings and discrepancies. Together with the prevailing view in doctrine, this book supports the opinion that competence to sanction a party representative in international arbitration should not fall within the remit of the arbitral tribunal, but should rather be left to national bar councils or even a global arbitration ethics council. Hence, to sanction a party representative is no alternative to drawing an adverse inference.

409 LANDROVE/GREUTER, 537.

Finally, although *astreintes* are available in some jurisdictions, there is no consensus in international arbitration about this legal concept. The only way to apply them, if not provided for in the respective *lex arbitri*, is by means of the parties' agreement, which seems to happen very rarely. To sum up, *astreintes* are considered as an alternative to adverse inference only if the parties have empowered the arbitral tribunal to impose such penalties in case of non-compliance.

§ 4 Conclusion

This chapter has set out the various sanctions that an arbitral tribunal can impose if parties do not voluntarily present evidence. In order to observe due process at all times and give a reluctant party a final chance to comply, an arbitral tribunal would be well advised to inform the parties of its intention before actually imposing a sanction.

From the point of view of the arbitral tribunal, sanctions are rather weak measures, since they cannot retrospectively undo the damage done to the proceedings as a result of non-compliance.[410] Nonetheless, some of the abovementioned measures can prove very helpful. Adverse inference is an important tool if a party refuses to reveal a piece of evidence. The legal framework as stated in institutional arbitration rules and the IBA Rules alike, as well as recent support from national courts, should therefore encourage arbitral tribunals not to be too hesitant and to use adverse inference by assessing the evidence.[411]

Regarding cost sanctions, it has been demonstrated that an arbitral tribunal can to some degree sanction a non-compliant party by allocating costs against it in the arbitral award. However, difficulties can arise in this regard in calculating the actual damages caused by the party's non-compliance.[412] Nonetheless, arbitral tribunals should deviate from the principle that costs follow the event where parties have hindered the taking of evidence. As regards sanctions against party representatives in international arbitration, this book has strongly argued against the sanction system as set forth in the IBA Guidelines. Although a general discussion of counsel ethics is welcome, and the initial initiatives of the IBA and the LCIA Guidelines are well intended, the arbitral tribunal should not be tasked with deciding on these matters. Rather,

410 REED, 100.

411 HOSANG, *Adverse Inferences*, 804 et seq.

412 REED, 100.

this should be left to either national bar councils or perhaps a global arbitration ethics council. Finally, monetary penalties such as *astreintes* should be imposed only if the respective *lex arbitri* contains such a sanction or if the parties have expressly agreed on their application.

This chapter has revealed that the arbitral tribunal is anything but powerless when faced with a party that is reluctant to produce evidence. Nevertheless, as the next chapter will demonstrate, there are situations in every arbitration where the arbitral tribunal's power is limited in many ways.

5

Gathering Evidence: Major Limitations

§ 1 Introduction

Parties who are willing to settle their disputes through arbitration choose this private system of justice with all its numerous advantages, such as procedural flexibility and speed, as well as the confidentiality of the proceedings and the finality of the arbitral award.[413] In addition, state courts usually do not get involved in the arbitral proceedings; the arbitrators therefore enjoy wide discretion in conducting the taking of evidence without interference.[414] In reflecting on these advantages, however, one might be tempted to forget that this great freedom has its flipside and always comes at a price. Regarding the taking of evidence, several important distinctions between state courts and arbitral tribunals are worth mentioning.[415] This chapter identifies the three main limitations of the arbitral tribunal regarding the power to gather evidence, which should pave the way towards a better understanding of why and when arbitral tribunals can and should resort to state courts for assistance.

§ 2 Temporary Lack of Jurisdiction

The first limitation concerns the jurisdiction of the arbitral tribunal. While state courts are, so to speak, always on duty, arbitral tribunals must be constituted before they can act as private juridical bodies.[416] Because the arbitral tribunal normally consists of either one or three arbitrators, its constitution can take quite some time.[417] If the parties do not agree on the arbitrators or even challenge them, this process can easily take several months. With regard to evidence, if parties wish to seek interim measures (e.g., securing the existence of evidence), state courts usually fill this jurisdictional vacuum.

413 BLACKABY et al., n. 7.02.

414 DUPEYRON, 463 et seqq.

415 BLACKABY et al., n. 7.16 et seqq.

416 BORN, *Int. Comm. Arb.*, 2450 et seq.; SCHAEFER, 524 et seq.

417 *See* e.g. COLOMBINI, n. 4; Art. 6 Swiss Rules; Art. 12 ICC Rules; Art. 5.2 LCIA Rules.

While for a long time the temporary lack of jurisdiction forced parties to apply to state courts for interim relief, international arbitration has developed alternative mechanisms.[418] They have done so primarily because turning to state courts often contradicts the parties' core intention of resolving their disputes through arbitration and therefore excluding state court jurisdiction as far as possible.[419] The fear that the dispute might become public and state courts' inexperience with international arbitration disputes are further reasons why parties prefer to seek interim relief directly from arbitration institutions.[420]

Hence, in recent years, almost every arbitration institution began to include standard provisions in its rules regarding emergency arbitrators.[421] Compared to state courts, these specialised arbitrators provide for a fast, confidential and efficient interim award.[422] Under the Swiss and ICC Rules, for example, an emergency arbitrator will render an arbitral award within 15 days of the date on which the secretariat transmits the file to him or her.[423] Moreover, the possible measures that emergency arbitrators can offer are not limited to those available in state courts, which are often bound to the respective *lex fori*.[424] Under most rules, unless the parties have agreed otherwise, provisions on emergency arbitrators apply automatically by choosing the respective institutional arbitration rules.[425] Nonetheless, the parties can still specify whether they would prefer to resort to state courts or seek relief from an emergency arbitrator.[426] Therefore, emergency arbitrators are considered a helpful supplement to interim relief from state courts.[427] Once the

418 *See* e.g. Art. 1449 CCP FR.

419 SANTACROCE, 284; Lew, 491.

420 SANTACROCE, 284; EHLE, *Emergency Arbitration*, 89.

421 *See* e.g. Art. 29 ICC Rules; Art. 9B LCIA Rules; Art. 6 ICDR Rules; Rule 30 SIAC Rules; Art. 43 Swiss Rules; WALZ, n. 13 et seqq. For a historic overview of emergency arbitrators, *see* COLOMBINI, n. 7 et seqq. and EHLE, *Emergency Arbitration*, 87 et seqq.

422 HOFMANN/FUCHS, 127; WALZ, n. 24 et seqq. On whether interim awards rendered by emergency arbitrators are considered enforceable under the NYC, *see* EHLE, *Emergency Arbitration*, 99.

423 Art. 43 (7) Swiss Rules; Art. 6 (4) Appendix V ICC Rules; WALZ, n. 24 et seqq.

424 *See* e.g. Art. 183 (2) PILA CH; EHLE, *Emergency Arbitration*, 90, 97; WALZ, n. 22 et seq.

425 Regarding emergency arbitrators, most institutional arbitration rules provide for an opt-out-clause; *see* e.g. Art. 29 (6) (b) ICC Rules; Art. 9B.14 (ii) LCIA Rules; Art. 43 (1) Swiss Rules.

426 *See* e.g. Art. 29 (7) ICC Rules; Art. 9B.12 LCIA Rules; Art. 6 (7) ICDR Rules; Art. 30 (3) SIAC Rules; for ICC and Swiss Rules in particular, *see* COLOMBINI, n. 114 et seqq.; HOFMAN/FUCHS, 118 et seq.; for strategic remarks regardin whether to opt for an emergency arbitrator or a state court, *see* LEVY D., 197 et seqq.

427 HOFMANN/FUCHS, 129.

arbitral tribunal has been constituted, however, the emergency arbitrator's power ends and his or her interim award can be examined and revised freely by the arbitral tribunal.[428]

In sum, the lack of jurisdiction prior to the constitution of the arbitral tribunal has become a minor issue, as parties can now often choose between state courts and emergency arbitrators. Usually, parties will opt for emergency arbitrators, due to their effectiveness and experience with arbitration disputes. Nonetheless, in some cases prior to the constitution of the arbitral tribunal, even an emergency arbitrator cannot provide enough help. For example, where a party requests that certain evidence be preserved because of the risk of potential destruction, emergency arbitrators lack coercive power to take the necessary legal steps to protect such evidence; which leads to the next limitation of the arbitral tribunal's power.

§ 3 Lack of Coercive Power

The second limitation is the lack of coercive power. Quite obviously, in contrast to state courts, arbitral tribunals cannot directly enforce their orders and awards. While state courts can use coercive power given to them by the respective state, arbitral tribunals can act solely within the powers conferred upon them by the parties.[429] As regards evidence, the arbitral tribunal is not completely helpless, as it can impose various sanctions on non-compliant parties. However, although adverse inference and cost sanctions are effective in many ways, they can be of limited use in certain situations–for example, where a party cannot be held responsible for the fact that a certain piece of evidence is unavailable.[430] In addition, if a party still refuses to produce evidence or even threatens to destroy relevant evidence, only state courts can solve the problem.[431] The same applies to circumstances where a party intends to make an *ex parte* application (i.e. without hearing the adverse party)–for example, to freeze bank accounts of the adverse party.[432] This

428 *See* e.g. Art. 6 (5) ICDR Rules; Art. 43 (8) Swiss Rules; SANTACROCE, 284; EHLE, *Emergency Arbitration*, 95.

429 BLACKABY et al., n. 5.11. However, from a philosophical point of view, one must acknowledge that arbitrators still have some sort of coercive power: parties will not wish to upset the arbitral tribunal equipped with the powers they have conferred upon it (*ibid.*, n. 7.29); WOLFF, 233.

430 KREINDLER, 103; WOLFF, 286.

431 DUPEYRON, 464; STEINBRÜCK, 20 et seq.

432 BLACKABY et al., n. 7.21; HOFMANN/FUCHS, 127 et seq.

competence is almost entirely reserved to state courts.[433] To take account of these shortcomings, various *leges arbitri* supplement the arbitral tribunal's powers by allowing national courts to step in and support the arbitral proceedings.[434]

§ 4 Third Parties

The third limitation is that the arbitral tribunal's powers are virtually always limited to the parties to the arbitration. Because of the consensual nature of arbitration, only the parties to the arbitration agreement can participate in the ensuing proceedings.[435] As a result, the arbitral tribunal has no jurisdiction over third parties–a reality which was cited as one of the three worst characteristics of international arbitration in a recent study.[436] This is in stark contrast to state court litigation, where parties' standing is determined not necessarily on a contractual basis, but more based on individual personal interests.[437] In order to protect these interests, any natural person or legal entity is free to commence court proceedings against any other.[438]

In complex international arbitral proceedings, relevant evidence is often found in the hands of third parties.[439] One option in this case is to approach the third party directly in a bid to obtain the respective evidence (e.g. in the form of a document or witness testimony).[440] However, this soon becomes problematic if the third party refuses to comply with the request. Unlike state courts, which can force third parties to appear before them to testify or reveal certain documents, arbitrators have no such powers.[441] The problem becomes even more complex if the third party resides outside the

433 For an exception, *see* Art. 26 (3) Swiss Rules, which expressly allows the arbitral tribunal to issue *ex parte* interim measures. This provision, inspired by Art. 265 (2) CCP CH, applies only in urgent cases, especially where communication of the request for an *ex parte* measure to the other party would prejudice the effectiveness of that measure (Zuberbühler et al.-OETIKER, Art. 26 Swiss Rules n. 14).

434 *See* e.g. Art. 184 (2) PILA CH; § 1050 CCP DE; S. 13 (2) IAA SG; BLACKABY et al., n. 5.11 et seq.; DUPEYRON, 465 et seq.

435 BREKOULAKIS, 1166; BORN, *Law and Practice*, ch. 1.01 n. 4 et seqq.; WAINCYMER, *Evidence*, 53 et seq.

436 DUPEYRON, 464; SCHAEFER, 529 et seq.; Queen Mary Survey (2018), 7 et seq.

437 BREKOULAKIS, 1166.

438 *Ibid.*

439 O'MALLEY, n. 3.93; HOFMANN/FUCHS, 127.

440 VARGA, 242.

441 KRSUL, 183.

territorial jurisdiction of the seat of arbitration.[442] If the third party is in any way closely connected to any of the arbitration parties (i.e. in their sphere of influence), the arbitral tribunal can put pressure on that party to persuade the third party to produce the evidence as requested. However, if the third party still refuses to cooperate voluntarily, the evidence needed can in most cases be gathered only by resorting to state courts.[443]

§ 5 Conclusion

This short overview has revealed that, despite the inherent procedural flexibility of international arbitration, there are certain points at which only state courts can provide effective support. Even if an emergency arbitrator can fill the jurisdictional vacuum prior to the constitution of the arbitral tribunal, this help is not enough if coercive power is needed–for example, if a party requests that evidence be preserved by means of a freezing order over certain assets of the adverse party. Last but not least, if evidence is in the control of third parties that are not willing to support the arbitral proceedings and refuse to produce the evidence voluntarily, the state courts serve as a last resort.

Although arbitrators and parties usually do not like the idea of involving state courts in ongoing arbitral proceedings, their assistance is often crucial to ensure the ultimate effectiveness of the arbitration.[444] Thus, the next chapter discusses the ways in which state courts can assist arbitral tribunals in taking evidence, and considers whether they in fact have a legal obligation to support arbitral tribunals in general and in the taking of evidence in particular.

442 *Ibid.*

443 *Ibid.*

444 SCHAEFER, 533; LEW, 492 et seq.

6

Court Assistance in the Taking of Evidence

§ 1 Introduction

As the previous chapter has demonstrated, court assistance in the taking of evidence is sometimes the only option. This chapter takes a closer look how this works in general, before moving to a comparative analysis of various *leges arbitri*. The issue is approached from three different angles. The first concentrates on when court assistance in the taking of evidence is needed and how this works in practice. Thus, in a short outline, various types of court assistance in taking evidence will be analysed in part two. However, the mere fact that court assistance is possible from a practical standpoint does not necessarily mean that it can or should be granted. Its legitimacy in general, and in the taking of evidence in particular, will therefore be examined in part three. This will show that both *leges arbitri* and (ad hoc and institutional) arbitration rules contain an option to resort to state courts in order to gather evidence. In addition, a closer look at the intention of the parties is necessary in order to confirm and strengthen the legitimacy of court assistance in the taking of evidence. However, such legitimacy does not, in itself, necessarily imply an obligation to grant assistance; thus, the final part of this chapter explores whether state courts are obliged to assist arbitral tribunals in the taking of evidence based on federal, constitutional and international public law.

§ 2 Measures of Court Assistance in Taking Evidence

A. Introduction

Throughout the arbitral proceedings, court assistance might become necessary in numerous situations. Prior to the constitution of the arbitral tribunal, the validity of the arbitration agreement may be questioned or interim measures sought.[445] While the arbitral tribunal is being established, state courts can assist in relation to the appointment and challenge of arbitrators.[446] During the arbitral proceedings, court assistance may be granted in relation to interim measures and the taking of evidence.[447] Once the arbitral award has been rendered, it may be challenged before state courts on various grounds, such as violation of the right to be heard or even breach of the *ordre public* (i.e. public policy).[448] Finally, at the enforcement stage, court assistance may be needed if a party refuses to comply with the arbitral award.[449]

This short outline provides only a glimpse of the situations in which court assistance may be necessary. As this thesis focuses on the taking of evidence, only measures concerning evidence will be examined.[450] In this regard, one should be aware that numerous *leges arbitri* contain only short provisions in this regard, stating merely that assistance from state courts in the taking of evidence may be sought. Consequently, there is no precise catalogue of the possible measures available in international arbitration; the ways in which and the extent to which courts can assist arbitral tribunals will therefore vary from jurisdiction to jurisdiction.[451] However, most types of assistance in relation to evidence can be classified as either interim measures or simple acts of court assistance in the taking of evidence. By means of various examples from *leges arbitri*, these types of assistance will be addressed next.

B. Interim Measures

Although interim measures will not be explored extensively in this book, a few remarks are nonetheless necessary because of their close connection to the taking of evidence. While numerous *leges arbitri* mention interim measures, these go by different names and their extent is rarely further specified.[452] An exception to this is the UNCITRAL ML, which provides a definition in Art. 17 (2):

445 LEW, 496 et seq.; BLACKABY et al., n. 7.09 et seqq.

446 Regarding the Swiss *lex arbitri see* Arts. 179 (2) and 180 (3) PILA CH.

447 LEW, 497 et seq.; BLACKABY et al., n. 7.13 et seqq.

448 BORN, *Law and Practice*, ch. 16.03 n. 21 et seqq.

449 BLACKABY et al., n. 11.01 et seqq.

450 For an extensive outline of the role of state courts in arbitration, *see* SUTTON et al., n. 7-001 et seqq.

451 Regarding measures taken by emergency arbitrators, *see* EHLE, *Emergency Arbitration*, 102 et seqq.

452 BLACKABY et al., n. 7.14; BOOG, n. 21 et seqq.

> "An interim measure is any temporary measure, whether in the form of an award or in another form, by which, at any time prior to the issuance of the award by which the dispute is finally decided, the arbitral tribunal orders a party to:
> (a) Maintain or restore the status quo pending determination of the dispute;
> (b) Take action that would prevent, or refrain from taking action that is likely to cause, current or imminent harm or prejudice to the arbitral process itself;
> (c) Provide a means of preserving assets out of which a subsequent award may be satisfied; or
> (d) Preserve evidence that may be relevant and material to the resolution of the dispute."

As Singapore has adopted the UNCITRAL ML to a significant extent, the IAA SG also refers to 'interim measures'.[453] By contrast, the Swiss, German and French *leges arbitri* speak of 'provisional and conservatory measures';[454] while English law[455] refers to 'court powers exercisable in support of arbitral proceedings'. Institutional arbitration rules take a similar approach, variously referring to 'interim measures' (ICDR Rules),[456] 'conservatory and interim measures' (ICC, LCIA and DIS Rules),[457] 'interim measures of protection' (Swiss Rules)[458] or 'interim relief' (SIAC Rules)[459]. Whatever the specific term may be, the goal of such interim measures remains the same: to grant temporary protection that safeguards the parties' rights from possible damage during the course of arbitration.[460] In the interest of simplification, the term 'interim measures' shall be used hereinafter, according to the definition set out in Art. 17 (2) UNCITRAL ML.

Under most of the examined *leges arbitri*, unless the parties have agreed otherwise, state courts and arbitral tribunals have concurrent jurisdiction to order interim measures.[461] Consequently, all examined institution arbitration

453 S. 3 and 12A IAA SG.

454 Art. 183 PILA CH; § 1041 (1) CCP DE; Art. 1449 CCP FR.

455 S. 44 (2) EAA 1996.

456 Art. 24 ICDR Rules.

457 Art. 28 ICC Rules; Art. 25.1 LCIA Rules; Art. 25 DIS Rules.

458 Art. 26 Swiss Rules.

459 Rule 30 SIAC Rules.

460 BORN, *Law and Practice*, ch. 11 n. 1; BERGER/KELLERHALS, n. 1236.

461 EHLE, *Concurrent Jurisdiction*, 158; BORN, *Law and Practice*, ch. 11.03 n. 25; *see* e.g. Art. 9 UNCITRAL ML, Art. 183 PILA CH; ZK-OETIKER, Art. 183 PILA CH n. 4; BSK-MABILLARD,

rules state that resorting to a state court to seek interim measures is not considered incompatible with the arbitration agreement or seen as a waiver thereof.[462] With regard to evidence, interim measures in relation to the preservation of evidence have significant relevance. Within the legal doctrine, such measures are considered almost unanimously as interim measures, even though the exact boundary between interim measures and ordinary measures for the taking of evidence is anything but clear-cut.[463] Especially at the outset of arbitration, before the constitution of the arbitral tribunal, parties may have a keen interest in ensuring that evidence is secured and preserved.[464] Examples include situations where a record of a building's construction must be made at a certain time (e.g. before completion of the construction),[465] or where a key witness must be examined because he or she is terminally ill.[466]

While all examined *leges arbitri* content themselves with rather short general statements that state courts can order interim measures, S. 44 (2) EAA 1996 is very specific and lists the matters in which they are competent to do so:

"Those matters are:

(b) the preservation of evidence;

(c) making orders relating to property which is the subject of the proceedings or as to which any question arises in the proceedings:

(i) for the inspection, photographing, preservation, custody or detention of the property, or

---

Art. 183 PILA CH n. 5; WALZ, n. 9 et seqq. In contrast, S. 44 (5) EAA 1996 is more restrictive, allowing state courts only to order interim measures if the arbitral tribunal has 'no power or is unable for the time being to act effectively' (MERKIN/FLANNERY, 177 et seq.). Under French law, the situation is comparable because once the arbitral tribunal is constituted, state courts are theoretically no longer competent to order interim measures (Art. 1449 CCP FR). However, as shown below, this view is supported by neither French legal doctrine nor case law (*see* p. 152 et seq. *infra*).

462 EHLE, *Concurrent Jurisdiction*, 159; BLACKABY et al., n. 7.24; *see* e.g. Art. 26 (9) UNCITRAL Rules; Art. 25.1 DIS Rules; Art. 28 (2) ICC Rules; Art. 26 (5) Swiss Rules; Rule 30 (3) SIAC Rules; Art. 25.3 LCIA Rules.

463 BERGER/KELLERHALS, n. 1247; BLACKABY et al., n. 737 et seq.; BORN, *Law and Practice*, ch. 11.01 n. 18; GIRSBERGER/VOSER, n. 1102; GÖKSU, n. 1905; VON SEGESSER, *Interim Measures*, 479; for a different view *see* WALTER et al., 135 et seq. These authors suggest that the arbitral tribunal can shift the burden of proof in cases where a party refuses to produce evidence or even interfere in the preservation of evidence. This opinion ignores the fact that evidence is often found in the hands of third parties where a simple shift of the burden of proof is not accurate. In contrast, BOOG argues that interim measures protect first and foremost the subjective rights of a party, while measures regarding the preservation of evidence concern only a matter of fact (n. 30). As a result, he considers such measures as interim measures only in the broadest sense.

464 BLACKABY et al., n. 7.37.

465 VON SEGESSER, *Interim Measures*, 479.

466 LEW et al., 595 et seq.

(ii) ordering that samples be taken from, or any observation be made of or experiment conducted upon, the property;

and for that purpose authorising any person to enter any premises in the possession or control of a party to the arbitration;

(d) the sale of any goods the subject of the proceedings."

This provision lists all types of interim measures available. Lit. (b) applies to cases where evidence is in the control of a third party, which the arbitral tribunals cannot obtain if that third party does not comply voluntarily.[467] The goal here is to preserve evidence (e.g. in the form of documents) which may cease to exist or may be impossible to find in the near future.[468] Moreover, lit. (c) mentions orders relating to the property of third parties.[469] Obviously, such measures exceed the powers of an arbitral tribunal. In construction disputes in particular, state courts may order that samples of a building be taken in order to prevent the property from being altered, destroyed or sold before the evidence is secured for use in arbitration.[470] Finally, according to lit. (d), state courts can also order the sale of perishable goods in order to preserve evidence or assets.[471] S. 44 (2) EAA 1996 thus sets out a few examples of how state courts in England can effectively support the arbitral proceedings by preserving evidence through interim measures.

C. Measures of Taking Evidence

In addition to interim measures, state courts can assist in the taking of evidence through a wide spectrum of possible measures, depending on the respective *leges arbitri*. In practice, however, in most cases either the attendance of witnesses or the production of documents is sought. As compared to interim measures, which aim to grant provisional relief (i.e. for a certain period of time only), ordinary measures for the taking of evidence aim to establish the relevant facts of the case. As for interim measures, the examined

467 *See.* e.g. *Assimina Maritime Ltd. v. Pakistan Shipping Corporation & Anor* [2004] EWHC 3005 (Comm.); for the corresponding provision regarding evidence in possession of a party, *see* S. 38 (6) EAA 1996.

468 MERKIN/FLANNERY, 140 et seq. Consequently, lit. (b) is not meant to order ordinary disclosure by a third party (HARRIS et al., S. 44 EAA 1996 n. 44D).

469 The corresponding provision as regards evidence in possession of a party is stated in S. 38 (4) EAA 1996.

470 S. 44 (2) (c) (ii) EAA 1996; SUTTON et al., n. 7-193.

471 MERKIN/FLANNERY, 183; *see* e.g. the example given by Lord Justice Clarke in *Cetelem S.A. v. Roust Holdings Ltd.*, [2005], EWCA 618 (Civ.), n. 65.

leges arbitri contain either general rules or detailed provisions stating that state courts will provide assistance to arbitral tribunals in the taking of evidence.

Art. 27 UNCITRAL ML contents itself with a general provision:

> "The arbitral tribunal or a party with the approval of the arbitral tribunal may request from a competent court of this State assistance in taking evidence. The court may execute the request within its competence and according to its rules on taking evidence."

The German and Swiss *leges arbitri* also contain similar short provisions.[472] In other countries, the respective provisions are more detailed. As previously shown, the arbitral tribunal's powers in relation to the taking of evidence are limited to the parties *(see* p. 82 et seq. *supra).* Thus, different *leges arbitri* recognise this issue by granting assistance as regards evidence in the control of third parties. For instance, Art. 1469 CCP FR is quite clear in this regard:

> "In case a party to the arbitral proceedings intends to rely upon a ... piece of evidence held by a third party, it may, upon the arbitral tribunal's invitation, file a claim against that third party before the President of the First Instance Court in order to obtain a copy thereof, or the submission of the document or piece of evidence."
>
> "If the President considers that the request is justified, he or she shall order the delivery or submission of an original, copy or abstracts, as the case may be, of the document or evidence, under the conditions and guarantees that he or she shall determine, and as need be, under penalty."

The main advantages of resorting to state courts in the taking of evidence–that is, their coercive powers ('under penalty') and jurisdiction over third parties–are perfectly reflected in this provision *(see in detail* p. 153 et seq. *infra).*

While the CCP FR speaks only of documents, S. 13 (2) IAA SG expressly mentions documents and witnesses:[473]

> "The High Court or a Judge thereof may order that a subpoena to testify or a subpoena to produce documents shall be issued to compel the attendance before an arbitral tribunal of a witness wherever he may be within Singapore."

In addition to the possibility to force third parties to produce documents or appear before a state court or an arbitral tribunal, one might also consider

472 Art. 184 (2) PILA CH; § 1050 (1) CCP DE.

473 *See also* S. 43 (1) EAA 1996.

expert evidence. The Dutch Arbitration Act is quite exceptional in this regard, as it empowers the arbitral tribunal to request expertise on foreign law through the assistance of state courts.[474]

D. Summary

In summary, state courts can assist by ordering either interim measures or ordinary measures for the taking of evidence–for example, forcing third parties to appear before a state court or directly before an arbitral tribunal to produce documents. Although there are many significant differences among jurisdictions, which will be discussed later in this book *(see* ch. 7 *infra),* it shall suffice here to conclude that most jurisdictions take a very arbitration-friendly stance by assisting arbitral tribunals in the taking of evidence.

§ 3 Court Assistance versus Court Intervention

A. Introduction

As previously shown *(see* p. 85 et seqq. *supra),* the assistance of state courts–in the form of either interim measures or ordinary measures for the taking of evidence–is a key factor in ensuring the ultimate effectiveness of arbitration in this regard. Before taking a closer look at the legitimacy of court assistance in the taking of evidence, a few general remarks about the relationship between state courts and arbitral tribunals are worth mentioning. While this relationship has been described as a mix of 'forced cohabitation and true partnership',[475] as well as 'judicial-arbitral cooperation',[476] PAULSSON describes the issue and the tension inherent therein as follows:[477]

> "The great paradox of arbitration is that it seeks the cooperation of the very public authorities from which it wants to free itself. "

Indeed, parties choose arbitration precisely because they do not want to settle their dispute in state court proceedings. Nonetheless, the help of state courts is often crucial. Many jurisdictions recognise the importance of international arbitration as an alternative dispute settlement mechanism and

474 S. 1044 CCP NL. The Dutch legislator decided that arbitral tribunals should also benefit from the European Convention on Information on Foreign Law (1968), which entered into force in the Netherlands in 1977.

475 BLACKABY et al., n. 7.01.

476 DUPEYRON, 467.

477 PAULSSON, 2.

commit themselves to support and assist arbitral tribunals–for example, by being Member States of international conventions such as the NYC or by modelling their *leges arbitri* on the UNCITRAL ML. In return, jurisdictions expect to have a certain degree of control during and after the arbitral process by implementing minimum standards (e.g. the right to be heard), and by recognising and enforcing international arbitral awards subject to certain requirements.[478] Depending on the side from which one looks at it, the involvement of state courts in arbitral proceedings can be seen as either helpful assistance or disturbing interference.[479] Because this issue opens up a broad field of technical and legal philosophical matters which would exceed the scope of this book, the following remarks focus on concerns regarding evidence.

While acknowledging that the issue must be examined separately per jurisdiction, several general conclusions can nonetheless be drawn. This will be done by considering the topic from the point of view of the UNCITRAL ML, on which many *leges arbitri* are modelled and which defines the way in which and the extent to which state courts can intervene in arbitral proceedings.[480] In addition, the IBA Rules–as *the* source regarding evidentiary matters in international arbitration–contain helpful guidance on how to approach state courts with regard to the taking of evidence. Because they apply even stricter standards than the IBA Rules as to how to seek assistance from state courts, the LCIA Rules are worth mentioning too. Finally, the question arises, from the parties' perspective, as to whether the possibility to seek assistance from state courts in the taking of evidence is actually covered by their intention.

B. UNCITRAL ML

1. Court Assistance in General

Art. 5 UNCITRAL ML establishes the overarching principle of limited court intervention–that is, a 'hands-off' approach:

> "In matters governed by this Law, no court shall intervene except where so provided in this Law."

The drafters of the UNCITRAL ML emphasised that although the wording of this provision could suggest that court intervention is negative, the intention was to clarify the expectations of parties and arbitrators alike with regard to

478 BLACKABY et al., n. 1.202 et seqq.

479 KREINDLER, 103; STEINBRÜCK, 44; *see also* Queen Mary Survey (2015), 7. Accordingly, national court intervention seems to be at least for 25% of the respondents a disadvantage of international arbitration.

480 For a closer analysis of various countries and their approach in this matter *see* ch. 7 *infra*.

the points in the arbitral proceedings at which state courts may get involved.[481] The term 'intervention' may thus also be read as 'assistance'.[482] Art. 5 UNCITRAL ML further clarifies that state courts have no inherent powers to interfere in arbitral proceedings to the surprise of the parties and the arbitral tribunal, except as set out in the UNCITRAL ML.[483] This involvement can be divided into two categories. The first category concerns issues regarding the appointment, challenge and termination of the mandate of arbitrators (Arts. 11, 13 and 14), the jurisdiction of the arbitral tribunal (Art. 16) and the setting aside of the arbitral award (Art. 34).[484] The second category comprises issues regarding the taking of evidence (Art. 27), recognition of the arbitration agreement (Art. 8) and interim measures (Arts. 9 and 17J), as well as recognition and enforcement of interim measures (Arts. 17H and I) and arbitral awards (Arts. 35 and 36).

2. Court Assistance in the Taking of Evidence

With regard to court assistance in the taking of evidence, Art. 27 UNCITRAL ML specifies as follows:

> "The arbitral tribunal or a party with the approval of the arbitral tribunal may request from a competent court of this State assistance in taking evidence. The court may execute the request within its competence and according to its rules on taking evidence."

Apparently, it was a major undertaking to reach an international consensus on how courts should assist in the taking of evidence. The question, therefore, was not *whether* but *how* such assistance may be granted.[485] The drafters began with a rather long and extensive article, and ended up with a limited provision which ultimately gained enough acceptance to be adopted.[486] This very fact indicates the complexity of the subject and the inconsistencies among the Member States of the UNCITRAL ML. In this regard, three issues were of major concern.

481 UNCITRAL, A/CN.9/264 (1985), 18, n. 3; UNCITRAL, Case Law (2012), Art. 5 UNCITRAL ML, n. 1-3. Because Art. 5 UNCITRAL ML refers only to 'matters governed by this Law', other concerns–such as the contractual relationship between arbitrators and parties or fixing the costs and fees of arbitration–are not included.

482 UNCITRAL, Summary Records of the 309th meeting (1985), n. 22, 25 and 40.

483 SCHAEFER, 533 et seq.; Mistelis-BREKOULAKIS et al., Art. 5 UNCITRAL ML, 847 et seq.

484 Art. 6 UNCITRAL ML.

485 HOLTZMANN/NEUHAUS, Art. 27 UNCITRAL ML, 734.

486 *Ibid.*, Art. 27 UNCITRAL ML, 735; UNCITRAL, A/CN.9/264 (1985), 58.

First, Art. 27 UNCITRAL ML refers only to 'court assistance in taking evidence', without further specifying the types of evidence.[487] According to the commission report, the scope of application was meant to be limited territorially.[488] Member States are thus at liberty to decide how to treat a request for the taking of evidence–that is, whether the court itself will take the evidence or whether that evidence will be provided directly to the arbitral tribunal.[489]

Second, concerns were voiced during the drafting process about the potential abuse of requests for court assistance.[490] While it was initially suggested that only the arbitral tribunal should be permitted to make requests for court assistance, the final draft also allows parties to do so, subject to the approval of the arbitral tribunal.[491] This puts the arbitral tribunal at the centre of the arbitral proceedings and avoids possible dilatory tactics, as well as conflicts with national rules on civil procedure.[492] Moreover, the arbitral tribunal itself can resort to state courts for assistance in the taking of evidence. Here again, because it takes evidence itself and decides how to assess that evidence itself, the arbitral tribunal should also be able to seek court assistance in this regard itself, unless the parties have expressly agreed otherwise.

Third, Art. 27 UNCITRAL ML applies only if the seat of arbitration is in the territory of a Member State.[493] Hence, court assistance in the taking of evidence is not available for a foreign arbitral tribunal or if the seat of arbitration is undetermined.[494] Although some drafters would have preferred that foreign tribunals also be able to seek court assistance in the taking of evi-

487 Mistelis-BREKOULAKIS et al., Art. 27 UNCITRAL ML, 889.

488 UNCITRAL, A/40/17 (1985), n. 223.

489 HOLTZMANN/NEUHAUS, Art. 27 UNCITRAL ML, 735.

490 *Ibid.*

491 *See also* UNCITRAL, A/CN.9/245 (1983), n. 40. During the drafting process it has been suggested by some representatives that because of the adversary principle, only parties should be allowed to make requests for court assistance.

492 UNCITRAL, A/CN.9/246 (1984), n. 94. *See* e.g. *Delphi Petroleum Inc. v. Derin Shipping and Training Ltd.*, Federal Court of Canada, 3 Dec. 1993, summarized in: UNCITRAL, A/CN.9/SER.C/ABSTRACTS/4, 11. In this decision, the Federal Court of Canada denied court assistance on the grounds of dilatory tactics of the requesting party; *see* furthermore *Vibroflotation A.G. v. Express Builders Co. Ltd.*, High Court of Hong Kong, 15 Aug. 1994, in: UNCITRAL, A/CN.9/SER.C/ABSTRACTS/5, 3. Here, a request for document production against a third party was denied because, according to the High Court of Hong Kong, such a request was not timely and 'months if not years away from the main evidential hearing in this arbitration'.

493 Art. 1 (2) UNCITRAL ML.

494 *See* e.g. *B.F. Jones Logistics Inc. et al. v. Rolko et al.*, Ontario Superior Court of Justice, Canada, 24 Aug. 2004, CanLII 21276. In contrast, *see* § 1050 CCP DE, which expressly allows foreign arbitral tribunals to obtain court assistance in the taking of evidence.

dence,[495] this idea was abandoned on the grounds that the UNCITRAL ML should not determine such a complex matter. Rather, solutions should be achieved by means of international conventions and bilateral treaties.[496] By contrast, the following comparative analysis will show that several jurisdictions have clearly adopted a more liberal approach in this respect.[497]

The evidence which can be taken depends on the rules of the respective Member State on the taking of evidence. As the comparative analysis conducted in this book will show, the reality is that many *leges arbitri* choose to offer assistance to foreign arbitral tribunals directly. However, the UNCITRAL ML takes a rather conservative approach by limiting the scope of the available assistance to the respective measures in the jurisdiction where such assistance is sought.

The territorial limitation of Art. 1 (2) UNCITRAL ML does not apply to interim measures for the preservation of evidence.[498] This exception takes account of the fact that interim measures might be needed at the outset of arbitration, when the seat is not yet determined, or if certain evidence is located in another jurisdiction than the seat of arbitration.[499] Unfortunately, this does not apply to the taking of evidence (Art. 27 UNICTRAL ML).

3. Result

The UNCITRAL ML introduces the basic principle that in order to support arbitration, state courts can step in during the proceedings where this possibility is provided for by the UNCITRAL ML itself. It has been shown that there are many situations in which state courts can support the arbitral proceedings. With regard to evidence, state courts can assist arbitral tribunals as long as the seat of arbitration is in the territory of the respective Member State. An exception in this respect concerns interim measures–for example, in relation to the preservation of evidence. Moreover, in order to avoid abuse in form of dilatory tactics, requests for court assistance always require the approval of the arbitral tribunal. Finally, the scope of possible assistance will be determined by the respective national rules of civil procedure. In conclusion, it may be said that–at least from a legislative point of view–there is an international consensus that state courts should assist

495 UNCITRAL, A./CN.9/WG.II/WP.44 (1983), 183, Art. E.

496 UNCITRAL, A/CN.9/245 (1983), n. 42 et seq; UNCITRAL, A/CN.9/246 (1984), n. 95 et seqq.; UNCITRAL, A/CN.9/264 (1985), 59 et seq.

497 *See* ch. 7 *infra*.

498 Art. 17 (2) (d) UNCITRAL ML. As regards measures of preservation of evidence as interim measures, *see* p. 87 et seqq. *supra*.

499 UNCITRAL, A/CN.9/WG.II/WP.108 (2000), n. 74 et seqq.

arbitral tribunals in the taking of evidence if the respective requirements are met. Whether this view is reflected in (institutional and ad hoc) arbitration rules will be explored next.

C. Arbitration Rules

1. IBA Rules

The IBA Rules, which were revised in 2010, now impose strict requirements as regards whether and when state courts can assist in the taking of evidence. They provide that court assistance may be sought only if the evidence–whether documentary evidence or witness evidence–is in the control of third parties.[500] As regards the parties themselves, the arbitral tribunal is empowered to sanction a recalcitrant party for its failure to provide evidence by drawing an adverse inference *(see* p. 56 et seqq. *supra)*. According to the IBA Rules, the arbitral tribunal has the widest discretion to grant or deny a request to seek state court assistance. Consequently, its decision is generally not open to challenge.[501] However, the comparative section of this book will show how this works in different *leges arbitri*.[502]

a. Documentary Evidence

The IBA Rules acknowledge that in some situations, documents must be obtained from third parties. However, strict requirements must be met in this regard. Art. 3 (9) IBA Rules reads as follows:

> "If a Party wishes to obtain the production of Documents from a person or organisation who is not a Party to the arbitration and from whom the Party cannot obtain the Documents on its own, the Party may, within the time ordered by the Arbitral Tribunal, ask it to take whatever steps are legally available to obtain the requested Documents, or seek leave from the Arbitral Tribunal to take such steps itself."
>
> "The Party shall submit such request to the Arbitral Tribunal and to the other Parties in writing, and the request shall contain the particulars set forth in Article 3.3, as applicable."
>
> "The Arbitral Tribunal shall decide on this request and shall take, authorize the requesting Party to take, or order any other Party to take, such

500 There are no similar provisions in regard to expert witnesses or inspections.

501 O'MALLEY, n. 4.71. A party would have to show that denying an evidence request would have a direct impact on the arbitral award–for example, by proving a violation of the right to be heard; *see also* the appellate remedies in Switzerland, p. 256 et seqq. *infra.*

502 *See* ch. 7 *infra.*

steps as the Arbitral Tribunal considers appropriate if, in its discretion, it determines that
(i) the Documents would be relevant to the case and material to its outcome,
(ii) the requirements of Article 3.3, as applicable, have been satisfied and
(iii) none of the reasons for objection set forth in Article 9.2 applies."

While Art. 27 UNCITRAL ML emphasises the role of the arbitral tribunal, the IBA Rules are even more specific in this respect.[503] Parties can thus make requests for court assistance only if they are unable to obtain the document themselves. In addition, the request itself must meet the requirements of Art. 3 (3) IBA Rules, as well as the absence of any reason listed in Art. 9 (2) IBA Rules. Instead of 'court assistance', the IBA Rules use the wording 'take whatever steps are legally available to obtain the requested Documents', without making further explanations. In legal doctrine, this wording is seen as allowing the possibility to seek assistance from state courts, among other things.[504] As an alternative, an arbitral tribunal can order a party that presumably knows where documents of a third party are located to assist in finding them.[505] If this is not possible, the arbitral tribunal must decide on the request by considering whether the strict conditions set out in (i) to (iii) have in fact been met.

Alternatively, the arbitral tribunal is at liberty to seek court assistance itself, quite similar to the possibility foreseen in Art. 27 UNCITRAL ML. Art. 3 (10) IBA Rules provides:

"At any time before the arbitration is concluded, the Arbitral Tribunal may (i) request any Party to produce Documents, (ii) request any Party to use its best efforts to take or (iii) itself take, any step that it considers appropriate to obtain Documents from any person or organisation."

Because of the danger of a violation of equal treatment, the IBA Rules provide for cascading measures with regard to court assistance: the tribunal must first grant the parties the right to be heard and only afterwards decide whether court assistance in the taking of evidence is necessary.[506]

503 O'MALLEY, n. 3.93.

504 *Ibid.*, n. 3.100; ZUBERBÜHLER et al., Art. 3 IBA Rules n. 210; IBA Review Subcommittee (2010), 11.

505 *See* e.g. *Waste Management, Inc. v. United Mexican States*, ICSID, ARB (AF)/00/3, 30 Apr. 2004, n. 30. In this ICSID case, the arbitral tribunal ordered the claimant to disclose all relevant documents in possession of a third party to the respondent.

506 O'MALLEY, n. 3.125. This course of action can be compared to the conditions to consider before drawing an adverse inference (*see* p. 56 et seqq. *supra*).

b. Witnesses

The wording of Art. 4 (9) IBA Rules is very similar to the provision on documentary evidence:

> "If a Party wishes to present evidence from a person who will not appear voluntarily at its request, the Party may, within the time ordered by the Arbitral Tribunal, ask it to take whatever steps are legally available to obtain the testimony of that person, or seek leave from the Arbitral Tribunal to take such steps itself."
> "In the case of a request to the Arbitral Tribunal, the Party shall identify the intended witness, shall describe the subjects on which the witness's testimony is sought and shall state why such subjects are relevant to the case and material to its outcome."
> "The Arbitral Tribunal shall decide on this request and shall take, authorize the requesting Party to take or order any other Party to take, such steps as the Arbitral Tribunal considers appropriate if, in its discretion, it determines that the testimony of that witness would be relevant to the case and material to its outcome."

By and large, reference may be made to the previous remarks on court assistance for documentary evidence according to Art. 3 (9) IBA Rules. Because Art. 4 (9) IBA Rules does not mention Art. 9 (2) IBA Rules, O'MALLEY rightly points out that, in addition to the conditions mentioned in Art. 4 (9) IBA Rules, the requesting party should demonstrate that none of the reasons for objection according to Art. 9 (2) IBA Rules applies.[507]

Regarding witnesses, the IBA Rules do not provide for the arbitral tribunal to resort to state courts on its own initiative. Art. 4 (10) IBA Rules states only that the arbitral tribunal is competent to order the examination of witnesses whose testimony has not yet been given in the arbitral proceedings. There is no indication that the drafters of the IBA Rules did not want to allow the arbitral tribunal to take 'any step that it considers appropriate'[508] in order to secure the attendance of witnesses. Therefore, Art. 4 (10) IBA Rules should be interpreted broadly by allowing the arbitral tribunal to seek court assistance with the examination of witnesses on its own initiative.

507 O'MALLEY, n. 4.70.

508 Art. 3 (10) IBA Rules.

2. Institutional Arbitration Rules

Almost all examined institutional arbitration rules are silent on the relationship between state courts and the arbitral tribunal.[509] In this regard, the LCIA Rules are an exception–Art. 22.2 states:

> "By agreeing to arbitration under the Arbitration Agreement, the parties shall be treated as having agreed not to apply to any state court or other legal authority for any order available from the Arbitral Tribunal (if formed) under Article 22.1, except with the agreement in writing of all parties."

The goal here is to strengthen the arbitration agreement by making it clear that where the parties agree to arbitrate under the LCIA Rules, they renounce the possibility to seek relief from state courts for anything that falls under the powers conferred on the arbitral tribunal according to Art. 22.1 LCIA Rules.[510] Consequently, this also relates to the arbitral tribunal's power to order document production, among other things.[511] While Art. 22.2 LCIA Rules refers only to matters set out in Art. 22.1 LCIA Rules, there are other situations in which resorting to state courts is within the scope of the LCIA Rules.[512] In comparison to the IBA Rules, Art. 22.2 LCIA Rules requires the consent of the other party to the arbitration to seek relief from state courts, rather than the approval of the arbitral tribunal. Neither the UNCITRAL ML nor the IBA Rules require such approval, so the LCIA Rules are thus even stricter in this regard. It is therefore conceivable that a party, even with the approval of the arbitral tribunal, may be unable to seek court assistance because the adverse party will not agree to it.

3. Result

Although they differ in their degree of detail, the IBA Rules and the LCIA Rules both provide for the possibility to seek assistance from state courts in the taking of evidence. Nonetheless, they impose very strict standards under which this is possible. The IBA Rules are very detailed in this respect, while the LCIA Rules content themselves with the general remark that court assistance can be sought only with the agreement of all parties. Both approaches

509 The only exception are provisions about concurrent jurisdiction in regard to interim measures *(see* p. 87 et seq. *supra).*

510 *See* e.g. Art. 22.1 LCIA Rules ('additional powers'); SCHERER et al., Art. 22 LCIA Rules n 38.

511 Arts. 22.1 (iv) and (v) LCIA Rules.

512 *See* e.g. Art. 23.5 LCIA Rules regarding the arbitral tribunal's jurisdiction and Art. 25.3 LCIA Rules concerning interim measures.

strive to prevent parties from reaching out to state courts without the approval of the arbitral tribunal or the other parties. Only this ensures that court assistance is actually in the interests of the respective arbitration.

Hitherto, the question of whether parties can seek assistance from state courts in the taking of evidence has been answered only from the point of view of the UNCITRAL ML and arbitration rules. Hence, the focus now shifts to the intention of the parties.

D. Intention of the Parties

Quite understandably, a party whose adversary is requesting court assistance in the taking of evidence might argue against such a course of action, for various understandable reasons. Most importantly, the parties will have chosen to arbitrate precisely because they did not want to settle their dispute before state courts; thus, every move in this direction could be considered an attempt to circumvent the arbitration agreement, including the arbitral tribunal's exclusive power over the arbitral proceedings.[513] In addition, one might argue that the requesting party is trying to impose the practices of a specific legal culture as regards matters of evidence, as opposed to the well-balanced approach to the taking of evidence in international arbitration.[514] Although these arguments are to a certain degree justified and comprehensible, from the parties' point of view, cogent arguments may also be made to support the opposite position.

First, it is important to ask whether resorting to state courts is really a circumvention of the arbitration agreement. Admittedly, the agreement to arbitrate implies an intention to settle the dispute through arbitration and not through state court litigation. It also implies an intention to play by the rules referred to in the arbitration agreement (e.g. institutional arbitration rules). These rules, as well as certain *leges arbitri*, oblige arbitrators and parties alike to act loyally–that is, 'in good faith'–in the conduct of the proceedings.[515] Thus, as SERAGLINI and ORTSCHEIDT argue, if parties do not act in good faith–for example, by withholding important evidence–court assistance is in fact justified by the parties' arbitration agreement.[516] Hence, the fact that a recalcitrant party is not acting in compliance with the arbitration

513 DUPEYRON, 467.

514 *Ibid.*, 467.

515 *See* e.g. Art. 2A (1) UNCITRAL ML; 1646 CCP FR; Art. 9 (7) IBA Rules; Art. 22 (1) ICC Rules; Art. 20 (7) ICDR Rules; Art. 14.5 LCIA Rules; Art. 15 (7) Swiss Rules.

516 SERAGLINI/ORTSCHEIDT, n. 806.

agreement authorises the arbitral tribunal to seek assistance from state courts. Presuming that the parties have not expressly excluded all types of court intervention, this rather extensive interpretation of the arbitration agreement may be applied.[517]

Whether one agrees or not, this book does not consider court involvement as a violation or circumvention of the arbitration agreement–quite the contrary. In fact, in most cases it can be seen as a confirmation of the arbitration agreement. Nonetheless, in order to avoid an extensive interpretation, as previously shown, the parties should define the exact conditions for seeking court assistance or even exclude this possibility entirely, either when drafting the arbitration agreement or in the case management conference.[518] In this way, one can easier discern whether resorting to state courts indeed represents a circumvention of the arbitration agreement. Consequently, an arbitral tribunal, in allocating the costs in the arbitral award, can sanction a party which has incurred costs and time delays by seeking state court assistance in violation of the arbitration agreement.[519]

Second, instead of undermining the role of the arbitral tribunal, resorting to state courts can actually reinforce the arbitral tribunal's status as the competent legal authority. In most situations, the arbitral tribunal has enough options to stop non-compliant parties (e.g. drawing an adverse inference or imposing cost sanctions). However, in extreme cases such as illegal (or even relevant criminal) conduct of a party, court assistance might prove useful or even mandatory as part of the arbitral tribunal's task of fulfilling its mandate.[520] Where a party seeks court assistance as a dilatory tactic (i.e. without seeking the arbitral tribunal's approval), most state courts will refuse to grant assistance on their own initiative anyway.[521]

Third, in respect of evidence, the scope for intrusive court intervention is very limited.[522] Although state courts must examine whether the content of the request is in line with the respective *lex arbitri*, its examination is not

517 *See also* Art. 34 (2) (a) (iv) UNCITRAL ML.

518 DUPEYRON, 470.

519 *Ibid.*, 471.

520 KREINDLER, 104 et seq.

521 *See* p. 136, p. 155, p. 169, p. 203 et seq. *and* p. 233 *infra*. Hence, under most *leges arbitri* and institutional arbitration rules, the approval of the arbitral tribunal to seek court assistance must first be obtained. In addition, depending on the respective *lex arbitri*, several other requirements must be met, such as a legitimate motive to seek court assistance or the inability of the arbitral tribunal to obtain the evidence itself.

522 DUPEYRON, 463, 467.

usually extensive and assistance will in most cases be granted.[523] Even if court assistance must be sought in countries with broad discovery/disclosure rights in their domestic civil procedure rules, the parties can define and limit the scope of the taking of evidence in the case management conference.[524] Hence, the fear that state courts will impose a foreign legal culture is in most cases unfounded.

Fourth, seeking state court assistance in the taking of evidence will lead to a better-informed arbitral tribunal, which can then render a more fact-grounded verdict.[525] Or, to put it differently, in the worst-case scenario, the respective state court will refuse to grant assistance and the arbitral tribunal will have to decide based on the available evidence. At best, however, assistance will be granted and the arbitral tribunal will be even more confident that it is rendering a fair verdict.

E. Summary

As previously discussed, court involvement in international arbitration may variously be seen as helpful assistance or disturbing interference. It has been shown that, based on the UNCITRAL ML and (ad hoc and institutional) arbitration rules, court assistance in the taking of evidence can be sought only if the respective conditions are met. In this regard, the approval of the arbitral tribunal is crucial. Regarding the parties' intentions, in most cases court assistance not only is in line with the arbitration agreement, but also reinforces the competence of the arbitral tribunal, which can render a more fact-grounded arbitral award as a result. Based on these findings, one may conclude that court assistance is in fact a means of supporting the arbitral proceedings, rather than interfering with them.

But does this mean that state courts must automatically provide assistance if all conditions for court assistance are met? Or, to put it another way, are they under a legal obligation to do so? Can state courts refuse to assist international arbitral tribunals in gathering evidence without reason? Or are they bound by constitutional or even international public law, obliging them to grant assistance subject to certain requirements? These questions are the subject of the last part of this chapter.

523 *Ibid.*, 467.

524 *See* p. 29 et seqq. *supra*.

525 DUPEYRON, 467.

§ 4 Obligation to Assist Arbitral Tribunals

A. Introduction

The previous analysis has shown the willingness of state courts to grant arbitral tribunals assistance in the taking of evidence. On the one hand, this fact can be seen as welcome support from arbitration-friendly jurisdictions for international arbitration. However, if this were the only reason why state courts granted assistance, it would leave the competent judge with wide discretion to decide whether to grant assistance in a specific case. The intention of the respective legislature is therefore crucial to resolve the issue at hand in cases which are not regulated in detail by law.[526] On the other hand, there may even be an obligation to assist. In order to recognise and enforce arbitral awards, all examined *leges arbitri* require that certain fundamental procedural guarantees be observed in the arbitral proceedings.[527] If these standards are met, the question arises as to whether state courts must not only recognise and enforce arbitral awards, but also provide assistance during the arbitral proceedings–for example, by ordering interim measures or the disclosure of evidence.[528]

In order to answer these questions, it is crucial to understand the legislature's intention as regards support for arbitral tribunals in general. This may be achieved by considering superior rules of law–that is, constitutional law and international public law.[529] If there were in fact an obligation to assist arbitral tribunals based on superior law, this process would involve more than just 'applying the law' and exercising judicial discretion. Consequently, this discretion would be significantly curtailed, with almost no room for different interpretation–regardless of what the competent judge might think of arbitration as an alternative to state court litigation.[530]

Thus, in a first step, the issue will be treated by examining the requirements for arbitral proceedings from a constitutional point of view. Since this book tries to make suggestions and propositions regarding court assistance in international arbitral proceedings in Switzerland, the focus is on the Swiss

---

526 STEINBRÜCK, 45.

527 GÖKSU, n. 963. In addition, arbitral awards can be challenged only under very limited conditions, such as violation of the equality of the parties or the right to be heard (BLACKABY et al., n. 1034 et seqq.; *see also* e.g. Art. 190 (2) PILA CH; § 1065 (1) i.c.w. § 1062 CCP DE; Art. 1520 CCP FR; S. 68 EAA 1996.

528 SCHOIBL, 525 et seq.; STEINBRÜCK, 47; with regard to the German situation, *see* GEIMER, 113 et seqq.

529 STEINBRÜCK, 42 et seqq.

530 *Ibid.*, 42, 46.

Constitution.[531] This is even more the case since although all examined *leges arbitri* emphasise the importance of fundamental procedural guarantees, as stated in many constitutions, their scope and meaning differ greatly among jurisdictions.[532] In a second step, the issue will be discussed in light of international conventions such as the ECHR, the NYC and the HEC. To provide the reader with insight at a purely European level, the ECICA and the EER will also be examined.

B. Swiss Constitutional Law

1. Introduction

Constitutions usually remain silent about arbitration and this is also true of the Swiss constitution.[533] Although the PILA CH provides for support of arbitral proceedings in general, it remains doubtful whether this automatically results in a duty to support arbitral tribunals based on constitutional law. In other words, does the arbitration-friendliness foreseen in the PILA CH (Arts. 183-185) derive from the Const. CH? In fact, neither the Const. CH nor the SFT nor the legal doctrine suggests expressly that state courts have an obligation to support arbitral tribunals.[534] Still, there are important connections between the *lex arbitri* (PILA CH) and the Const. CH–for example, as regards access to justice and the right to be heard.

The fundamental procedural guarantees are set forth in Arts. 29-32 Const. CH and determine the procedural requirements of state court proceedings. While Art. 29 Const. CH contains general procedural guarantees, Art. 29a Const. CH focuses on access to justice; followed by Art. 30 Const. CH, which sets out a person's right to have his or her case heard by a legally constituted, competent, independent and impartial court. Finally, Arts. 31 and 32 Const. CH address criminal matters such as the deprivation of liberty (Art. 31) and criminal proceedings (Art. 32). With regard to the taking of evidence, access to justice and the right to be heard are of particular relevance and will thus be considered next.

531 For the German perspective *see* STEINBRÜCK, 48 et seqq.

532 POUDRET/BESSON, n. 546.

533 As an exception, many Latin American States have constitutionalized arbitration, *see* e.g. Art. 202 Const. PA; Art. 253 and 258 Const. VE; Art. 57 Const. UY; Art. 116 Const. CO; Art. 43 Const. CR; Art. 23 Const. SV; Art. 248 Const. PY; Arts. 62, 63 and 139 (1) Const. PE; *see also* ch. V, Art. 5 Const. FR (1791): 'The right of citizens to finalize their disputes through arbitration cannot be infringed by the acts of the Legislative Power.'

534 For the German perspective, *see* GEIMER, 126 et seqq., 187 et seq. He argues that since the German legislator allows arbitration, there is a duty to support abirtral tribunals e.g. in the taking of evidence.

2. Access to Justice

Art. 29a Const. CH reads as follows:

> "In a legal dispute, every person has the right to have their case determined by a judicial authority. The Confederation and the Cantons may by law preclude the determination by the courts of certain exceptional categories of case."

This constitutional guarantee equips 'every person' (i.e. natural persons and legal entities) with an individual right in the form of access to at least one judicial authority which determines their case, irrespective of whether it derives from criminal, civil or administrative proceedings, or of whether factual or legal questions are concerned.[535] Moreover, in certain fields of law, exceptions and restrictions can be made at both federal and cantonal level; this is the case, for instance, as regards political matters such as acts of the Federal Assembly or the Federal Council.[536] Another example would be to limit the appellate proceeding before the SFT to legal questions and exclude the incorrect establishment of facts.[537] As regards the assistance of arbitral proceedings by state courts, no limitations are foreseen by law at either federal or cantonal level.

Usually, the arbitral proceedings will be examined retrospectively only if one of the parties tries to set aside the arbitral award–for example, by claiming that the right to be heard or the right of equal treatment has been violated.[538] One could therefore ask whether Art. 29a Const. CH could be seen as a constitutional obligation to provide sufficient access to justice *during* the arbitral proceedings–for example, by providing assistance in the taking of evidence.[539] In this respect, the opinion of Waldmann and Steinbrück deserves approval. Accordingly, it is at the parties' discretion to exclude state court jurisdiction and this also applies to access to justice.[540] However, applying the case law of the ECtHR by analogy, this is possible only if the renunciation takes place

535 DFT 143 III 193, cons. 5.4; DFT 141 I 172, cons. 4.4.1; SGK-KLEY, Art. 29a Const. CH n. 13; OFK-BIAGGINI, Art. 29a Const. CH n. 4; BSK-WALDMANN, Art. 29a Const. CH n. 4, 10.

536 *Ibid.*, n. 18; SGK-KLEY, Art. 29a Const. CH n. 20.

537 Art. 97 (1) FSCA CH, but *see* the exceptions listed therein.

538 Art. 190 (2) (d) PILA CH; *see also* p. 266 et seqq. *infra*.

539 *See also* STEINBRÜCK as regards the situation in Germany (64 et seqq.) and the reference to GEIMER (140 and 187 et seq.); SCHLOSSER, 273, 281.

540 BSK-WALDMANN, Art. 29a Const. CH n. 30; STEINBRÜCK, 66.

voluntarily–that is, if it is 'free, permissible and unambiguous', and does not represent a complete waiver of every fundamental procedural guarantees as stated in Art. 6 (1) ECHR.[541]

In sum, it follows that if one can exclude access, there is no constitutional obligation to support arbitral proceedings under its title. Parties are therefore free to decide the degree to which they wish to exclude state court assistance in the taking of evidence. It will be shown that, even at the level of statutory law (i.e. Art. 184 (2) PILA CH), state courts are not automatically forced to provide assistance.[542] Nonetheless, one must bear in mind that the mere fact that court assistance in the taking of evidence is not a constitutional obligation does not liberate state courts from the need to consider whether they must render assistance based on statutory law. Otherwise, this would result in a denial of justice.

3. Right to be Heard

As under most laws, according to the PILA CH, the parties and the arbitral tribunal have full discretion to tailor the arbitral proceedings, subject only to the requirement to observe the principle of equal treatment of the parties and the right to be heard.[543] That is why, according to Art. 190 (2) (d) PILA CH, arbitral awards can be challenged through an adversarial procedure on the grounds of violation of the principle of equal treatment or the right to be heard. As regards evidence, the right to be heard is *the* central procedural guarantee. Its constitutional basis is found in Art. 29 (2) Const. CH. While this provision usually refers only to state court proceedings, the SFT has decided and confirmed several times that it is no different from Art. 190 (2) (d) PILA CH and thus also applies to arbitral proceedings.[544] Whether this also implies an obligation to assist arbitral tribunals, rather than just to ensure that minimum procedural guarantees are observed, depends on how the SFT defines the right to be heard.

Because arbitral awards can be challenged only on the limited grounds set out in Art. 190 PILA, there is a considerable volume of case law on the right to be heard, which specifies and interprets its scope of application.[545]

541 *Nourredine Tabbane v. Switzerland*, ECtHR, App no. 41069/12, n. 26 et seq., 1 Mar. 2016; STEINBRÜCK, 68.

542 *See* p. 250 et seqq. *infra*.

543 Art. 182 (3) PILA CH.

544 DFT 142 III 360, cons. 4.1.1; DFT 4A_342/2015 of 26 Apr. 2016, cons. 4.1.1; DFT 4A_172/2015 of 29 Sept. 2015, cons. 4.1; DFT 4A_402/2010 of 17 Feb. 2011, cons. 3.1; DFT 130 III 235, cons. 5; DFT 128 III 234, cons. 4b; DFT 127 III 576, cons. 2c; DFT 119 II 386, cons. 1b; DFT 117 II 346, cons. 1a.

545 DUTOIT, Art. 190 PILA CH n. 26 et seqq.; BSK-PFISTERER, Art. 190 PILA CH n. 64 et seqq.

Accordingly, the right to be heard is violated, for example, if the parties did not have the possibility to present their case and evidence, take part in the proceedings and be assisted and represented before the arbitral tribunal.[546] With regard to the right to present the case, the SFT has specified that the arbitral tribunal has a minimum duty to consider all information, arguments, evidence and evidence requests presented by the parties if they are relevant to the decision to be rendered.[547] Furthermore, the wording 'in an adversarial proceeding'[548] means that a party can comment on the evidence presented by the adverse party and refute it with its own evidence.[549]

After the previous remarks, one could easily conclude that since the SFT's interpretation of the right to be heard is quite broad and this principle also applies to arbitral proceedings, state courts are obliged to assist in the gathering of evidence based on federal and constitutional law.[550] However, while the SFT has extended the right to be heard in favour of the parties in certain circumstances, it has also limited this right in others. As regards evidence, the SFT has stated that an arbitral tribunal does not violate the right to be heard if it refuses to examine evidence because the fact to be proven is already established or because the presented evidence will not convince the arbitral tribunal to change its finding.[551] Thus, the possibility to examine witnesses and experts is not unlimited, and the arbitral tribunal can exercise its discretion to impose time limits or refuse to allow certain questions because of their irrelevance to the case.[552] The SFT has further held that as long as the right to be heard is not simply ignored, which would result in a denial of justice, even an incorrect assessment of evidence cannot be challenged.[553] In addition, because the parties can specify that the arbitral award need not be reasoned, there is no constitutional right to receive a reasoned arbitral

546 DFT 130 III 35, cons. 5; BSK-PFISTERER, Art. 190 PILA CH n. 63.

547 DFT 4A_606/2013 of 2 Sept. 2014, cons. 5; DFT 4A_360/2011 of 31 Jan. 2012, cons. 5.1; DFT 4A_46/2011 of 16 May 2011, cons. 4.3.1; DFT 133 III 235, cons. 5.2; DFT 121 III 331, cons. 3b.

548 Art. 190 (2) (d) PILA CH.

549 DFT 133 III 139, cons. 6.1; HABERBECK, 1414 et seq.

550 Art. 190 (2) (d) PILA CH i.c.w. Art. 29 (2) Const. CH.

551 DFT 4A_342/2015 of 26 Apr. 2016, cons. 4.1.1; DFT 4A_246/2014 of 15 Jul. 2015, cons. 6.1; DFT 4A_386/2010 of 3 Jan. 2011, cons. 7.2. The so-called 'anticipated assessment of evidence' can therefore be examined only from the limited angle of a violation of public policy (Art. 190 (2) (e) PILA CH; HABERBECK, 1422 et seqq.; for a different view *see* GÖKSU, n. 2087).

552 DFT 4A_544/2014 of 24 Feb. 2015, cons. 3.4.

553 DFT 127 III 576, cons. 2e and f; DFT 121 III 331, cons. 3a.

award.[554] To summarise, there is no constitutional duty to support arbitral proceedings under the right to be heard.

4. Result

From the preceding discussion, it is difficult to argue that state courts have a constitutional obligation to assist arbitral tribunals in the taking of evidence. First and foremost, although the PILA CH provides for the possibility for courts to assist[555] arbitral tribunals, there is no explicit constitutional basis suggesting the same.[556] Or, to put it differently, arbitration-friendliness is not the same as a constitutional obligation to assist arbitral tribunals.[557]

Second, neither the Swiss legislature nor the SFT supports the view that a constitutional obligation to assist arbitral tribunals exists, based on the reasoning that minimum procedural guarantees must be granted in arbitral proceedings. By imposing strict requirements on such proceedings, such as equal treatment and the right to be heard, the Swiss legislature wanted to afford arbitral awards equal status to state court decisions.[558] In addition, in order to provide for fast and efficient arbitral proceedings, the reasons for challenging an arbitral award are very limited under the PILA CH and parties can generally appeal only to the SFT.[559] That is why minimum procedural guarantees are even more important. These guarantees will be examined in detail in chapter eight of this book.[560] Finally, as previously discussed *(see* p. 107 *supra),* there is no reassessment of evidence or examination of how the arbitral tribunal exercised its discretion to conduct the arbitral proceedings. Thus, the Swiss legislature and the SFT are concerned only that certain minimal procedural guarantees are observed during the arbitral proceedings. To imply a direct constitutional obligation to assist arbitral tribunals during the course of arbitration (i.e. in the taking of evidence) would not be in line with this intention.[561]

554 DFT 134 III 186, cons. 6.1; DFT 133 III 235, cons. 5.2; DFT 116 II 373, cons. 7b.; for a different view *see* HABERBECK, 1417 et seqq.; ZK-OETIKER, Ar. 189 PILA CH n. 59 et seqq.; BUCHER, n. 351; BESSON, n. 400 et seq.

555 Arts. 183 (2) and 184 (2) PILA CH.

556 STEINBRÜCK, 132 et seq.

557 *Ibid.*, 65.

558 BSK-PFISTERER, Art. 190 PILA CH n. 1; GÖKSU, n. 1978.

559 According to Art. 192 PILA CH, parties can even exclude all appeals against the arbitral award if neither party has a domicile, a place of habitual residence or a place of business in Switzerland. Alternatively, the partial exclusion of one or several reasons to challenge the arbitral award as stated in Art. 190 (2) PILA CH is also possible.

560 *See* p. 256 et seqq. *infra*.

561 STEINBRÜCK, 64 et seqq.

Third, a constitutional obligation to assist arbitral tribunals would exist only if the ability to challenge an arbitral awards did not suffice to protect the minimum procedural guarantees of the parties.[562] In this case, instead of just examining retrospectively whether those guarantees were observed (i.e. *after* the arbitral award has been rendered), state courts would have to observe and protect these guarantees *during* the arbitral proceedings based on the constitution–for example, by assisting in the taking of evidence.[563] As previously discussed, this is clearly not the case–at least, not in Switzerland. In order to make Switzerland an attractive forum for arbitration, the Swiss legislature requires the courts to take a 'hands-off' approach during the course of arbitration, with the possibility only to examine arbitral awards after they have been rendered.

Finally, it may be summarised that Swiss courts assist arbitral tribunals in the taking of evidence not because of a constitutional duty, but simply because the Swiss legislature wishes to attract and support international arbitral proceedings, and thus to promote Switzerland as an arbitration-friendly jurisdiction. Thus, in assessing whether to grant assistance, a Swiss court is not bound by any direct constitutional obligation, but must decide according to the provisions as set forth in the PILA CH.[564]

C. International Public Law

1. Introduction

At least from the Swiss point of view, there is no constitutional obligation to assist international arbitral tribunals. Under international public law, the situation is not much different.[565] Although several international conventions state that minimum procedural guarantees must be observed in arbitral proceedings, they do not expressly state how far this obligation goes and what it implies. Nonetheless, various important decisions have helped with the interpretation of the issue. In this case, the question is again whether the need to observe these guarantees also obliges state courts to assist arbitral tribunals during the arbitration proceedings–for example, with regard to the taking of evidence. This question will be answered next by examining several international conventions such as the ECHR,[566] the NYC and the HEC.

562 *Ibid.*, 62.

563 *Ibid.*

564 Art. 183 (2) and Art. 184 (2) PILA CH; *see* p. 223 et seqq. *infra*.

565 STEINBRÜCK, 52 et seq.

566 As its name implies, the ECHR is largely considered a purely European convention. However, looking at Member States such as Russia and Turkey, the examination of the ECHR under the title of international public law seems to be justified.

It is important to stress that, at the level of international public law, the minimum procedural guarantees are worded even more carefully and generally than in the Const. CH. Thus, although these conventions are meant to have a synchronous effect in all Member States, their adoption and execution vary from one jurisdiction to another.[567] As stated previously in the introduction to this part of the chapter *(see* p. 103 *supra)*, the issue of whether a possible obligation to assist state courts based on international public law exists can only partially be answered globally; it should rather be considered separately per jurisdiction. The following remarks will thus–where possible–concentrate on the issues and consequences in and for Switzerland.

2. European Convention on Human Rights

a. Introduction

Since its establishment in 1950, the ECHR has been adopted in 47 countries in Europe. It entered into force in Switzerland in 1974.[568] With regard to minimum procedural guarantees, Art. 6 (1) ECHR reads as follows:

> "In the determination of his civil rights and obligations ..., everyone is entitled to a fair and public hearing within a reasonable time by an independent and impartial tribunal established by law."

As one of the fundamental and by far most important provisions of the ECHR, Art. 6 (1) ECHR grants access to a court combined with several minimum procedural guarantees.[569] Quite obviously, the wording of Art. 6 (1) ECHR is very general, allowing for broad interpretation. Therefore, the ECtHR has had many possibilities to express its views on the term 'fair hearing' and its meaning as regards evidence.[570] The ECtHR has held that this term includes, among other rights, equality of arms, which allows a party to present its case–including evidence–'under conditions that do not place him at a substantial

567 STEINBRÜCK, 53 et seq. He states that since customary international public law (*Völkergewohnheitsrecht*) provides no requirements with regard to arbitral proceedings, such a basis may be found in contractual international public law (*Völkervertragsrecht*) such as the ECHR or the NYC.

568 *See* the current status.

569 *See* ECtHR Annual Report 2018, 171 et seq. Accordingly, more than 24% of the 1068 cases brought before the ECtHR have concerned a violation of the right to a fair trial; Karpenstein/Mayer-MEYER, Art. 6 EMRK n. 5.

570 For an overview, *see* HARRIS D. et al., Art. 6 ECHR, 413 et seqq.; RAINEY et al., 291 et seqq.; HK-EMRK-LADEWIG et al., Art. 6 EMRK n. 139 et seqq.; Karpenstein/Mayer-MEYER, Art. 6 EMRK n. 100 et seqq.

disadvantage *vis-à-vis* his opponent'.[571] Furthermore, it has stated that parties have a right to a fair procedure for the taking of evidence–that is, to have the opportunity 'to have knowledge of and comment on the observations filed or evidence adduced by the other party'.[572] Regarding the admissibility of evidence and the way it should be assessed, the ECtHR has also held that Art. 6 (1) ECHR does not regulate these matters, but leaves them to national laws and courts.[573]

Thus far, the SFT and the ECtHR have examined the relationship between the ECHR and arbitration several times. In addition, the topic is much debated in legal doctrine.[574] Although there are all sorts of interesting questions to be answered in this conversation, the following remarks aim to establish whether the ECHR actually obliges Member States and their courts to assist arbitral tribunals in the taking of evidence, or whether they must merely ensure that minimum procedural guarantees were observed in the arbitral proceedings.

b. Case Law of the ECtHR

The ECtHR has ruled several times on the applicability of the ECHR to arbitral proceedings in general, as well as the admissibility of a waiver of the rights derived from the ECHR in arbitral proceedings in particular. In contrast to various authors who have suggested that the ECHR does not apply to arbitral proceedings at all, the ECtHR has clearly stated that a 'tribunal established by law' as foreseen in Art. 6 (1) ECHR should not necessarily be understood as a classic court of law; 'it may comprise a body set up to determine a limited number of specific issues, provided always that it offers the appropriate guarantees'.[575] The ECHR is therefore also applicable to arbitral tribunals, at least to a certain degree.

571 *Dombo Beheer B.V. v. the Netherlands*, ECtHR, no. 14448/88, n. 33, 27 Ocotber 1993; HARRIS D. et al., Art. 6 ECHR, 409 et seqq.; RAINEY et al., 291 et seqq.; Dörr et al.-GRABENWARTER/PABEL, ch. 14 n. 4, 93; HK-EMRK-LADEWIG et al., Art. 6 EMRK n. 96 et seqq.; STEINBRÜCK, 57 et seq.; It is noteworthy that a 'fair hearing' according to Art. 6 (1) ECHR is anything but a closed term with strict requirements. Derived from the case law of the ECtHR, it is interpreted widely and remains open to new interpretations (HARRIS D. et al., Art. 6 ECHR, 409). In addition, whether a hearing was in fact 'fair' can be determined only by looking at the proceedings as a whole (RAINEY et al., 291).

572 *Ruiz-Mateos v. Spain*, ECtHR, no. 12952/87, n. 63, 23 Jun. 1993.

573 *Schenk v. Switzerland*, ECtHR, no. 00010862/84, n. 46, 12 Jul. 1988; *Roland Volkmer v. Germany*, ECtHR, no. 39799/98, n. 4, 22 Nov. 2001; *see also Tamminen v. Finnland*, ECtHR, no. 40847/98, n. 38-42, 15 Jun. 2004, where the national court violated Art. 6 (1) ECHR because it refused to hear a witness for unfair and contradictory reasons.

574 For an extensive overview, *see* BESSON, 413 et seqq.; KODEK, n. 8.

575 BESSON, 401; *Lithgow and Others v. the United Kingdom*, ECtHR, no. 9006/80; 9262/81; 9263/81; 9265/81; 9266/81; 9313/81; 9405/81, n. 201, 8 Jul. 1986.

In this regard, the ECtHR distinguishes between compulsory and voluntary arbitration.[576] Consequently, if arbitration is imposed by law and the parties have no other option than to settle their dispute through arbitration, Art. 6 (1) ECHR is fully applicable.[577] First and foremost, this applies to sports-related arbitration, where the players usually have no choice but to submit to the respective federation rules, which will contain an arbitration clause.[578] In contrast, according to the *Tabbane* case, if parties choose arbitration voluntarily, they automatically waive certain rights as set forth in the ECHR, and in this case the right of access to a court is not absolute.[579] As a consequence, a waiver *per se* is not a violation of the ECHR.[580] Provided that the parties waive their rights freely, permissibly and unambiguously, the ECtHR considers that this does not violate the ECHR, as long as it is not a complete waiver of all rights under Art. 6 (1) ECHR.[581] Moreover, the waiver must be accompanied by minimum guarantees corresponding to its gravity (e.g. to freely choose an arbitrator or to be represented by a lawyer).[582] Although the ECtHR does not further specify which rights can be waived and which cannot, it seems that this issue is considered on a case-by-case basis rather than according to a dogmatic rule, subject only to the abovementioned conditions.[583]

c. Case Law of the Federal Tribunal

Not as detailed as the case law of the ECtHR, but noteworthy nonetheless, are the decisions of the SFT and its approach to the ECHR and arbitral proceedings.

576 *Mutu et Pechstein v. Switzerland*, ECtHR, no. 40575/10 and 67674/10, n. 95, 2 Oct. 2018.

577 *Bramelid and Malmström v. Sweden*, ECtHR, no. 8588/79 and 8589/79, n. 30 et seqq., 12 Dec. 1983. In this case, according to the Swedish Company Act of 1944, a dispute between a parent company and its subsidiary company had to be settled in arbitration by law.

578 *Mutu et Pechstein v. Switzerland*, ECtHR, no. 40575/10 and 67674/10, n. 98, 109 et seqq., 2 Oct. 2018.

579 *Nourredine Tabbane v. Switzerland*, ECtHR, App no. 41069/12, n. 26 et seq., 1 Mar. 2016.

580 *Ibid.*, n. 25; *Deweer v. Belgium*, ECtHR, no. 6903/75, n. 49, 27 Feb. 1980.

581 *Mutu et Pechstein v. Switzerland*, ECtHR, no. 40575/10 and 67674/10, n. 103 et seqq., 2 Oct. 2018; *Nourredine Tabbane v. Switzerland*, ECtHR, App no. 41069/12, n. 26 et seq., 1 Mar. 2016; *Eiffage S.A. et autres v. Switzerland*, ECtHR, no. 1742/05, 15 Sept. 2009; *Transport Fluviais do Sado S.A. v. Portugal*, ECtHR, no. 35943/02, 16 Dec. 2003; *Osmo Suovaniemi and others v. Finland*, ECtHR, no. 31737/96, 23 Feb. 1999; *Pfeifer and Plankl v. Austria*, ECtHR, no. 10802/84, 25 Feb. 1992; Karpenstein/Mayer-MEYER, Art. 6 EMRK n. 59; BESSON, 400.

582 *Nourredine Tabbane v. Switzerland*, ECtHR, App no. 41069/12, n. 16 and 27, 1 Mar. 2016; *Osmo Suovaniemi and others v. Finland*, ECtHR, no. 31737/96, 23 Feb. 1999.

583 BESSON (405), making reference to *Osmo Suovaniemi and others v. Finland*, ECtHR, no. 31737/96, 23 Feb. 1999.

In some early cases in the 1980s, the SFT stated that because the arbitral tribunal is not a 'tribunal established by law', Art. 6 (1) ECHR does not apply to arbitration, where the parties are at liberty to choose the arbitrators.[584] A few years later, the SFT changed its mind, stating that Art. 6 (1) ECHR also applies to private arbitral tribunals and especially with regard to the correct composition of the court and the arbitral tribunal, respectively.[585] In subsequent decisions, the SFT clarified that since the ECHR is not mentioned under the reasons to challenge an arbitral award according to Art. 190 (2) PILA CH, it is therefore not *directly* applicable; but it can be used *indirectly* to interpret and substantiate this article.[586] How this should work in practice has not yet been decided. Hence, there are no clear conditions as to how the ECHR should be used to interpret Art. 190 (2) PILA CH or which principles and rights apply with regard to arbitration.

d. Result

Further to the previous remarks, it must be asked whether there is an obligation to assist arbitral tribunals in the taking of evidence, based on the fact that the ECHR is also partially applicable to arbitral proceedings. It has been shown that, according to the case law of the ECtHR, a 'fair hearing' involves similar principles such as the right to be heard pursuant to the Const. CH.[587] While the SFT has clearly stated that the ECHR is not directly applicable to arbitral proceedings, but rather serves as a means to interpret the minimum procedural guarantees as set forth in Art. 190 (2) PILA CH, the ECtHR is not as explicit. It has held that in voluntary arbitration, the ECHR is applicable in principle, although not without limitations. Parties can therefore waive certain rights, as long as they freely agree to this, it is permissible under law and the waiver is made unambiguously.

In light of these findings, it is evident that the ECtHR obliges arbitral tribunals as well as national courts only to ensure that minimum procedural guarantees have been observed in the arbitral proceedings. Besides the fact

584 DFT 112 Ia 166, cons. 3a with reference to a further unpublished decision of 9 Feb. 1984, cons. 3d. For opinions against that reasoning, *see* BANGERT, 54 et seqq.; BESSON, 401.

585 DFT 117 Ia 166, cons. 5a. This change in opinion can easily be explained by the reasoning of the *Lithgow* decision of the ECtHR, which has been rendered in the meantime (*see* fn 575 *supra*).

586 DFT 142 III 360, cons. 4.1.2; DFT 4A_246/2014 of 15 Jul. 2015, cons. 7.2.2; DFT 4A_198/2012 of 14 Dec. 2012, cons. 3.1; DFT 4A_238/2011 of 4 Jan. 2012, cons. 3.1.2; DFT 4A_404/2010 of 19 Apr. 2011, cons. 3.5.3; DFT 4A_43/2010 of 29 Jul. 2010, cons. 3.6.1; DFT 4A_612/2009 of 10 Feb. 2010, cons. 2.4.1; DFT 4A_320/2009 of 2 Jun. 2010, cons. 1.5.3; DFT 4A_370/2007 of 21 Feb. 2007, cons. 5.3.2; DFT 4P.105/2006 of 4 Aug. 2006, cons. 7.3.

587 *Ibid.*; *see* p. 110 *supra*.

that there is no explicit obligation in the ECHR for state courts to assist tribunals, various other reasons contradict the existence of such an obligation. First, to conclude that such an obligation exists would not be coherent with the aforementioned case law of the ECtHR and the SFT. Although both suggest that the ECHR applies under certain conditions as regards minimum procedural guarantees, it would go too far to conclude that an obligation exists to assist arbitral tribunals in the taking of evidence.[588] At least in Switzerland, the ECHR serves only as a means to assist with the interpretation of minimum procedural guarantees as stated in Art. 190 (2) PILA CH. Consequently, no further obligation can be derived therefrom.

Second, for the same reason that was presented with regard to the Const. CH, a duty to assist arbitral tribunals in the taking of evidence based on the ECHR would exist only if state courts were obliged to supervise arbitration during the course of the proceedings themselves, and not merely after the arbitral award has been rendered *(see* p. 109 *supra).* This is clearly not the case; rather the contrary.[589] By agreeing to settle the dispute through arbitration, the parties deliberately renounce certain rights provided by the ECHR.[590] Moreover, because the arbitral award takes effect only after it has been rendered and a violation of procedural rules can be addressed by challenging the arbitral award, there is no obligation for state courts to supervise the arbitration to achieve a 'precautionary prevention of procedural violations'.[591]

3. New York Convention

a. Introduction

The NYC–which was established in 1958 and has 160 Member States–is the most important convention in the field of international arbitration.[592] It applies to arbitral awards rendered in a state other than that in which recognition and enforcement are sought.[593] Moreover, it comes into play not only as regards

588 STEINBRÜCK, 64.

589 KODEK, n. 60 et seqq.

590 *See* the aforementioned decision *Nourredine Tabbane v. Switzerland*, ECtHR, App no. 41069/12, n. 26 et seq., 1 Mar. 2016.

591 KODEK, n. 60. According to KODEK, the only exceptions would concern cases where the arbitral proceedings are excessively lengthy. In this respect, *see R v. Switzerland*, stating that a violation of the ECHR can be assumed only when a case is pending before a state court and not before an arbitral tribunal prior to the application made to the ECtHR (*R v. Switzerland*, ECtHR, no. 10881/84, 4 Mar. 1987).

592 UNCITRAL NYC Guide, Preface n. 1. It entered into force on 7 Jun. 1959 and Switzerland joined it on 30 Aug. 1965; Wolff-LIEBSCHER, Preliminary Remarks, n. 1; Balthasar-SOLOMON, n. 1; Mistelis et al.-MISTELIS/DI PIETRO, Introductory Remarks NYC, 1; PAULSSON, 1; Kronke et al.-BAGNER, Art. I NYC, 20 et seq.; *see* the current status.

593 Art. I (1) NYC.

the recognition and enforcement of arbitral awards (Arts. III–VI NYC), but also as regards the upholding of the arbitration agreement (Art. II NYC). If the respective arbitration agreement meets the conditions of Art. II (1) NYC, state courts must respect that agreement. Art. II (3) NYC reads as follows:

> "The court of a Contracting State, when seized of an action in a matter in respect of which the parties have made an agreement within the meaning of this article, shall, at the request of one of the parties, refer the parties to arbitration, unless it finds that the said agreement is null and void, inoperative or incapable of being performed."

As long as the arbitration agreement is not invalid in the sense of this article, state courts must support it in order to respect the parties' choice. Whether this obligation also includes support for arbitral tribunals in the taking of evidence will be considered below.

b. Art. II (3) NYC

This question can be answered only in general if the terms 'null and void, inoperative or incapable of being performed' are interpreted uniformly and not according to the respective applicable national law.[594] The question has been answered differently in various jurisdictions. While the scope of the wording 'null and void, inoperative or incapable of being performed' may overlap, its meaning is either understood as being internationalised or interpreted according to the respective national law.[595] The internationalised approach, adopted by French and US scholars and courts, holds that a valid arbitration agreement should be interpreted in light of international standards such as international public policy[596] or internationally recognised breach of contract defences such as duress and fraud.[597] However, most other jurisdictions, such as Switzerland[598] and Germany,[599] refer–by analogy to Art. V (1) (a) NYC–to the law chosen by the parties or, in the absence of such a

594 STEINBRÜCK, 72.

595 Kronke et al.-SCHRAMM et al., Art. II NYC, 104.

596 Paris Court of Cassation, 30 Mar. 2004, 1st Civil Chamber, 02-12259; *St. Hugh Williams v. NCL (Bahamas) LTD.*, 686 F.3d 1169 (11th Cir. 2012); *Bautisa v. Star Cruises*, 396 F.3d 1289, 1302 (11th Cir. 2005).

597 *Rhone Mediterranee Compagnia Francese di Assicurazioni e Riassicurazioni v. Achille Lauro*, 712 F.3d 50 (3d Cir. 1983), in: Y.B. Comm. Arb. 1984, 474 et seqq.; Kronke et al.-SCHRAMM et al., Art. II NYC, 104; UNCITRAL NYC Guide, Art. II n. 104; Wolff-WILSKE/FOX, Art. II (3) NYC n. 307.

598 DFT 4A_279/2010 of 25 Oct. 2010, cons. 2; DFT 5C.215/1994 of 21 Mar. 1995, cons. 2b.

599 STEINBRÜCK, 72 et seq.

choice, to the law of the country in which the award was rendered.[600] Consequently, the question of whether Art. II (3) NYC obliges national courts to support arbitral tribunals in the taking of evidence must be answered separately per jurisdiction.

Although the views on this matter differ from jurisdiction to jurisdiction, there is always a tendency to uphold the arbitration agreement and thus to apply Art. II (3) NYC only in drastic cases.[601] In order to assert or deny an obligation to assist arbitral tribunals, Steinbrück argues that Art. II (3) NYC can be interpreted either extensively or restrictively.[602] In cases where an arbitration agreement is not 'incapable of being performed', but the parties have not agreed on the exact procedure as regards the constitution of the arbitral tribunal, national courts may be bound to support the arbitral proceedings based on the NYC by appointing an arbitrator.[603] In contrast, Steinbrück further suggests that there are also cases in which Art. II (3) NYC should be understood as a limitation of court assistance.[604] For instance, if arbitral proceedings cannot be commenced or if the arbitral tribunal simply refuses to act despite the existence of a valid arbitration agreement, court assistance will not prove as helpful and could even run contrary to the parties' intention.[605] Based on the NYC, national courts can therefore assist only if it is within the intention of the parties. Otherwise, arbitral awards will be neither recognised nor enforced because the arbitral proceedings were not in accordance with the agreement of the parties.[606]

c. Result

The foregoing examination shows that the NYC does not provide a clear answer to the question of whether Art. II (3) NYC obliges national courts not only to respect arbitration agreements, but also to assist arbitral tribunals in the taking of evidence. Even if Art. II (3) NYC is interpreted uniformly, it remains dubious whether such an obligation exists. In addition, the possible restrictive interpretation of Art. II (3) NYC reveals that there are also situations in which court assistance would contradict the parties' intention. Hence, because

---

600 *Ibid.*, 104; Y.B. Comm. Arb. 2003, n. 620 et seqq.; Wolff-WILSKE/FOX, Art. II (3) NYC n. 290.

601 UNCITRAL NYC Guide, Art. II n. 103 et seqq.; Wolff-WILSKE/FOX, Art. II (3) NYC n. 292.

602 STEINBRÜCK, 75 et seqq.

603 *Ibid.*, with reference to *Etat d'Israël v. Société NIOC*, Paris Court of Cassation, 1 Feb. 2005, 1st Civil Chamber, in: Rev. Arb. 2005, 693 et seqq.

604 STEINBRÜCK, 79 et seqq.

605 Kronke et al.-SCHRAMM et al., Art. II NYC, 107; STEINBRÜCK, 80.

606 Art. V (1) (d) NYC.

there seems to be no clear-cut answer according to Art. II (3) NYC, the question must be answered by considering the overall intention of the NYC.

As its title states, the NYC aims first and foremost to facilitate the recognition and enforcement of arbitral awards to the 'greatest extent possible'.[607] The NYC therefore serves as a minimum standard, while leaving Member States free to apply more liberal rules.[608] This is demonstrated best by Art. V NYC, which states that arbitral awards must be recognised and enforced unless certain exceptions apply, such as where one party was unable to present its case.[609] Nonetheless, the NYC does not further specify those exceptions; nor does it say when arbitral awards should be enforced or annulled. It states merely that unless there are insurmountable obstacles, arbitral awards must be recognised and enforced.[610]

As the connection between arbitration agreements and the recognition and enforcement of arbitral awards was discussed late in the drafting process, Art. II NYC was added at the last minute to the text of the convention.[611] This explains why important issues such as the precise scope of application and the law governing the interpretation of Art. II NYC are not addressed. However, it seemed crucial to emphasise the importance of the arbitration agreement as the foundation of arbitration itself and ultimately the recognition and enforcement of arbitral awards.[612] Hence, apart from Art. II (3) NYC, this article harmonises the understanding of the arbitration agreement in general, as well as its formal requirements.

In sum, Art. II NYC prevents parties from having recourse to state courts if they have agreed to settle their dispute through arbitration. It lays the foundations for the recognition and enforcement of arbitral awards by emphasising the importance of the arbitration agreement. This is in line with the overall intention of the NYC: to establish general requirements as regards the recognition and enforcement of arbitral awards, but not to regulate the process itself.[613] Consequently, no obligation to assist arbitral tribunals during the proceedings (e.g. with the taking of evidence) can be derived from Art. II NYC or the convention as a whole.[614]

607 UNCITRAL NYC Guide, Art. II n. 5.

608 Art. VII (1) NYC.

609 Art. V (1) (b) NYC.

610 Kronke et al.-KRONKE, Introduction, 2.

611 UNCITRAL NYC Guide, Art. II n. 2.

612 Kronke et al.-SCHRAMM et al., Art. II NYC, 38 et seq.

613 BORN, *Law and Practice*, ch. 1.04 n. 28.

614 STEINBRÜCK, 89.

4. Hague Evidence Convention

a. Introduction

In a further step, it will be examined whether an obligation to assist international arbitral tribunals exists under the HEC, which was established in 1970. This convention has proved a very useful tool in international litigation, helping parties to obtain evidence abroad by means of international judicial assistance.[615] So far, the HEC has been adopted by 63 Member States; it entered into force in Switzerland in 1995.[616] Regarding arbitration, there is a broad consensus among Member States and legal scholars that the HEC is not applicable directly to arbitral proceedings, because only 'judicial authorities' can submit requests to foreign national courts in order to obtain evidence.[617] The reality is thus that the HEC is not used directly in arbitral proceedings. In this respect, a distinction must be made between the issue of the direct applicability of the HEC to arbitral proceedings and its indirect use where court assistance is sought in support of arbitral proceedings.[618] This applies to cases in which an arbitral tribunal requests assistance from a state court at the seat of arbitration, which then sends a letter of request to a state court based in another jurisdiction. While this scenario does not seem to present any significant difficulties,[619] the following remarks concentrate on a possible direct application which would force state courts of Member States to render assistance in the taking of evidence based on the HEC.

615 *See* the HEC Questionnaire (2014), 25 et seq.

616 *See* the current status.

617 Art. 1 HEC; HEC Handbook (2016), n. 93; BLACKABY et al., n. 6.131; SAATHOF, 62; BORN, *Int. Comm. Arb.*, n. 2422 et seq.; BORN, *Law and Practice*, ch. 9.02 n. 32; STEINBRÜCK, 129 et seq.; MüKo-PABST, Art. 1 HEC n. 9; KLAUS, 302, fn 21; KNEISEL/LECKING, 153; GAUTHEY/MARKUS, n. 831 et seqq. Even though GAUTHEY/MARKUS consider the fact that arbitral tribunals render arbitral awards as judicial acts, they agree that they are certainly not 'judicial authorities of a contracting state'. Accordingly, they are not within the HEC's scope of application; *see also* HEC Questionnaire (2009), 40 et seq. According to this questionnaire, very few jurisdictions have been approached directly by arbitral tribunals based on the HEC. These requests have either been denied or transmitted to the respective competent state authority; HEC Questionnaire (2004), 11 et seq.; *see also* the commentary of Australia as regards arbitration, noting that 'there is nothing within the Convention to prevent its use by two parties in circumstances where both parties consent to it having such additional application.'

618 WIRTH/HOFFMANN-NOWOTNY, 70; for the procedure of indirect court assistance *see* p. 120 *infra*.

619 WIRTH/HOFFMANN-NOWOTNY, 70; GAUTHEY/MARKUS, n. 833; KNÖFEL, *Judicial Assistance*, 284 et seqq.; HEC Recommendations (2003), n. 38; HEC Special Commission (1985), 1679.

b. Drafting Process

So far, few authors suggest that the HEC should be directly applicable to arbitral proceedings.[620] They suggest that instead of first submitting a request to the competent state court at the seat of arbitration, which will then send a letter of request to the competent authority of the Member State in which the requested evidence is located, international arbitral tribunals should be able to submit direct requests to national courts abroad. In this case, the court approached would be obliged–subject to the requirements of the HEC–to render assistance in the taking of evidence.

This argument is anything but new and has been proposed since the very beginning of the HEC drafting process, as well as during the drafting of the UNCITRAL ML in 1985.[621] During the discussions on Art. 27 UNCITRAL ML *(see* p. 93 et seqq. *supra),* it was suggested that international court assistance should not be governed by the UNCITRAL ML, but rather remain within the field of international cooperation.[622] This position can also be explained by the fact that the drafters of the UNCITRAL ML knew that, at the same time, a special commission of the Hague Conference on Private International Law was discussing the possibility of using the HEC in the context of arbitral proceedings.[623] The idea was to add an additional protocol to the HEC, allowing arbitral tribunals to submit direct evidence requests to the respective authority of a Member State.[624] Within the special commission, opinion on this possibility was divided.[625] Despite the technical feasibility of the protocol, the majority of commission members raised doubts about its usefulness.[626] In the end–and probably also because the drafting process of the UNCITRAL ML had already been completed without the inclusion of a provision obliging national courts to assist international arbitral tribunals in the taking of evidence–the commission abandoned the idea.[627] In addition, and in contrast to the former view, the special commission questioned the practicability of the protocol because of the many different types of arbitral

620 MEIER, 120; KNÖFEL, *Judicial Assistance*, 284 et seqq.; Geimer/Schütze-KNÖFEL, Art. 1 HEC, n. 16; Guideline Judicial Assistance in Civil Matters CH (2013), 5.

621 ROTHSTEIN, 84 et seqq.; KNÖFEL, *Judicial Assistance*, 299 et seqq.

622 UNCITRAL, 18th session, A/CN.9/263 (1985), 59.

623 KNÖFEL, *Judicial Assistance*, 300.

624 HEC Special Commission (1985), 1679.

625 *Ibid.*

626 UNCITRAL, Summary Records of the 325th meeting (1985), n. 57.

627 HEC Special Commission (1985), 1679; AMRAM, n. 254; UNCITRAL, A/40/17 (1985), n. 225.

tribunals (ad hoc and institutional) that exist.[628] More recently, the view that the HEC is not applicable to arbitral proceedings in practice has also been reflected in the latest questionnaire of HEC Member States in 2008.[629]

c. Criticism

It is beyond controversy that an arbitral tribunal is not a 'judicial authority of a contracting state', but rather a private body acting without a permanent jurisdiction or coercive powers.[630] However, with regard to the term 'judicial', the situation is not as clear.[631] Because arbitral awards have similar effects to state court decisions, the arbitrator's task may be considered and qualified as a 'judicial' act in the sense of Art. 1 HEC.[632] Arguing strongly in favour of the direct applicability of the HEC to arbitral proceedings, KNÖFEL suggests that instead of interpreting Art. 1 HEC too strictly, it should rather be read in light of the HEC's overall aim to 'improve mutual judicial co-operation in civil or commercial matters'.[633] In assimilating arbitral awards to state court decisions, this cooperation should also be established as regards arbitration.[634] Concerning the drafters' objection that 'it would be difficult, if not impossible'[635] to apply the HEC to different kinds of arbitral tribunals, KNÖFEL argues further that despite the heterogeneity of arbitral proceedings, Member States have a keen interest in promoting international arbitration and should consequently extend the HEC's applicability to arbitral proceedings in their jurisdictions.[636]

Moreover, and as regards disclosure proceedings, Rothstein states that in addition to the IBA Rules, using the HEC in arbitral proceedings could help to harmonise arbitral disclosure proceedings, as well as *leges arbitri*.[637] In contrast to Knöfel, he suggests that instead of interpreting the HEC too broadly and applying it to arbitral proceedings, it should rather be modified first in order to fit within the context of international arbitration.[638]

628 HEC Special Commission (1985), 1679; KNÖFEL, *Judicial Assistance*, 301.

629 HEC Questionnaire (2009), 40 et seqq.; ROTHSTEIN, 86.

630 Art. 1 HEC; KNÖFEL, *Judicial Assistance*, 301; GAUTHEY/MARKUS, n. 832.

631 Art. 1 HEC; AMRAM, n. 19. The term 'judicial' is therefore not defined.

632 GAUTHEY/MARKUS, n. 831; KNÖFEL, *Judicial Assistance*, 301.

633 HEC Preambel; KNÖFEL, *Judicial Assistance*, 301.

634 *Ibid.*

635 HEC Special Commission (1985), 1679.

636 KNÖFEL, *Judicial Assistance*, 301 et seq.

637 ROTHSTEIN, 87; Art. 23 HEC.

638 ROTHSTEIN, 86.

Indeed, the HEC's direct applicability to arbitral proceedings could contribute to their effectiveness. In order to provide clarity, in addition to a 'judicial authority', Art. 1 HEC should include an 'arbitral tribunal'. This amendment would have several procedural consequences, as discussed below, focusing on the situation in Switzerland.

d. Procedural Consequences

I. Non-Exclusivity

It is worth mentioning that if arbitral tribunals could avail of the HEC directly, Switzerland would have to amend its first reservation, which declares that the HEC applies exclusively to its Member States.[639] As Art. 184 (2) PILA CH also provides for court assistance in the taking of evidence in international arbitral proceedings, neither possibility should be given priority. While the HEC's exclusive character might apply to state court proceedings, this is certainly not the case with arbitral proceedings. As a result, the HEC would represent just one of various possible means to obtain evidence–for instance, in addition to the aforementioned domestic legal basis or another international treaty.[640] Indeed, Art. 27 (c) HEC explicitly empowers Member States to permit, 'by internal law or practice, methods of taking evidence other than those provided for in this Convention'.[641]

In this regard, the US approach should also be mentioned. In *Société Nationale Industrielle Aérospatiale v. U.S. Dist. Court*, the US Supreme Court argued that by virtue of Art. 27 HEC, both the HEC and the domestic rules (FRCP USA) may be used to obtain evidence located in the US and thus there is no exclusivity.[642] Switzerland could therefore amend its first reservation to the HEC and open up the possibility for arbitral tribunals to avail of the HEC directly. In a similar way to diplomatic officers, consular agents and commissioners (Art. 18 HEC), arbitral tribunals could therefore be empowered to seek evidence.

639 *See* the reservations.

640 Geimer/Schütze-KNÖFEL, Introduction, n. 28; Art. 11a (4) PILA CH; MüKo-PABST, Preliminary Remarks n. 11 with reference to the fact Art. 1 HEC is modelled as a discretionary clause; KLAUS, 302: *see also* p. 128 et seqq. *infra*.

641 From the point of view of Swiss criminal law, there is no danger of 'felonies and misdemeanours against the state or unlawful activities on behalf of a foreign state' pursuant to Art. 271 SCC CH. Since arbitral tribunals are *per se* private institutions, their taking of evidence, even through an international treaty such as the HEC, would not endanger the sovereignty of any state (*see* BSK-HUSMANN, Art. 271 SCC CH n. 18 et seqq.).

642 *Société Nationale Industrielle Aérospatiale v. U.S. Dist. Court*, 482 U.S. 522 (1987); *see also* p. 208 *infra*.

If Member States were to expand the scope of application of the HEC to arbitral tribunals–either by making each a separate reservation or by agreeing to amend the convention as a whole–this would positively influence international arbitral proceedings. Consequently, arbitral tribunals could choose to seek evidence under either the HEC or the respective *lex arbitri*. In jurisdictions which do not offer court assistance in the taking of evidence pursuant to their *lex arbitri*, but which are also Member States of the HEC, state courts could provide assistance based solely on the HEC without any need to amend national law.

II. Requesting Arbitral Tribunal

Regarding the requesting authority, the special commission's concerns regarding the many types of arbitral tribunals can easily be rebutted.[643] According to Arts. 3 (a-d) HEC, a letter of request must not only specify who is seeking to obtain what evidence, but also provide further information regarding the parties, including their names and legal representatives, as well as an overview of the dispute in question, including all necessary information thereto. As a consequence, irrespective of whether the letter of request comes from an ad hoc or institutional arbitral tribunal, the competent authority will be perfectly aware of whom it concerns.

III. Jurisdiction

In Switzerland, the 'central authority' pursuant to Arts. 2 and 24 HEC is determined by the Federal Office of Justice (FOJ), which usually appoints a Cantonal Supreme Court.[644] As a result, there are 26 central authorities.[645] Alternatively, letters of requests can be addressed to the FOJ in Berne, which acts as a subsidiary central authority and forwards the request to the respective competent Cantonal instance.[646] In very few Cantons will this jurisdiction be different from that where court assistance in the taking of evidence is sought under Art. 184 (2) PILA CH. Taking the example of Berne, while the respective District Court renders assistance pursuant to the PILA CH, it is the Cantonal Supreme Court which executes letters of request in accordance with the

643 HEC Special Commission (1985), 1679; KNÖFEL, *Judicial Assistance*, 301.

644 Art. 11 PILA CH; *see* the database of Swiss Localities and Courts; Art. 6 HEC; *see also* Art. 7 (6a and 7) of the Organisation Ordinance for the Federal Department of Justice and Police (SR 172.213.1).

645 *See* the list of the central authorities.

646 *See* the second reservation of Switzerland; Guideline Judicial Assistance in Civil Matters CH (2013), 21.

HEC.[647] However, since this District Court acts as the single cantonal instance too, jurisdiction under the HEC does not substantially deviate from the situation under the PILA CH.[648]

IV. Participation of the Parties and the Arbitral Tribunal

Under Art. 7 HEC, the parties concerned and their representatives can participate in the taking of evidence. This also applies to the requesting judicial authority–that is, an arbitral tribunal if the respective Member State made a declaration in this respect.[649] According to the fourth reservation of Switzerland, subject to the consent of the executing state court, members of the requesting judicial authority may be present during the taking of evidence.[650] In sum, from the point of view of due process, the HEC's participation rights regarding the parties to the arbitration and the arbitral tribunal are very welcome and go even further than Art. 184 (2) PILA CH.[651]

V. Applicable Law and Procedure

Although the executing authority will normally apply its own law, this does not exclude the consideration of foreign procedure, 'unless this is incompatible with the internal law of the state of execution or is impossible of performance by reason of its international practice and procedure or by reason of practice difficulties'.[652] Applied to arbitral proceedings, it follows that the specific procedural rules of the respective arbitration could be taken into account unless one of the grounds previously mentioned applies. Consequently, an arbitral tribunal could seek to cross-examine a witness or allow affidavits, subject to the consent of the respective witness.[653] Moreover, this is in line with the proposed Art. 184 (3) PILA, which states that, on request, a state court can apply or consider different (i.e. foreign) procedural forms.[654]

VI. Costs

Regarding costs, the overall principle stated in the HEC is that in general, assistance in the taking of evidence will not lead to any reimbursement of

647 Art. 8 (1) EG ZSJ BE.

648 Art. 356 (2) (c) CCP CH by analogy.

649 Art. 8 HEC.

650 *See* the reservations; Guideline Judicial Assistance in Civil Matters CH (2013), 25.

651 *See* p. 233 *infra*.

652 Art. 9 HEC; MüKo-PABST, Art. 9 HEC n. 4 et seqq.; Geimer/Schütze-KNÖFEL, Art. 9 HEC n. 2 et seqq.

653 Guideline Judicial Assistance in Civil Matters CH (2013), 24.

654 *See in more detail* p. 242 et seq. *infra*.

taxes or costs of any nature.[655] As an exception thereto, the state of execution can require the state of origin to reimburse the costs occasioned by the use of a special (foreign) procedure.[656] Because in Swiss court proceedings court assistance in the taking of evidence will always lead to costs, Art. 14 HEC would have to be amended in order to exclude arbitral proceedings from the overall principle.[657] Otherwise, there would be an unjustified imbalance between the cost regulations pursuant to the PILA CH and the HEC.

VII. Duration of Proceedings

Finally, one must stress that the HEC's direct applicability to arbitration could also lead to a faster and more efficient process for obtaining court assistance in the taking of evidence. In this respect, it is often said that this process is cumbersome, time consuming and costly.[658] In contrast, and according to Art. 9 HEC, letters of request must 'be executed expeditiously'.[659] Although this provision does not specify the timeframe within which these letters must be dealt with, let alone any sanction in case of delay, authorities of Member States are nonetheless required to handle evidence requests as quickly as possible.[660] The most recent available statistics show that most evidence requests are answered within approximately four months, with only small divergences between jurisdictions.[661] While four months can be a long time in international arbitration, this timeframe would be much longer in case of indirect court assistance–that is, through the state courts at the seat of arbitration, via the central authority in the assisting jurisdiction to the assisting court, back to the central authority, then to the court at the seat of arbitration and ultimately to the requesting arbitral tribunal.[662]

655 Art. 14 HEC; Geimer/Schütze-KNÖFEL, Art. 14 HEC n. 1; MüKo-PABST, Art. 14 HEC n. 2; *see also* Art. 26 HEC, which does not apply to Switzerland (Guideline Judicial Assistance in Civil Matters CH (2013), 26).

656 Art. 14 HEC i.c.w. Art. 9 (2) HEC.

657 Art. 95 (1) CCP CH; *see also* p. 255 et seqq. *infra*.

658 *See* e.g. BSK-SCHNEIDER/SCHERER, Art. 184 PILA CH n. 56.

659 *See also* Arts. 5 and 6 HEC, where the requested authorities are bound to act 'promptly' and 'forthwith'.

660 MüKo-PABST, Art. 9 HEC n. 10; Geimer/Schütze-KNÖFEL, Art. 9 HEC n. 15.

661 HEC Questionnaire (2014), 18 et seq. While Switzerland executes most evidence requests within two months, the same requests take six months to a year to be answered in France and the US.

662 ROTHSTEIN, 63; SCHOIBL, 527 et seq.

e. Result

The previous discussion has shown that although the HEC is barely mentioned in connection with arbitral proceedings, the idea of its direct application in the field of arbitration is anything but new. The issue came up not only during the drafting process, but also more recently, as international arbitration has become increasingly attractive.

While the direct applicability of the HEC to arbitration would indeed facilitate international arbitral proceedings, Member States still seem to prefer its indirect use via state courts only.[663] Were this preference to shift, nothing would prevent them from extending the HEC's scope of application to arbitral proceedings; as previously shown, few amendments would be necessary in this respect. Since the HEC is by far the most important international convention in relation to the taking of evidence, this idea is certainly worth considering, although it remains to be seen whether an international consensus can be reached among Member States. To sum up, at present, the HEC is not generally available directly for arbitral proceedings.

5. Summary

From the foregoing, it may be concluded that there is no obligation for courts to assist arbitral tribunals in the taking of evidence, whether under the ECHR, the NYC or the HEC. Regarding the ECHR, it has been demonstrated that both the ECtHR and the SFT oblige arbitral tribunals only to observe minimum procedural guarantees during the arbitral proceedings.[664] Particularly in Switzerland, the ECHR serves only as a tool to interpret those minimum procedural guarantees at the level of federal law. Consequently, there is no duty to comply with the ECHR during the arbitral proceedings, but only once the arbitral award has been rendered. Furthermore, the NYC—which aims to uphold arbitration agreements—does not give a clear-cut answer as to whether this also includes assisting arbitral tribunals in the taking of evidence.[665] While there are good arguments to support answering this question both positively and negatively, a conclusive answer may be found by considering the NYC's overall intention. Instead of imposing strict requirements as regards the arbitral proceedings themselves, the NYC emphasises the importance of the arbitration agreement and its connection to the recognition and enforcement of arbitral awards. As a consequence, there is

663 HEC Questionnaire (2009), 40 et seqq.; HEC Questionnaire (2004), 11 et seq.

664 *See* p. 104 et seqq. *and* p. 110 et seqq. *supra*.

665 *See* p. 116 et seq. *supra*.

no duty to assist arbitral tribunals in the taking of evidence. Finally, as a more theoretical discourse (but with practical suggestions), the potential direct application of the HEC to arbitral proceedings has been discussed.[666] It has been pointed out that, despite the current reluctance to apply the HEC in arbitral proceedings, this idea is worth considering in future amendments of the HEC. This would not only facilitate and accelerate arbitral proceedings, but also promote international arbitration as an alternative dispute settlement mechanism.

D. European Law

1. Introduction

In a purely European context, and in addition to the conventions at the level of international public law, a European convention and a European regulation are notable regarding the taking of evidence. While the European Convention on International Commercial Arbitration (ECICA) addresses arbitral proceedings in a more general way, the European Evidence Regulation (EER) specifically provides for the taking of evidence in almost all EU Member States. The following will thus examine whether an obligation can be deduced from the ECICA and the EER.

2. ECICA and the Paris Agreement

Shortly after the establishment of the NYC, the ECICA was introduced in 1961; so far, it has 31 Member States, of which only 16 have ratified the convention.[667] Switzerland is not among the Member States. As a product of the UN Economic Commission for Europe, and with the goal of simplifying arbitration between Western and Eastern European countries, the ECICA addresses the arbitral tribunal as well as the parties, and therefore the arbitral proceedings themselves.[668] Because it thus has a different scope from the NYC, it is often considered as a supplement thereto.[669]

As regards the existence of a possible obligation to assist arbitral tribunals, Art. IV ECICA is of major importance, since it allows the parties to tailor the arbitral proceedings at their widest discretion (i.e. also in relation to the

666 *See* p. 118 et seqq. *supra*.

667 *See* the current status; Despite its name, there are also non-european Member States such as Azerbajian, Burkina Faso, Cuba and Kazakhstan. In contrast, a few European countries, such as Switzerland and the United Kingdom, are not part of it.

668 HASCHER, n. 1. BERGER/KELLERHALS, n. 143.

669 PITKOWITZ, 93.

taking of evidence).[670] According to Art. IV (1) ECICA, if the parties choose ad hoc arbitration, they can designate the arbitrators, the seat of arbitration and the rules of the arbitral proceedings. By contrast, where the parties have neither agreed upon the rules of the arbitral proceedings nor appointed an arbitrator who could decide in this regard, the ECICA provides for either a special committee or the president of the respective chamber of commerce to do so.[671] On the one hand, this mechanism has facilitated arbitral proceedings between parties from Western and Eastern European countries; but in arbitral proceedings solely between parties from Western Member States, it has proved rather impractical and complicated.[672]

As a result, several of these (Western) Member States entered into a separate agreement which replaced Arts. IV (2)-(7) ECICA.[673] Art. 1 of the so-called Paris Agreement reads as follows:

> "If the arbitral Agreement contains no indication regarding the measures referred to in paragraph 1 of Article IV of the European Convention on International Commercial Arbitration as a whole, or some of these measures, any difficulties arising with regard to the constitution or functioning of the arbitral tribunal shall be submitted to the decision of the competent authority at the request of the party instituting proceedings."[674]

According to this agreement, the 'competent authority' is responsible for rendering assistance, rather than a chamber of commerce or a special committee. The Paris Agreement itself does not further specify the 'competent authority'. Although the unofficial German version speaks of 'state courts', the official French and English texts refer to the 'competent authority'.[675] While the main goal of the ECICA was to simplify West-East arbitration and therefore to appoint special authorities (a chamber of commerce or a special committee) instead of state courts to grant assistance, the Paris Agreement changed this mechanism in relation to arbitral proceedings between its

670 HASCHER, n. 33. However, considering Art. IX (1) (b) ECICA, it becomes clear that the recognition and enforcement of an arbitral award can be refused on the grounds of a violation of the right to present one's case (*see also* Art. V (1) (b) NYC).

671 Art. IV (3) ECICA. The same procedure applies to cases where parties fail to appoint the arbitrators (Art. IV (2) ECICA).

672 PITKOWITZ, 96.

673 Agreement Relating to Application of the European Convention on International Commercial Arbitration (1962). Except the Republic of Moldova, which joined the agreement in 1998, all other Member States are Western European countries (Austria, Belgium, Denmark, France, Germany, Italy and Luxembourg).

674 Art. 1, para. 2 Paris Agreement.

675 STEINBRÜCK, 69 et seq.

Member States.[676] This historical background seems to indicate that the rationale behind the Paris Agreement was to shift the competence of either the chamber of commerce or a special committee back to the state courts as the authorities responsible for rendering assistance.[677]

In sum, both the ECICA and the Paris Agreement foresee the possibility for authorities to render assistance during the arbitral proceedings–but nothing more. The extent to which these authorities will or must grant assistance remains unclear. In addition, the international jurisdiction is not regulated. Therefore, both the ECICA and the Paris Agreement merely confirm that there are some situations in which court assistance may be needed and therefore provide mechanisms to resolve the issue, without regulating much more. To interpret this as an obligation to effectively support the arbitral tribunal would thus be too far-fetched.

3. European Evidence Regulation

As regards evidence, in contrast to the ECICA and the Paris Agreement, the EER is not only newer, but also more specific.[678] It entered into force in 2004 and applies directly between all 28 EU Member States, except Denmark.[679] As regards Switzerland, it is thus not applicable.[680] As between the 28 EU Member States, the EER replaces the HEC.[681] The EER allows the courts of one Member State either to submit evidence requests to the competent court in another Member State where the evidence is located or to take evidence directly in that Member State.[682] Regarding the applicability of the EER to arbitral proceedings, the discussion centres on the term 'court' in Art. 1 EER–referring to the authority which can submit an evidence request. As with the term 'judicial authority' within the HEC, the prevailing view among authors of legal doctrine is that an arbitral tribunal cannot fulfil the requirements of a court in the sense of the EER.[683] Consequently, in order to obtain evidence

676 HASCHER, n. 38; STEINBRÜCK, 68 et seqq.

677 HASCHER, n. 95; STEINBRÜCK, 69 et seq.

678 SCHÜTZE, *Rechtsverfolgung*, n. 317 et seqq.

679 *See* the current status.

680 However, the EER can be still useful in situations where Switzerland makes an evidence request according to the HEC in a Member State of both the HEC and the EER. In this situation, the requested court could make further requests with the help of the EER (KNÖFEL, *Judicial Assistance*, 307 et seq.).

681 Art. 21 (1) EER; EER Report (2007), 2.

682 Art. 1 EER.

683 *See* p. 120 *supra;* SCHOIBL, 521 et seq.; MüKo-RAUSCHER, Art. 1 EER, n. 1; Rauscher-VON HEIN, Art. 1 EER, n. 9 with further references; KNÖFEL, *Judicial Assistance*, 303 with further references; EER Study (2007), 18, 102.

abroad, an arbitral tribunal must take the indirect route of seeking assistance from a national court, which will then act according to the mechanism set out in the EER by either submitting a request to the competent foreign court or directly taking evidence in the respective Member State.[684]

So far, there have been no cases in which an arbitral tribunal has used the EER and submitted an evidence request directly. Nonetheless, Knöfel suggests the EER's direct applicability in order to bypass the lengthy and cumbersome process of indirect court assistance in the taking of evidence.[685] In this respect, he proposes–in keeping with his arguments as regards the HEC–that the term 'court' in Art. 1 EER should be interpreted functionally, and consequently that arbitral tribunals should fall under the scope of Art. 1 EER.[686] One must admit that the direct applicability of the EER to arbitral proceedings would indeed contribute to their effectiveness. In contrast to the HEC, which specifies no express timeframe for responding to evidence requests, the EER states that they must be executed without delay or at the latest within 90 days of receipt.[687] What is more, subject to the law of the Member State in which the evidence is located, the arbitral tribunal can ask that the taking of evidence take place according to the procedural rules as specified in the arbitration agreement (e.g. cross-examination).[688] Finally, if the law of the respective Member State so provides, the parties can be present when the evidence is taken or can ask to take evidence directly in another Member State.[689]

In summary, although the EER's direct applicability to arbitral proceedings would facilitate the taking of evidence in international contexts, most authors deny such a possibility due to the clear wording of 'courts of a Member State'.[690] Still, in light of the soaring popularity of international arbitration, the EER should be available not only for state courts of Member States, but also for international arbitral tribunals. Instead of interpreting the term

684 KNÖFEL, *Judicial Assistance*, 305. For the equivalent procedure under the HEC, *see* p. 118 *supra*.

685 KNÖFEL, *Judicial Assistance*, 305.

686 *Ibid.*, 306 et seq.; *see* in this respect e.g. § 1055 CCP DE and Art. 387 CCP CH (as regards domestic arbitration), which give arbitral awards the same effect as final and binding court judgments.

687 Art. 10 (1) EER. However, one should be aware that the time limit of 90 days increasingly seems to cause trouble in practice–*see* EER Impact Assessment (2018), 42 et seqq.; (EER Report (2007), 3; EER Study (2007), 40).

688 Art. 10 (3) EER; *see also* the possibility of using video and conference calls (Art. 10 (4) EER).

689 Arts. 11 (1) and 17 EER. The direct taking of evidence is only be performed on a voluntary basis without the need of coercive measures (Art. 17 (2) EER).

690 *See also* KNÖFEL, *Judicial Assistance*, 305, with further references in fn 148.

'court' too broadly, the EU could thus explicitly include arbitral tribunals in the EER's scope of application in a future amendment. Still, at present, no obligation derives from the EER to support arbitral tribunals directly in the taking of evidence.

4. Result

Although the ECICA, the Paris Agreement and the EER all address court assistance, their actual significance varies considerably. On the one hand, while the ECICA and the Paris Agreement are still in force and applicable to arbitral proceedings in European Member States, they have nonetheless lost a great deal of their importance due to the improved relationships between Western and Eastern European countries. On the other hand, the EER–which could make a valuable contribution towards increasing the effectiveness of procedures for the taking of evidence in international arbitration–is not currently applicable to arbitration. It follows, therefore, that state courts have no obligation to directly assist arbitral tribunals in the taking of evidence, whether under the ECICA, the Paris Agreement or the EER.

E. Summary

This part of the chapter has discussed the possible existence of an obligation to assist arbitral tribunals based on superior law (i.e. either constitutional or international public law). As regards the Const. CH and the ECHR, it has been shown that they are concerned only that certain minimum procedural guarantees be observed during the arbitral proceedings. Furthermore, the NYC aims to uphold arbitration agreements and to facilitate the recognition and enforcement of arbitral awards, but says little about the arbitral proceedings themselves (e.g. the taking of evidence). For their part, the ECICA and Paris Agreement merely confirm that in certain situations, state courts must support arbitral proceedings and nothing more. Finally, several arguments have been presented in favour of the direct applicability of the HEC and the EER to international arbitral proceedings, which unfortunately is not currently the case. In sum, no obligation to assist arbitral tribunals in the taking of evidence exists based on the Const. CH or international conventions, either European or universal. Whether state courts are obliged to assist international arbitral tribunals in the taking of evidence is therefore a question of the respective national law and thus an issue of legal policy.[691]

691 STEINBRÜCK, 89.

§ 5 Conclusion

The main focus of this chapter has been to provide the reader with a general understanding of court assistance in the taking of evidence in international arbitration. This has been done by exploring the subject from three different angles. While the first part focused on how this works in practice, the second part considered the legal bases and the intention of the parties. The third part then examined the possible existence of an obligation for courts to assist in the taking of evidence based on the Const. CH and international public law.

In the first part, in order to arrive at a general understanding of how state courts can support arbitral tribunals in the taking of evidence, the situations in which such support is needed and the means by which it is granted were discussed. In this regard, interim measures are central to temporarily protect the parties' rights from possible damage during the course of arbitration; while ordinary measures for the taking of evidence aim to establish the relevant facts of the case. The second part discussed the divergent perceptions of court assistance in general, and concerning the taking of evidence in particular, as either helpful assistance or disturbing intervention. The prevailing view in international arbitration seems to advocate a hands-off approach, setting strict standards regarding the involvement of state courts in arbitral proceedings and particularly in the taking of evidence. The UNCITRAL ML and (ad hoc and institutional) arbitration rules thus provide for court assistance in the taking of evidence, subject to the consent of the arbitral tribunal or even the adverse party. From the parties' point of view, court assistance in the taking of evidence not only is in line with the arbitration agreement, but will also reinforce the status of the arbitral tribunal and lead to a more substantiated arbitral award. As a result, it can truly be seen as assisting, rather than interfering in, the arbitration. The third and final part demonstrated that there is no obligation to assist arbitral tribunals in the taking of evidence under either Swiss constitutional or international public law. The decision of whether and to what extent the courts of a jurisdiction will grant assistance in the taking evidence is therefore an issue of legal policy and depends on the laws of the respective country.

From an arbitration practitioner's perspective, the lack of international common practice is, to put it bluntly, unsatisfactory. As pointed out *(see* p. 2 *supra),* indirect court assistance in international arbitral proceedings is in most cases not an option, due to the lengthy and cumbersome process involved. Parties and arbitrators have therefore a keen interest in being able to resort directly to foreign state courts in order to obtain evidence. As views on how international arbitral tribunals should be supported vary among countries, it is indeed difficult to make general statements and suggestions. However, since this book aims to analyse the status quo concerning court assistance in the taking of evidence in aid of international arbitral proceedings in Switzerland, a comparative analysis of several jurisdictions seems useful in this regard. Thus, the focus shall now shift to various other countries and their respective approaches–whether liberal or conservative–to the issue at hand. This comparative study will inform the analysis of the status quo in Switzerland. The following chapter therefore concentrates on the legal bases and technical mechanisms on the one hand and on the respective legislator's intention to offer court assistance in the taking of evidence on the other hand.

7

International Arbitration and Taking of Evidence: A Comparative Study

§ 1 Introduction

Since the theoretical foundations of court assistance in the taking of evidence in international arbitration have been set out in the previous chapter, this chapter concentrates on more practical aspects. The extent to which state courts grant assistance varies significantly from jurisdiction to jurisdiction; from a practitioner's point of view, it is therefore crucial to understand these differences and provide for them in the tactical strategies of a case.[692] In addition, this chapter lays the groundwork for the analysis of the situation in Switzerland that follows. This chapter therefore outlines how court assistance in the taking of evidence in aid of international arbitral proceedings is provided in several key forums for arbitration: France, England, the USA and Germany.[693] Although these countries are best known for their arbitration-friendly stance, the outcome as regards court assistance in the taking of evidence is anything but uniform. Instead of merely listing various country reports or even making a comprehensive comparison, the following remarks concentrate on elaborating key evidentiary issues.

The first and most important issue concerns the question of whether the respective jurisdictions directly grant assistance in the taking of evidence to international arbitral tribunals–that is, without making a detour via international judicial assistance *(see* p. 118 et seqq. *supra)*. The second issue relates to the competence to make an evidence request and the possibility to exclude court assistance in the taking of evidence. The third issue focuses on the scope of evidence sought and the law according to which evidence may be sought, and from whom (i.e. the parties to the arbitration and/or third parties). It will be examined whether evidence can be obtained only according

692 DUPEYRON, 472.

693 Although it is not (yet) considered one of the most popular forums for arbitration, recent ICC statistics have shown the importance of Germany not only in terms of arbitrators and parties to arbitration, but also regarding the number of disputes filed in Germany under the ICC Rules; for a short outline how court assistance in taking evidence is modeled in the USA, England and Wales as well as France, *see also* BRADSHAW, 639 et seqq.

to the respective *lex arbitri* or whether national civil procedure rules or even foreign forms of evidentiary procedure are also applicable. A section on the target of evidence will further show how a party or third party can defend itself against an evidence request. The fourth issue focuses on the competence of the *juge d'appui*–that is, the judge of support in the country in which assistance is sought. In this regard, crucial aspects such as the scope of discretion in general, and how far the *juge d'appui* can examine the legitimacy of the evidence request and the arbitration agreement, will be addressed. As a fifth issue, in order to avoid unnecessarily lengthening the arbitral proceedings, it is important to know whether the decision of the *juge d'appui* as regards an evidence request can be challenged and if so, on what grounds.

§ 2 Germany

A. Introduction

Since the fundamental amendments to the German *lex arbitri* in 1998–namely, the 10th book of the CCP DE (§ 1025 et seqq.)–arbitration in Germany has been facilitated in many ways and the country has become an increasingly attractive forum for international arbitration.[694] The new provisions were largely an adoption of the UNCITRAL ML and therefore strive to make Germany an attractive seat of arbitration by strengthening the status of arbitral tribunals and facilitating cooperation between arbitral tribunals and state courts.[695] In this regard, and as stated in the UNCITRAL ML, § 1026 CCP DE provides that a state court may take action only insofar as provided by the 10th book of the CCP DE.[696] Because Germany–unlike Switzerland–does not have separate statutes for domestic and international arbitration, § 1025-1066 CCP DE are the main source regarding arbitral proceedings.[697] Nonetheless, the 10th book of the CCP DE sometimes refers to other provisions on German court litigation in other parts of the CCP DE.

694 KREINDLER et al., n. 1.6 et seqq.; Balthasar-BALTHASAR, 379, n. 1; *see also* the statistical data of DIS arbitration in Germany.

695 Parliamentary Documentation 13/5274 (1996), 22 et seq., 34; KREINDLER et al., n. 1.32; WOLFF, 243; MüKo-MÜNCH, Vorbemerkungen zu § 1025, n. 175.

696 Art. 5 UNCITRAL ML; *see also* S. 1 (c) EAA 1996.

697 MüKo-MÜNCH, § 1025 CCP DE, n. 3 et seqq.; KREINDLER et al., n. 1.36.

B. Legal Bases

Like many other *leges arbitri*, the CCP DE provides for court assistance in the taking of evidence in aid of arbitral proceedings. § 1050 CCP DE reads as follows:

> "(1) The arbitral tribunal or a party with the approval of the arbitral tribunal may request from a court assistance in taking evidence or performance of other judicial acts which the arbitral tribunal is not empowered to carry out.
> (2) Unless it regards the application as inadmissible, the court shall execute the request according to its rules on taking evidence or other judicial acts.
> (3) The arbitrators are entitled to participate in any judicial taking of evidence and to ask questions."

The competent court for assistance in the taking of evidence is the local court (*Amtsgericht*) in whose district the evidence request will be carried out–that is, the place of residence of the witness or third party.[698] In proceedings before a local court under § 1050 CCP DE, the parties need not be represented by a lawyer admitted to the German bar.[699] This can be especially relevant and beneficial in international arbitral proceedings with lawyers from foreign jurisdictions.[700]

Although almost all provisions of the 10th book of the CCP DE apply only to arbitral proceedings whose seat is located in Germany, there are certain exceptions.[701] According to § 1025 (2) CCP DE, court assistance in the taking of evidence is also granted to arbitral tribunals whose seat has not yet been determined, as well as to international arbitral tribunals with their seat outside Germany. In this regard, the CCP DE goes even further than the UNCITRAL ML and can be considered as a 'deliberate German offer of cooperation to international arbitration'.[702] To this day, such provisions are rare in *leges*

698 § 1062 (4) CCP DE; Parliamentary Documentation 13/5274 (1996), 64; SCHWAB/WALTER, ch. 17 n. 11; MüKo-MÜNCH, § 1050 CCP DE n. 13; RÜTZEL et al., 162.

699 § 1062 (4) CCP DE i.c.w. § 78 (1) CCP DE.

700 BeckOK-WILSKE/MARKERT, § 1050 CCP DE n. 8; Böckstiegel et al.-SACHS/LÖRCHER, § 1050 CCP DE, n. 1; BeckKuKo-HARTMANN, § 1050 CCP DE n. 4; RÜTZEL et al., 162.

701 § 1025 (1) CCP DE.

702 Art. 1 (2) UNCITRAL ML; WOLFF, 244; Stein/Jonas-SCHLOSSER, § 1050 CCP DE n. 28; SCHWAB/WALTER, ch. 17 n. 12; EBERL/EBERL, § 1 n. 33; Wieczorek/Schütze-SCHÜTZE, § 1050 n. 3 CCP DE; BeckOK-WILSKE/MARKERT, § 1050 CCP DE n. 3.2; STEINBRÜCK, 386 et seq.; RÜTZEL et al., 161.

arbitri, so the broadened scope of § 1050 CCP DE is thus truly in the interests of international arbitration.[703] It remains to be seen whether other countries will be influenced by § 1025 (2) read with § 1050 CCP DE and adopt the same approach. So far, only Austria has implemented an almost identical provision based on the model of the CCP DE.[704]

C. Competence to Seek Court Assistance

1. Primacy of the Arbitral Tribunal

As stated in Art. 27 UNCITRAL ML, according to § 1050 (1) CCP DE, the approval of the arbitral tribunal is necessary in order to resort to state courts for assistance in the taking of evidence.[705] This strengthens the position of the arbitral tribunal as the authority in charge of the arbitral proceedings. In addition, this provision aims to prevent possible delaying tactics of the parties.[706] Thus, if the arbitral tribunal considers an evidence request to be irrelevant or inadmissible, it can refuse consent to resort to state courts.[707] In this regard, one could argue that this risks violating the right to be heard.[708] This would indeed be the case if the arbitral tribunal ignored an evidence request completely or denied it without reasonable grounds. However, as long as the arbitral tribunal–which is obliged to treat the parties equally and observe the right to be heard–respects the mandatory provisions of the CCP DE, the parties' agreement on the procedural rules and the optional provisions of law, it is at liberty to conduct the arbitral proceedings at its full discretion.[709] Consequently, as long as it acts within these boundaries, there is no risk of violating the right to be heard.[710] If a party nonetheless wants to take action against a refusal to resort to state courts, parties can either challenge this decision directly or challenge the arbitral award if the arbitral tribunal has denied the request without justification and this denial has in some way influenced the arbitral award.[711]

703 *See* e.g. similiar provisions in S. 2 (3) i.c.w. S. 43 and 44 EAA 1996 (p. 169 *infra*).

704 § 577 (2) i.c.w. § 602 CCP AU; SCHUMACHER, n. 165 fn 260.

705 *See also* Art. 182 (2) PILA CH; S. 43 (2) EAA 1996; SCHMIDT-AHRENDTS/DE JONG, 285.

706 Parliamentary Documentation 13/5274 (1996), 51.

707 Wieczorek/Schütze-SCHÜTZE, § 1050 CCP DE n. 2; MüKo-MÜNCH, § 1025 CCP DE, n. 18; STEINBRÜCK, 388; EBERL/EBERL, § 1 n. 38; HK-SAENGER, § 1050 n 2.

708 MüKo-MÜNCH, § 1025 CCP DE, n. 18.

709 § 1042 (1) and (4) CCP DE; Parliamentary Documentation 13/5274 (1996), 46 et seq.

710 MüKo-MÜNCH, § 1025 CCP DE n. 18.

711 § 1059 (1) (d) CCP DE; EBERL/EBERL, § 1 n. 38; *see* p. 146 et seqq. *infra*.

In addition to the possibility for a party to seek court assistance in the taking of evidence, the arbitral tribunal itself can make an evidence request if it deems this appropriate in order to establish the facts of the case.[712] As a consequence, § 1050 (3) CCP DE entitles the arbitral tribunal to participate in the taking of evidence and to ask questions.[713] This right, which is not included in the UNCITRAL ML, allows the arbitral tribunal to get a first-hand impression of the taking of evidence.[714] Therefore, arbitrators must be notified in advance when the taking of evidence takes place.[715] Still, they are at liberty to make use of their right and there is no obligation to participate.[716]

2. Exclusion of Court Assistance in Taking Evidence

Since arbitration is a field predominantly influenced by the parties' discretion, one might ask whether the assistance of state courts may be excluded by the parties. As stated in the previous chapter (*see* p. 100 et seqq. *supra*), court assistance in the taking of evidence is in most cases in the interests of the parties. However, the parties might still want to exclude assistance in the taking of evidence through state courts altogether–for instance, for time, cost or confidentiality reasons.[717] In legal doctrine, in the absence of an explicit legal basis, it is controversial whether a complete waiver of § 1050 CCP DE is in fact possible. Schlosser takes the view that although the parties cannot renounce the rights as foreseen in § 1050 CCP DE in advance, in the sense of a total waiver of minimum legal protection, a partial waiver of the right to resort to state courts should nevertheless be possible.[718]

By contrast, Münch suggests that because assistance according to § 1050 CCP DE serves the interests of the parties, they are also at liberty to renounce this assistance altogether.[719] This applies even more so, he argues, because the arbitral tribunal must act first and foremost according to the procedural rules that the parties have agreed upon; only in the absence of such rules may

712 § 1050 (1) and § 1042 (4) CCP DE.

713 In addition to the arbitral tribunal, parties are also entitled to participate in the taking of evidence (*see* § 357 CCP DE).

714 Parliamentary Documentation 13/5274 (1996), 51; WOLFF, 266; STEINBRÜCK, 404 et seqq.

715 SCHWAB/WALTER, ch. 17 n. 17; Stein/Jonas-SCHLOSSER, § 1050 CCP DE n. 18; RÜTZEL et al., 162.

716 § 1042 (4) 2nd sentence CCP DE; MüKo-MÜNCH, § 1050 CCP DE n. 34; Stein/Jonas-SCHLOSSER, § 1050 CCP DE n. 17 et seq.; BeckOK-WILSKE/MARKERT, § 1050 CCP DE n. 15; Wieczorek/Schütze-SCHÜTZE, § 1050 CCP DE n. 30.

717 STEINBRÜCK, 411.

718 Stein/Jonas-SCHLOSSER, § 1050 CCP DE n. 3; STEINBRÜCK, 409 et seqq.

719 MüKo-MÜNCH, § 1025 CCP DE n. 12.

the arbitral tribunal decide at its own discretion.[720] Similarly, Wolff and Schütze state that if parties can exclude certain types of evidence (e.g. witnesses examination), they should also be able to exclude assistance from state courts in taking evidence.[721]

This view deserves approval and is confirmed by considering the issue from the basic concept of arbitration: namely, to provide a private and consensual legal sphere through which parties can obtain 'a final and binding decision on a dispute ..., without reference to a court of law'.[722] If this applies to arbitration in general, it must also apply to the process of taking evidence. Furthermore, one should bear in mind that if the parties waive the possibility to resort to state courts in one arbitration, this does not preclude them from seeking such assistance again in another. Consequently, the exclusion of § 1050 CCP DE is always temporary and not a permanent renouncement of minimum principles of legal protection.[723]

D. Spectrum of Evidence and its Target

1. Evidence According to a Party Agreement

Before exploring the scope of evidence available pursuant to the CCP DE, the respective state court must examine whether the parties have explicitly excluded certain evidence.[724] If the parties, as previously discussed *(see* p. 137 et seq. *supra),* can exclude court assistance as a whole, this also applies to different types of evidence.[725] For instance, parties may exclude all evidence other than documentary evidence.[726] This can be done either by explicitly excluding discovery/disclosure proceedings in the arbitration agreement or by way of reference to institutional arbitration or the IBA Rules.[727] Still, if evidence is gathered contrary to a party agreement, this serves as a reason to annul the arbitral award.[728] Most often, however, an arbitral tribunal will not introduce evidence which was gathered against a contrary agreement between the parties.

720 § 1050 (3) and (4) 1st sentence CCP DE.

721 Wieczorek/Schütze-SCHÜTZE, § 1050 CCP DE n. 8; WOLFF, 256 et seq.

722 BLACKABY et al., n. 1.04 et seq.; BORN, *Law and Practice,* ch. 1.01 n. 3 et seqq.

723 STEINBRÜCK, 412.

724 § 1042 (4) CCP DE; MüKo-Münch, § 1050 CCP DE n. 25; SCHWAB/WALTER, ch. 17 n. 9; EBERL/EBERL, § 1 n. 44; WOLFF, 262.

725 Wieczorek/Schütze-SCHÜTZE, § 1050 CCP DE n. 8.

726 *See* fn 139 *supra.*

727 *See* e.g. Art. 22.2 LCIA Rules; Art. 3 (9) IBA Rules.

728 § 1059 (2) (1.) (d) CCP DE.

2. Evidence According to the CCP DE

a. In General

According to § 1050 CCP DE, parties may seek assistance in relation to either the taking of evidence or 'other judicial acts', such as the ordering of documents to be served by public notice or abroad.[729] As regards the taking of evidence, the requested state court will carry out the request in accordance with its rules on taking evidence, unless it considers this inadmissible *(see* p. 140 et seqq. *infra).*[730] Accordingly, all sorts of evidence can be sought under the CCP DE, such as examination of witnesses (§ 373 et seqq. CCP DE), parties (§ 445 et seqq. CCP DE) and experts (§ 402 et seqq. CCP DE); production of documents[731] (§ 142, § 415 et seqq. CCP DE); inspections (§ 371 et seqq. CCP DE); and the administration of oaths[732] (§ 391-393, § 410, § 478-484 CCP DE).[733] The parties are entitled to participate in the taking of evidence.[734]

b. Independent Evidentiary Proceeding

As already discussed *(see* p. 87 et seq. *supra),* state courts and emergency arbitrators have parallel competence to order interim measures prior to the constitution of the arbitral tribunal. However, because of the lack of coercive power, assistance from an emergency arbitrator is not always suitable in situations where the preservation of evidence is urgent and assistance from state courts is thus required. In such cases, § 485 et seqq. CCP DE can prove very helpful. In circumstances where a party fears the potential destruction of evidence prior to constitution of the arbitral tribunal, § 485 et seqq. CCP DE provides for a special procedure in the form of an 'independent evidentiary proceeding'. Accordingly, and subject to the approval of the adverse

729 Parliamentary Documentation 13/5274 (1996), 51; Böckstiegel et al.-SACHS/LÖRCHER, § 1050 CCP DE n. 1. Wieczorek/Schütze-SCHÜTZE, § 1050 CCP DE n. 2, 14; MüKo-MÜNCH, § 1025 CCP DE n. 7; BeckOK-WILSKE/MARKERT, § 1050 CCP DE n. 3; SCHWAB/WALTER, ch. 17 n. 3; EBERL/EBERL, § 1 n. 34.

730 § 1050 (2) i.c.w. § 355 et seqq. CCP DE. This is in line with Art. 27 UNCITRAL ML, according to which 'the court may execute the request within its competence and according its rules on taking evidence'.

731 While § 142 CCP DE concerns documents from third parties, § 432 CCP DE allows state courts to order production of records or documents of public authorities in aid of arbitration.

732 Wieczorek/Schütze-SCHÜTZE, § 1050 CCP DE n. 10; SCHAEFER, 536.

733 LACHMANN, n. 1621; EBERL/EBERL, § 1 n. 30, 47; Zöller-GEIMER, § 1050 CCP DE n. 8; HK-SAENGER, § 1050 CCP DE n. 3; MüKo-MÜNCH, § 1050 CCP DE n. 6; Stein/Jonas-SCHLOSSER, § 1050 CCP DE n. 6; BeckOK-WILSKE/MARKERT, § 1050 CCP DE n. 4; Prütting/Gehrlein-PRÜTTING, § 1050 CCP DE n. 2; RÜTZEL et al., 72 et seqq., 161.

734 § 357 CCP DE; for the attendance of the arbitral tribunal, *see* § 1050 (3) CCP DE.

party, or in cases where there is a concern that evidence might be lost or will become difficult to use, a state court may order inspections, the examination of witnesses or the preparation of an expert review. Although the demarcation between measures in relation to the preservation of evidence as interim measures and ordinary measures for the taking of evidence is not always apparent, German legal doctrine considers preservation measures pursuant to § 485 et seqq. CCP DE as interim measures in the sense of § 1033 CCP DE.[735] This provision reads as follows:

> "An arbitration agreement does not rule out that a court may order, before or after arbitration proceedings have commenced, and upon a party having filed a corresponding petition, that a provisional measure or one serving to provide security be taken with regard to the subject matter of the dispute being dealt with in the arbitration proceedings."

The independent evidentiary proceeding should therefore be distinguished from the assistance available under § 1050 CCP DE, where temporal urgency is not the major concern. Regardless of whether the arbitral tribunal has already been established, the preservation of evidence can be an issue in the arbitral proceedings themselves. Thus, because it is considered an interim measure, an independent evidentiary proceeding is also possible during the arbitral proceedings–that is, once the arbitral tribunal has been established.[736]

3. Foreign Types of Evidence

While the types of evidence that may be sought in accordance with the CCP DE usually cause no problems, it remains doubtful whether a German court could nonetheless apply foreign forms of taking evidence. According to a minority of authors, if the parties in an international arbitration agree on cross-examination or document production in accordance with the IBA Rules, the German courts must apply these foreign forms of taking evidence without further ado.[737]

735 OLG Brandenburg, 16 Feb. 2011, 13 U 11/10, cons. II, 3; SCHWAB/WALTER, ch. 17 n. 12; MüKo-MÜNCH, § 1033 CCP DE n. 7; Stein/Jonas-SCHLOSSER, § 1033 CCP DE n. 1; Wieczorek/Schütze-SCHÜTZE, § 1033 CCP DE n. 5; Zöller-GEIMER, § 1033 CCP DE n. 9; Musielak/Voit-VOIT, § 1033 CCP DE n. 2; Prütting/Gehrlein-PRÜTTING, § 1033 CCP DE n. 2; for a different view, *see* LACHMANN, n. 2892.

736 On the question of whether the approval of the arbitral tribunal to initiate an independent evidentiary proceeding is indeed necessary after the establishment of the arbitral tribunal, *see* Stein/Jonas-SCHLOSSER, § 1033 CCP DE n. 1; STEINBRÜCK, 407 et seq.; STEINBRÜCK, Note on OLG Düsseldorf, 7 Feb. 2008, I-20 W 152/07, in: 8 Iprax 424 et seqq. (2010); for a different view *see* MüKo-MÜNCH, § 1033 CCP DE n. 8 et seq.; VARGA, 249.

737 LACHMANN, n. 1636; SCHWAB/WALTER, ch. 17 n. 8.

From the German perspective, there are several arguments against this liberal approach. First of all, and quite obviously, it is against the plain wording of § 1050 (2) CCP DE.[738] In addition, § 1026 CCP DE expressly states that state courts may take action only in accordance with the provisions of the 10th book of the CCP DE. The German courts are therefore not bound by any internal agreements between the parties on the arbitral proceedings in general and the taking of evidence in particular.[739] Nonetheless, if the parties have explicitly excluded certain types of evidence which are permissible under the CCP DE, this choice must be respected.[740] Second, although foreign types of evidence are in some cases in the interests of the parties, the intention behind § 1050 (2) CCP DE was to avoid broad US-style discovery proceedings.[741] Because evidence often belongs to third parties, § 1050 (2) CCP DE protects these third parties from unwelcome foreign intrusion.[742] Although it may at times be accurate to interpret § 1050 CCP DE broadly in the interests of the parties, this is certainly not the case here.

In contrast to the aforementioned arguments against foreign types of evidence, Steinbrück suggests a pragmatic middle way to handle this issue. Although the CCP DE does not provide for any foreign forms of evidence, he argues, German courts ought to transform these measures until they conform to the CCP DE, subject to the German *ordre public*.[743] As a sort of compromise, this approach still avoids US-style discovery, but at the same time allows the competent *juge d'appui* to examine the extent to which the foreign form of evidence can be transformed and adapted to proceedings pursuant to the CCP DE.[744] This not only is in the interests of international arbitration, but also promotes Germany as a seat of arbitration. Because this view is not substantiated by law, it remains doubtful as to how German judges of support will react when confronted with an evidence request containing foreign types of evidence, such as cross-examination or the examination of a party

738 § 1050 (2) CCP DE: Unless it regards the application as inadmissible, the court shall execute the request according to its rules on taking evidence or other judicial acts.

739 STEINBRÜCK, 397.

740 § 1042 (3) CCP DE; SCHWAB/WALTER, ch. 17 n. 8; SCHÜTZE, *Ermessensgrenzen*, 3; *see also* SCHMIDT-AHRENDTS/DE JONG, who suggest the amendment of § 1050 to ensure that German courts take evidence only in accordance with the agreement of the parties–for example, that witnesses be cross-examined instead of only questioned by the judge and the arbitrator(s), respectively (285).

741 Parliamentary Documentation 13/5274 (1996), 51.

742 STEINBRÜCK, 398.

743 *Ibid.*, 404.

744 *Ibid.*, 403.

as a witness.[745] So far, few relevant decisions of German courts have been rendered in this regard and it remains to be seen how widely § 1050 CCP DE will be interpreted.[746]

4. International Judicial Assistance in Taking Evidence

Besides the aforementioned assistance in the taking of evidence, state courts can provide assistance by requesting foreign state courts to gather evidence by means of international judicial assistance (e.g. through the HEC or the EER).[747] However, this course of action is unpopular in most situations, due to the lengthy and costly process involved. Since these international treaties are not open for direct use in arbitral proceedings, the best alternative is to approach a state court directly in the jurisdiction in which the evidence is located.

5. Target of Evidence

As regards the target of an evidence request, a distinction must be made between the parties to the arbitration and third parties.[748] If a party refuses to reveal evidence in its control, state courts cannot force the reluctant party to reveal it; but this will be considered by the arbitral tribunal when assessing the evidence.[749] In this regard, possible privilege must be taken into account before drawing any adverse inference.[750]

The situation is different regarding third parties–for example, if there is a request for document production or their examination as witnesses. Under the CCP DE, such a request will be granted only if it could reasonably be expected by the respective third party or to the extent that such party is not entitled to refuse to testify.[751] Accordingly, third parties can refuse to reveal documents or to give testimony based on personal privilege (e.g. a personal relationship with one of the parties as spouse or fiancé) or factual privilege

745 *Ibid.*; *see also* SCHMIDT-AHRENDTS/DE JONG, suggesting that in order to facilitate the arbitral proceedings and ensure that the respective state court judge does not have to take evidence in a way that he or she is not normally entitled nor accustomed to, witnesses should be ordered to testify directly before the arbitral tribunal (286).

746 RÜTZEL et al., 163.

747 *See* p. 118 et seqq. *supra;* Stein/Jonas-SCHLOSSER, § 1050 CCP DE n. 23 et seqq.; Wieczorek/Schütze-SCHÜTZE, § 1050 CCP DE n. 37; EBERL/EBERL, § 1 n. 31; WOLFF, 253; VARGA, 247 et seq. In Germany, the HEC entered into force in 1979 (*see* the current status).

748 VON ENZBERG/ROHRSSEN, 14 et seq.

749 BeckOK-VON SELLE, § 142 CCP DE n. 17; RÜTZEL et al., 162.

750 RÜTZEL et al., 80, 163 et seq.

751 § 142 et seqq. CCP DE i.c.w. § 385-390 CCP DE; WOLFF, 266; Böckstiegel et al.-SACHS/LÖRCHER, § 1050 CCP DE n. 9 et seq.; RÜTZEL et al., 80 et seqq.

(e.g. if a document or testimony would reveal a technical or trade secret).[752] Refusing to produce a document or give testimony without sufficient grounds can lead to fines or even coercive detention.[753] However, if the respective state court forces a third party to produce evidence, this decision can be challenged by means of a miscellaneous appeal (*sofortige Beschwerde*) to the regional court (*Landgericht*).[754]

E. Competence of the *Juge d'Appui*

1. Scope of Discretion

Regardless of whether the conditions pursuant to § 1050 CCP DE are fulfilled, the respective *juge d'appui* has no choice but to grant or deny assistance.[755] For instance, there is no discretion to grant assistance in cases where the conditions are not met because of an inadmissible requested method of taking evidence.[756] Furthermore, as a basic principle of international court assistance, state courts will not examine the usefulness, appropriateness or relevance of an evidence request. Only the arbitral tribunal is entitled to do so.[757] Thus, if the arbitral tribunal has explicitly requested to examine a witness under oath, the *juge d'appui* seized is not at liberty to deem this request unnecessary because the witness statement is considered reliable; unless, of course, it is legally not permissible.[758]

In contrast, if the arbitral tribunal does not specify the manner in which a witness should be examined and thus does not exclude the administration of oath, the *juge d'appui* can decide freely whether an oath is necessary.[759] After the evidence has been taken, the result will be introduced into the arbitral proceedings. The assessment of evidence and its consequences (i.e. whether a fact is proved) forms part of the arbitral proceedings and not of the

752 § 383 and § 384 as well as the exception in § 385 CCP DE. In addition to this civil procedural rules, German criminal law can impose sanctions on members of certain professions revealing client information in the context of their profession (§ 203 CC DE); *see also* RÜTZEL et al., 80 et seqq.

753 § 390 CCP DE.

754 § 567 (1) (2.) CCP DE.

755 Zöller-GEIMER, § 1050 CCP DE n. 6; EBERL/EBERL, § 1 n. 44; HK-SAENGER, § 1050 CCP DE n. 5.

756 § 1050 (2) CCP DE.

757 § 1042 (4) 2nd sentence CCP DE; MüKo-MÜNCH, § 1050 CCP DE n. 24; SCHWAB/WALTER, ch. 17 n. 8.

758 Stein/Jonas-SCHLOSSER, § 1050 CCP DE n. 13; Musielak/Voit-VOIT, § 1050 CCP DE n. 4; BeckOK-WILSKE/MARKERT, § 1050 CCP DE n. 9; SCHWAB/WALTER, ch. 17 n. 16.

759 Stein/Jonas-SCHLOSSER, § 1050 CCP DE n. 13.

state court proceedings pursuant to § 1050 CCP DE.[760] As a consequence, only the assessment of evidence which is taken by a state court is part of the arbitral proceedings, and not the taking of evidence itself.[761]

2. Principle of Subsidiarity

According to § 1050 (1) CCP DE, the respective *juge d'appui* will assist in the taking of evidence only if the arbitral tribunal is not empowered to take the evidence itself.[762] The extent to which the arbitral tribunal must explain why it cannot take the evidence itself remains contentious. On the one hand, it is obvious that if the arbitral tribunal is legally authorised to obtain evidence and can do so without further ado, state courts cannot be approached for assistance.[763] Thus, arbitral tribunals cannot resort to state courts merely because they consider it inconvenient to take the evidence themselves.[764]

Situations in which the arbitral tribunal could act autonomously, but only with a disproportionately significant effort, are more problematic.[765] For example, a third-party witness located abroad may likely refuse to testify.[766] Consequently, because § 1050 CCP DE does not address this situation and § 1026 CCP DE specifies that state courts can take action only where provided so explicitly by law, the arbitral tribunal will first have to try to examine the witness at his or her place of residence. Obviously, the chances of success are very low, so the question arises as to whether § 1050 CCP DE may be applied by analogy.[767]

760 Böckstiegel et al.-SACHS/LÖRCHER, § 1050 CCP DE n. 11; Musielak/Voit-VOIT, § 1050 CCP DE n. 8; EBERL/EBERL, § 1 n. 50; HK-SAENGER, § 1050 CCP DE n. 7; WOLFF, 267.

761 Musielak/Voit-VOIT, § 1050 CCP DE n. 8.

762 § 1050 (1) CCP DE.

763 SCHWAB/WALTER, ch. 17 n. 4; Wieczorek/Schütze-SCHÜTZE, § 1050 CCP DE n. 7; Böckstiegel et al.-SACHS/LÖRCHER, § 1050 CCP DE n. 4.

764 Wieczorek/Schütze-SCHÜTZE, § 1050 CCP DE n. 7.

765 Stein/Jonas-SCHLOSSER, § 1050 CCP DE n. 11; Zöller-GEIMER, § 1050 CCP DE n. 8; HK-SAENGER, § 1050 CCP DE n. 4; RÜTZEL et al., 162 et seq.

766 WOLFF, 254; MüKo-MÜNCH, § 1025 CCP DE, n. 26; EBERL/EBERL, § 1 n. 42.

767 Stein/Jonas-SCHLOSSER, § 1050 CCP DE n. 11; BeckOK-WILSKE/MARKERT, § 1050 CCP DE n. 3; for a different view, *see* LACHMANN, n. 1627. He argues that because of considerable demarcation difficulties in deciding at which stage one can presume that the effort of the arbitral tribunal is too significant to take evidence, § 1050 CCP DE should be applied only *stricto sensu*–that is, exclusively if the arbitral tribunal is not legally empowered to take evidence.

By filling this legal gap, one must consider the fact that §1026 CCP, like its counterpart in Art. 5 UNCITRAL ML, strives to limit court intervention, but not possible assistance by state courts.[768] Applying §1050 CCP DE by analogy thus would allow not for additional intervention by state courts, but rather for assistance which goes only slightly further than the strict wording of §1050 CCP DE.[769] This argument is supported by the intention of §1050 CCP DE as a whole–namely, to assist arbitral tribunals where they are unable to effectively conduct the taking of evidence. According to Hartmann, §1050 CCP DE should be interpreted and applied broadly and thus encompass cases in which the gathering of evidence would be disproportionately burdensome for the arbitral tribunal.[770] This is also in the interests of the parties that wish to gather such evidence, regardless of whether the state court seized acts because the arbitral tribunal cannot legally gather evidence or because it is almost impossible to do so.[771] Apart from these arguments, there is no hint that the German legislature deliberately intended to exclude such situations from the scope of application of §1050 CCP DE. All in all, there are several good reasons to apply §1050 CCP DE by analogy in circumstances where it would involve a disproportionately significant effort for the arbitral tribunal to gather the evidence itself.

3. Examination of the Arbitration Agreement

Because §1050 CCP DE serves only to assist arbitral proceedings, one might ask whether the *juge d'appui* has any scope to examine the validity of the arbitration agreement. This question has been subject to controversial discussions in German legal doctrine. A minority of authors argue that the validity of the arbitration agreement can be examined only on a prima facie basis–that is, a motion under §1050 CCP DE must be denied if the arbitration agreement is obviously invalid.[772] However, the prevailing view suggests that since the arbitral tribunal is competent to decide on the validity of the arbitration agreement and therefore on its own jurisdiction (competence-competence), state courts are not entitled to review the validity of the arbitration agree-

768 UNCITRAL, (2012), Art. 5 UNCITRAL ML n. 1.

769 STEINBRÜCK, 394; EBERL/EBERL, §1 n. 42.

770 KuKo-HARTMANN, §1050 CCP DE n. 1.

771 STEINBRÜCK, 394.

772 SCHWAB/WALTER, §1050 CCP DE, n. 10; LACHMANN, n. 1634; Stein/Jonas-SCHLOSSER, §1050 CCP DE, n. 13; Musielak/Voit-VOIT, §1050 CCP DE, n. 5; STEINBRÜCK, 419 et seq.; HK-SAENGER, §1050 CCP DE n. 6.

ment under § 1050 CCP DE.[773] If there is a dispute as regards the arbitration agreement, the parties can challenge the competence of the arbitral tribunal according to § 1040 (3) CCP DE. Allowing for a full review of the arbitration agreement in proceedings pursuant to § 1050 CCP DE would indeed circumvent § 1040 (3) CCP DE.[774] This competence is reserved for the higher regional court and not the local court, pursuant to § 1050 CCP DE.[775] Apart from that, the arbitration agreement can of course be examined in the context of the recognition and enforcement of an arbitral award under the NYC, but not during court assistance in the taking of evidence.[776]

F. Appellate Remedies

If all conditions under § 1050 CCP DE are fulfilled, the *juge d'appui* will render his or her decision in the form of a court order (*Beschluss*).[777] In cases where only one party has made an evidence request, the right to be heard must be granted to the adverse party prior to rendering a decision.[778] Reading the CCP DE in its strictest sense, a remedy against an order pursuant to § 1050 CCP DE is not possible.[779] The intention is clear: to keep state court intervention to a minimum and thus simplify and speed up the arbitral proceedings.[780] Nonetheless, it is widely accepted that parties can initiate an immediate miscellaneous appeal (*sofortige Beschwerde*) to the regional court (*Landgericht*)

773 § 1040 (1) CCP DE; MüKo-MÜNCH, § 1050 CCP DE n. 21; Böckstiegel et al.-SACHS/LÖRCHER, § 1050 CCP DE, n. 6; EBERL/EBERL, § 1 n. 43; Zöller-GEIMER, § 1050 CCP DE n. 6; BeckOK-WILSKE/MARKERT, § 1050 CCP DE n. 10; BeckKuKo-HARTMANN, § 1050 CCP DE n. 4; Wieczorek/Schütze-SCHÜTZE, § 1033 CCP DE n. 23. SCHÜTZE distinguishes between situations where a motion under § 1050 CCP DE is initiated by a party or the arbitral tribunal itself. While in the first case an examination is possible, it does not apply to the latter situation because of competence-competence in accordance with § 1040 CCP DE.

774 For another view *see* Steinbrück, 420; WOLFF, 260.

775 § 1062 (1) (2.) CCP DE i.c.w. § 1059 (2) (1.) (a) and (c) CCP DE.

776 Art. III (3) and V (1) (a) NYC.

777 § 1063 (1) CCP DE.

778 Böckstiegel et al.-SACHS/LÖRCHER, § 1050 CCP DE n. 8. Therefore, in order to avoid lengthening state court proceedings, the parties should make an evidence request together if they agree that certain evidence should be gathered or the arbitral tribunal itself initiates a proceeding pursuant to § 1050 CCP DE (MüKo-MÜNCH, § 1050 CCP DE n. 28).

779 § 1065 (1) i.c.w. § 1062 (1) CCP DE *e contratrio.*

780 BeckOK-WILSKE/MARKERT, § 1065 CCP DE n. 1.

if a motion under § 1050 CCP DE is denied.[781] In contrast, there is no remedy against a court order granting the motion.[782] This follows from the fact that an immediate miscellaneous appeal is possible only against a decision denying a request, not granting one.[783]

As previously discussed (*see* p. 143 *supra*), the proceeding under § 1050 CCP DE should be viewed separately from the arbitral proceedings in which the evidence which has been taken by the state court will be assessed. That is why in general, violations of procedural rules during the taking of evidence in accordance with § 1050 CCP DE cannot be challenged before the arbitral tribunal. Nevertheless, such violations can be the subject of a challenge to the arbitral award if there is a connection between the violation and the reasons for seeking annulment of the arbitral award pursuant to § 1059 (2) CCP DE.[784] An example is a situation where the *juge d'appui* orders cross-examination of a witness, even though this has been explicitly excluded by the parties.[785] If one can demonstrate that there is a separate agreement between the parties which has been violated, and it may be assumed that this violation influenced the arbitral award, the higher regional court (*Oberlandesgericht*) may annul it.[786]

Up to 2011, there seem to have been no cases in which arbitral awards were set aside because the arbitral tribunal disregarded an explicit agreement between the parties. However, this changed in 2011 with a decision of the Higher Regional Court of Frankfurt am Main.[787] The court reasoned that procedural orders which have been expressly approved by the parties and which amend or change the agreed procedural rules are to be seen as a separate agreement between the parties.[788] In the respective case, the arbitral

781 § 567 (1) (2.) CCP DE; Stein/Jonas-SCHLOSSER, § 1050 CCP DE n. 17; EBERL/EBERL, § 1 n. 46; BeckOK-WILSKE/MARKERT, § 1050 CCP DE n. 14; Musielak/Voit-VOIT, § 1050 CCP DE n. 6; Prütting/Gehrlein-PRÜTTING, § 1050 CCP DE n. 3; for another view *see* MüKo-MÜNCH, § 1050 CCP DE n. 28. He refers to the competence of the Higher Regional Court (*Oberlandesgericht*) according to § 159 CCA DE.

782 SCHWAB/WALTER, ch. 17 n. 13; WOLFF, 264.

783 § 567 (1) (2.) CCP DE.

784 EBERL/EBERL, § 1 n. 50; SCHWAB/WALTER, ch. 17 n. 14; Böckstiegel et al.-SACHS/LÖRCHER, § 1050 CCP DE n. 11; Musielak/Voit-VOIT, § 1050 CCP DE n. 8; Stein/Jonas-SCHLOSSER, § 1050 CCP DE n. 21 et seq.; MüKo-MÜNCH, § 1050 CCP DE n. 33.

785 § 1059 (2) (1.) (d) CCP DE; MüKo-MÜNCH, § 1059 CCP DE n. 37.

786 § 1059 (2) (1.) (d) CCP DE; § 1062 (1) (4) CCP DE.

787 OLG Frankfurt am Main, 17 Feb. 2011, 26 Sch 13/10; § 1059 (2) (1.) (d) CCP DE; MARGHITOLA, 231 et seqq.; WAGNER/BÜLAU, 8 et seqq.; RÜTZEL et al., 182 et seq.

788 OLG Frankfurt am Main, 17 Feb. 2011, 26 Sch 13/10, n. 57; regarding the difference between procedural orders and party agreements, *see* WAGNER/BÜLAU, 13 et seq.

tribunal refused to order document production in violation of an explicit agreement between the parties.[789] In addition, in terms of causality, it was held that because of the severity of the violation, it could have influenced the arbitral award.[790] In this respect, the Court stated that it would indeed be speculative to examine in too much detail whether the arbitral award could have turned out differently.[791]

Although in this case the violation of the agreement between the parties did not arise in the context of court assistance in the taking of evidence, the approach followed by the Higher Regional Court of Frankfurt demonstrates that–as opposed to the discretion of the arbitral tribunal to tailor the arbitral proceedings, which mostly cannot be challenged–party autonomy must be taken seriously and failure to do so can lead to the annulment of the arbitral award.[792] Applied to court assistance in the taking of evidence, one can therefore conclude that under German law, a violation of an agreement during the taking of evidence will be taken seriously, provided that it influenced the arbitral award.

G. Summary

§ 1050 CCP DE takes a very arbitration-friendly stance in various ways. First and most importantly, it does not distinguish between domestic and international arbitration, so court assistance in the taking of evidence is also granted to foreign arbitral tribunals. This direct court assistance considerably simplifies and shortens the process of taking evidence in international arbitration.

Second, from a tactical point of view, the arbitral tribunal must approve a request to seek state court assistance in the taking of evidence, to avoid delaying tactics. The arbitral tribunal can even seek court assistance itself if it considers this necessary. In the ongoing proceedings, the arbitral tribunal can actively participate in the taking of evidence before state courts and ask questions, which confirms and strengthens its position. By contrast, the parties can also exclude this process altogether pursuant to § 1050 CCP DE, without waiving their right to minimum legal protection.

Third, a broad spectrum of possible measures for the taking of evidence is available under the CCP DE. Such measures also include the independent

789 OLG Frankfurt am Main, 17 Feb. 2011, 26 Sch 13/10, n. 64.

790 *Ibid.*, n. 66; MARGHITOLA, 241.

791 OLG Frankfurt am Main, 17 Feb. 2011, 26 Sch 13/10, n. 66.

792 MARGHITOLA, 239 et seqq.; WAGNER/BÜLAU, 11.

evidentiary proceeding prior to and during the arbitral proceedings, in cases where there is a risk that certain evidence may potentially be destroyed. Although only measures for the taking of evidence that accord with the CCP DE are permissible, it has been shown that in cases where foreign types of evidence are requested, they can theoretically be transformed and adapted to the extent that they correspond to the CCP DE. Concerning the target of evidence, parties cannot–in contrast to witnesses–be forced to reveal evidence in their control. Rather, this fact will be considered when assessing the evidence in the arbitral proceedings. The situation is different as regards third parties, which can be forced to reveal evidence in their possession, unless this would be unreasonable or there are legal grounds to refuse to testify or reveal a certain document, including a technical or trade secret.

Fourth, as regards the competence of the *juge d'appui*, his or her scope of discretion is limited. If the conditions of § 1050 CCP DE are met, assistance must be granted and vice versa. Moreover, the *juge d'appui* is not entitled to examine the usefulness, appropriateness or relevance of an evidence request. This exercise is left to the arbitral tribunal which conducts the taking of evidence. The same applies to the assessment of evidence which does not form part of § 1050 CCP DE, but rather of the arbitral proceedings. A further competence–or rather, duty–of the *juge d'appui* is to examine whether the arbitral tribunal could take the requested evidence itself. In this regard, assistance should be granted not only if the arbitral tribunal is legally not entitled to do so, but also where this would involve a disproportionately significant effort. As regards the arbitration agreement, the *juge d'appui* has no power to fully examine it, because of the principle of competence-competence. The challenge to the arbitration agreement is thus part of a separate proceeding, according to § 1042 (3) CCP DE.

Finally, although the CCP DE does not expressly provide for this, the parties can appeal to the local court if a motion under § 1050 CCP DE is denied. If it is granted, an appeal is not possible. Because the proceeding according to § 1050 CCP DE does not form part of the arbitral proceedings, violations of procedural rules during the taking of evidence before a state court generally cannot be challenged during the arbitral proceedings. This is possible only if there is a link between the violation of procedural rules and the reasons for annulling the arbitral award according to § 1059 (2) (d) CCP DE–for example, if the taking of evidence before a state court violated an agreement between the parties and influenced the arbitral award. In such case, the higher regional court could annul the arbitral award. As seen in the decision of the Higher Regional Court of Frankfurt, the bar to affirm such a violation is not set too high.

All in all, § 1050 CCP DE is a very helpful and flexible tool for international arbitral proceedings. Varga even argues that the fact that § 1050 CCP DE provides an easily accessible tool to gather evidence through the German courts should motivate parties to comply voluntarily with the arbitral tribunal's orders, and thus that § 1050 CCP DE will become unnecessary in many cases.[793] Admittedly, the very arbitration-friendly German approach, which also allows for the provision of court assistance in the taking of evidence to foreign arbitral tribunals, is remarkable. Nevertheless, it remains questionable why the liberal German approach has gone almost unnoticed, both nationally and internationally. So far, there are almost no reported relevant court decisions concerning the scope of application of § 1050 CCP DE.[794] This might not necessarily imply its insignificance, but could rather be because decisions of lower first instance courts (regional courts) are frequently unreported.

In addition, German courts which receive an evidence request can assist in the taking of evidence only in accordance with the types of evidence set out in the CCP DE. As previously discussed (*see* p. 140 et seqq. *supra*), German legal doctrine almost unanimously argues that no foreign forms of evidence can be taken in international arbitral proceedings before German courts. As long as this view prevails, § 1050 CCP DE will very likely remain insignificant.[795] It remains to be seen whether the German courts will take a more flexible approach by trying to adapt an evidence request containing a foreign form of evidence until it is compatible with the CCP DE.[796]

§ 3 France

A. Introduction

Thanks to the presence of the ICC headquarters and a very liberal arbitration regime, France is one of the most popular forums for international arbitration.[797] This is confirmed by the pro-arbitration stance of both the Paris Court of Appeal and the Court of Cassation.[798] The French *lex arbitri* was revised in 2011, when important case law was codified and arbitration-friendly provi-

793 VARGA, 236 et seq.; *see also* WOLFF, 268.

794 RÜTZEL et al., 163.

795 *Ibid.*, 161.

796 STEINBRÜCK, 422; as a possible model, *see* e.g. Art. 184 (2) Draft-PILA CH.

797 DERAINS/KIFFER, n. 1; Balthasar-BALTHASAR/ZIADE, n. 1; MOURRE, *France*, 1; BORN, *Int. Comm. Arb.*, 141.

798 Balthasar-BALTHASAR/ZIADE, n. 3; MOURRE, *France*, 2.

sions were implemented.[799] Its provisions form part of the fourth book of the CCP FR, which is divided into two parts. While the first part (Arts. 1442-1503 CCP FR) applies to domestic arbitration, the second part (Arts. 1504-1527 CCP FR) deals with international arbitration. These articles apply where 'international trade interests are at stake'.[800] To avoid having two different statutes containing identical rules for both domestic and international arbitration, Art. 1506 CCP FR specifies which provisions of domestic arbitration also apply to international arbitration.[801]

Obviously, the provisions that apply to international arbitration are often more liberal than the domestic provisions. For instance, the arbitration agreement need not be in writing, while in domestic arbitration, the written form is mandatory.[802] As discussed below *(see* p. 156 *infra),* the parties enjoy remarkable freedom in tailoring the arbitral proceedings by modifying Art. 1506 CCP FR at their discretion. Lastly, although it is not based on the UNCITRAL ML, the CCP FR is in many ways influenced by it.[803]

B. Legal Bases

1. Prior to the Constitution of the Arbitral Tribunal

The CCP FR foresees the possibility of court assistance in the taking of evidence both before and after the arbitral tribunal has been established. In cases where evidence is sought or must be preserved prior to the constitution of the arbitral tribunal, the arbitral tribunal itself can order conservatory or provisional measures (interim measures), and even combine them with an *astreinte*.[804] Still, in cases where coercive power is needed, court assistance in the taking of evidence is possible pursuant to Art. 1449 CCP FR:

> "The existence of an arbitration agreement, insofar as the arbitral tribunal has not yet been constituted, shall not preclude a party from applying to a court for measures relating to the taking of evidence or provisional or conservatory measures."
>
> "Subject to the provisions governing conservatory attachments and judicial security, application shall be made to the President of the Tribunal de grande instance (Court of First Instance) or of the Tribunal de com-

799 BORN, *Int. Comm. Arb.*, 142 et seq.

800 Art. 1504 CCP FR.

801 CLAY, Art. 1506 CCP FR, 179 et seqq.; JARROSSON/PELLERIN, n. 85.

802 Art. 1443 and 1507 CCP FR; GAILLARD/DE LAPASSE, n. 28.

803 MOURRE, *France*, 2; DERAINS/KIFFER, n. 1.

804 Art. 1468 CCP FR.

merce (Commercial Tribunal) who shall rule on the measures relating to the taking of evidence in accordance with the provisions of Article 145 and, where the matter is urgent, on the provisional or conservatory measures requested by the parties to the arbitration agreement."

The competent state judge is either the president of the court of first instance or the Commercial Tribunal.[805] Where the need for evidentiary measures is urgent–for instance, to preserve evidence from potential loss–one might conclude that Art. 1449 CCP FR can be used only before the arbitral tribunal has been established, since the provision refers only to this stage of the arbitral proceedings.[806] Indeed, as Gaillard/De Lapasse argue, because Art. 1468 (1) CCP FR provides that an arbitral tribunal is competent to order interim measures and combine them with an *astreinte* as an indirect coercive measure, the French legislature did not consider it necessary to implement parallel competence between state courts and arbitral tribunals.[807]

This view has long been criticised and in French legal doctrine, it is widely accepted that in some cases after the arbitral tribunal has been established, the only way to impose suitable interim measures–for example, in relation to the preservation of evidence–is to resort to state courts.[808] This parallel competence should not be seen as an inconvenience, but rather as helpful assistance that should facilitate smooth arbitral proceedings and effective legal protection.[809] This view is in line not only with the generally accepted principle in international arbitration of parallel competence to order interim measures between the arbitral tribunal and state courts, but also with the position of Art. 1449 CCP FR in the French *lex arbitri*. It appears under chapter one, which deals with the arbitration agreement without any mention of what happens once the arbitral tribunal has been established.[810] Furthermore, according to the legislative material, Art. 1449 CCP FR has been drafted in order to set the boundaries of court intervention prior to constitution of the arbitral tribunal,

805 Art. 1449 CCP FR thus deviates from the usual competence of the *juge d'appui* pursuant to Art. 1505 CCP FR.

806 CHAINAIS, n. 70.

807 GAILLARD/DE LAPASSE, n. 14; LOQUIN, n. 271.

808 CALLÉ/DARGENT, Art. 145 CCP FR n. 11; RACINE, n. 307; JARROSSON/PELLERIN, n. 18; CHAINAIS, n. 15; DUPREY, 17; AUDIT/D'AVOUT, n. 1403; BÉGUIN/MENJUCQ, n. 1829; CACHARD, n. 1233; CHAINAIS, n. 69 et seqq.; for another view, *see* DUPEYRON, 466; CLAY, Art. 1449 CCP FR, 56; GAILLARD/DE LAPASSE, n. 12, 14.

809 CHAINAIS, n. 73, 76.

810 Arts. 1442–49 CCP FR; JARROSSON/PELLERIN, n. 18.

without mentioning the situation thereafter.[811] In sum, there are good reasons to apply Art. 1449 CCP FR also after the constitution of the arbitral tribunal.

Hitherto, however, these opinions have not led to any amendments to Art. 1449 (1) CCP FR, such as deletion of the wording 'insofar as the arbitral tribunal has not yet been constituted'.[812] Nonetheless, under the old *lex arbitri*, French Courts have confirmed that although Art. 145 CCP FR is no longer available after the establishment of the arbitral tribunal, interim measures according to Arts. 808 et seqq. CCP FR *(see* p. 158 *infra)* should still be available in urgent cases during the arbitral proceedings.[813] It is therefore desirable that the French courts confirm this view under the new *lex arbitri*.

2. After the Constitution of the Arbitral Tribunal

Once the arbitral tribunal has been established, it itself is equipped with the power to force parties to produce evidence and can even attach an *astreinte* to such an order.[814] Nonetheless, when third parties are involved, court assistance is crucial. Thus, Art. 1469 CCP FR, inspired by Art. 184 (2) PILA CH,[815] reads as follows:

> "(1) If one of the parties to arbitral proceedings intends to rely on a notarized (acte authentique) or private (acte sous seing privé) deed to which it was not a party, or on evidence held by a third party, it may, upon the arbitral tribunal's invitation, have that third party summoned before the President of the Court of First Instance for the purpose of obtaining a copy thereof (expédition) or the production of the deed or item of evidence.
>
> (2) Articles 42 through 48 shall determine which Court of First Instance has territorial jurisdiction in this regard.
>
> (3) Application shall be made, heard and decided as for expedited proceedings (référé).
>
> (4) If the President considers the application well-founded, he or she shall order that the relevant original, copy or extract of the deed or item of evidence be issued or produced, under such conditions and guarantees as he or she determines, and, if necessary, attach penalties to such order.

811 Rapport to the Premier Minister (2011), 33; JARROSSON/PELLERIN, n. 18.

812 CHAINAIS, n. 77.

813 Paris Court of Cassation, 13 Jun. 2002, 2nd Civil Chamber, 00-20077; HORY, note on *Société Akzo Nobel et autres v. SA Elf Atochem*, Versailles Court of Appeal, 8 Oct. 1998, 2nd Chambre Civile, in: Rev. Arb. 1999, 57 et seqq.

814 Art. 1467 (3) CCP FR.

815 CLAY, *Arbitrage*, 134; CLAY, Art. 1469 CCP FR, 104; RACINE, n. 697.

(5) Such order is not readily enforceable.
(6) It may be appealed within fifteen days following service (signification) of the order."

Quite similar to the respective provision in state court proceedings, state courts will provide assistance *vis-à-vis* recalcitrant third parties.[816] Here again, the competent judge is the president of the court of first instance according to the rules of territorial jurisdiction of Arts. 42-48 CCP FR–that is, the judge where the third party is domiciled or the evidence will be taken.[817] Because there are third parties involved, it is not the *juge d'appui* pursuant to Art. 1505 CCP FR who is competent, but rather the respective president of the court of first instance (also called the 'judge of evidence'), deciding in an expedited proceeding.[818]

3. Support for Foreign Arbitral Tribunal

In contrast to other *leges arbitri*, the French approach is quite liberal and sets no strict boundaries as regards the application of its *lex arbitri*. Arts. 1504 et seqq. CCP FR therefore apply if 'international trade interests are at stake'.[819] In this regard, the Paris Court of Cassation has confirmed that, irrespective of the applicable law, the seat of arbitration or the nationality of the parties, an arbitration is considered international when it affects international trade interests.[820]As an example, a dispute is considered 'international' if it concerns a cross-border transfer of goods, even if both parties are French.[821] Thus, if more than one state is involved economically, the arbitration is considered international.[822] The question of whether the international arbitration regime applies therefore depends more on economic aspects than on

816 Art. 138 CCP FR; NOUGEIN/DUPEYRÉ, n. 226.

817 *Ibid.*, n. 227.

818 CLAY, Art. 1469 CCP FR, 105; JARROSSON/PELLERIN, n. 29; RACINE, n. 697; LOQUIN, n. 338.

819 Art. 1504 CCP FR; DERAINS/KIFFER, n. 3 et seq.; Balthasar-BALTHASAR/ZIADE, n. 6; CADIET/JEULAND, n. 1063.

820 Art. 1504 CCP FR; *Institut national de la santé et de la recherche médicale (INSERM) v. Fondation Letten F. Saugstad, Paris Court of Cassation, 26 Jan. 2011, 1st Civil Chamber, 09-10198; Société Uni-Kod v. Société Ouralkali,* Paris Court of Cassation, 30 Mar. 2004, 1st Civil Chamber, in: Rev. Arb. 2005, 959; DERAINS/KIFFER, n. 3 et seq.; Balthasar-BALTHASAR/ZIADE, n. 6; CADIET/JEULAND, n. 1063.

821 *Société Pangee v. Société Fancefert,* Paris High Court, 13 Jul. 1999, in: Rev. Arb. 1995, 625 (2.).

822 *M. Ch. Di Sabatino et autre v. Société Animated Ventures et autres,* Paris Court of Appeal, 7 Oct. 2014, in: Rev. Arb. 2015, 531; for other examples *see* CALLÉ/DARGENT, Art. 1504 CCP FR n. 2; CLAY, Art. 1504 CCP FR, 171 et seqq.

legal aspects; unlike in other countries, where the seat of arbitration or the residence of a party is a key factor in determining the applicable *lex arbitri*.[823] From the perspective of a foreign arbitral tribunal, this approach is welcome, since it allows for court assistance in the taking of evidence pursuant to the CCP FR without any connection to France beyond the location of evidence there.

C. Competence to Seek Court Assistance

1. Primacy of the Arbitral Tribunal

Like most *leges arbitri*, Art. 1469 (1) CCP FR states that the party seeking court assistance in the taking of evidence must first obtain the consent of the arbitral tribunal.[824] Since it is the arbitral tribunal that conducts the arbitral proceedings (Art. 1467 CCP FR), its prior consent strengthens its position and avoids dilatory tactics or unnecessary evidence requests.[825] Consequently, when presented with an evidence request, the respective arbitral tribunal is at liberty to grant or decline it, and there are very limited possibilities to challenge its decision.[826]

Unlike under Art. 27 UNCITRAL ML and other *leges arbitri*, the arbitral tribunal itself is not competent to seek court assistance in the taking of evidence.[827] This possibility was discussed in the drafting process of the new French arbitration provisions, but unfortunately was ultimately abandoned.[828] However, although the arbitral tribunal is vested with significant power to conduct the taking of evidence and even to order *astreintes*, it should also be able to resort to state courts for assistance in the taking of evidence.[829] Not least, this would be in line with Art. 1467 (1) CCP FR, which allows the arbitral tribunal to take all 'necessary steps' as regards the taking of evidence.

823 Art. 176 (1) PILA CH, S. 2 (1) EAA 1996; CALLÉ/DARGENT, Art. 1504 CCP FR n. 1; CLAY, Art. 1504 CCP FR, 107; Balthasar-BALTHASAR/ZIADE, n. 6 et seqq.; for the 'delocalisation of the seat of arbitration', *see* LOQUIN, n. 344 et seqq.

824 CLAY, *Arbitrage*, 135.

825 JARROSSON, 337; Loquin, n. 336.

826 JARROSSON, 337; RACINE, n. 697; BÉGUIN/MENJUCQ, n. 1948; NOUGEIN/DUPEYRÉ, n. 227; SERAGLINI/ORTSCHEIDT, n. 339; *see also* Art. 1469 (4) CCP FR, stating that document production will be granted 'If the President considers the application well-founded, ...'.

827 NOUGEIN/DUPEYRÉ, n. 227; CLAY, *Arbitrage*, 135; SERAGLINI/ORTSCHEIDT, n. 339.

828 BÉGUIN/MENJUCQ, n. 1948; *see also* Art. 184 (2) PILA CH; § 1050 (1) CCP DE.

829 Art. 1467 (3) CCP FR.

2. Exclusion of Court Assistance in Taking Evidence

In contrast to the discussions in other jurisdictions, it appears that the complete exclusion of court assistance in the taking of evidence as a violation of minimum legal protection in arbitration has not yet been discussed in French legal doctrine.[830] Nonetheless, there are several reasons that support this possibility. Besides those presented in the discussion of German law *(see* p. 137 et seq. *supra),* the CCP FR explicitly allows for the parties to exclude court assistance in the taking of evidence. According to Art. 1506 CCP FR, subject to the mandatory rules as foreseen in Arts. 1504-1527 CCP FR, the parties are at liberty to exclude the listed provisions, such as those relating to court assistance in the taking of evidence, prior to and after the constitution of the arbitral tribunal.[831] This guarantees the parties to international arbitral proceedings remarkable freedom, as opposed to the stricter rules applicable to domestic arbitration.[832] In sum, although in most cases the complete exclusion of court assistance in the taking of evidence makes little sense, under French law it is nonetheless a possibility.

D. Spectrum of Evidence and its Target

1. Evidence According to a Party Agreement

When it comes to the taking of evidence and the procedural rules, the parties enjoy broad discretion in tailoring the arbitral proceedings.[833] As it is already possible to exclude any court assistance in the taking of evidence, this is all the more so the case in relation to specific types of evidence, such as witness testimonies. This may be done either by explicitly limiting the scope of discovery/disclosure in the arbitration agreement or by referring to institutional arbitration rules or the IBA Rules.[834] Thus, if the parties have explicitly excluded a specific type of evidence, the respective state court must respect this choice and decline any request in this regard.[835] Likewise, if the taking

---

830 AUDIT/D'AVOUT mention only that in certain situations, parties may have an interest in excluding court assistance and the arbitration agreement should therefore be examined in order to find out whether such an exclusion took place (n. 1400).

831 Art. 1506 (1) i.c.w. Art. 1449 CCP FR and Art. 1506 (3) i.c.w. Art. 1469 CCP FR.

832 For instance, in international arbitral proceedings, the arbitration agreement does not have to be in writing (Art. 1506(1) i.c.w. Art. 1443 CCP FR *e contratrio*); Balthasar-BALTHASAR/ZIADE, n. 5; BÉGUIN/MENJUCQ, 1053; JARROSSON/PELLERIN, n. 90.

833 Art. 1509 CCP FR.

834 *See.* e.g. Art. 22.2 LCIA Rules; Art. 3 (9) IBA Rules.

835 CALLÉ/DARGENT, Art. 1509 CCP FR n. 7.

of evidence before a state court is contrary to an explicit agreement between the parties, this will serve as grounds for the annulment of the arbitral award if it influences the arbitral award.[836] In most cases, however, the arbitral tribunal will be reluctant to introduce evidence into the arbitral proceedings which was gathered contrary to a party agreement.

2. Evidence According to the CCP FR

a. Prior to the Constitution of the Arbitral Tribunal

As stated in Art. 1449 (2) CCP FR, state courts may either assist in the taking of evidence prior to the constitution of the arbitral tribunal under the conditions set out in Arts. 145 et seqq. CCP FR or, in urgent cases, impose provisional or conservatory measures. Art. 145 CCP FR reads as follows:

> "If, before legal proceedings commence, there is a legitimate reason to preserve or establish evidence upon which the resolution of a dispute may depend, measures relating to the taking of evidence may be ordered, upon the request of any concerned party, by way of a petition to a court (sur requête) or expedited proceedings (référé)."

In contrast to interim measures, no urgency need be proved when starting a proceeding according to Art. 145 CCP FR.[837] Before any production of evidence is ordered, the requesting party must prove that there is a 'legitimate reason' for this measure–that is, that it is useful and will most likely have an influence on the outcome of the proceedings.[838] If this condition is fulfilled, any measure which is 'legally admissible' can be ordered in the two different proceedings as foreseen in Art. 145 CCP FR.[839] The main difference between a petition to a court (*sur requête*) and an expedited proceeding (*référé*) relates to their (non-) adversarial character.[840] The adversarial expedited proceeding is often needed in cases where the opinion of an expert is sought (Arts. 232 et seqq. CCP FR) and the parties are invited to express their views on his or her mission.[841] Meanwhile, proceedings *sur requête*–that is, *ex parte* measures–are non-adversarial and offer a wide range of possible measures, derived from either Arts. 232 et seqq. CCP FR or case law, such as examination

836 Art. 1520 (3) CCP FR; *see* p. 164 *infra*.

837 CALLÉ/DARGENT, Art. 145 CCP FR n. 40.

838 DUPEYRON/VALENTINI, 542; CHAINAIS, n. 21; DEVOT/LAURENT-BELLUE, 19.

839 Paris Court of Cassation, 27 Feb. 2014, 2nd Civil Chamber, 13-10.013.

840 Arts. 484 (expedited proceeding) and 493 (*ex parte* measures) CCP FR; DUPEYRON/VALENTINI, 548.

841 *Ibid.*; CALLÉ/DARGENT, Art. 145 CCP FR n. 78.

of witnesses under oath[842] (Arts. 199 et seqq.), document production[843] by third parties[844] (Art. 11 CCP FR), on-site investigations[845] and expert reports.[846] These *ex parte* measures represent a highly effective tool, especially in order to preserve evidence without the possibility for the defendant to challenge such measures in an adversarial proceeding prior to their execution.[847]

In urgent cases, interim measures may also be sought. Art. 808 CCP FR states the following:

> "In all cases of urgency, the President of the Court of First Instance may order in an expedited proceeding all measures that do not encounter any serious challenge or which the existence of the dispute justifies."

Without going into too much detail, it is important to note that this provision aims primarily to preserve evidence–for example, by protecting goods from the threat of loss or destruction by keeping them in good condition. This will prove helpful not only prior to the establishment of the arbitral tribunal, but also thereafter. It remains to be seen whether the French legislature will consider this fact in a possible future revision of its *lex arbitri*.

b. After the Constitution of the Arbitral Tribunal

Once the arbitral tribunal has been constituted–that is, once the arbitrators have accepted their mandate–the possibilities for the taking of evidence are very limited, in terms of both the target (*see* p. 160 et seq. *infra*) and the scope of evidence.[848] Pursuant to Art. 1469 (1) CCP FR, parties can seek to obtain from third parties only documents which are either notarised or private.[849] If the respective president of the court of first instance considers the evidence request well founded, the third party must deliver the original document, or a copy or extract therefrom.[850] Because the respective state court judge can conduct the proceeding under Art. 1469 CCP FR 'under such con-

842 Under French law, parties can be examined as witnesses (Art. 205 CCP FR).

843 Paris Court of Cassation, 11 Apr. 1995, Commercial Chamber, 92-20985; CALLÉ/DARGENT, Art. 145 CCP FR n. 69.

844 Paris Court of Cassation, 26 May 2011, 2nd Civil Chamber, 10-20048; CALLÉ/DARGENT, Art. 145 CCP FR n. 70.

845 DEVOT/LAURENT-BELLUE, 20.

846 Paris Court of Cassation, 11 Oct. 1995, 2nd Civil Chamber, 92-20496; BÉGUIN/MENJUCQ, n. 1829.

847 Paris Court of Cassation, 19 Mar. 2015, 2nd Civil Chamber, 14-14.389; Art. 493 CCP FR.

848 Art. 1456 (1) CCP FR.

849 Although only documentary evidence can be sought under Art. 1469 CCP FR and the word 'private' is not clearly defined, the range of documents seems to be very broad.

850 Art. 1469 (4) CCP FR.

ditions and guarantees as he or she determines', the presence of the parties is also allowed, at least in theory.[851]

Apart from document production, no other evidence can be sought–neither an examination of witnesses nor any inspection or expert report.[852] In the absence of any visible legislative intent to exclude such types of evidence, one must conclude that this is because the arbitral tribunal is competent to take all 'necessary step concerning evidentiary and procedural matters', even under threat of an *astreinte*. Still, as previously discussed, document production is often connected to witnesses.[853] This is why it would be welcome if Art. 1469 CCP FR were extended to examination of witnesses and other types of evidence.

3. Foreign Types of Evidence

In general, it may be said that the French courts will not execute evidence requests relating to US-style discovery.[854] Prior to constitution of the arbitral tribunal, Art. 1449 CCP FR explicitly states that the taking of evidence must be conducted in compliance with Art. 145 CCP FR. As a result, only measures for the taking of evidence pursuant to French law, as stated in Arts. 145 et seqq. CCP FR, are permissible. The situation is not much different once the arbitral tribunal has been established. Art. 1469 (4) CCP FR states that evidence requests will be granted under the conditions determined by the president of the court of first instance.[855] In practice, this is regularly done according to French law.[856] Although the parties enjoy wide discretion to tailor the taking of evidence within the arbitral proceedings–for instance, by agreeing on foreign measures for the taking of evidence–this does not apply to the proceeding before state courts pursuant to Art. 1469 CCP FR. Since the French legislature has not allowed for evidence requests in the style of US-discovery, document production will therefore be ordered according to French law. What STEINBRÜCK has suggested for German law–that is, that foreign types of evidence be adapted until they are compliant with domestic law–thus seems not possible under French law.[857]

851 Art. 1469 (4) CCP FR.

852 GAILLARD/DE LAPASSE, n. 22; CLAY, *Arbitrage*, 134; RACINE, n. 697; BÉGUIN/MENJUCQ, n. 1948; SERAGLINI/ORTSCHEIDT, n. 338.

853 *See* p. 41 *supra*.

854 DUPEYRON/VALENTINI, 542, 550; JARROSSON, 338; *see also* the reservation of France as regards Art. 23 HEC (*see* the reservations).

855 Art. 1469 (4) CCP FR.

856 DEVOT/LAURENT-BELLUE, 20.

857 *See* p. 141 *supra*.

4. International Judicial Assistance in Taking Evidence

As an alternative, although this is seldom used in practice, the French courts can also assist in the taking of evidence by means of international judicial assistance pursuant to the HEC or the EER.[858] As previously discussed *(see p. 2 et seqq. supra)*, parties are very reluctant to choose this route due to the lengthy and cumbersome process involved, and instead will generally seek court assistance pursuant to Arts. 1449 and 1469 CCP FR.

5. Target of Evidence

Regardless of whether evidence is sought from a party to the arbitration or a third party, possible privileges such as commercial or technical confidentiality, as well as attorney-client privilege, must be respected at all times.[859] Third parties who are parents, direct relatives or a (divorced) spouse of one of the parties may refuse to testify.[860] Regardless of whether he or she is called by a party to the arbitration or a third party, if a witness refuses to testify without legitimate reason, he or she can be charged with a civil fine of up to EUR 10,000.[861]

Prior to constitution of the arbitral tribunal, evidence can be sought from anyone, irrespective of the target of evidence or whether the evidence request has been granted by a petition to court (*sur requête*) or in an expedited proceeding (*référé*). While the target of evidence in an adversarial expedited proceeding can seek to avoid the taking of evidence as a whole, or at least limit its extent, this is logically not possible as regards *ex parte* measures.[862] In this proceeding, the respective measures can be avoided or modified only upon request, once they have already been executed.[863] After the arbitral tribunal has been established, evidence can be sought only from third parties located in France. As regards the parties to the arbitration, the arbitral tribunal will usually order a party to produce evidence under threat of an *astreinte* or, as an alternative, will draw an adverse inference in case of non-compliance with evidence orders. Nonetheless, if the taking of evidence from a third party according to Art. 1469 CCP FR is requested, this takes the

858 JARROSSON, 338. In France, the HEC entered into force in 1974 (*see* the current status).

859 CALLÉ/DARGENT, Art. 145 CCP FR n. 112; DEVOT/LAURENT-BELLUE, 22; as regards examination of witnesses *see* Art. 206 CCP FR.

860 Art. 206 CCP FR.

861 Art. 207 CCP FR.

862 DEVOT/LAURENT-BELLUE, 22; Arts. 484 et seqq. CCP FR (expedited proceeding) and Arts. 493 et seqq. CCP FR (*ex parte* measures).

863 Art. 497 CCP FR.

form of an adversarial expedited proceeding, in which the third party can be forced to produce evidence, where necessary combined with an *astreinte*.[864] A third party may also appeal the decision of the respective state court within 15 days of the date of grant of the evidence request.[865]

E. Competence of the *Juge d'Appui*

1. Scope of Discretion

Strictly speaking, and as previously discussed *(see* p. 152 *supra),* the judge who provides assistance prior to or after the constitution of the arbitral award is not the *juge d'appui* in the sense of Art. 1505 CCP FR (i.e. the president of the Paris Court of First Instance), but rather the respective judge where the evidence is located or the witness is domiciled.[866] In deciding whether court assistance in the taking of evidence should be granted, the respective judge has full discretion, subject only to the requirements as stated in Arts. 1449 and 1469 CCP FR.[867] However, the judge has no scope to assess the evidence taken, which is left completely to the arbitral tribunal.[868]

Prior to constitution of the arbitral tribunal, the respective judge will usually grant the request if there is a legitimate reason to gather the evidence–for example, if it is useful and relevant in the context of the case at hand.[869] If the requesting party already has enough evidence to prove its case or if the request itself is too vague or far reaching, it will most likely be denied.[870] In contrast, if the request is granted, the respective judge is at liberty to modify the requested evidence production pursuant to Arts. 145 et seqq. CCP FR 'as to what is sufficient for the resolution of the dispute by endeavouring to select the simplest and least onerous ones'.[871] In proceedings as stated in Art. 1469 CCP FR after the arbitral tribunal has been constituted, the respective 'judge of evidence' will execute the evidence request as long as it is 'well-founded'. The fact that the respective state court judge can then take the evidence 'under such conditions and guarantees as he or she determines'

---

864 Art. 1469 (3) CCP FR.

865 Art. 1469 (6) CCP FR; *see also* p. 163 et seq. *infra*.

866 In case of Art. 1469 CCP FR, the respective judge is called the 'judge of evidence'.

867 JARROSSON, 337 et seq.; NOUGEIN/DUPEYRÉ, n. 227.

868 Paris Court of Cassation, 10 Jan. 2013, 2nd Civil Chamber, 12-12.375; DEVOT/LAURENT-BELLUE, 24; in respect of the *juge d'appui* in accordance with Art. 1505 CCP FR *see* BÉGUIN/MENJUCQ, n. 1900.

869 DUPEYRON/VALENTINI, 542.

870 Paris Court of Cassation, 18 Feb. 1986, 2nd Civil Chamber, 84-10620.

871 Art. 147 CCP FR.

indicates that the judge is not strictly bound by the evidence request, but can modify it at his or her discretion. Lastly, if it is necessary to put pressure on the third party, an *astreinte* will be attached to the order to produce specific documentary evidence.

2. Principle of Subsidiarity

Contrary to other *leges arbitri*, the CCP FR does not mention whether it is possible to have recourse to state courts if the arbitral tribunal could take the evidence itself.[872] This makes perfect sense, since Art. 1469 CCP FR addresses only evidence held by third parties, over which the arbitral tribunal has no *imperium*.[873] Nevertheless, one might ask–as a minimum requirement–whether state courts should not examine whether the arbitral tribunal has at least tried to make third parties comply with an evidence request on a voluntary basis.[874] However, it appears that this view is supported neither by legal doctrine nor by French case law.

3. Examination of the Arbitration Agreement

The question of whether the judge of evidence can express a view on the validity of the arbitration agreement has not yet been discussed, either in French legal doctrine or in case law. As regards competence-competence, the CCP FR addresses the examination of the arbitration agreement both prior to and after the constitution of the arbitral tribunal. Art. 1448 CCP FR states:

> "When a dispute subject to an arbitration agreement is brought before a court, such court shall decline jurisdiction, except if an arbitral tribunal has not yet been seized of the dispute and if the arbitration agreement is manifestly void or manifestly not applicable."

Consequently, in a proceeding under Art. 1449 CCP FR, the respective judge will examine whether the arbitration agreement is manifestly void or inapplicable.[875] This is therefore a very restricted and limited prima facie examina-

872 In contrast, *see* e.g. § 1050 (1) CCP DE: The arbitral tribunal or a party with the approval of the arbitral tribunal may request from a court assistance in taking evidence or performance of other judicial acts *which the arbitral tribunal is not empowered to carry out* (emphasis added).

873 SERAGLINI/ORTSCHEIDT, n. 338; AUDIT/D'AVOUT, n. 1403; BÉGUIN/MENJUCQ, n. 1948; CLAY, *Arbitrage*, 134; GAILLARD/DE LAPASSE, n. 14; JARROSSON, 336.

874 *See also* the suggestion for Swiss domestic arbitration in DIKE-BRUNNER/STEININGER, Art. 375 CCP CH n. 7.

875 JARROSSON, 332; BÉGUIN/MENJUCQ, n. 1817.

tion.[876] However, in most cases–especially in institutional arbitral proceedings–if an arbitration agreement is invalid, this will be discussed long before an evidence request is brought before state courts.[877] The situation is different once the arbitral tribunal has been established. Art. 1455 CCP FR states:

> "If an arbitration agreement is manifestly void or manifestly not applicable, the judge acting in support of the arbitration shall declare that no appointment need be made."

Because this provision clearly addresses only the *juge d'appui* (Art. 1505 CCP FR), and not the judge of evidence in accordance with Art. 1469 CCP FR, the arbitration agreement cannot be examined under this provision. Rather, if a party wants to challenge the competence of the arbitral tribunal after the arbitral tribunal has been constituted, it can do so by challenging the arbitral award, where the validity of the arbitration agreement can be examined extensively.[878] Finally, the examination of the arbitration agreement during court assistance in the taking of evidence must be distinguished from its examination in the context of recognition and enforcement of an arbitral award under the NYC.[879]

F. Appellate Remedies

A decision on court assistance in the taking of evidence issued prior to constitution of the arbitral tribunal–whether issued against a future party to the arbitration or a third party–can be challenged before the respective court of appeal within 15 days.[880] The respective state court will render its decision in the form of a '*décision provisoire*'–that is, an interim order.[881] As previously discussed (*see* p. 157 *supra*), unlike where evidence is ordered in an expedited proceeding, *ex parte* measures can be challenged only if they have been denied.[882] However, if they have already been executed, they can still be avoid-

876 *Ibid.*; According to the Paris Court of Cassation, the existence of a valid arbitration agreement already excludes the possibility that it is manifestly void or not applicable (FOUCHARD, note on Paris Court of Cassation, 1 Dec. 1999, 1st Civil Chamber, in: Rev. Arb. 2000, 96 et seqq.).

877 JARROSSON, 332.

878 Art. 1520 (1) CCP FR; BÉGUIN/MENJUCQ, n. 1818; Paris Court of Cassation, 6 Oct. 2010, 1st Civil Chamber, 08-20563.

879 Arts. III (3) and V (1) (a) NYC.

880 Art. 490 (3) CCP FR (expedited proceeding) and Art. 496 CCP FR (*ex parte* measures).

881 Arts. 484 CCP FR (expedited proceeding) and 493 CCP FR (*ex parte* measures).

882 Art. 496 CCP FR.

ed or modified upon the request of either party.[883] If an evidence request is presented during the arbitral proceedings, the state court's decision can be appealed before the respective court of appeal within 15 days of service of the decision.[884] As this decision is analogous to a decision issued in an expedited proceeding, it can be challenged whether it has been granted or denied.[885]

The taking of evidence according to Arts. 1449 and 1469 CCP FR may be distinguished from the assessment of evidence by the arbitral tribunal. Thus, if a party wants to challenge the taking of evidence due to a violation of the procedural rules applicable to the arbitral proceedings, this can be done only by challenging the arbitral award on the grounds that due process has been violated or the arbitral tribunal has not complied with its mandate.[886] As an example–albeit purely theoretical–consider the situation where a state court orders a third party to testify even though witness examination has been explicitly excluded by the parties.[887] If this testimony has a significant influence on the arbitral award, the arbitral award may be challenged before the respective court of appeal within one month of the date on which the arbitral award is rendered.[888]

G. Summary

From an analysis of the French *lex arbitri*, it is clear that this not only affords the parties broad discretion in tailoring the arbitral proceedings, but also provides for assistance in the taking of evidence both prior to and after the constitution of the arbitral tribunal. First, instead of requiring the fulfilment of various conditions, such as the applicable law, the seat of arbitration or the nationality of the parties, court assistance in the taking of evidence will be granted as long as international trade interests are at stake.[889] This simplification, which is unique in international arbitration, is highly welcome–even more so since in such cases evidence is often located in several different countries. In these situations, it is unnecessarily cumbersome if the availability of state court assistance hinges on whether the international arbitral

883 Art. 497 CCP FR.

884 Art. 1469 (6) CCP FR.

885 Art. 1469 (3) i.c.w. Arts. 484 et seqq. CCP FR; CLAY, Art. 1469 CCP FR, 105.

886 Arts. 1520 (3) and (4) CCP FR.

887 *See also Société Filali Film Alimentaire SARL v. Société Bielloni Convertin Spa*, Paris Court of Appeal, 4 Nov. 2014, in: Rev. Arb. 2014, 1037.

888 *Ibid.*; Art. 1523 CCP FR.

889 *See* p. 154 *supra*.

tribunal has its seat in the respective country or whether a certain law is applicable to the matter in dispute.[890]

Second, and unsurprisingly, the arbitral tribunal's consent must be obtained before court assistance in the taking of evidence can be sought. Prior to constitution of the arbitral tribunal, court assistance can also be requested *ex parte*. Unlike under other *leges arbitri*, the arbitral tribunal cannot resort to state courts on its own initiative. Since the arbitral tribunal is already competent to conduct the taking of evidence and even to impose *astreintes* as it sees fit, this should also apply to its competence to seek court assistance by itself as a 'necessary step' concerning evidentiary matters.[891] Moreover, the parties are at liberty to exclude court assistance in the taking of evidence altogether or in relation to specific forms of evidence.

Third, as regards the scope and target of evidence, the situation differs depending on whether the arbitral tribunal has been constituted. Prior to constitution of the arbitral tribunal, a wide range of evidentiary measures can be imposed both on third parties and on the future parties to the arbitration. Because the types of evidence must accord with Art. 145 CCP FR, no foreign types of evidence may be sought. Once the arbitral tribunal has been constituted, evidence can be taken from third parties only and the scope of evidence is limited to document production according to French law. Third parties can even be forced to produce such evidence under threat of an *astreinte*. Since document production is often related to the examination of witnesses, Art. 1469 CCP FR should be extended to encompass witness examination and other types of evidence. Moreover, regardless of whether court assistance in the taking of evidence is sought prior to or after the constitution of the arbitral tribunal, it would be desirable and in the interests of international arbitration if state courts could take evidence according to foreign law.[892]

Fourth, both prior to and after the constitution of the arbitral tribunal, the respective state court judge has broad discretion in deciding whether to grant or deny court assistance, and in deciding how evidence will be taken. As regards the principle of subsidiarity, the CCP FR makes no mention of whether the arbitral tribunal can take the evidence itself and if and when state courts come into play in this regard. This may be explained in part because Art. 1469 CCP FR refers only to third parties as targets of evidence, from whom the arbitral tribunal is *per se* unable to take evidence because of its lack of *imperium*. Furthermore, it remains doubtful whether the court must ex-

890 STEINBRÜCK, 32.

891 Art. 1467 (1) CCP FR.

892 *See* e.g. the proposed Art. 184 (3) PILA CH.

amine whether the arbitral tribunal tried to take the evidence from a third party on a voluntary basis. Regarding the examination of the arbitration agreement, once again, the situation differs depending on whether the arbitral tribunal has been constituted. Prior to constitution of the arbitral tribunal, examination is possible on a prima facie level only. Thereafter, the judge of evidence, pursuant to Art. 1469 CCP FR, is no longer competent to examine the arbitration agreement; this can be done only post-arbitration by challenging the arbitral award and therefore the arbitration agreement.

Finally, the decision of state courts to assist in the taking of evidence may be challenged both prior to and after constitution of the arbitral tribunal. If evidence is taken before a state court contrary to an explicit agreement between the parties (e.g. which provides for documentary evidence only), the arbitral award can be challenged if this had an influence on the arbitral award.

By and large, the French *lex arbitri* takes a very liberal approach as regards court assistance in the taking of evidence. In this regard, its application to international arbitration is highly beneficial and parties should not be too hesitant to initiate an evidence request if relevant evidence is located in France. On the one hand, this applies to situations prior to constitution of the arbitral tribunal where the target of evidence may be caught by surprise through an *ex parte* proceeding. On the other hand, it might become necessary during the arbitral proceedings, even though only documents can be obtained from third parties.

§ 4 England

A. Introduction

England in general, and London specifically, are among the most popular forums for international arbitration.[893] This is confirmed by the consistently high caseload of the LCIA and the fact that the vast majority of parties to LCIA arbitration are not English residents.[894] The English *lex arbitri* is substantially codified by the Arbitration Act of 1996, which provides a detailed legal framework for both domestic and international arbitration.[895] Case law also plays a vital role in further interpreting and substantiating the English *lex arbitri*.[896] The EAA 1996 came into force in 1997 and generally applies where the seat of arbitration is in England and Wales or Northern Ireland, irrespective of

893 Balthasar-ILLMER, n. 1; ANDREWS/LANDBRECHT, n. 1; BORN, *Int. Comm. Arb.*, 148.

894 LCIA Report (2018), 8 et seq.

895 RAWDING et al., n. 18-3.

896 EAA 1996 Report (1996), n. 9.

the chosen substantive law.[897] As set out below (*see* p. 196 *infra*), it applies to evidentiary and other procedural matters even if the seat of arbitration is outside the English territory or has not been determined.[898]

Although it is not based on the UNCITRAL ML and is much broader in its application, the structure and language of the EAA 1996 are clearly and intentionally inspired by the UNCITRAL ML.[899] For instance, like Art. 5 UNCITRAL ML, S. 1 (c) EAA 1996 states that no court should intervene unless there is an explicit legal basis to do so.[900] Although more broadly drafted than Art. 5 UNCITRAL ML, the EAA 1996 aims to limit state court intervention.[901] In this way, the parties have plenty of space to conduct the arbitral proceedings at their discretion, subject only to the mandatory provisions as listed in schedule 1 of the EAA 1996 and the general duty to 'do all things necessary for the proper and expeditious conduct of the arbitral proceedings'.[902] Still, once the assistance of a state court is sought pursuant to the EAA 1996, that court has wide discretion in deciding whether and to what extent such assistance should be granted or denied.

B. Legal Bases

Under the EAA 1996, court assistance in the taking of evidence can be sought either by securing the attendance of witnesses (S. 43 EAA 1996) or by exercising other powers in support of arbitral proceedings (S. 44 EAA 1996). S. 43 EAA 1996 reads as follows:

> "(1) A party to arbitral proceedings may use the same court procedures as are available in relation to legal proceedings to secure the attendance before the tribunal of a witness in order to give oral testimony or to produce documents or other material evidence.
>
> (2) This may only be done with the permission of the tribunal or the agreement of the other parties.

897 Ss. 2 (1) and 3 EAA 1996; MERKIN/FLANNERY, 15. For the sake of brevity, the following will only refer to the *English* Arbitration Act, well aware that it applies to Wales and Northern Ireland too.

898 S. 2 (3) EAA 1996.

899 EAA 1996 Report (1996), n. 1, 4; ANDREWS, preface (viii); SHEPPARD, Introduction n. 4; ANDREWS/LANDBRECHT, n. 40, 161; STEINBRÜCK, 104.

900 This provision concerns only the first part of the EAA 1996 and, for instance, does not apply to consumer arbitration agreements as set out in the second part (*see* Ss. 89 et seqq. EAA 1996).

901 Instead of 'shall' as in Art. 5 UNCITRAL ML, the EAA 1996 uses 'should'; EAA Report (1996), n. 19 et seqq.; MERKIN/FLANNERY, 10.

902 Ss. 4 and 40 EAA 1996; ANDREWS, n. 1.11; DEY et al., n. 511.

(3) The court procedures may only be used if–

(a) the witness is in the United Kingdom, and

(b) the arbitral proceedings are being conducted in England and Wales or, as the case may be, Northern Ireland.

(4) A person shall not be compelled by virtue of this section to produce any document or other material evidence which he could not be compelled to produce in legal proceedings."

What is more, S. 44 EAA 1996 equips the respective state court with a broad range of possible assistance measures for the taking of evidence:

"(1) Unless otherwise agreed by the parties, the court has for the purposes of and in relation to arbitral proceedings the same power of making orders about the matters listed below as it has for the purposes of and in relation to legal proceedings.

(2) Those matters are:

(a) the taking of the evidence of witnesses;

(b) the preservation of evidence;

(c) making orders relating to property which is the subject of the proceedings or as to which any question arises in the proceedings:

(i) for the inspection, photographing, preservation, custody or detention of the property, or

(ii) ordering that samples be taken from, or any observation be made of or experiment conducted upon, the property;

and for that purpose authorising any person to enter any premises in the possession or control of a party to the arbitration;

(d) the sale of any goods the subject of the proceedings;

(e) the granting of an interim injunction or the appointment of a receiver.

(3) If the case is one of urgency, the court may, on the application of a party or proposed party to the arbitral proceedings, make such orders as it thinks necessary for the purpose of preserving evidence or assets.

(4) If the case is not one of urgency, only on the application of a party to the arbitral proceedings (upon notice to the other parties and to the tribunal) made with the permission of the tribunal or the agreement in writing of the other parties.

(5) In any case the court shall act only if or to the extent that the arbitral tribunal, and any arbitral or other institution or person vested by the parties with power in that regard, has no power or is unable for the time being to act effectively.

(6) If the court so orders, an order made by it under this section shall cease to have effect in whole or in part on the order of the tribunal or of any such arbitral or other institution or person having power to act in relation to the subject-matter of the order.
(7) The leave of the court is required for any appeal from a decision of the court under this section."

In both cases, the competent court is usually[903] the Commercial Court or the Circuit Commercial Court, which is part of the Business and Commercial Courts of England and Wales and which forms part of the High Court in London (EWHC).[904] As an exception to the rule that the EAA 1996 applies only if the seat of arbitration is in England and Wales or Northern Ireland, Ss. 43 and 44 EAA 1996 are available even if the seat of arbitration is outside the English territory or has not yet been determined.[905] In this regard, the EAA 1996 differs from the rather narrow scope of application as foreseen in the UNCITRAL ML.[906] Although this approach is not enshrined in many *leges arbitri*, the English legislature considers court assistance in the taking of evidence to support foreign arbitrations as a natural necessity.[907] As a consequence, the HEC and the EER are in most cases superfluous in arbitral proceedings.[908]

C. Competence to Seek Court Assistance

1. Primacy of the Arbitral Tribunal

Court assistance in the taking of evidence under the EAA 1996 can be sought either autonomously by the parties if they both agree–in contrast to the usual stance in international arbitration; or, as under most other *leges arbitri* and the UNCITRAL ML, with the approval of the arbitral tribunal.[909] In both cases, the goal is to respect party autonomy as set out in the arbitral agreement and the position of the arbitral tribunal in charge of the arbitration.[910] How-

903 It should be noted that in some cases, some applications must be started in the Commercial Court (*see* e.g. Rules 58.1 (2) (k) and 62.1 (3) CPR 1998; CPR 1998 Practice Direction 62.3, para. 2.3.

904 S. 105 (1) EAA 1996; S. 2 High Court and County Courts Order 1996; DEY et al., n. 551.

905 S. 2 (3) EAA 1996.

906 Art. 1 (2) UNCITRAL ML.

907 EAA Report (1996), n. 25; SHEPPARD, S. 2 EAA 1996 n. 4.

908 SHEPPARD, S. 43 EAA 1996 n. 5.

909 Ss. 43 (2) and 44 (4) EAA 1996; *see also* e.g. Art. 27 UNCITRAL ML; Art. 184 (2) PILA CH; § 1050 (1) CCP DE.

910 EAA Report (1996), n. 213.

ever, the situation is different in urgent cases–mostly prior to constitution of the arbitral tribunal–where a party may seek remedy from the court unilaterally in order to preserve evidence or assets.[911] What is more, pursuant to S. 33 EAA 1996, the arbitral tribunal must act fairly and impartially by giving each party the possibility to present its case. The arbitral tribunal is not obliged to agree to all evidence requests initiated by one of the parties to the arbitration; but likewise, it cannot unreasonably refuse an evidence request according to Ss. 43 and 44 EAA 1996 if there are reasonable grounds to grant it.[912]

It remains unclear whether the arbitral tribunal itself can seek court assistance in the taking of evidence. Neither S. 43 nor S. 44 EAA 1996 empowers the arbitral tribunal to do so explicitly. However, in the absence of any contrary agreement between the parties, the arbitral tribunal is empowered by law to decide 'whether and to what extent the tribunal should itself take the initiative in ascertaining the facts and the law'.[913] It is noteworthy and surprising that such an inquisitorial approach, which is generally foreign to common law, has found its way into the EAA 1996.[914] In light of this provision and the overall intention of the EAA 1996, the arbitral tribunal itself should also be able to seek court assistance in the taking of evidence on its own initiative, pursuant to Ss. 43 and 44 EAA 1996.[915] That said, as English case law has pointed out, arbitrators should not exceed their powers by, for example, directly and unilaterally contacting witnesses.[916] To avoid such a situation, the parties are at liberty to limit the vast powers of the arbitral tribunal in this regard.[917]

2. Exclusion of Court Assistance in Taking Evidence

Since arbitration is *per se* a sphere in which the parties have broad discretion in tailoring the arbitral proceedings, they may wish to exclude court assistance in the taking of evidence altogether. However, under English law, this is only partially possible. Since S. 43 EAA 1996 is a mandatory rule, its exclusion is void.[918] In contrast, assistance according to S. 44 EAA 1996, as a

911 S. 44 (3) EAA 1996; MERKIN/FLANNERY, 179.

912 HARRIS et al., S. 43 EAA 1996 n. 43C.

913 S. 34 (2) (g) EAA 1996.

914 MERKIN/FLANNERY, 141; HARRIS et al., S. 34 EAA 1996 n. 34K.

915 TOMS, 17.

916 *Norbrook Laboratories Ltd v. Tank* [2006] EWHC 1055 (Comm.).

917 S. 34 (1) EAA 1996: It shall be for the tribunal to decide all procedural and evidential matters, subject to the right of the parties to agree any matter.

918 S. 4 (1) i.c.w. Schedule 1 EAA 1996; SHEPPARD, S. 43 EAA 1996 n. 1; HARRIS et al., S. 43 EAA 1996 n. 43A.

non-mandatory provision, may be excluded.[919] To make things clear, the parties would be well advised to include an express statement on the exclusion of assistance according to S. 44 EAA 1996. In this regard, the EWHC has specified that in order to exclude S. 44 EAA 1996, neither a specific form of words nor a 'very clear express' agreement is necessary.[920] Rather, the court considered that a general clause excluding state court legal proceedings until the dispute is heard and determined by arbitrators will suffice to exclude S. 44 EAA 1996.[921] Finally, the question of a complete loss of minimum legal protection does not arise under the EAA 1996, since the parties cannot completely waive the right to court assistance in the taking of evidence under S. 43 EAA 1996.

D. Spectrum of Evidence and its Target

1. Evidence According to a Party Agreement

In the same way that parties can exclude court assistance in the taking of evidence under S. 44 EAA 1996 as a whole, certain types of evidence may also be excluded. This is usually done by way of an explicit limitation of discovery/disclosure in the arbitration agreement or by making reference to institutional arbitration rules or the IBA Rules.[922] State courts must respect this choice by denying any evidence request which is contrary to an agreement between the parties. However, the chances that a state court will take evidence in violation of such an agreement are very low. This is because the arbitral tribunal is bound by any agreement between the parties in relation to evidentiary issues, and the parties themselves will most likely not make an evidence request which is inconsistent with their own agreement.[923] Nevertheless, if evidence is taken contrary to an explicit agreement between the parties, this will serve as grounds to challenge an award based on a 'failure by the tribunal to conduct the proceedings in accordance with the procedure agreed by the parties'.[924] This may be the case, for instance, if the tribunal itself initiates court assistance to examine a witness while the parties have agreed on documentary evidence only. If this witness examination has a substantial influence on the arbitral award, there is a good chance that a subsequent challenge to the arbitral award based on S. 68 (2) (c) EAA 1996 will succeed.

919 S. 4 (2) i.c.w. Schedule 1 EAA 1996 *e contrario*; SUTTON et al., n. 7-192.

920 *B v. S* [2011] EWHC 691 (Comm.), n. 8, 9, 78-90.

921 *Ibid.*, n. 2.

922 *See* e.g. Art. 22.2 LCIA Rules; Art. 3 (9) IBA Rules.

923 S. 34 (1) EAA 1996.

924 S. 68 (2) (c) EAA 1996; *see* p. 180 et seqq. *infra*.

2. Evidence According to the EAA 1996

a. In General

Ss. 43 and 44 EAA 1996 offer a wide range of measures for assistance in the taking of evidence. While S. 43 EAA 1996 concerns securing the attendance of a witness who is located in England, S. 44 EAA 1996 has a much broader focus. Because of the general rule that no state court should intervene except as provided by the EAA 1996, the list in S. 44 is exhaustive.[925]

b. Securing the Attendance of Witnesses

S. 43 EAA 1996 is inspired by Art. 27 UNCITRAL ML and serves to bring witnesses before the arbitral tribunal in order to give testimony or produce documents or other material evidence. This provision therefore has a broad scope of application which goes beyond the mere examination of witnesses. As a first condition, the witness must be in England (as opposed to S. 44 (2) (a) EAA 1996) and, in the absence of any clear indication, he or she must probably be an English resident rather than simply be located in England at the time of service of the witness summons.[926]

The second condition requires that arbitral proceedings be conducted on the English territory. Because S. 43 EAA 1996 is explicitly excluded as a whole from the general requirement that the seat of arbitration be within England (S. 2 (3) EAA 1996), arbitral proceedings can be held temporarily in England to make use of the powers of S. 43 EAA 1996.[927] An arbitral tribunal with its seat in France could therefore request the English courts to examine a certain witness located in England, if the arbitral tribunal itself or the French courts cannot act effectively.[928] This second condition makes it quite clear that S. 43 EAA 1996 is available only once the arbitral tribunal has been constituted.[929] If both conditions are met, the court procedures of the CPR 1998 may be used in the arbitral proceedings.[930] As a consequence, a witness will be summoned according to Pt. 34 CPR 1998 and the respective practice directions will apply.[931]

925 S. 1 (c) EAA 1996; MERKIN/FLANNERY, 180.

926 S. 43 (3) (a) EAA 1996; SHEPPARD, S. 43 EAA 1996 n. 5.

927 SHEPPARD, S. 43 EAA 1996 n. 5; MERKIN/FLANNERY, 170; SUTTON et al., n. 7-212; O'CALLAGHAN/FINNIS, n. 20-112.

928 Ss. 44 (2) (a) and (5) EAA 1996.

929 This stands in sharp contrast to cases of urgency pursuant to S. 44 (3) EAA 1996 according to which state courts can make orders for the preservation of evidence or assets.

930 S. 43 (1) EAA 1996.

931 *See* CPR 1998 Practice Direction 34A (depositions and court attendance by witnesses; paras. 1.1-3.4) and 62 (arbitration; paras. 7.1-7.3).

Although this is mentioned under S. 43 (1) EAA 1996, the term 'other material evidence' remains unclear. In contrast, the English courts have ruled on several occasions on the (non-) availability of disclosure from third parties under S. 43 EAA 1996. In *BNP Paribas v. Deloitte & Touche LLP*, the High Court held that S. 43 EAA 1996 gives no right to order disclosure from third parties.[932] Consequently, instead of applying for the production of classes of documents as in disclosure proceedings under Rule 31.17 CPR 1998, an application pursuant to S. 43 EAA 1996 must specifically identify the party to the arbitration agreement against which the remedy is sought and a description of the documents in question.[933] Regarding disclosure, it is up to the arbitral tribunal–and not the assisting state court–to decide whether and to what extent to grant disclosure.[934]

c. Court Powers Exercisable in Support of Arbitral Proceedings

S. 44 EAA 1996 aims to redefine the relationship between arbitral tribunals and state courts by providing the state courts with several powers in case the arbitral tribunal cannot act, either at all or effectively.[935] Also, where the conditions of S. 43 EAA 1996 are not met, an application pursuant to S. 44 (2) (a) EAA 1996 may be made.[936] As can be seen in S. 44 EAA 1996, the state courts have considerable scope to assist in the taking of evidence. Consequently, under the respective conditions, the English courts may assist in relation to the taking of evidence regarding witnesses[937] (lit. a), preservation of evidence[938] (lit. b), measures concerning property[939] (lit. c), the

932 *BNP Paribas v. Deloitte & Touche LLP* [2003] EWHC 2874 (Comm.), n. 12; O'CALLAGHAN/FINNIS, n. 20-115.

933 *Stuart Peter and Anor v. Skylet Andrew* [2009] EWHC 1511 (QB), n. 3; *Tajik Aluminium Plant v. Hydro Aluminium AS & Ors* [2006] EWCA 1218 (Civ.), 24 et seqq.; *BNP Paribas v. Deloitte & Touche LLP* [2004] EWHC 2874 (Comm.), n. 14; *see also Assimina Maritime Ltd. v. Pakistan Shipping Corp* [2004] EWHC 3005 (Comm.), n. 16; *South Tyneside Borough Council v. Wickes Building Supplies* [2004] EWHC 2428 (Comm.), n. 23 (i).

934 S. 34 (2) (d) EAA 1996: '...whether any and if so which documents or classes of documents should be disclosed between and produced by the parties and at what stage'. The former rule of S. 12 (6) (b) EAA 1950 contained the state court's power to order disclosure, which has been handed over to the arbitral tribunal under the EAA 1996 (*Tajik Aluminium Plant v. Hydro Aluminium AS & Ors* [2006] EWCA 1218 (Civ.), n. 26; SUTTON et al., n. 7-213).

935 EAA Report (1996), n. 214.

936 SUTTON et al., n. 7-198. This applies to cases where either witnesses are located and/or the arbitration is conducted outside of England (S. 43 (3) EAA 1996).

937 MERKIN/FLANNERY, 180 et seqq.; SUTTON et al., n. 7-198; SHEPPARD, S. 44 EAA 1996 n. 3.

938 MERKIN/FLANNERY, 182 et seq.; SUTTON et al., n. 7-199; SHEPPARD, S. 44 EAA 1996 n. 4.

939 MERKIN/FLANNERY, 183; SUTTON et al., n. 7-200; SHEPPARD, S. 44 EAA 1996 n. 5.

sale of goods[940] (lit. d) and interim injunctions[941] (lit. e). As with S. 43 EAA 1996, third parties will not be ordered to disclose documents.[942] For instance, an English court will most likely grant a request from an arbitral tribunal with its seat in Switzerland to inspect a certain property in England which belongs to a party if the arbitral tribunal and the Swiss courts are unable to act effectively.[943]

In English case law, there have been some discussions on the scope of the assistance provided by state courts in urgent cases.[944] S. 44 (3) EAA 1996 authorises a state court to 'make such orders as it thinks necessary for the purpose of preserving evidence or assets'. In *Cetelem v. Roust* the EWCA had to decide whether S. 44 (3) EAA 1996 encompasses the powers as stated in Ss. 44 (1) and (2) EAA 1996. It held that S. 44 (3) EAA 1996 is not restricted to orders for the preservation of evidence or assets; the court can make any order as provided in subsection (2), as long as it is 'necessary for the purpose of preserving evidence or assets'.[945] Furthermore, it applied a rather broad interpretation of S. 44 (3) EAA 1996, defining 'assets' not only as tangible assets, but also as choses in action, including contractual rights.[946]

3. Foreign Types of Evidence

Both Ss. 43 and 44 EAA 1996 equip state courts assisting in arbitration with the same powers as are available in state court proceedings.[947] This seems to indicate that the English courts will assist in the taking of evidence only pur-

940 MERKIN/FLANNERY, 183; SUTTON et al., n. 7-201.

941 *Ibid.*, n. 7-202; MERKIN/FLANNERY, 183 et seqq.; SHEPPARD, S. 44 EAA 1996 n. 7; O'CALLAGHAN/FINNIS, n. 20-95 et seqq.

942 *See* p. 173 *supra.*

943 S. 2 (3) EAA 1996 i.c.w. Ss. 44 (2) (a) and (5) EAA 1996; HARRIS, S. 2 EAA 1996 n. 2E.

944 MERKIN/FLANNERY, 179 et seq.; O'CALLAGHAN/FINNIS, n. 20-61 et seqq. Regarding the term 'urgency', *see Travelers Insurance Co Ltd v. Countrywide Surveyors Ltd* [2010] EWHC 2455 (TCC), n. 4: 'Section 44 (3) of the 1996 Act was intended to be invoked in exceptional circumstances where, for example, the critical evidence was about to be lost forever or where there was a risk that it would be destroyed or otherwise tampered with, such as to make it of no probative value.'; *Starlight Shipping Co v. Tai Ping Insurance Co Ltd.* [2007] EWHC 1893 (Comm.), n. 22: 'Urgency, in this context must have reference to the question whether or not arbitrators could reach any decision on the point in any relevant timescale.'

945 *Cetelem SA v. Roust Holding Ltd* [2005] EWCA 618 (Civ.), n. 49.

946 *Ibid.*, n. 57; *see also AB v. CD* [2014] EWHC 1 (QB), n. 19 et seq.; *Euroil Ltd v. Cameroon Offshore Petroleum Sarl* [2014] EWHC 12 (Comm.), n. 12 et seq.; HARRIS et al., S. 44 EAA 1996 n. 44H; SHEPPARD, S. 44 EAA 1996 n. 7; SUTTON et al., S. 44 EAA 1996 n. 7-194; O'CALLAGHAN/FINNIS, n. 20-62.

947 S. 43 (1) and S. 44 (1) EAA 1996.

suant to the CPR 1998.[948] Assisting state courts are therefore not bound by any agreement between the parties concerning either a foreign law applicable to the substance of the dispute or foreign procedural rules governing the arbitral proceedings when assisting in the taking of evidence. As a consequence, the method as proposed by Steinbrück under German law–that is, to adapt foreign types of evidence until they are compliant with domestic law–seems questionable under English law.[949] In *Commerce & Industry Insurance Co. (Canada) v. Lloyd's Underwriters*, the EWHC denied a request to examine a witness according to US-style discovery.[950] Unsurprisingly, this request was considered 'inappropriate' in the sense of S. 2 (3) EAA 1996.[951] It is therefore possible that English courts may allow evidence requests according to a foreign law and adapt them to comply with English law, as long as they do not substantially differ from proceedings under the CPR 1998.

4. International Judicial Assistance in Taking Evidence

In common with the approach taken under German and French law, Ss. 43 and 44 EAA 1996 overcome the difficulties presented by the HEC and EER–that is, the lengthy and cumbersome process involved–by providing direct assistance to international arbitral tribunals.[952] The parties to arbitration thus will most likely not initiate a request by means of the HEC or EER, but directly approach an English court based on Ss. 43 and 44 EAA 1996.[953] Theoretically, it seems possible that an arbitral tribunal may also approach an English court in order to request court assistance via another foreign state court. However, due to the lengthy process that this would involve, the arbitral tribunal is more likely to try to approach that foreign court directly.

5. Target of Evidence

Regarding the target of evidence, a clear distinction must be drawn between Ss. 43 and 44 EAA 1996. While the former serves to force third parties to produce evidence, the latter is available only against the parties to the arbitration. To secure the attendance of witnesses according to S. 43 EAA 1996, third parties can be ordered, by means of a witness summons, to give testimony or

948 TOMS, 15.

949 *See* p. 141 et seq. *supra*.

950 *Commerce and Industry Co, Canada v. Certain Underwriters of Lloyds of London* [2002] EWHC 2 All ER, 211.

951 *Ibid.*

952 SHEPPARD, S. 43 EAA 1996 n. 5.

953 In Great Britain and Northern Ireland, the HEC entered into force in 1976 (*see* the current status).

produce evidence for an ongoing arbitration. However, one must bear in mind that a third party who receives a witness summons can object if privilege applies or if the requested documents are not relevant to the proceedings. S. 43 (4) EAA 1996 is quite clear on this point:

> "A person shall not be compelled by virtue of this section to produce any document or other material evidence which he could not be compelled to produce in legal proceedings."

For instance, nobody can be forced to reveal documents which are protected by attorney-client privilege.[954] To set aside a witness summons, the potential witness must make an application to the court that issued it (in arbitration, usually the EWHC).[955] In contrast, a witness who fails to comply with a witness summons without sufficient reason risks being in contempt of court, which may incur a fine or even imprisonment.[956] Finally, as previously mentioned *(see* p. 173 *supra),* state courts cannot order disclosure of documents from a third-party witness under S. 43 EAA 1996.

On the other hand, there is some debate as to whether S. 44 EAA 1996 can be used against third parties. The legislative materials of the EAA 1996 state merely that S. 44 EAA 1996 may have effect on third parties without saying that they are a direct target.[957] In *Cruz City 1 Mauritius Holding v. Unitech Ltd.* it was held that because of the wording in S. 44 EAA 1996, which states 'for the purposes of and in relation to arbitral proceedings', S. 44 EAA 1996 applies only between the parties to the arbitration.[958] Moreover, because this provision applies even if the seat of arbitration is outside the English territory, the respective judge will consider it unlikely that a state court could make orders against third parties domiciled anywhere in the world.[959] This view is arguably correct, even though it would be desirable if S. 44 EAA 1996 had the same broad scope of application in proceedings as S. 43 EAA 1996.

954 Rules 31.3 (1) (b) and 31.19 CPR 1998; SUTTON et al., n. 7-213; SHEPPARD, S. 43 EAA 1996 n. 6; HARRIS et al., S. 43 EAA 1996 n. 43G; BURROWS, n. 22.61.

955 Rule 34.3 (4) CPR 1998; CPR 1998 Practice Direction 34A, para. 2.2.

956 Rule 34.10 CPR 1998; Pt. 81 CPR 1998; CPR 1998 Practice Direction 34A, para. 4.11; O'CALLAGHAN/FINNIS, n. 20-114; SUTTON et al., n. 7-214; *see also* the official form of a witness summons.

957 EAA Report (1996), n. 214.

958 *Cruz City 1 Mauritius Holding v. Unitech Ltd. & Ors* [2014] EWHC 3704 (Comm.), n. 48; confirmed in *DTEK Trading S.A. v. Morozov & Anor* [2017] EWHC 94 (Comm.); for a summary of the previous contrary case law *see PJSC Vseukrainskyi Aktsionernyi Bank v. Sergey Maksimov & Ors* [2013] EWHC 3203 (Comm.), n. 72 et seqq.

959 *Cruz City 1 Mauritius Holding v. Unitech Ltd. & Ors* [2014] EWHC 3704 (Comm.), n. 49.

E. Competence of the *Juge d'Appui*

1. Scope of Discretion

Court assistance in the taking of evidence according to the English *lex arbitri* must always be read in combination with S. 2 (3) EAA 1996 (last para.):

> "The court may refuse to exercise any such power if, in the opinion of the court, the fact that the seat of the arbitration is outside England and Wales or Northern Ireland, or that when designated or determined the seat is likely to be outside England and Wales or Northern Ireland, makes it inappropriate to do so."

State courts therefore have wide discretion in deciding whether to grant or deny assistance in the taking of evidence and the boundary of this provision must be determined by case law. The aim of S. 2 (3) EAA 1996 is to avoid possible conflicts with another jurisdiction.[960] In case of a conflict, the respective state court is therefore entitled to deny its assistance. An example is *Commerce & Industry Insurance Co. (Canada) v. Lloyd's Underwriters*.[961] In arbitral proceedings conducted in New York, a claimant requested an *ex parte* order for two witnesses in England to attend for examination under US law, to make a deposition in a discovery proceeding. Although the court argued that it had jurisdiction based on S. 2 (3) i.c.w. S. 44 (2) (a) EAA 1996, they refused the request on several grounds. First, the EWHC held that discovery proceedings do not form part of English law and consequently state courts have no power to order a witness for examination for the sole purpose of determining whether he or she has information which may help in the case at hand:

> "The procedure adopted under the curial law differs in this respect from that which applies under our law in a way which, on this ground alone, makes it inappropriate in my view to make the order now being sought."[962]

This would suggest that as long as the foreign law–or rather, the way of taking evidence under a foreign law–does not substantially differ from English law, an evidence request may be considered 'appropriate'. It is therefore at least conceivable that English courts could adapt evidence requests pursuant to

960 EAA Supplementary Report (1997), n. 15.

961 *Commerce and Industry Co, Canada v. Certain Underwriters of Lloyds of London* [2002] EWHC 2 All ER (Comm.); MERKIN/FLANNERY, 181 et seq.; ILLMER/STEINBRÜCK, 337 et seq.; HARRIS et al., S. 44 EAA 1996 n. 44H.

962 *Commerce and Industry Co, Canada v. Certain Underwriters of Lloyds of London* [2002] EWHC 2 All ER (Comm.), 205.

foreign law until they are compatible with English law.[963] Although this first argument in itself was sufficient to reject the request, the EWHC further stated that the requesting party had presented no evidence regarding the importance of the examination to the arbitration:

> "The greater the likely inconvenience to the witness, the greater the need to satisfy the court that he can give evidence which is necessary for the just determination of the dispute."[964]

As the application had been made *ex parte*, this statement is unsurprising; it would most likely not been made if the arbitral tribunal itself or a party with the consent of the arbitral tribunal had initiated the request. This decision shows how the English courts can use their discretion according to S. 2 (3) EAA 1996 to find a balance between assisting foreign arbitral proceedings and protecting third-party witnesses based in England.[965]

2. Principle of Subsidiarity

Irrespective of whether the matter is urgent, according to S. 44 (5) EAA 1996, state courts can act only insofar as the arbitral tribunal cannot take the evidence itself:

> "In any case the court shall act only if or to the extent that the arbitral tribunal, and any arbitral or other institution or person vested by the parties with power in that regard, has no power or is unable for the time being to act effectively."

They can therefore act only if the arbitral tribunal either has no power or is unable to act quickly or effectively enough.[966] This applies to situations where the arbitral tribunal has not yet been constituted[967] or lacks coercive power–for example, to enforce a freezing order or restrain a (third) party from doing something.[968] Logically, this does not apply to S. 43 EAA 1996, where the parties *per se* cannot force a third party to produce evidence. As far as can be seen, cases in which the taking of evidence by the arbitral tribunal

963 For this approach under German law, *see* p. 141 *supra*.

964 *Commerce and Industry Co, Canada v. Certain Underwriters of Lloyds of London* [2002] EWHC 2 All ER (Comm.), 211.

965 ILLMER/STEINBRÜCK, 338.

966 EAA Report (1996), n. 215; for the similar German approach, *see* § 1050 (1) CCP DE.

967 *Euroil Ltd. v. Cameroon Offshore Petroleum SARL* [2014] EWHC 12 (Comm.), n. 11; *Permasteelisa Japan KK v. Bouyguesstroi & Anor* [2007] EWHC 3508 (TCC), n. 42; *Cetelem S.A. v. Roust Holdings Ltd.*, [2005], EWCA 618 (Civ.), n. 71; DEY et al., n. 554.

968 MERKIN/FLANNERY, 177 et seq. with reference to *Pacific Maritime (Asia) Ltd. v. Holystone Overseas Ltd* [2007] EWHC 2319 (Comm.), n. 80.

would involve a disproportionately significant effort, and where state court assistance is therefore sought according to S. 44 EAA 1996, have not been the subject of any debate in English legal doctrine or case law. Still, this scenario could easily be included under the term 'unable ... to act effectively'.[969]

S. 44 (5) EAA 1996 acknowledges the overall principle of the EAA 1996 by giving the arbitral tribunal full control over the arbitral proceedings.[970] Because the arbitral tribunal is vested with the necessary powers, not at least as regards evidentiary issues, under S. 44 EAA 1996 state courts will examine whether the arbitral tribunal itself could not act effectively.[971] Also, because S. 44 (5) EAA 1996 makes direct reference to arbitration institutions, state courts must consider whether, in an arbitration held under institutional arbitration rules, an emergency arbitrator could act more effectively.[972] Indeed, in an LCIA arbitration in 2016 (*Gerald Metals SA v. Timis & Ors*), it was held that parties cannot resort to state courts for a 'second attempt' if the relief sought through an emergency arbitrator is unsuccessful.[973] Finally, according to S. 44 (6) EAA 1996, state courts are competent to decide that any order made under S. 44 EAA 1996 may be varied or set aside by the arbitral tribunal once it has been constituted or any time during the arbitral proceedings.[974] It is therefore at the discretion of the respective court to pronounce on the longevity of its orders.[975]

3. Examination of the Arbitration Agreement

Thus far, the possibility to examine the arbitration agreement under Ss. 43 and 44 EAA 1996 does not seem to have been the subject of debate in English legal doctrine or case law. According to S. 30 (1) (a) EAA 1996, the competence-competence principle means that the arbitral tribunal is competent to decide whether there is a valid arbitration agreement.[976] If there is a dispute regarding the validity of the arbitration agreement, a party may object to the

969 S. 44 (5) EAA 1996.

970 S. 34 EAA 1996; O'CALLAGHAN/FINNIS, S. 44 EAA 1996 n. 20-71.

971 As regards the power of the arbitral tribunal to order disclosure instead of state courts *see NB Three Shipping Ltd. v. Harebell Shipping Ltd* [2004] EWHC 2001 (Comm.), n. 14.

972 SUTTON et al., n. 7-195; *see* e.g. Art. 29 ICC Rules; Art. 43 Swiss Rules; Rule 30 SIAC Rules.

973 *Gerald Metals SA v. Timis & Ors* [2016] EWHC 2327, n. 7.

974 MERKIN/FLANNERY, 199.

975 SUTTON et al., n. 9-197. Because an arbitral tribunal has no power over third parties, SUTTON et al. suggest that the state court in charge can make an order that lasts for the duration of the proceedings.

976 EAA Report (1996), n. 137 et seqq.; HARRIS et al., S. 30 EAA 1996 n. 30C; *see also* S. 9 (4) EAA 1996 as regards the examination of the arbitration agreement under a stay of legal proceedings.

arbitral tribunal's jurisdiction pursuant to S. 31 EAA 1996 and state courts therefore will not examine the arbitration agreement under Ss. 43 and 44 EAA 1996.[977] Furthermore, the examination of the arbitration agreement is possible in the context of recognition and enforcement of an arbitral award under the NYC.[978]

F. Appellate Remedies

As regards orders under S. 44 EAA 1996, the leave of the court is required for any appeal.[979] In comparison to other *leges arbitri*, this provision is unique.[980] It aims to limit the role of the court and ensures a high degree of finality–regarding not only S. 44 EAA 1996, but also many other provisions in the EAA 1996.[981] Consequently, if a state court finds that there are no flaws in an order of S. 44 EAA 1996 that would constitute sufficient grounds for an appeal, the request under S. 44 (7) EAA 1996 will most likely be denied. Since this provision gives wide discretion to the respective state court, it remains to be seen whether English courts will interpret this broadly or narrowly. However, there seems to be a consensus that it is possible to apply to the EWHC without permission if the state court did not have jurisdiction at the outset[982] or if the court's refusal to leave to appeal was arbitrary, unfair or even against Art. 6 EHRC.[983] Applying the rules of appellate remedies against an arbitral award by analogy, an appeal may be filed with the EWHC in London within 28 days of the parties being notified of the decision under S. 44 EAA 1996.[984]

In the absence of any explicit legal bases, the aforementioned appeal procedure also applies to S. 43 EAA 1996. In this regard, the procedure mentioned under S. 44 EAA 1996 likewise applies accordingly. A distinction must

977 SUTTON et al., n. 2-012.

978 Arts. III (3) and V (1) (a) NYC.

979 S. 44 (7) EAA 1996.

980 See e.g. the approach under German (p. 146 et seqq. *supra*), French (p. 163 et seq. *supra*), US (p. 212 et seq. *infra*) and Swiss law (p. 256 et seqq. *infra*).

981 *See* e.g. Ss. 12 (6), 17 (4), 18 (5), 21 (6), 24 (6), 25 (5) and 42 (5) EAA 1996; *Cetelem SA v. Roust Holding Ltd* [2005] EWCA 618 (Civ.), n. 24: *CGU International Insurance Plc & Ors v. AstraZeneca Insurance Co Ltd* [2006] EWCA 1340 (Civ.), n. 3 as regards S. 69 EAA 1996 (appeal on point of law): 'It enacts a concern, in the interest of party autonomy, privacy and finality, that such awards should not be readily transferred to the courts for appellate review.'; SUTTON et al., n. 8-128.

982 *Cetelem SA v. Roust Holding Ltd* [2005] EWCA 618 (Civ.), n. 25.

983 *CGU International Insurance Plc & Ors v. AstraZeneca Insurance Co Ltd* [2006] EWCA 1340 (Civ.), n. 98.

984 S. 70 (3) EAA 1996.

be made, however, regarding the assessment of evidence, which falls under the exclusive competence of the arbitral tribunal and not any state court under S. 43 or 44 EAA 1996.

The threshold for challenging an arbitral award is high. Although S. 68 (2) (c) EAA 1996 provides that an arbitral award may be set aside due to a 'failure by the tribunal to conduct the proceedings in accordance with the procedure agreed by the parties', this can be done only by showing that the conditions set out in S. 68 (1) EAA 1996 are met. Accordingly, a party must demonstrate that there has been a serious irregularity which affected the arbitral tribunal, the proceedings or the award. This is no easy task; thus, the EAA 1996 ensures a high degree of finality regarding arbitral awards.[985] With regard to the timeframe for appeal, according to S. 70 (3) EAA 1996, an appeal must be brought before the EWHC within 28 days of the date of the award.

G. Summary

Like the approaches taken in the *leges arbitri* of Germany and France, the English approach is very liberal in many ways and seeks to preserve party autonomy and contractual choice. First, although the EAA 1996 usually applies only if the seat of arbitration is in the English territory, court assistance in the taking of evidence is explicitly excluded from this requirement. The parties are therefore at liberty to make requests for the attendance of witnesses or to avail of additional state court powers in support of the arbitral proceedings.

Second, unlike other *leges arbitri*, the arbitral tribunal's consent to seek court assistance is not necessary if both parties agree to this course of action.[986] In exceptional urgent cases, a party may resort to a state court *ex parte* in order to preserve evidence or assets. In the absence of any explicit legal basis, the arbitral tribunal, in executing its mandate to decide whether and to what extent it should take the initiative in ascertaining the facts and law, can seek court assistance in taking evidence itself. If the parties wish to exclude this possibility, they can only exclude the powers according to S. 44 EAA 1996; this is not possible with regard to S. 43 EAA 1996, which has mandatory application.

Third, while the attendance of a witness to testify or produce evidence under S. 43 EAA 1996 can be requested only if that witness is located and the arbitral proceedings are conducted in England, the spectrum of possible measures under S. 44 EAA 1996 is much broader. According to S. 43 EAA 1996,

985 MERKIN/FLANNERY, 305.

986 *See e.g.* p. 169 *supra*.

third parties can be forced to appear before an arbitral tribunal to give evidence, but this provision cannot be used to request disclosure from third parties under the CPR 1998. Because S. 43 EAA 1996 relates to third parties, they do not have to reveal evidence which is irrelevant or protected by privilege. In contrast, orders under S. 44 EAA 1996 can be imposed only on the parties to the arbitration. Unlike S. 43 EAA 1996, if the case is urgent and evidence or assets must be preserved, S. 44 EAA 1996 plays a role even before the constitution of the arbitral tribunal. As regards foreign types of evidence which are requested to be executed before an English court, this depends on how narrowly the appropriateness rule set out in S. 2 (3) EAA 1996 is interpreted; a clear-cut answer in this regard is therefore not possible.

Fourth, the respective *juge d'appui* has wide discretion in deciding whether and to what extent court assistance in the taking of evidence should be granted. As previously discussed (*see* p. 177 et seqq. *supra*), state courts can deny court assistance in the taking of evidence solely on the grounds that the seat of arbitration, which is or will likely be outside of England, would make this inappropriate. Obviously, this leaves a lot of room for interpretation. As regards evidence, English courts seem to deny evidence requests from foreign arbitral tribunals if they are substantially different from English law. In addition, the importance of the taking of evidence and its link to the outcome of the arbitration must be demonstrated in order to obtain assistance. As a consequence, the English courts will consider the usefulness, appropriateness and relevance of the request, unlike under German law, for example. Moreover, assistance will be granted only if the arbitral tribunal cannot take the evidence itself. This is mostly the case if the arbitral tribunal has not yet been constituted or if evidence is sought from third parties. This should also apply to situations where the taking of evidence by the arbitral tribunal would involve a disproportionately significant effort. Finally, a state court whose assistance is sought under Ss. 43 and 44 EAA 1996 is not entitled to conduct a full examination of the arbitration agreement, but only on a prima facie basis. The extensive examination forms part of a separate procedure under the EAA 1996 (*see* p. 179 *supra*).

Finally, to minimise state court involvement in arbitral proceedings, the leave of the assisting state court is required to make an appeal. The threshold for granting or denying such a request remains at the discretion of the respective state court. However, if it never actually had jurisdiction or if the refusal to appeal was arbitrary, unfair or in breach of Art. 6 EHRC, the parties can appeal to the EWHC. Moreover, it has been demonstrated that the EAA 1996 imposes a high threshold for challenging an arbitral award and therefore guarantees a high degree of finality.

All in all, the English *lex arbitri* and case law take a very pro-arbitration stance. Therefore, if the parties wish to force witnesses to appear before the arbitral tribunal or use the powers of the English courts to support arbitral proceedings, they should not be too hesitant to initiate an evidence request. However, the issue of whether the English courts will consider evidence appropriate nonetheless remains.

§ 5 USA

A. Introduction

In recent years, international arbitration in the USA has become increasingly popular. The caseload of the ICDR continues to grow, promoting the USA as an attractive forum for arbitration.[987] Unlike the detailed provisions of English law, the approach under US law is in many ways different. On the one hand, the US courts have adopted a very arbitration-friendly stance, acknowledging and enforcing arbitral agreements and awards. On the other hand, however, the US *lex arbitri* is one of the most wide-ranging and complex arbitral legal frameworks at the federal, state and international levels.[988] This is also true when it comes to assisting international arbitral tribunals in gathering evidence.[989] Since a comprehensive examination of the relevant procedures in all fifty states would exceed the scope of the present discussion, the following analysis will concentrate on the issue at a purely federal and international level, including federal court decisions applying federal and international law.

Arbitration at the federal level is mainly governed by the Federal Arbitration Act (FAA USA), which was first enacted in 1925 and forms part of the USC (Title 9). In contrast to other *leges arbitri*, it is not based on the UNICTRAL ML, which has served as a model for the laws in only eight out of fifty US states.[990] Due to the age of the FAA USA, many aspects of arbitration have been defined by case law over time.[991] Besides chapter one, which mainly governs domestic arbitration matters, the NYC and the so-called

987 In 2019, the ICDR dealt with 9,737 commercial cases; *see* the 2019 statistics.

988 SHORE et al., Introduction, 6.

989 O'MALLEY, n. 3.107.

990 This applies for the states of California, Connecticut, Florida, Georgia, Illinois, Louisiana, Oregon and Texas (*see* the current status); for a summary of the predominant arbitral legal frameworks among the fifty states, *see* AMIRFAR et al., 1 et seqq.; SALOMON/FRIEDRICH, *Obtaining Evidence*, 558 et seqq.

991 Balthasar-NIEDERMAIER, n. 5.

Panama Convention[992] are applicable, due to their implementation into the FAA USA in 1970 and 1990 in chapters two and three respectively.[993] While the FAA USA sometimes applies to international arbitral proceedings -for instance, to refer the parties to arbitration or vacate an arbitral award–this does not apply to evidentiary issues if the seat of arbitration is outside the US.[994] Thus, § 7 FAA USA, which governs the possibility to summon witnesses to assist with arbitration–applies only to arbitral proceedings with their seat in the USA; international arbitral proceedings with their seat abroad are therefore excluded.[995] The question thus arises as to whether there are other possibilities to obtain evidence located in the USA to assist in international arbitration.

B. Legal Bases

1. Federal Rules of Civil Procedure

The FRCP USA provide for a wide range of different discovery measures in state court litigation.[996] In international arbitration, however, it is commonly accepted that broad discovery rights are not available, subject to a divergent agreement between the parties, the arbitration rules and the discretion of the arbitral tribunal.[997] The reasons for this resistance towards broad discovery are clear when the matter is considered from the parties' point of view, since they are seeking a faster, less expensive alternative to state court litigation. Moreover, the parties in international arbitration often have different ideas and approaches as to how to the taking of evidence should be conducted (*see* p. 7 et seqq. *supra*).

992 Inter-American Convention on International Commercial Arbitration.

993 SALOMON/FRIEDRICH, *Obtaining Evidence*, 555.

994 § 206 and § 303 FAA USA; *see also* Art. II (3) NYC; STEINBRÜCK, 168 et seqq.; NYC Bar Committee Report (2010), 38; as regards vacating an arbitral award under the FAA USA *see* p. 212 et seq. *infra*.

995 § 7 FAA USA only confers enforcement authority on the 'district court for the district in which such arbitrators, or a majority of them, are sitting; *see also National Broadcasting Company Inc NBC v. Bear Stearns Co Inc SBC TV*, (2d Cir.1999), in: Y.B. Comm. Arb. 1999, 886; FRIEDMAN/LAVAUD, 4; SALOMON/FRIEDRICH, *FAA*, 352 et seqq.

996 Rule 26-37 FRCP USA; SALOMON/FRIEDRICH, *Obtaining Evidence*, 587 et seqq.

997 DELANEY/FRUCHTER, 21; *see also* Art. 21 (10) ICDR Rules: 'Depositions, interrogatories, and requests to admit as developed for use in US court procedures generally are not appropriate procedures for obtaining information in an arbitration under these Rules.'

What is more, the US courts have confirmed several times that pre-trial discovery is generally not available in arbitral proceedings.[998] Nevertheless, discovery has been granted in arbitral proceedings with their seats outside the USA in very few exceptional urgent cases–primarily maritime cases–in order to preserve evidence.[999] As an example, in *Deiulemar Compagna v. Pacific Eternity*, a US District Court ordered an inspection of a damaged engine of a ship which was soon scheduled to leave US waters. In the ongoing proceedings, the Court of Appeals of the 4th Cir. stated that although discovery rules typically do not apply to arbitral disputes, their application in the present case was justified due to 'extraordinary circumstances', as otherwise the requested information would be unavailable.[1000]

As far as can be seen, this case law in maritime law has not yet led to any similar decisions in other areas of law, let alone to a common principle regarding when and under what conditions foreign arbitral tribunals can seek discovery under the FRCP USA. Nonetheless, it is noteworthy that direct discovery pursuant to the FRCP USA is not altogether excluded in international arbitration, but is reserved for extraordinary circumstances, which seem to be defined on a case-by-case basis. Furthermore, discovery under the FRCP USA might be available through 28 USC § 1782.

2. 28 USC § 1782

a. General Scope of Application

US statute law provides a powerful litigation and investigation tool, empowering US district courts to assist in discovery in aid of a 'foreign or international tribunal'. 28 USC § 1782 (hereinafter '§ 1782') reads as follows:

> "(a) The district court of the district in which a person resides or is found may order him to give his testimony or statement or to produce a document or other thing for use in a proceeding in a foreign or international tribunal, including criminal investigations conducted before formal accusation.
>
> The order may be made pursuant to a letter rogatory issued, or request made, by a foreign or international tribunal or upon the application of

998 *Burton v. Bush*, 614 F.2d 389 (4th Cir. 1980), n. 5: 'When contracting parties stipulate that disputes will be submitted to arbitration, they relinquish the right to certain procedural niceties which are normally associated with a formal trial. ... One of these accoutrements is the right to pre-trial discovery.'

999 *In re Application of the Petition of Compania Chilena de Navegacion*, 2004 WL 1084243 (E.D.N.Y 2004); *Deiulemar Compagna v. M/V. Allegra*, 198 F.3d 473 (4th Cir. 1999); *In Re Deiulemar di Navigazione S.P.A.*, 153 F.R.D. 592, 593 (E.D. La. 1994); STEINBRÜCK, 188 et seq.

1000 *Deiulemar Compagna v. M/V. Allegra*, 198 F.3d 473, 476, 479 (4th Cir. 1999).

> any interested person and may direct that the testimony or statement be given, or the document or other thing be produced, before a person appointed by the court. By virtue of his appointment, the person appointed has power to administer any necessary oath and take the testimony or statement.
> The order may prescribe the practice and procedure, which may be in whole or part the practice and procedure of the foreign country or the international tribunal, for taking the testimony or statement or producing the document or other thing. To the extent that the order does not prescribe otherwise, the testimony or statement shall be taken, and the document or other thing produced, in accordance with the Federal Rules of Civil Procedure.
> A person may not be compelled to give his testimony or statement or to produce a document or other thing in violation of any legally applicable privilege.
> (b) This chapter does not preclude a person within the United States from voluntarily giving his testimony or statement, or producing a document or other thing, for use in a proceeding in a foreign or international tribunal before any person and in any manner acceptable to him."

However, the application of § 1782 in international arbitration remains unclear. The increasing split among US courts and in legal doctrine not only is confusing, but also suggests that, to be on the safe side, arbitration practitioners should resist trying to make use of § 1782, especially in private commercial arbitration. However, the following examination shows that this conclusion is not appropriate in all circumstances. This follows from a closer look at US case law, especially a ground-breaking Supreme Court decision from 2004. Therefore, before examining § 1782 according to the common structure, as with the previous examined *leges arbitri*, the questionable applicability of this section in arbitration must first be discussed.

b. Legislative Background

§ 1782 was enacted in 1948 to assist foreign state courts with discovery.[1001] In 1964 the word 'court' in § 1782 was replaced with the wording 'foreign or international tribunal', to broaden the scope of this section and avoid its appli-

1001 H.R. Rep. 1052, 88th Cong. 1st Sess. (1963), 9; BENTO, 32 et seqq.; The history of discovery in aid of foreign proceedings goes indeed much further back; *see Intel Corp. v. Advanced Micro Devices, Inc.*, 542 U.S. 241, 247 et seqq. (2004); MARTINEZ-FRAGA, 38 et seqq.; BEALE et al., 56 et seqq.; O'MALLEY/EATON, 112 et seqq.; NYC Bar Committee Report (2010), 2 et seqq.

cation being restricted merely to conventional courts.[1002] It was expected that other countries would initiate similar reforms.[1003] Reading this passage, one might easily conclude that arbitral tribunals are included.[1004] Unfortunately, however, US Congress (hereinafter 'Congress') never defined the term 'foreign or international tribunal' sufficiently specifically.[1005] It merely stated the following:

> "The word 'tribunal' is used to make it clear that assistance is not confined to proceedings before conventional courts. For example, it is intended that the courts have discretion to grant assistance when proceedings are pending before investigating magistrates in foreign countries. (...). In view of the constant growth of administrative and quasi-judicial proceedings all over the world, the necessity for obtaining evidence in the United States may be as impelling in proceedings before a foreign administrative tribunal or quasi-judicial agency as in proceedings before a conventional foreign court. Subsection (a) therefore provides the possibility of U.S. judicial assistance in connection with all such proceedings."[1006]

Although the wording remains vague, one may conclude that Congress' overall intention was to broaden the scope of international court assistance in the taking of evidence by increasing the powers of district courts in this respect.[1007]

c. Case Law

I. Introduction

In light of the legislative history, it is unsurprising that for a long time, the use of § 1782 in international arbitral proceedings was non-existent or denied.[1008]

1002 H.R. Rep. 1052, 88th Cong. 1st Sess. (1963), 9; Sen. Rep. 1580, 88th Cong. 2nd Sess. (1964), 3788; ELUL/MOSQUERA, n. 408. In addition, the replacement meant a combination between the former 22 USC § 270 to 270g which only addressed international tribunals, while the former 28 USC § 1782 to 1785 referred to foreign courts. The revisions in 1964 has therefore resulted in a combination of both provisions (*see also* SMIT, *International Tribunals*, 1264 et seqq.; SMIT, *Section 1782 Revisited*, 3).

1003 H.R. Rep. 1052, 88th Cong. 1st Sess. (1963), 20; SMIT, *International Litigation*, 1019; MARTINEZ-FRAGA, 38; BENTO, 54 et seq.

1004 BORN, *Law and Practice*, ch. 9 n. 30.

1005 ELUL/MOSQUERA, n. 393 et seq.

1006 H.R. Rep. 1052, 88th Cong. 1st Sess. (1963), 9.

1007 *In re Request for Assistance from Ministry of Legal Affairs of Trinidad and Tobago petition Jospeh Azar*, 848 F.2d 1151, 1154 (11th Cir. 1988).

1008 *Application of Medway Power Ltd.*, 985 F. Supp. 402 (S.D.N.Y. 1997); *National Broadcasting Company Inc NBC v. Bear Stearns Co Inc SBC TV*, (2d Cir.1999), in: Y.B. Comm. Arb. 1999, 884 et seqq.; *Republic of Kazakhstan v. Biedermann International*, (5th Cir. 1999), in: Y.B. Comm. Arb. 2000, 918 et seqq.

Accordingly, arbitral tribunals and parties were forced to gather evidence in the USA through international judicial assistance under treaties such as the HEC.[1009] This situation changed dramatically following the Supreme Court's decision *Intel Corp. v. Advanced Micro Devices, Inc.* (hereinafter '*Intel*') in 2004.[1010] As a logical consequence, this shift in case law has led to a broad debate in legal doctrine and a split among various circuits. It therefore remains very unclear whether there is in fact a legal basis for US-style discovery in aid of international arbitration. Nevertheless, there are some commonalities among the decisions of various circuits. The following discussion tries to shed some light on the applicability of § 1782 by analysing various US court decisions prior to and after *Intel*. Needless to say, given the vast case law on § 1782, the discussion focuses on a selective examination rather than a comprehensive overview.

II. Decisions prior to Intel

Following the amendment of § 1782 in 1964, US courts from the 2d and 5th Cir. had several possibilities to express their views on the term 'foreign or international tribunal'.[1011] In *Application of Technostroyexport*, an NY district court (2d Cir.) stated bluntly that an arbitrator or an arbitration panel is a tribunal in the sense of § 1782.[1012] However, the court did not further elaborate on its decision, but denied the request for discovery because it had been made *ex parte*. The same applied in *Trygg-Hansa Ins. Co., Ltd.*, where discovery was sought in arbitral proceedings in England, but was denied because the district court (5th Cir.) considered the request an attempt to circumvent English disclosure rules.[1013] Here again, the district court mentioned nothing regarding the applicability of § 1782 to arbitral proceedings. By contrast, in *Application of Medway Power Ltd.*, an NY district court (2d Cir.) denied discovery in aid of an arbitration held under the EAA 1996 because an arbitral tribunal was not considered a 'foreign and international tribunal'.[1014] The

1009 For the relationship between the HEC and § 1782, *see* p. 208 *infra*. As an exception to this, there have been a few rare cases in which arbitral tribunals have been supported by ordering discovery according to the FRCP USA (*see* p. 185 *supra*).

1010 *Intel Corp. v. Advanced Micro Devices, Inc.*, 542 U.S. 241 (2004); STRONG, 302 et seq.

1011 *See* e.g. in the case of a letter rogatory by a Director of Inspection under the Income Tax Act of the Government of India in *Letters Rogatory Issued by Director of Inspection of Government of India*, 385 F.2d 1017 (2d Cir. 1967).

1012 *Application of Technostroyexport*, 853 F. Supp. 695, 697 (S.D.N.Y. 1994).

1013 *In re Trygg-Hansa Ins. Co., Ltd.*, 896 F. Supp. 624 (E.D. La. 1995).

1014 *Application of Medway Power Ltd.*, 985 F. Supp. 402 (S.D.N.Y. 1997).

court argued that in amending § 1782, Congress intended to assist only official 'governmental agencies exercising a judicial or quasi-judicial' role, and that consequently arbitral tribunals are excluded.[1015]

Two years later, in 1999, the decision in *National Broadcasting Company, Inc. and NBC Europe, Inc., v. Bear Stearns & Co., Inc.* (hereinafter '*NBC*') was even clearer:[1016] the 2d Cir. held that an ICC arbitration conducted in Mexico was not a proceeding under a foreign or international tribunal in the sense of § 1782.[1017] The court held that although it has been argued that the term 'foreign or international tribunal' is ambiguous and does not necessarily include or exclude arbitral tribunals, the legislative history shows that Congress had in mind only 'governmental entities, such as administrative or investigative courts, acting as state instrumentalities or with the authority of the state'.[1018] This stems from the fact that the term 'international tribunal' in the new § 1782 came from the former 22 USC § 270-270g, enacted in 1930 to compel witnesses to appear in state arbitral proceedings between Canada and the USA.[1019]

Furthermore, the court held that allowing foreign arbitral tribunals to make use of § 1782 would be in stark contrast to court assistance in the taking of evidence in domestic arbitration pursuant to § 7 FAA USA, which is far more limited.[1020] This result, the court reasoned, could not have been intended by Congress. Finally, the 2d Cir. Court of Appeals argued that the application of wide-ranging discovery rights under § 1782 to arbitration would also contradict the basic principle of arbitration: that is, to provide an efficient and cost-effective alternative to litigation.[1021] If it were applied to international arbitration, there would be a risk that a party could *ex parte* initiate discovery according to § 1782 and therefore misuse this option for tactical reasons, which would not be in the interests of arbitration.

1015 *Ibid.*, 402, 403 et seq. In addition, reference was made to *Application of Technostroyexport*, 853 F. Supp. 695 (S.D.N.Y. 1994; made in the same 2d Cir.) stating that this decision has been rendered on no precedent authority and therefore it was not binding (404).

1016 *National Broadcasting Company Inc NBC v. Bear Stearns Co Inc SBC TV*, (2d Cir.1999), in: Y.B. Comm. Arb. 1999, 884 et seqq.; BEALE et al., 61 et seqq.; ROBERTSON/FRIEDMAN, 68 et seq.

1017 The decision confirmed was *In re Application of National Broadcasting Co.*, No. M-77, 1998 WL 1994 (S.D.N.Y. 1998).

1018 *National Broadcasting Company Inc NBC v. Bear Stearns Co Inc SBC TV*, (2d Cir.1999), in: Y.B. Comm. Arb. 1999, 888.

1019 SMIT, *International Tribunals*, 1264 et seqq.

1020 *See* p. 183 *supra; see also* SALOMON/FRIEDRICH, *Obtaining Evidence*, 554 et seqq.; *National Broadcasting Company Inc NBC v. Bear Stearns Co Inc SBC TV*, (2d Cir.1999), in: Y.B. Comm. Arb. 1999, 886.

1021 *Ibid.*, 890 et seq.

Shortly after *NBC*, the 5th Cir. rendered a very similar decision in an investment arbitration between Kazakhstan and a US investor. In *Republic of Kazakhstan v. Biedermann Int.* (hereinafter '*Republic of Kazakhstan*'), the Court of Appeals of the 5th Cir. largely followed the reasoning in *NBC*.[1022] In doing so, it emphasised the comparison between § 1782 and § 7 FAA USA. Accordingly, the latter provision permits arbitration panels to serve a witness summons only within the federal district in which the arbitrators, or a majority of them, are sitting. Under § 1782, however, not only foreign and international tribunals, but also 'every interested party', can initiate discovery requests. Therefore, the Court of Appeals stated:

> "It is not likely that Congress would have chosen to authorize federal courts to assure broader discovery in aid of foreign private arbitration than is afforded its domestic dispute-resolution counterpart. ... Empowering arbitrators or, worse, the parties, in private international disputes to seek ancillary discovery through the federal courts does not benefit the arbitration process."[1023]

The decisions prior to *Intel* leave little room for interpretation; private international tribunals are clearly excluded from the scope of application of § 1782. First, only 'state-sponsored' entities will thus benefit from discovery rights under § 1782. Second, if § 1782 were used in international arbitration, there would be a clear imbalance between domestic and international arbitration held in the USA. Third, the often time-consuming discovery process is at odds with the very essence and goal of international arbitration, which is to provide an efficient and cost-effective instrument to settle international commercial disputes. In sum, the use of § 1782 in international arbitral proceedings seemed out of the question for the time being–at least in the 2d and 5th Cirs.

III. Intel

i. Factual Background

In the 2004 *Intel* case, Advanced Micro Devices, Inc. (hereinafter 'AMD') filed an antitrust complaint against Intel Corporation (hereinafter 'Intel') before the Directorate-General for Competition (DG-Competition) of the

1022 *Republic of Kazakhstan v. Biedermann International*, (5th Cir. 1999), in: Y.B. Comm. Arb. 2000, 918 et seqq.; BEALE et al., 63 et seq.; ROBERTSON/FRIEDMAN, 69 et seqq.

1023 *Republic of Kazakhstan v. Biedermann International*, (5th Cir. 1999), in: Y.B. Comm. Arb. 2000, 921 et seq.

Commission of the European Communities.[1024] Pursuing this complaint, AMD applied to the District Court for the Northern District of California, requesting Intel to produce certain documents in accordance with § 1782. After the Californian district court denied the application because it lacked authority, the Court of Appeals of the 9th Cir. reversed this decision, ordering the district court to rule on the merits of AMD's application. Subsequently, Intel appealed to the Supreme Court, which issued several guidelines on how to deal with requests under § 1782 before remanding the case to the district court.

Without doubt, *Intel* represents a landmark in the history of § 1782, since it paved the way for discovery in international arbitral proceedings where evidence is sought to be obtained in the USA.[1025] Although this decision was rendered *obiter dicta*–that is, with non-binding effect for lower courts, because it was not primarily about a foreign arbitral tribunal–the Supreme Court offered some helpful insight into how to interpret and apply § 1782, which at times runs contrary to what was decided by the 2d and 5th Cirs. *(see* p. 188 et seqq. *supra).*[1026] The consequences of *Intel* are thus crucial as regards obtaining evidence in the USA for international arbitration. The following analysis focuses on how the US Supreme Court in *Intel* tackled the three main reasons raised in *NBC* and *Republic of Kazakhstan* against the use of § 1782 in arbitral proceedings, as well as the '*Intel* factors'.

ii. 'Foreign and International Tribunal'

The first and most important issue concerns the term 'foreign and international tribunal'. As seen in the cases prior to *Intel*, by looking at the historical background of § 1782, several courts reached the clear conclusion that Congress did not intend to include arbitral tribunals at all.[1027] Although not speaking explicitly of arbitral tribunals, it is still startling that in *Intel*, Justice Ginsburg stated very quickly that since the DG-Competition is an adjudicative body involved in taking evidence and acting as a first-instance decision maker whose decisions can be reviewed, it may be considered a 'foreign or

1024 *Intel Corp. v. Advanced Micro Devices, Inc.*, 542 U.S. 241, 246 (2004); MARTINEZ-FRAGA, 44; BEALE et al., 64 et seqq.; O'MALLEY/EATON, 114; NYC Bar Committee Report (2010), 19 et seqq.

1025 MARTINEZ-FRAGA, 43.

1026 *Ibid.*, 45.

1027 *See* p. 188 et seqq. *supra*.

international tribunal' in the sense of § 1782.[1028] To support this view, she made reference to Smit, who served as director of the Columbia Law School project–in which Justice Ginsburg herself was an associate director–which assisted the law commission in drafting the new § 1782.[1029] According to a passage in an article written by Smit in 1965, one year after the enactment of § 1782, the term 'tribunal' encompasses:

> "All bodies exercising adjudicatory powers, and includes investigating magistrates, administrative and arbitral tribunals, and quasi-judicial agencies, as well as conventional civil, commercial, criminal, and administrative courts ..., but also arbitral tribunals or single arbitrators."[1030]

Besides the fact that arbitral tribunals are explicitly mentioned by Smit, one might easily also consider them to be first-instance decision makers, taking evidence in the arbitral proceedings and rendering an arbitral award which is subject to review depending on the respective *lex arbitri*.[1031] Accordingly, § 1782 could be used in aid of international arbitration, irrespective of any other requirement such as the applicable law, the seat of arbitration or the nationality of the parties. Despite this very arbitration-friendly approach taken in *Intel*, one must acknowledge that Smit adopted this same liberal approach back in 1965, a year after § 1782 was revised.[1032] In an earlier publication of Smit from 1962, to which Congress explicitly referred in the legislative materials on § 1782, (private) international arbitral tribunals are not mentioned at all.[1033] However, this does not necessarily lead to the conclusion that Congress deliberately excluded arbitral tribunals from the scope of application of this provision.

Looking at the legislative history of § 1782, it may be assumed that although Congress adopted rather broad wording, it is hard to justify an interpretation that the primary focus was on private international arbitral tribunals as understood today.[1034] In 1964, although international arbitra-

1028 *Intel Corp. v. Advanced Micro Devices, Inc.*, 542 U.S. 241, 255 et seq, (2004); MARTINEZ-FRAGA, 45; MALAMENT, 1219 et seq. It is noteworthy that in 1964, the time of the important amendment to § 1782, the DG-Competition had not yet been founded (*see* O'MALLEY/EATON, 118).

1029 *Intel Corp. v. Advanced Micro Devices, Inc.*, 542 U.S. 241, 258 (2004); VALENTINE, 397.

1030 *Ibid.*; SMIT, *International Litigation*, fn 71; SMIT, *Section 1782 Revisited*, 5 et seqq.

1031 MARTINEZ-FRAGA, 46.

1032 MALAMENT, 1224; STRONG, 303 et seq.

1033 SMIT, *International Aspects*, 1031 et seqq.; *see also* SMIT, *International Tribunals*, 1264 et seqq. (1962).

1034 ROTHSTEIN, 79.

tion was slowly gaining importance, it had not yet become the instrument of choice to settle international commercial disputes. This can be seen in the fact that multilateral treaties concerning international arbitration such as the NYC and the Panama Convention had not yet been ratified in the USA.[1035] By the same token, however, the USA was by no means a 'dead man's land' for arbitration at this time.[1036] Following the end of World War II, the USA entered into several treaties of friendship, commerce and navigation, especially between 1946 and 1968,[1037] which often included clauses on the reciprocal acknowledgment and enforcement of arbitral awards.[1038] What is more, in 1966 the USA ratified the ICSID Convention.[1039] It may thus be concluded that–contrary to what was held in *NBC*–Congress neither expressly included nor excluded international arbitral tribunals from the scope of application of § 1782.[1040] Rather, the clear aim was to improve international court assistance–albeit that at the time, this was mainly in the field of international litigation.[1041] In this regard, *Intel* goes even further by emphasising the broad scope given to the term 'foreign and international tribunal'.

iii. Domestic v. International Arbitration

The second issue concerns the difference between domestic and international arbitration.[1042] Regarding the difference between § 1782 and § 7 FAA USA, the Supreme Court reached a different conclusion from that in *NBC* and *Republic of Kazakhstan*.[1043] The latter decisions suggested that Congress could not have intended to introduce a disparity between domestic and international arbitration with regard to who can request discovery, which district court may decide and what evidence may be sought. The reasoning in *Intel* was rather different:

> "Section 1782 is a provision for assistance to tribunals abroad. It does not direct United States courts to engage in comparative analysis to determine whether analogous proceedings exist here."[1044]

1035 STRONG, 304; ROTHSTEIN, 72 et seqq. The NYC was ratified in 1970 and the Panama Convention in 1990; *see* the current status of the NYC, and the Panama Convention.

1036 *Contra* GODFREY, 503.

1037 COYLE, 308; STEINBRÜCK, 215 et seq.; ILLMER/STEINBRÜCK, 332 et seq.

1038 STEINBRÜCK, 216; *see* e.g. the Treaty of Friendship, Commerce and Navigation between the USA and Germany from 1956, Art. VI (2).

1039 *See* the current status.

1040 *National Broadcasting Company Inc NBC v. Bear Stearns Co Inc SBC T V.* (2d Cir.1999), in: Y.B. Comm. Arb. 1999, 888; STEINBRÜCK, 213; MALAMENT, 1224.

1041 MARTINEZ-FRAGA, 40.

1042 *See* p. 183 *supra;* MALAMENT, 1234 et seqq.

1043 *See* p. 189 et seqq. *supra.*

1044 *Intel Corp. v. Advanced Micro Devices, Inc.*, 542 U.S. 241, 263 (2004).

First, the Supreme Court makes it clear that there is no legal basis or principle stating that domestic and international arbitration must be treated equally.[1045] §1782 only and specifically addresses tribunals *abroad* and says nothing of the situation in domestic arbitration, which is a separate issue.[1046] Going one step further, Smit even argued that instead of narrowing §1782, either §7 FAA USA should be revised based on the model of §1782 or §1782 should also be applied to domestic arbitration.[1047] One must also bear in mind that a district court whose assistance is sought under §1782 always has wide discretion to decide whether and to what extent to grant such assistance.[1048] Consequently, in the case of requests made *ex parte*, assistance may depend on the consent of the arbitral tribunal in charge.[1049]

Second, as previously discussed, in some circumstances §7 FAA USA can even be invoked in international arbitral proceedings.[1050] In the same manner, §7 FAA USA does not purely apply to domestic arbitration; it can also be applied to domestic arbitration in the USA, as long there is an international arbitral tribunal seated in the country.[1051] From a systematic point of view, *Intel* therefore suggests that the differences between domestic and international court assistance in the taking of evidence are no reason to deny this assistance to foreign arbitral tribunals.

iv. Discovery in Arbitral Proceedings: Intel Factors

Third, it remains to be considered whether the use of §1782 in international arbitral proceedings would in fact run contrary to the essence and nature of

1045 *See also Hallmark Capital Corporation*, 534 F. Supp. 2d 951, 956 et seq. (D. Minn. 2007); Regarding the different approaches to arbitrability in domestic and international arbitration, *see Mitsubishi v. Soler Chrysler-Plymouth*, 473 U.S. 614, 615 (1985); *Scherk v. Alberto-Culver Co.*, 417 U.S. 506 (1974).

1046 NYC Bar Committee Report (2010), 38 et seq.

1047 SMIT, *Section 1782 Revisited*, 7, fn 31. He even argues that US courts have inherent power to order discovery according to 28 USC §1782 in domestic arbitration.

1048 *Intel Corp. v. Advanced Micro Devices, Inc.*, 542 U.S. 241, 264 et seqq. (2004): 'A district court is not required to grant a §1782 (a) discovery application simply because it has the authority to do so.'; MALAMENT, 1232 et seq., 1236.

1049 *See* e.g. *Application of Technostroyexport*, 853 F. Supp. 695, 697 (S.D.N.Y. 1994).

1050 *See* p. 183 *supra*; STEINBRÜCK, 222.

1051 SMIT, *Section 1782 Revisited*, 7 et seq. He argues for the broadest possible interpretation of 'international', which is if any of the parties or arbitrators is not a citizen or resident of the USA; for the difference between 'foreign and international' tribunal, *see also* NYC Bar Committee Report (2010), 32 et seqq.

arbitration.[1052] Indeed, discovery under the FRCP USA–subject to a divergent agreement between the parties–is uncommon in international arbitral proceedings,[1053] and can end up in lengthy and cumbersome battles over discovery requests.[1054] Moreover, according to § 1782, any 'interested person' can initiate a request for discovery, even without the prior consent of the arbitral tribunal. Consequently, as argued in *NBC* and *Republic of Kazakhstan*, there is a danger that § 1782 may be misused for tactical reasons by either party.[1055] The question of discovery should therefore be answered prior to the arbitral proceedings by the parties themselves or, in the absence of any agreement, by the arbitral tribunal.[1056]

In *Intel*, however, to address the concern over allegedly lengthy discovery proceedings, the Supreme Court stated:

> "The dissent sees a need for 'categorical limits' to ward off 'expensive, time-consuming battles about discovery'. ... There is no evidence whatsoever, in the 40 years since § 1782 (a)'s adoption, ... of the cost, delays, and forced settlements the dissent hypothesizes."[1057]

In light of the broad discussion of the appropriateness of US discovery, the Supreme Court's respective remarks are incisive. Besides the statutory requirements, Justice Ginsburg then set out several discretionary guidelines to deal with discovery requests under § 1782. Simply put, a court presented with a § 1782 request always has wide discretion to decide whether to grant or deny

1052 *National Broadcasting Company Inc NBC v. Bear Stearns Co Inc SBC TV*, (2d Cir. 1999), in: Y.B. Comm. Arb. 1999, 890; *Republic of Kazakhstan v. Biedermann International*, (5th Cir. 1999), in: Y.B. Comm. Arb. 2000, 922 et seq.; *see also* the dissenting opinion of Justice Breyer in *Intel Corp. v. Advanced Micro Devices, Inc.*, 542 U.S. 241, 267 et seqq. (2004).

1053 BORN, *Law and Practice*, ch. 9.01 n. 19; BERGER/KELLERHALS, n. 1329; GIRSBERGER/VOSER, n. 994; VÁRADY et al., 674; MARTINEZ-FRAGA, 55; GODFREY, 506 et seq.; *see also* Art. 21 (10) ICDR Rules.

1054 *Republic of Kazakhstan v. Biedermann International*, (5th Cir. 1999), in: Y.B. Comm. Arb. 2000, 922 et seq.; CONLEY, 67 et seq.

1055 *Ibid.*; *National Broadcasting Company Inc NBC v. Bear Stearns Co Inc SBC TV*, (2d Cir. 1999), in: Y.B. Comm. Arb. 1999, 890.

1056 *Ibid.*; *Republic of Kazakhstan v. Biedermann International*, (5th Cir. 1999), in: Y.B. Comm. Arb. 2000, 922 et seq.

1057 *Intel Corp. v. Advanced Micro Devices, Inc.*, 542 U.S. 241, 264, fn 17 (2004); MALAMENT, 1233. This fact is even acknowledged in a decision denying the use of § 1782 in arbitral proceedings; *see La Comision Ejecutiva Hidroelecctrica v. El Paso*, 617 F.Supp.2d 481, 487 (S.D. Tex. 2008): 'The Supreme Court may yet be moved by the stronger gravitational pull of international comity, concomitant with international commerce, to apply § 1782 to arbitral tribunals.'

it.[1058] In this regard, the court ought to examine not only who is seeking discovery, but also from whom and for what reason.[1059] More specifically, the Supreme Court identified five discretionary factors which district courts ought to consider:

"1. The person from whom discovery is sought. § 1782 will most likely not be granted if it is invoked against a party over which the arbitral tribunal has jurisdiction.[1060] As previously discussed, under most institutional arbitration rules, the arbitral tribunal can order a party to produce evidence and even impose sanctions in case of non-compliance.[1061] In contrast, without § 1782, evidence from non-participants would be unobtainable."[1062]

"2. The nature of the foreign tribunal as a first-instance decision maker whose decision is subject to review, as well as the character of the proceedings underway abroad–that is, the rules applicable to the arbitral proceedings concerning discovery (e.g. institutional arbitration rules or the IBA Rules), as well as the stage at which the arbitral proceedings currently stand."[1063]

"3. The receptivity of the foreign tribunal to court assistance under § 1782.[1064] If assistance is not desired–for instance, because the arbitral tribunal refused to give its consent to a request under § 1782–it will most likely be denied."

"4. Whether the § 1782 request is an attempt to circumvent foreign evidence-gathering restrictions."[1065]

"5. Whether the § 1782 request is unduly intrusive or burdensome.[1066] Such requests for 'fishing expeditions' may be rejected or restricted."[1067]

1058 *Intel Corp. v. Advanced Micro Devices, Inc.*, 542 U.S. 241, 255 (2004): 'The statute authorizes, but does not require, a federal district court to provide assistance … .' For an extensive outline of the *Intel* factors *see* BENTO, 50 et seqq.

1059 *Ibid.*, 264, 264 et seqq.

1060 *Ibid.*, 264.

1061 *See* p. 27 et seqq. *and* p. 57 et seqq. *supra*.

1062 *Ibid.*

1063 *Ibid.*, 243, 264; BEALE et al., 100; *see* e.g. *Caratube Intl. Oil Company, Llp.*, 730 F. Supp. 2d 101, 106 et seq. (D.C.C. 2010).

1064 BEALE et al., 97 et seqq.; *Intel Corp. v. Advanced Micro Devices, Inc.*, 542 U.S. 241, 264 (2004).

1065 *Ibid.*, 244 et seq., 265.

1066 *Ibid.*, 245, 265.

1067 BEALE et al., 101.

At first sight, these factors, together with the statutory requirements of § 1782, seem clear enough to equip district courts with the necessary guidance to grant or deny discovery requests.[1068] However, because the decision did not expressly address arbitral tribunals, it remained unclear how US courts would react to *Intel*.

IV. Decisions after Intel

The decisions following *Intel* could not differ more with regard to their interpretation of the case itself and the ensuing consequences in the respective disputes.[1069] While in some circuits there seems to be a logical line of case law, the picture in others is very inconsistent. For the sake of clarity, the following decisions have been presented chronologically, according to their circuit. One must pay close attention to the distinction between decisions of district and circuit courts on the one hand, and the fact that in some circuits, district courts do not follow the previous rulings of the respective circuit courts on the other.

i. 2d Circuit

After *Intel*, in dealing with requests pursuant to § 1782, district courts in the 2d Cir. took a more liberal view as opposed to the prior stance taken in *NBC* in 1999.[1070] For instance, in *OJSC Ukrnafta v. Carpatsky Petroleum Corp.*, based on the criteria in *Intel*, it was held that a private SCC arbitration was within the scope of § 1782.[1071] In other decisions, district courts cited a misguided line of case law differentiating between purely private arbitrations and those conducted by UNCITRAL, which was seen as 'a body operating under the United Nations'.[1072] Quite obviously, although the UNCITRAL Rules were drafted by UNCITRAL, this commission itself–unlike arbitration institutions–is not an administering body in arbitral proceedings conducted under the UNCITRAL Rules.[1073]

1068 *Intel Corp. v. Advanced Micro Devices, Inc.*, 542 U.S. 241, 266 (2004): 'Having held that § 1782 (a) authorizes, but does not require, discovery assistance, we leave it to the courts below to ensure an airing adequate to determine what, if any, assistance is appropriate.'

1069 STRONG, 303; NYC Bar Committee Report (2010), 21 et seqq.; BENTO, 110 et seqq.

1070 *See also* the NYC Bar Committee Report (2010), strongly arguing for the use of § 1782 in aid of international arbitral proceedings (44 et seq.).

1071 *Ukrnafta v. Carpatsky Petroleum Corp.*, 2009 WL 2877156, 1 (D. Conn. 2009).

1072 *Ibid.*, 4; *In re Arbitration between Norfolk Southern Corporation et al.*, 626 F. Supp. 2d 882, 885 (N.D. Ill. 2009); *see also* the investment arbitration disputes in this respect; *In re Government of the Lao People's Democratic Republic*, Case 1:15-MC-00018, 5 et seq. (D. n. Mar. I. 2016; *Chevron Corp. v. Jonathan S. Shefftz*, 754 F. Supp. 2d 254 (D. Mass. 2010); STRONG, 311 et seqq.; *Oxus Gold PLC*, MISC 06-82 (D.N.J. 2007).

1073 STRONG, 308; TIMÁR/KRAAYVANGER, 70.

In the 2016 case of *Kleimar N.V.*, an NY district court confirmed an *ex parte* application under §1782 in aid of arbitration held in London under the LMAA.[1074] Regarding the precedent in *NBC*, rendered in the same circuit, the district court bluntly stated that unfortunately, the 2d Cir. has not yet approved the Supreme Court's reasoning in *Intel*.[1075] Quite unusually, by citing several decisions rendered outside the 2d Cir., the district court considered itself no longer bound by *NBC* in light of these persuasive decisions.[1076] Consequently, after confirming that the requirements of *Intel* had been met, the request made under §1782 was granted. This reasoning was recently confirmed in 2019 in *In re Children's Investment Fund Foundation*, in which an NY district court granted §1782 discovery in aid of an arbitration held under the LCIA Rules.[1077]

ii. 5th and 3d Circuit

By contrast, the 5th Cir.–which handed down the decision in *Republic of Kazakhstan* in 1999–stood firmly behind its precedent and denied an *ex parte* request under §1782 in aid of an arbitration in Switzerland.[1078] In *La Commission Ejecutiva Hidroelecctrica v. El Paso*, the district court noted that in *Intel*, the Supreme Court never intended to include arbitral tribunals, even though it cited Smit's article in which arbitral tribunals were explicitly mentioned.[1079] The 5th Cir. argued that this reference was made only to justify that §1782 applies to quasi-judicial agencies and administrative courts such as the

1074 *Kleimar N.V.*, 220 F. Supp. 3d 517 (S.D.N.Y. 2016); *see also* the related request in the 7th Cir. which has also been granted: *N.V. v. Benxi Iron & Steel Am., Ltd.*, No. 17-cv-01287 (N.D. Ill. 2017).

1075 *Kleimar N.V.*, 220 F. Supp. 3d 517, 521 (S.D.N.Y. 2016).

1076 *Ibid.*, 521 et seq. citing *Consorcio Ecuatoriano v. JAS Forwarding (USA)*, 685 F.3d 987 (11th Cir. 2012); *Winning (HK) Shipping Co. Ltd.*, No. 09-22659 (S.D. Fla. 2010; 11th Cir.); *In re Owl Shipping, LLC*, No. 14-5655 (D.N.J. 2014; 3d Cir.).

1077 *In re Children's Inv. Fund Found. (UK), Sir Christopher Hohn, & Axon Partners, LP*, No. 18-MC-104 (VSB) (S.D.N.Y. 2019).

1078 *La Comision Ejecutiva Hidroelecctrica v. El Paso*, 617 F.Supp.2d 481 (S.D. Tex. 2008); confirmed in *El Paso Corp. v. La Comission Ejecutiva Hidroelectrica*, 341 Fed. Appx. 31 (5th Cir. 2009). Respecting the arbitral tribunal's opinion that itself would have denied a request for discovery because it had been made *ex parte*, the District Court of the S.D. of Texas noted that even if it had the power to order discovery under §1782, it would not do so 'out of respect for the efficient administration of the Swiss arbitration' (*La Comision Ejecutiva Hidroelecctrica v. El Paso*, 617 F.Supp.2d 481, 487 (S.D. Tex. 2008).

1079 *La Comision Ejecutiva Hidroelecctrica v. El Paso*, 617 F.Supp.2d 481, 486 (S.D. Tex. 2008); BEALE et al., 74 et seqq.; O'MALLEY/EATON, 116.

DG-Competition.[1080] Ironically, the same request for documents submitted to the District Court of Delaware in the 3d Cir. led to a different result. This court simply stated that Intel indicated that § 1782 applies to foreign private arbitration, but unfortunately did not explain why.[1081] In the subsequent appeal, the Court of Appeals of the 3d Cir. dismissed the appeal without expressing itself further on § 1782, because the parties merely waited for the arbitral award to be rendered; the whole issue has thus become moot.[1082]

iii. 11th Circuit

In the 11th Cir., several other district courts applied a functional approach to the issue as illustrated in *Intel*, arguing that 'it is the function of the body that makes it a "tribunal", not its formal identity as "governmental" or "private" institution', but rather its adjudicatory function:[1083]

> "Where a body makes adjudicative decisions responsive to a complaint and reviewable in court, it falls within the widely accepted definition of 'tribunal', the reasoning of Intel, and the scope of § 1782 (a), regardless of whether the body is, governmental or private."

Thus, in *Roz Trading Ltd.*, a Georgia district court concluded that an arbitral panel of the International Arbitral Centre of the Austrian Federal Economic Chamber in Vienna fell within the scope of § 1782.[1084] Conversely, in *Operadora DB Mexico* a district court from the same circuit reached the opposite conclusion regarding an ICC arbitral tribunal, upholding the reasoning in *NBC* and *Republic of Kazakhstan* that the word 'tribunal' refers only to governmental (i.e. state-sponsored) entities.[1085] In addition, it held that the re-

1080 *La Comision Ejecutiva Hidroelecctrica v. El Paso*, 617 F.Supp.2d 481, 486 (S.D. Tex. 2008): 'Smit does not speak for the Supreme Court. Until, and, if, the Supreme Court itself adopts Hans Smit's statements as its own within the text of the opinion itself, Hans Smit's opinions on arbitral tribunals has no more weight and authority than any other article. Smit's opinion is not even Supreme Court *dicta*.'

1081 *Comision Ejecutiva Hidroelecctrica del Rio Lempa v. Nejapa Power Company, LLC*, WL 4809035 (D. Del. 2008).

1082 *Comision Ejecutiva Hidroelecctrica del Rio Lempa v. Nejapa Power Company LLC*, 341 Fed. Appx. 821 (3d Cir. 2009).

1083 *See* e.g. *In re Roz Trading Ltd.*, 469 F. Supp. 2d 1221, 1228 (N.D. Ga. 2006).

1084 *Ibid.*

Ibid., 1226; BEALE et al., 69 et seqq.

1085 *Operadora DB Mexico, S.A. DE C.V.*, Case No. 6:09-cv-Orl-22G JK., 23 (M.D. Fla. 2009): 'Because the ICC Panel is the product of a private agreement to resolve disputes independently of state-sponsored tribunals, the court finds that Congress and the Supreme Court would not casually extend § 1782 to such proceeding without some deliberation.' *See also* O'MALLEY/EATON, 117 et seq.

view process of the ICC arbitration did not satisfy the requirements of *Intel* because the arbitral award was 'judicially reviewable' only within very narrow boundaries.[1086]

One year later, in *Winning (HK) Shipping Co. Ltd.* which was conducted under the LMAA, another district court again reached a different conclusion.[1087] Because the arbitration at hand was governed by the EAA 1996 and the arbitral award was therefore reviewable by an English court, the arbitral tribunal was considered a first-instance decision maker in the sense of *Intel*.[1088] Unfortunately, no further explanations of the differences between the review process under ICC and LMAA arbitration were given. In 2012, however, *Consorcio Ecuatoriano v. JAS Forwarding (USA)* shed some light on this issue, at least in the 11th Cir.[1089] The Court of Appeals held that the Centre of Arbitration and Conciliation of the Guayaquil Chamber of Commerce in Ecuador does render first-instance decisions which are subject to judicial review.[1090] Unfortunately, in 2014 the same court vacated this ruling without examining the phrase 'foreign or international tribunal'.[1091] However, it did emphasise the functional approach taken by the Supreme Court in *Intel* and cited Smit's article which explicitly mentioned arbitration tribunals.[1092]

iv. Other Circuits

In other circuits, the situation is even more confusing. District courts in the 1st and 8th Cirs. have considered § 1782 applicable to arbitrations under the ICC Rules, as well as to an Israeli arbitration, based mainly on the legislative history of § 1782 and the reasoning in *Intel*.[1093] Furthermore, interpreting the word 'foreign tribunal' broadly and stating that congress intended to broaden the scope of § 1782, the 6th Cir. reversed the prior district court's order and

1086 *Operadora DB Mexico, S.A. DE C.V.*, Case No. 6:09-cv-Orl-22GJK., 20 et seq. (M.D. Fla. 2009).

1087 *Winning (HK) Shipping Co. Ltd.*, No. 09-22659 (S.D. Fla. 2010); BEALE et al., 83 et seq.; regarding arbitration under the LMAA *see also Kleimar N.V.*, 220 F. Supp. 3d 517 (S.D.N.Y. 2016); *In re Owl Shipping, LLC*, No. 14-5655 (D.N.J. 2014).

1088 *Ibid.*, 18 et seq.

1089 *Consorcio Ecuatoriano v. JAS Forwarding (USA)*, 685 F.3d 987 (11th Cir. 2012); VÁRADY et al., 692 et seq.; MALAMENT, 1229 et seq.

1090 *Consorcio Ecuatoriano v. JAS Forwarding (USA)*, 685 F.3d 987, 996 et seqq. (11th Cir. 2012).

1091 *Consorcio Ecuatoriano v. JAS Forwarding (USA)*, 747 F.3d 1262 (11th Cir. 2014).

1092 *Ibid.*, 1270 fn 4; MALAMENT, 1216 et seq., 1221 et seq.

1093 *In re Babcock Borsig AG*, 583 F. Supp. 2d 233 (D. Mass. 2008; 1st Cir.); *Hallmark Capital Corporation*, 534 F. Supp. 2d 951 (D. Minn. 2007; 8th Cir.) *see also* the decisions regarding investment arbitration mentioned in BLACKMAN/STIEFLER, fn 40 et seq.; STRONG, 306 et seqq.; ALFORD, 136, fn 56.

remanded the case so the district court determines again if discovery pursuant to § 1782 could be granted.[1094] Their counterparts in the 4th, 9th and 10th Cirs., however, denied its application. In *Finserve Group Ltd.*, a district court of the 4th Cir. argued, concerning an LCIA arbitration in London, that 'the Court questions whether the LCIA would be considered to be a 'foreign tribunal' under the statute, as there appears there is no judicial review'.[1095] Without further discussing this point, the request was denied as the LCIA was not receptive to the request.[1096]

What is more, in several decisions of the 9th Cir., requests for court assistance in arbitration under § 1782 were denied based on the reasoning of the 2d and 5th Cirs. prior to *Intel*. In *Dubey*, the district court distinguished between 'purely private arbitrations established by private contract and state-sponsored arbitral bodies' such as the DG-Competition.[1097] By following the reasoning in *NBC* and *Republic of Kazakhstan*, it denied a request under § 1782 requesting discovery in an AAA arbitration held in California.[1098] A decision rendered in the 10th Cir. likewise found an ICC arbitration to be outside the scope of § 1782.[1099]

Finally, district court decisions both granting and denying requests for court assistance in arbitration under § 1782 have been handed down in the 7th Cir. In *Norfolk Southern Corp.*, a district court agreed to the flawed assumption that § 1782 does not apply to purely private arbitral tribunals, but does apply to arbitration under the UNCITRAL Rules and administrated by UNCITRAL itself.[1100] Moreover, it followed *NBC* and *Republic of Kazakhstan* by making a clear distinction between state-sponsored tribunals and purely private arbitral tribunals.[1101] The same reasoning was applied in *TJAC Waterloo*, a construction dispute in which a request under § 1782 was denied to a

1094 *Abdul Latif Jameel Trans. Co. v. Fedex Corp.*, No. 19-5315, 10 et seqq., 18 (6th Cir. 2019); BENTO, 119 et seqq.

1095 *Finserve Group Ltd.*, No. 4:11-mc-2044-RBH, 4 (D.S.C. 2011); regarding judicial review, *see also* the decisions from the 11th Cir., p. 199 et seq. *supra*.

1096 *Finserve Group Ltd.*, No. 4:11-mc-2044-RBH, 5 (D.S.C. 2011); *see also In re Servotronics, Inc.*, No. 2:18-mc-00364-DCN (D.S.C. 2018).

1097 *Dubey*, 949 F. Supp. 2d 990, 994 (D.C. California 2013).

1098 *See also* the subsequent decisions after *Dubey* in the 9th Cir.; *Grupo Unidos Por El Canal S.A.*, No. 14-mc-80277-JST (N.D. Cal. 2015); *In re Government of the Lao People's Democratic Republic*, 1:15-MC-00018 (D. n. Mar. I. 2016).

1099 *Grupo Unidos Por El Canal, S.A.*, No. 14-mc-00226-MSK-KMT, 15 et seq. (D.C. Colo. 2015).

1100 *In re Arbitration between Norfolk Southern Corporation et al*, 626 F. Supp. 2d 882, 885 (N.D. Ill. 2009); *see also* p. 197 *supra*.

1101 *Ibid.*

private arbitration held in London.[1102] In another decision which was closely connected to *Kleimar (see* p. 198 *supra),* a district court within the 7th Cir. applied a similar functional approach to that applied in the 11th Cir. and held that the LMAA is a foreign tribunal according to § 1782.[1103]

v. Summary

Unfortunately, there is not only a split among the circuits, but at times also within them. In light of this, it is difficult to determine commonalities. This problem is vividly demonstrated in requests made under § 1782 in the same dispute, which ended in conflicting decisions in different circuits.[1104] Nonetheless, one can detect several lines of argumentation among the US courts. With regard to those decisions which denied the application of § 1782 to arbitration, it seems commonly accepted among these courts that § 1782 does at least apply to state-sponsored tribunals whose decisions are subject to review, as stated in *Intel.*[1105] Therefore, most courts in the 4th, 5th, 7th, 9th, 10th and 11th Cirs. have excluded only arbitral tribunals from the scope of application of § 1782. A minority of decisions within these circuits have distinguished between purely private arbitration and arbitration conducted under the UNICTRAL Rules. As previously discussed, this assumption is clearly misguided.[1106] In contrast, decisions granting requests under § 1782 in the 1st, 2nd, 3rd and 8th Cirs. have been justified either by referring to the legislative history of *Intel* or by applying a functional approach to the issue. The use of this approach has led to varied results.

d. Intermediate Result

The foregoing discussion has focused on the use of § 1782 by US courts in the field of international arbitration. The result is disturbing, to put it mildly. At this point, only a clear-cut decision from the Supreme Court or an amendment of § 1782 would afford sufficient guidance and clarity on whether and under what conditions this section is applicable to arbitration. In the meantime, US courts are left with the legislative history of § 1782 and the reasoning in *Intel*. Regarding the legislative materials, it has been shown that Congress

1102 *TJAC Waterloo, LLC*, No. 3:16-mc-9CAN (N.D. Ind. 2016).

1103 *N.V. v. Benxi Iron & Steel Am., Ltd.*, No. 17-cv-01287, 12 et seqq. (N.D. Ill. 2017).

1104 The several decisions rendered in the dispute between *La Comision Ejecutive Hidroelectrica* and *El Paso* show vividly how inconsistently § 1782 is handled among US courts; *see* p. 198 *supra*.

1105 *Intel Corp. v. Advanced Micro Devices, Inc.*, 542 U.S. 241, 254 et seq. (2004).

1106 *See* p. 197 *supra*.

neither expressly included nor excluded arbitral tribunals from the scope of application of § 1782. Although the primary focus of this provision is not arbitration, the goal was to improve international court assistance in general. With regard to the tension between court assistance in the taking of evidence in domestic (under the FAA USA) and foreign (under § 1782) arbitration, it has been demonstrated that there is no obligation to treat requests equally.

Still, the main question remains as to whether US-style discovery in fact runs contrary to the essence of arbitration and the expectations of arbitrators and the parties. According to *Intel*, if § 1782 is read not only with the statutory requirements which have been further interpreted by the Supreme Court, but also with the five discretionary factors set out in *Intel*, the risk of imposing US discovery in foreign proceedings is considerably minimised. The question at hand has been treated differently not only by various US courts, but also in legal doctrine. A minority of authors have embraced the reasoning of *NBC* and *Republic of Kazakhstan*, arguing that neither the legislative history nor *Intel* itself suggests that § 1782 should be used in relation to arbitral proceedings.[1107] Yet the majority seem to have embraced the use of § 1782 in arbitration.[1108] These authors mainly argue that, together with the *Intel* factors, § 1782 can be used in arbitration without disturbing the proceedings. They further argue that an appropriate use of § 1782 may be very beneficial. Whether this is in fact true will be analysed in the following section, applying the same structure as was followed in the previous examinations of *leges arbitri*.

C. Competence to Seek Court Assistance

1. Primacy of the Arbitral Tribunal

A request under § 1782 is initiated through either a letter rogatory, a request by a foreign or international tribunal or a simple application by 'any interested person'. This latter possibility presents one of the main problems arising from § 1782: the 'interested person' might be either a party to the arbitration or even a third party.[1109] As previously discussed, this was strongly criticised

1107 STRONG, 315 et seqq.; GODFREY, 475 et seqq.; CONLEY, 45 et seqq.

1108 BORN, *Law and Practice*, ch. 9 n. 30; BLACKABY et al., n. 7.44; MALAMENT, 1217 et seqq.; BEALE et al., 51 et seqq.; NYC Bar Committee Report (2010), 1 et seqq.; STEINBRÜCK, 205 et seqq.; KRAAYVANGER et al., 161 et seqq.; ILLMER/STEINBRÜCK, 329 et seqq.; SMIT, *Section 1782 Revisited*, 5 et seqq.; differentiated O'MALLEY/EATON, 118; ROTHSTEIN, 61 et seqq.

1109 *Intel Corp. v. Advanced Micro Devices, Inc.*, 542 U.S. 241, 255 et seq., 256 (2004): 'No doubt litigants are included among, and may be the most common example of, the 'interested person(s)' who may invoke § 1782 (a) … .'

in *NBC* and *Republic of Kazakhstan*.[1110] While there is no danger if the arbitral tribunal itself is allowed to make a request, the situation is different if assistance is sought *ex parte* either by one of the parties to the arbitration or by any other person. Practice shows that § 1782 is mostly invoked *ex parte* and, as a consequence, the primacy of the arbitral tribunal is obviously undermined.[1111] Although in *Intel* the Supreme Court imposed no 'categorical limits' on the wording of § 1782, it stated that the receptivity of the foreign tribunal to court assistance (the third *Intel* factor) should be taken into account.[1112] This central requirement has been acknowledged in a number of cases, with requests under § 1782 often denied because they had not been approved by the arbitral tribunal.[1113] It is therefore unsurprising that authors who favour the use of § 1782 in international arbitration consider the approval of the arbitral tribunal to be a key prerequisite.[1114]

What is more, the approval of the arbitral tribunal addresses in part the second and fourth *Intel* factors, taking into account the 'character of the proceedings underway abroad' by examining whether the request under § 1782 is an attempt to circumvent foreign evidence-gathering restrictions.[1115] As previously discussed (*see* p. 96 et seqq. *supra*), many institutional arbitration rules as well as the IBA Rules require the arbitral tribunal's consent on evidentiary matters such as court assistance in the taking of evidence.[1116] The arbitral tribunal, as opposed to the respective state court, is therefore best placed to decide whether and to what extent assistance should be granted.[1117] Within these boundaries, the arbitral tribunal is unlikely to risk violating the right to be heard by deciding what is best for the respective arbitration. This

1110 *See* p. 189 et seq. *supra*.

1111 GODFREY, 510; CONLEY, 66; ROTHSTEIN, 64 et seq.

1112 *Intel Corp. v. Advanced Micro Devices, Inc.*, 542 U.S. 241, 255 et seq., 264 (2004).

1113 *Application of Technostroyexport*, 853 F. Supp. 695, 697 (S.D.N.Y. 1994); *Hallmark Capital Corporation*, 534 F. Supp. 2d 951, 957 (D. Minn. 2007); *In re Babcock Borsig AG*, 583 F. Supp. 2d 233, 241 (D. Mass 2008; 1st Cir.); *see also In re Roz Trading Ltd.*, 469 F. Supp. 2d 1221, 1229 (N.D. Ga. 2006); Instead of seeking the approval of the arbitral tribunal in charge, the district court in Georgia assumed receptivity merely on the grounds that the rules applicable to the arbitral proceedings under the Arbitral Center of the Austrian Federal Economic Chamber in Vienna allowed for foreign court assistance in the taking of evidence (BEALE et al., 97 et seq.).

1114 MALAMENT, 1241; BEALE et al., 97 et seqq.; SMIT, *Section 1782 Revisited*, 8 et seq.; NYC Bar Committee Report (2010), 30 et seqq.; KRAAYVANGER et al., 164; ILLMER/STEINBRÜCK, 341 et seq.; BORN, *Law and Practice*, ch. 9 n. 30.

1115 *See* p. 196 *supra*; BEALE et al., 100 et seq., 102.

1116 *See* e.g. Art. 27 (4) UNCITRAL Rules; Art. 25 (7) Swiss Rules; Art. 25 (3) ICC Rules; Art. 3 (9) IBA Rules.

1117 NYC Committee Report (2010), 31.

would be the case only if the evidence sought were absolutely relevant to the case and the arbitral tribunal's refusal would therefore be disproportionate and unnecessary.

Intel further suggests that the foreign arbitration need not be pending, but only in 'reasonable contemplation'.[1118] Applied to arbitral proceedings, it follows that § 1782 can be used even before the constitution of the arbitral tribunal. As the arbitral tribunal has not yet been constituted, one might ask how a state court should deal with the receptivity factor in such situations. As already demonstrated, many institutional arbitration rules provide for the appointment of emergency arbitrators in such situations *(see* p. 80 *supra).*[1119] Thus, if the arbitration is governed by an institution which provides for the appointment of an emergency arbitrator, the consent of that emergency arbitrator should be sought first. By contrast, if there is no emergency arbitrator available, a request under § 1782 should generally be denied.[1120] Still, in circumstances where evidence might be lost or destroyed and assistance under § 1782 is sought *ex parte,* the respective state court should exercise its discretion in favour of arbitration. The arbitral tribunal which will subsequently be constituted can still refuse to introduce the evidence taken under § 1782 into the proceedings when assessing the evidence.[1121]

2. Exclusion of Court Assistance in Taking Evidence

Both the plain wording of § 1782 and the discretionary factors set out in *Intel* support a conclusion that the parties can exclude court assistance in the taking of evidence pursuant to § 1782. This may be done in the arbitration agreement either explicitly or by reference to a set of institutional arbitration rules and/or the IBA Rules. While the former possibility might be used from time to time, the latter scenario is much more common.[1122] At the outset of a dispute, it can be difficult to predict where evidence might be sought in the subsequent proceedings. Thus, the exclusion of § 1782 is usually not addressed directly in the arbitration agreement, but rather in arbitration rules in relation to court assistance in the taking of evidence.[1123] Taking the second

1118 *Intel Corp. v. Advanced Micro Devices, Inc.*, 542 U.S. 241, 258 et seq. (2004); *see also In re Letter of Request from the Crown Prosecution Service of the United Kingdom*, 870 F.2d 868, 687, 691 (D.C. Cir. 1989), a decision also rendered by Justice Ginsburg, who at this time worked as a circuit judge.

1119 *See* e.g. Art. 29 ICC Rules; Rules 30 SIAC Rules; Art. 43 Swiss Rules.

1120 ROTHSTEIN, 79.

1121 *Ibid.*, 80; *see* e.g. Art. 9 (1) IBA Rules.

1122 MARTINEZ-FRAGA, 87 et seqq.

1123 *See* e.g. Art. 22.2 LCIA Rules; Arts. 3 (9) and 4 (9) IBA Rules.

Intel factor into account–that is, the nature of the proceedings underway abroad–it follows that state courts should respect the parties' choice to exclude § 1782 altogether.[1124] As a result, such a renunciation should not be at odds with the right to minimum legal protection.

D. Spectrum of Evidence and its Target

1. Evidence According to a Party Agreement

Like the exclusion of § 1782 as a whole, a state court whose assistance is sought under § 1782 should consider whether the parties excluded certain types of evidence in the arbitration agreement or by reference to arbitration rules (third *Intel* factor). Thus, the state court should consider whether the parties have agreed on certain evidentiary mechanisms, such as those stated in the IBA Rules. Here again, the fourth *Intel* factor addresses the issue when discussing the circumvention of foreign evidence-gathering restrictions. As an example, in *Caratube International Oil Company*, the District Court of Columbia denied discovery because the requesting party tried to circumvent not only the agreed ICSID Convention, but also the IBA Rules.[1125] Besides arbitration rules, the fourth *Intel* factor also addresses laws that forbid discovery.[1126] Even if the respective state court grants discovery despite a divergent agreement between the parties, this will serve as a reason to annul the arbitral award.[1127] Usually, however, the arbitral tribunal will not even introduce evidence into the arbitral proceeding which was gathered without authorisation under § 1782.

2. Evidence According to 28 USC § 1782

In the process of taking evidence, either state courts (i.e. federal courts in the US) will follow the foreign 'practice and procedure' *(see* p. 186 *supra)* or, if the order does not prescribe otherwise, the FRCP USA (Rules 26 et seqq. FRCP USA) will apply.[1128] Thus, one might ask to what extent they will do so. Reading § 1782, it is evident that it mentions only two types of evidence–witness testimony and document production:

> "The district court ... may order him to give his testimony or statement or to produce a document or other thing for use in a proceeding ... ."

1124 *See* p. 196 *supra.*

1125 *Caratube International Oil Company, Llp.*, 730 F. Supp. 2d 101, 107 et seqq. (D.D.C. 2010); Art. 43 ICSID Convention; Art. 3 (9) IBA Rules.

1126 *See* e.g. § 1050 (2) CCP DE.

1127 S. 10 (a) (4) FAA USA; Art. V (1) (c) NYC; *see also* p. 213 *infra.*

1128 § 1782 (a).

Distinguishing between testimony and statements, Congress intended that district courts could also order that parties and other individuals whose statements would not be considered 'testimony' under foreign law be heard.[1129] In addition, because § 1782 primarily serves to obtain evidence from third parties, interrogatories (Rule 33 FRCP USA) and admissions (Rule 36 FRCP USA), which are specifically tailored to preparations for trial, are not usually available through § 1782.[1130] 'Testimony' therefore refers to classical depositions–that is, a witness examination before a court-authorised person to ask certain questions relevant to the case.[1131] Regarding document production, § 1782 distinguishes between documents and 'other things'. According to Rule 34 FRCP USA, this includes not only documents in the common sense, but also electronically stored information. In addition, it remains unclear what is meant by the term 'other things'. In the absence of any indication in § 1782, it would seem that this does not refer to inspections in the sense of Rule 34 (a) (2) FRCP USA, but rather to objects in one's possession which may be subject to inspection and tests, such as machines or motors.[1132]

3. Foreign Types of Evidence

While in most cases a court whose assistance is sought under § 1782 will proceed according to the FRCP USA, it might also take into account the foreign practice and procedure.[1133] As a consequence, US courts can take evidence according to the rules agreed in the arbitration. Nevertheless, whether a US court will in fact take evidence according to foreign law depends mostly on the discretion of the respective state court.[1134] As seen in other *leges arbitri*, state courts usually take evidence according to their own law only.[1135] Therefore, this provision illustrates the very open US approach to international court assistance.

This notwithstanding, it is unsurprising that evidence is usually taken according to the FRCP USA. Often, parties deliberately choose to initiate a request under § 1782 precisely because US discovery is much broader than

1129 SMIT, Section 1782 Revisited, 1026.

1130 *In re Order for Labor Court of Brazil*, 466 F. Supp. 2d 1020, 1033 (N.D. Ill. 2006); *In re Ishiara Chemical Co., Ltd.*, 121 F. Supp. 2d 209, 224 et seq. (E.D.N.Y. 2000).

1131 Rule 27 et seqq. FRCP USA.

1132 Advisory Committee FRCP USA (1970).

1133 § 1782: 'The order may prescribe the practice and procedure, which may be in whole or part the practice and procedure of the foreign country of the international tribunal, for taking the testimony or statement or producing the document or other thing.'

1134 SMIT, *International Litigation*, 1028.

1135 *See e.g.* as regards Germany; p. 140 et seqq. *supra*.

that available under most laws. If the request is made with the consent of the arbitral tribunal and the statutory requirements and the other discretionary factors are fulfilled, discovery will most likely be granted. In contrast, if a request under § 1782 is sought *ex parte*, usually to circumvent foreign evidence-gathering restrictions (fourth Intel factor), the request should be denied, in order to uphold the parties' agreement whereby evidentiary issues should be governed by the arbitral tribunal. Consequently, there is no 'foreign discoverability' rule, based on either § 1782 or its legislative history, according to which requests must also be permissible under foreign law.[1136] It may be summarised that although § 1782 allows for evidence to be taken according to foreign law, this is seldom done because requests under § 1782 are usually made in an attempt to avail of the broad discovery foreseen in the FRCP USA.

4. International Judicial Assistance in Taking Evidence

Instead of choosing § 1782 to obtain evidence located in the USA, the parties may also choose to use the HEC as a time-tested tool.[1137] Indeed, it has been argued that since the USA is a Member Party to the HEC, the only way to obtain evidence through international court assistance is via this convention. Even though the HEC does indeed serve as a relevant convention in this field, it would be sub-optimal if this were the only way to obtain evidence in the USA. Fortunately, the Supreme Court has shed light on this issue by making clear that the HEC is only one alternative to the FRCP USA, rather than the exclusive procedure through which court assistance in international arbitration may be obtained.[1138] This follows not only from the Supreme Court's decision, but also from the text of the HEC itself.[1139] Among other reasons, this seems to be justified given the often lengthy and costly process involved in obtaining evidence through the HEC, compared to that under the FRCP USA.[1140] In sum, through the lens of an arbitration practitioner, it is welcome that the HEC route is just one, and not the only, way to obtain evidence in the USA.[1141]

1136 *Intel Corp. v. Advanced Micro Devices, Inc.*, 542 U.S. 241, 259 et seqq. (2004): 'A foreign nation may limit discovery within its domain for reasons peculiar to its own legal practices, culture, or traditions–reasons that do not necessarily signal objection to aid from United States Federal Courts' (261); *see also Bayer*, 146 F.3d 188, 193 et seq. (3d Cir. 1998).

1137 In the USA, the HEC entered into force in 1972; *see* the current status.

1138 *Société Nationale Industrielle Aérospatiale v. U.S. Dist. Court*, 482 U.S. 522 (1987).

1139 Art. 27 (c) HEC: 'The provisions of the present Convention shall not prevent a Contracting State from–... c) permitting, by internal law or practice, methods of taking evidence other than those provided for in this Convention.'

1140 *Société Nationale Industrielle Aérospatiale v. U.S. Dist. Court*, 482 U.S. 522, 543 (1987); *Schindler Elevator Corp. v. Otis Elevator Co.*, 657 F. Sup. 2d 525, 530 (D.N.J. 2009); ABDOLLAHI, 778 et seqq.

1141 *Ibid.*, 800.

5. Target of Evidence

As regards the target of evidence, evidence can be taken only from a 'person' who 'resides or is found' in a certain district. This person need not necessarily be domiciled there; it seems to suffice if he or she is staying in the district temporarily.[1142] If the target of evidence is a legal entity, the party requesting assistance under § 1782 must show that this entity undertakes 'systematic and continuous local activities' in the district.[1143] In *Intel*, an important difference was made between the parties to the arbitration and third parties.[1144] Because the foreign or international tribunal has jurisdiction over the parties–as opposed to third parties–discovery requests against a party to the ongoing proceedings will most likely be denied (first *Intel* factor).[1145] Applied to arbitral proceedings, if certain evidence could be produced by a party but it refuses to do so, the arbitral tribunal can respond by drawing an adverse inference or allocating the costs accordingly.[1146] By granting requests under § 1782 mainly in cases where evidence lies outside the reach of the parties to the arbitration, the risk of misuse of this section by a party to the arbitration is dramatically reduced.[1147] In addition, US courts will provide assistance where arbitral tribunals cannot obtain evidence because of their lack of *imperium*.[1148]

Irrespective of whether the target of evidence is a party to the arbitration or a third party, § 1782 makes it clear that privileges apply at all times:

> "A person may not be compelled to give his testimony or statement or to produce a document or other thing in violation of any legally applicable privilege."

While the legislative history does not further explain which privileges under which law apply, US courts seem to respect them under both US and foreign law, as long as there is 'authoritative proof' that privilege exists

1142 SMIT, *Section 1782 Revisited*, 9 et seq.; *In re Edelmann*, 295 F.3d 171, 179 et seqq. (2d Cir. 2002). Regarding the requirement that a person can be forced to attend a hearing only within 100 miles of where he or she resides or regularly transacts business, *see* Rule 45 (c) (1) (A) FRCP USA); *In re Edelmann*, 295 F.3d 171, 181 (2d Cir. 2002).

1143 SMIT, *Section 1782 Revisited*, 10; ELUL/MOSQUERA, n. 398; *Kleimar N.V.*, 220 F. Supp. 3d 517, 521 (S.D.N.Y. 2016); *In Re Godfrey*, 526 F. Supp. 2d 417, 422 (S.D.N.Y. 2007); *Qualcomm Inc.*, 162 F. Supp. 3d 1029, 1035 (N.D. Cal. 2016). Regarding the non-extraterritorial scope of § 1782, *see also* SMIT, *Section 1782 Revisited*, 10 et seqq.

1144 *Ibid.*, 264.

1145 *Ibid.*; BEALE et al., 99 et seq.; MALAMENT, 1240. 2.

1146 *See* p. 56 et seqq. *supra*.

1147 BEALE et al., 99 et seq.

1148 *Ibid.*

under foreign law.[1149] According to the FRCP USA, the scope of discovery is as follows:

> "Parties may obtain discovery regarding any nonprivileged matter that is relevant to any party's claim or defense and proportional to the needs of the case, considering the importance of the issues at stake in the action, the amount in controversy, the parties' relative access to relevant information, the parties' resources, the importance of the discovery in resolving the issues, and whether the burden or expense of the proposed discovery outweighs its likely benefit."[1150]

A person faced with a request to produce evidence pursuant to § 1782 can initiate a motion to quash or modify a discovery order ('protective order') by showing that discovery would force that person to reveal 'a trade secret or other confidential research, development, or commercial information'.[1151] If the person fails to obey the discovery order without sufficient reason, the court can, for instance, draw an adverse inference and treat the non-compliance as contempt of court.[1152] In addition, the disobedient party can be forced to pay the expenses caused by the failure to produce evidence.[1153]

In addition to the statutory factors, the fifth *Intel* factor states that unduly intrusive or burdensome requests pursuant to § 1782 should be rejected or restricted.[1154] As a consequence, fishing expeditions–such as requests for extensive categories of documents, for documents which are sought in bad faith for the purpose of harassment or for irrelevant material–will be denied.[1155] In this regard, a little 'inconvenience alone will not justify an order to quash a subpoena that seeks potentially relevant testimony'.[1156] In order to maximize the chances that a court will grant discovery under § 1782, parties would be well advised to narrow their discovery requests accordingly.

1149 *In re Veiga*, 746 F. Sup. 2d 8, 26 (D.D.C. 2010); *Metallgesellschaft AG v. Hodapp*, 121 F.3d 77, 80 (2d Cir. 1997).

1150 Rule 26 (b) (1) FRCP USA.

1151 Rule 26 (c) (1) (g) FRCP USA; Rule 45 (d) (3) (iii) FRCP USA.

1152 Rule 37 (b) (2) (A) FRCP USA.

1153 Rule 37 (b) (2) (B) FRCP USA.

1154 *Intel Corp. v. Advanced Micro Devices, Inc.*, 542 U.S. 241, 265 (2004).

1155 *In re Petition for Asia Mar. Pac. Ltd.*, 253 F. Supp. 3d 701, 705 (S.D.N.Y. 2015); *Brandi-Dohrn v. IKB Deutsche Industriebank AG*, 673 F.3d 76, 81 (2d Cir. 2012); *Euromepa S.A. v. R. Esmerian, Inc.*, 51 F.3d 1095, 1101 (2d Cir. 1995).

1156 *Anwar v. Fairfield Greenwich Ltd.*, 297 F.R.D. 223, 226 (S.D.N.Y. 2013).

E. Competence of the *Juge d'Appui*

1. Scope of Discretion

The previous discussion has shown that the use of § 1782 is always discretionary. This follows not only from the discretionary *Intel* factors, but also from § 1782 itself.[1157] When this section is supplemented by the discretionary factors, the concerns raised in *NBC* and *Republic of Kazakhstan* can be largely eliminated. In this regard, the arbitral tribunal's consent to a § 1782 request plays a central role.[1158] Further, the fear of excessive discovery in international arbitration seems to be unfounded, given that the discretionary factors ensure that discovery is granted only in limited circumstances.[1159] Moreover, one should bear in mind that discretion is the byword not only before the state courts, but also before the arbitral tribunal, which will carefully weigh whether and how to introduce and assess evidence gathered under § 1782. For instance, if the parties agreed to proceed according to the IBA Rules, there are several requirements regarding whether and under what circumstances evidence can be introduced into the arbitral proceedings (*see* p. 36 et seqq., p. 42 et seqq. *supra*).[1160]

2. Principle of Subsidiarity

§ 1782 is silent regarding whether a foreign or international tribunal can take the requested evidence itself. *Intel* states only that discovery will most likely be denied if it is sought against a party over which the foreign or international tribunal has jurisdiction, as opposed to third parties which are out of reach. Because there is no 'exhaustion requirement' to seek discovery under § 1782, it is left to the discretion of the state court in charge to 'consider a party's failure first to attempt discovery measures in the foreign jurisdiction'.[1161] In *Malev Hungarian Airlines*, the Court of Appeals of the 2d Cir. stated that any 'exhaustion requirement' would be in conflict with the purpose of § 1782:

1157 The word 'may' is found six times in § 1782; SMIT, *Section 1782 Revisited*, 15.

1158 *In re Babcock Borsig AG*, 583 F. Supp. 2d 233, 241 (D. Mass. 2008): 'In a situation where the foreign tribunal restricts discovery, granting the application could undermine the statute's objective.'

1159 BEALE et al., 96.

1160 *See* e.g. *Grupo Unidos Por El Canal, S.A.*, No. 14-mc-00226-MSK-KMT, 23 (D.C. Colo. 2015).

1161 ELUL/MOSQUERA, n. 406; *In re Roz Trading Ltd.*, 469 F. Supp. 2d 1221, 1229 et seq. (N.D. Ga. 2006); *In re Babcock Borsig AG*, 583 F. Supp. 2d 233, 241 (D.C. Mass. 2008); *Europepa S.A. v. R. Esmerian, Inc.*, 51 F.3d 1095, 1098 (2d Cir. 1995); *Malev Hungarian Airlines*, 964 F.2d 97, 100 (2d Cir. 1992).

namely, to improve international court assistance and to prompt foreign jurisdictions to introduce similar provisions based on the US model.[1162] This again demonstrates the very liberal approach taken by the USA.

3. Examination of the Arbitration Agreement

Aside from the need to verify what the arbitration agreement says about the applicable arbitration rules, there is little debate in US legal doctrine regarding the examination of the arbitration agreement.[1163] As it is still controversial whether § 1782 actually applies to arbitral proceedings, the examination of the arbitration agreement plays a crucial role–albeit mainly with the aim of distinguishing between arbitral proceedings and state court litigation. State courts whose assistance is sought under § 1782 will therefore take a closer look at the second *Intel* factor by examining the nature of the foreign tribunal as a first-instance decision maker whose decisions are subject to review. Because of the vast divergence among US circuits, a prior study of decisions on § 1782 is crucial to test the receptivity of US courts to requests for assistance in arbitral tribunals. Moreover, the arbitration agreement can of course be examined in the context of the recognition and enforcement of an arbitral award under the NYC.[1164]

F. Appellate Remedies

As previously discussed *(see* p. 210 *supra),* the target of evidence under § 1782 can initiate a motion to quash or modify the discovery request.[1165] If it is granted nevertheless, the parties can appeal the 'judgment' within 30 days of entry of the decision with the respective court of appeals in the circuit in which the relevant district court is based.[1166] The review mainly involves questions of law and not findings of fact (unless they were 'clearly erroneous').[1167] The court of appeals may either deny the appeal or reverse and remand the case to the district court with instructions in the sense of its decision.[1168]

1162 *Ibid.*

1163 BEALE et al., 104 et seqq.

1164 Arts. III (3) and V (1) (a) NYC.

1165 Rule 26 (c) (1) (g) FRCP USA; Rule 45 (d) (3) (iii) FRCP USA.

1166 Rule 54 FRCP USA; 28 USC § 1291 and § 1294 (1); Rule 4 (a) (1) (A) FRAP USA.

1167 Rule 52 (a) (6) FRCP USA; HAY, n. 211.

1168 *Ibid.*

The question of how to vacate an arbitral award based on the taking of evidence pursuant to §1782 is different. In the USA, this process is regulated by the FAA USA.[1169] Accordingly, an international arbitral award rendered in the USA can be vacated upon the application of any party by the district court at the place where the arbitral award was rendered within three months of the date on which it was rendered.[1170] This might be the case where the arbitral tribunal allowed a request under §1782 despite an explicit agreement to the contrary between the parties. If the taking of evidence had a significant influence on the arbitral award, this could serve as a reason to vacate the arbitral award because the arbitrator(s) violated due process or exceeded their powers.[1171] In this regard, US courts usually establish a high bar for such applications, acknowledging the broad discretion of arbitrators in relation to evidentiary matters.[1172]

G. Summary

The foregoing examination of court assistance in the taking of evidence in the USA is the most complex so far, with regard to both the legal bases and the extent to which evidence can be taken. First, the question of the legal bases for assistance of international arbitral tribunals is very ambiguous; the ongoing dispute as to whether §1782 applies to international arbitration will therefore most likely continue. In this regard, a clear answer from the Supreme Court would be highly desirable.[1173] In the meantime, considering the second *Intel* factor–that is, to examine the nature of the foreign tribunal as a first-instance decision maker–US courts whose assistance is sought under §1782 are equipped with guidelines to assess whether such assistance should be granted. As an alternative, one might ask whether this question should rather be answered at the legislative level by explicitly mentioning arbitral tribunals in §1782.[1174] Until then, as the previous overview of case law has demonstrated, it is crucial to understand which circuits are more likely to grant a request under §1782 for assistance in international arbitral proceedings. Finally, it is

1169 ORLOWSKI, n. 506; for the dispute in legal doctrine as to whether §10 FAA USA also applies to international arbitration, *see ibid.*, 507 et seq.

1170 §10 (a) and §12 FAA USA.

1171 §10 (a) (4) FAA USA; ORLOWSKI, n. 521 et seqq.

1172 *Ibid.*; *see* e.g. *Kolel Beth Yechiel Mechil of Tartikov, Inc. v. YLL Irrevocable Trust*, 729 F.3d 99, 107 (2d Cir. 2013).

1173 TIMÁR/KRAAYVANGER, 71.

1174 ROTHSTEIN, 79.

important to bear in mind that without § 1782, international arbitral tribunals would have to take the lengthy and burdensome route of seeking international court assistance through the HEC.[1175]

Second, the competence to make a request pursuant to § 1782 has been one of the main arguments against its use in international arbitration.[1176] In contrast to the arbitral tribunal, which can initiate a request according to § 1782 in certain circuits, the ability for 'any interested person' to do likewise is problematic. § 1782, as it stands today, should thus be read together with the third *Intel* factor, taking into account the receptivity of the arbitral tribunal. Although practice shows that § 1782 is almost always sought *ex parte*, such requests should be granted only in exceptional urgent cases. At the legislative level, in order to avoid delaying tactics, § 1782 could be amended by allowing the parties to arbitration to make such requests only with the prior consent of the arbitral tribunal.[1177] Moreover, the parties are at liberty to exclude discovery under § 1782 altogether.

Third, the scope of evidence is limited to document production, witness testimony and inspection of objects. In most cases, evidence is obtained under the FRCP USA or, as an alternative, in accordance with foreign law. However, usually the person seeking discovery under § 1782 does so to make use of broad discovery rights which are mostly unavailable in other jurisdictions. Regarding the target of evidence, evidence can be gathered from natural persons or legal entities. If the target is a party to the arbitration (as opposed to a third party), assistance should be denied, since the arbitral tribunal has jurisdiction over that party and thus has means to address any non-compliance in evidentiary matters (first *Intel* factor). Still, if discovery is ordered against a third party, privileges may apply to shield that person from giving evidence. This is not only foreseen in § 1782, but also addressed in the fifth *Intel* factor, which prohibits unduly intrusive or burdensome requests.

Fourth, even more so than under English law (*see* p. 177 et seqq. *supra*), the US courts enjoy wide discretion to grant or deny assistance in the taking of evidence. This is obvious not only from an examination of § 1782, but first and foremost from an examination of the *Intel* factors, which provide guide-

1175 As an exception to this, *see* the rare cases in which court assistance in the taking of evidence has been granted under § 7 FAA USA (p. 183 *supra*). This problem was even acknowledged in *NBC*, but ultimately considered less significant in light of the trouble which would arise from the applicability of § 1782 to international arbitration (*National Broadcasting Company Inc NBC v. Bear Stearns Co Inc SBC TV*, 165 F.3d 184, fn 8 (2d Cir.1999); Y.B. Comm. Arb. 1999, 890.

1176 *See* p. 190 *supra*.

1177 ROTHSTEIN, 79.

lines for the exercise of this discretion. The *Intel* factors address crucial aspects such as the consent of the arbitral tribunal to request discovery and the autonomy of the parties to determine how the arbitration should be conducted. Furthermore, delaying tactics are avoided by paying attention to the reason for requesting discovery under § 1782 and considering whether the request is an attempted 'fishing expedition'. Moreover, there is no 'exhaustion requirement', obliging state courts to consider whether the requested evidence could have been obtained in the foreign proceedings. Finally, because the applicability of § 1782 to arbitral proceedings remains unclear to date, a state court will examine the arbitration agreement to determine whether arbitration is underway and, if so, what the parties have agreed in their arbitration agreement.

Finally, a decision under § 1782 granting or denying discovery can be challenged by either party before the respective court of appeals. However, as assistance under § 1782 is often sought *ex parte*, the battle between parties before the respective district court can take quite a long time. What is more, if the assistance is granted under § 1782 contrary to an explicit agreement between the parties and influences the arbitral award, the arbitral award may even be vacated before the district court where the arbitral award was rendered. In this regard, the bar is set high, since the US courts respect the discretion of the parties, arbitrators and arbitration itself as an alternative dispute settlement mechanism.

In contrast to the *leges arbitri* previously examined in this chapter, the US approach is in many ways different and more complex. Regarding US discovery, although the approach to international arbitration (with justification) appears largely hands-off, it has been shown that if § 1782 is read and applied together with the *Intel* factors, its use will not endanger the arbitral proceedings, but will rather be highly beneficial. Hitherto, the fears expressed in *NBC* and *Republic of Kazakhstan* have remained unjustified. Not least, this is evident from the relatively few cases in which § 1782 has been applied to arbitral proceedings.[1178] Still, given the ambiguity regarding § 1782 and its use in international arbitration, further guidance from the Supreme Court–or, even better, the amendment of this section–would be highly welcome.

1178 BEALE et al., 109.

§ 6 Conclusion

Under the previous comparative analysis, court assistance in the taking of evidence has been addressed from various angles. In this regard, several findings are of major importance for the subsequent examination and evaluation of the situation in Switzerland. First, as regards the subject of direct assistance, all examined *leges arbitri* allow for the provision of assistance irrespective of additional requirements, such as the location of the seat of arbitration or the nationality of the parties. Evidence located in these countries can therefore be obtained within a shorter timeframe than under international treaties such as the HEC. However, in the USA, it remains doubtful whether a request under § 1782 will in fact be granted; the result will depend mainly on how the district courts interpret § 1782 and the *Intel* factors.[1179]

Second, as regards the competence to seek court assistance in the taking of evidence, the approaches diverge. While under German and French law, the arbitral tribunal's approval must be obtained before seeking assistance, this does not apply in England and the USA. Under the EAA 1996, assistance can be granted if–as an alternative to the arbitral tribunal's consent–both parties agree to the request. The approach under § 1782 is quite different: court assistance may be sought by 'any interested person'. As previously discussed, this section should always be read together with the third *Intel* factor, concerning the receptivity of the arbitral tribunal to the request for assistance.[1180] All in all, while the arbitral tribunal's approval is central, there may be cases in which *ex parte* requests are granted due to exceptional circumstances, such as the imminent loss of evidence, both prior to and after constitution of the arbitral tribunal. Finally, with regard to the parties' discretion to tailor the arbitral proceedings, court assistance in the taking of evidence can in most cases be excluded. One exception to this is in England, where the attendance of witnesses (S. 43 EAA 1996) cannot be waived due to its mandatory nature.[1181]

Third, court assistance in the taking of evidence will be granted either strictly, according to the law at the place where the evidence is sought, or even pursuant to the law and procedure of the requesting foreign arbitral tribunal. While the former situation applies under German and French law, the latter is possible in England and the USA. What is common in all four jurisdictions is that at times, evidence will be taken not only according to the

1179 *See* p. 202 *supra*.

1180 *See* p. 203 *supra*.

1181 *See* p. 170 *supra*.

respective *lex arbitri*, but also pursuant to national rules of civil procedure. Specifically, in the USA, the availability of the broad discovery rights under the FRCP USA in international arbitration has led to heated debates. However, if discovery is granted after taking into account the *Intel* factors, discovery will be much narrower.[1182] Concerning the target of evidence, evidence can mainly be obtained from third parties over whom the arbitral tribunal has no jurisdiction. This is best illustrated in France, where the arbitral tribunal is vested with the power to impose *astreintes* on non-compliant parties.[1183]

Fourth, state courts requested to assist in the taking of evidence enjoy wide discretion. Except in Germany, where this discretion seems limited, if the respective conditions are fulfilled, the courts in all other examined jurisdictions are at liberty to grant or deny assistance. This is particularly clear in the USA, where court discretion plays a key role in applying the *Intel* factors. Furthermore, while in some jurisdictions, such as Germany and England, evidence will be taken only if the arbitral tribunal itself is unable to do so, this view has been explicitly rejected by the US courts.[1184] Finally, the arbitration agreement should not be examined. Accordingly, in a first step, state courts will explore whether the evidence request stems from an arbitral tribunal, before analysing in a second step whether the agreement includes any provisions on evidentiary matters.

Finally, all examined jurisdictions provide for appellate proceedings against a decision of a state court granting or denying court assistance. Moreover, if court assistance in the taking of evidence is in any way a violation of the procedural rules as agreed by the parties, this can serve as a reason to annul the arbitral award. In this regard, the appellate procedure under English law is unique. Accordingly, to limit the role of the court and ensure a high degree of finality, the approval of the state court that rendered the decision is necessary to challenge an arbitral award.

1182 *See* p. 203 *supra*.

1183 *See* p. 153 *supra*.

1184 *See* p. 211 *supra*.

8

Court Assistance in the Taking of Evidence in Switzerland

§ 1 Introduction

A. Preliminary Remarks

The preceding comparative analysis has laid the foundations for an examination of the Swiss status quo. Thus, where appropriate, the findings of the previous chapter will be considered in assessing how Switzerland deals with court assistance in the taking of evidence. After a general introduction to Switzerland as a forum for arbitration and the dualistic nature of its *lex arbitri*, the subject will be examined in detail according to the structure followed in the preceding comparative analysis. In doing so, some tactical insights will be presented on how best to increase the chances of successfully obtaining court assistance in the taking of evidence.

B. Popularity of Switzerland as a Seat of Arbitration

International arbitration in Switzerland enjoys a long tradition dating back to the 19th century, when Geneva was named as the seat of arbitration in a dispute between the US and the UK arising from the American Civil War.[1185] Ever since, Geneva has enjoyed a sterling reputation as a forum for interstate dispute settlement–not least thanks to the presence of the WTO Dispute Settlement Body and the OSCE Court of Conciliation and Arbitration.[1186]

International arbitration has also become increasingly influential in the private sector and today Switzerland is one of the most important forums for international arbitration worldwide.[1187] This is evident in the increasing

1185 FCDisp PILA CH Revision (2018), 7168; KAUFMANN-KOHLER/RIGOZZI, n. 1.105; Arroyo-HOFBAUER, n. 1.; For an extensive overview of arbitration in Switzerland, *see* the Swiss Historical Dictionary.

1186 *See* the recent decisions of the WTO dispute settlement body and the OSCE Court of Conciliation and Arbitration; regarding other arbitral tribunals and similar bodies, *see* KAUFMANN-KOHLER/RIGOZZI, n. 1.109.

1187 Int. Arbitration in CH Study (2017), 22; EU Study (2014), 181; FCDisp PILA CH Revision (2018), 7167 et seq.; SCHERER, 3; Arroyo-HOFBAUER, n. 10.

number of international arbitrations held in Switzerland under both the ICC and the Swiss Rules.[1188] For instance, in 2017 a total of 810 new ICC cases were filed, involving parties from more than 142 countries; Geneva and Zurich were among those cities most frequently selected as seats of arbitration.[1189] In addition to arbitrators from England and France, Swiss arbitrators are frequently chosen as a highly professionalised and sophisticated group of practitioners.[1190] Moreover, in 2008, several cantonal chambers of commerce founded the Swiss Chambers' Arbitration Institution (SCAI), which governs domestic and international arbitration under the Swiss Rules.[1191] The SCAI's caseload is consistently high and is usually dominated by international arbitration.[1192] In addition to arbitration under the ICC and the Swiss Rules, several specialist arbitration institutions are active in the area of sports and intellectual property.[1193]

Several key factors underpin Switzerland's popularity as a forum for arbitration.[1194] The country's traditional neutrality and political stability are crucial in this regard[1195]–especially when parties to arbitration may fear the partiality of the courts in their home countries. The aim is to settle disputes in a stable country, with both a clear and easily intelligible *lex arbitri* and arbitration-friendly case law.

The PILA CH, which entered into force in 1987, governs international arbitration and currently consistent of just 19 articles.[1196] It is available in several languages and is commonly considered concise and modern. As an overall approach, the PILA CH emphasises the autonomy of the parties and limits inference by state courts.[1197] For instance, the parties are free to

1188 KAUFMANN-KOHLER/RIGOZZI, n. 1.110 et seqq.; Arroyo-HOFBAUER, n. 1.

1189 ICC Dispute Resolution Bulletin 2018, 52, 60; EU Study (2014), 181; Queen Mary Survey (2018), 9 et seq.

1190 ICC Dispute Resolution Bulletin 2018, 58 et seq.

1191 This institution, originally named the Swiss Chamber Court of Arbitration and Mediation was renamed as the SCAI in 2012; *see* the historial overview.

1192 SCAI Statistics (2018), 4.

1193 *See* FCDisp PILA CH Revision (2018), 7182 et seq.; the Court of Arbitration for Sport (CAS), headquartered in Lausanne and established in 1983; the Basketball Arbitral Tribunal (BAT), headquartered in Geneva and established in 2006; the World Intellectual Property Organization (WIPO), headquartered in Geneva and established in 1994.

1194 Int. Arbitration in CH Study (2017), 22 et seq.

1195 Arroyo-HOFBAUER, n. 30.

1196 Arts. 176-194 PILA CH.

1197 Arts. 182 (1) and 183-185 PILA CH.

choose the applicable procedural rules (e.g. by referring to a set of institutional arbitration rules).[1198] Moreover, the SFT, as a 'one-stop shop', is the only court with competence to set aside arbitral awards, and then usually only within a six-month period.[1199] Because of the very restrictive grounds on which arbitral awards may be challenged, fewer than 10% of such attempts generally succeed.[1200] Finally, Switzerland's geographical location at the heart of Europe and its sophisticated infrastructure (e.g. hotels, conference venues) cannot be underestimated.[1201]

C. Open Dualism of the Lex Arbitri

Switzerland has adopted a dualistic system in its *lex arbitri*.[1202] Consequently, unlike in countries such as Germany and England, which have monistic *leges arbitri*, there are separate sets of rules for domestic and international arbitration. While domestic arbitration is governed by the third part of the CCP CH (Arts. 353-399; entered into force in 2011), the 12th chapter of the PILA CH sets out the rules for international arbitration (Arts. 176-194; entered into force in 1987).[1203] This chapter of the PILA CH exclusively governs international arbitration, except where it refers directly to the CCP CH (e.g. regarding the taking of evidence).[1204] Thus, in general, in the absence of any reference in this regard, the analogous application of the CCP CH is excluded.[1205] Nevertheless, the parties are free to opt out of the 12th chapter of the PILA CH and instead apply the third part of the CCP CH (and vice versa).[1206] In this regard, the 'open dualism' between the PILA CH and

1198 Art. 182 (1) PILA CH.

1199 Art. 191 PILA CH; DASSER/WÓJTOWICZ, 282.

1200 *Ibid.*, 280; EU Study (2014), 183.

1201 Arroyo-HOFBAUER, n. 35; regarding the recent data on the influence of international arbitration on the Swiss market, *see* Int. Arbitration in CH Study (2017), 33 et seq.

1202 AMBAUEN, n. 9, 24 et seqq.; Arroyo-JERMINI/BERNARDONI, ch. I, pt. II, n. 1.

1203 The rules on arbitration served as a model in the drafting of the domestic arbitration rules of the CCP CH (FCDisp CCP CH (2006), 7392).

1204 Art. 184 (2) PILA CH; CR-BUCHER, Art. 176 PILA CH n. 37; DUTOIT, Art. 176 PILA CH n. 14; *see also* the effort under the revised PILA CH to provide a comprehensive *lex arbitri* (FCDisp PILA CH Revision (2018), 7173).

1205 ZK-OETIKER, Art. 176 PILA CH n. 2, 116; BERGER/KELLERHALS, n. 88; Arroyo-ORELLI, Art. 176 PILA CH n. 3; BSK-PFIFFNER/HOCHSTRASSER, Art. 176 PILA CH n. 4.

1206 Art. 176 (2) PILA CH; Art. 353 (2) CCP CH; for the strict requirements of such an opt-out, *see* DFT 4A_256/2013 of 19 Nov. 2013, cons. 1.2.3 et seq.; ZK-OETIKER, Art. 176 PILA CH n. 97 et seqq.; Arroyo-ORELLI, Art. 176 PILA CH n. 28 et seqq.; BERGER/KELLERHALS, n. 107 et seqq.; BSK-PFIFFNER/HOCHSTRASSER, Art. 176 PILA CH n. 40 et seqq.

CCP CH undermines the broad discretion of the parties to tailor the arbitral proceedings according to their needs.[1207]

According to Art. 176 PILA CH, the rules of international arbitration apply to all arbitrations if the seat of arbitration is in Switzerland and if (at the time the arbitration agreement is concluded)[1208] at least one of the parties does not have its domicile, its registered office or its habitual residence in Switzerland.[1209] The applicability of the 12th chapter of the PILA CH therefore depends on a formal requirement, rather than on a substantive requirement such as an international connection (i.e. the 'internationality' of the dispute).[1210] Since the requirement of Art. 176 PILA CH is not geographical, the arbitral proceedings can be conducted elsewhere (i.e. outside Switzerland).[1211] The approach here is therefore in line with the general stance adopted under German, English and US law, and does not go as far as the very liberal French approach, which requires only that 'international trade interests are at stake'.[1212]

In this regard, the UNCITRAL ML goes further too. Its rules apply in general to 'international commercial arbitration', giving the terms 'international' and 'commercial' very broad definitions.[1213] Still, as regards assistance in the taking of evidence (Art. 27 UNCITRAL ML), this will be granted only if the seat of arbitration is within the territory in which the UNCITRAL ML is enacted.[1214] Although the UNCITRAL ML was established in 1985, two years before the PILA CH entered into force, it initially had no significant direct influence on the Swiss *lex arbitri*.[1215] However, in light of the success of the UNCITRAL ML and its influence on many *leges arbitri*, the Swiss legislature recently decided to modernise the PILA CH to align it with the latest in-

1207 In the ongoing revision of the PILA CH, the idea of a monistic *Code unique* was proposed, but ultimately rejected (see FCDisp PILA CH Revision (2018), 7175 et seq.); for a historical overview and criticism of the open dualism, *see* AMBAUEN, n. 24 et seqq., 570 et seqq.

1208 *See* Art. 176 (1) Draft-PILA CH.

1209 For the definition of domicile and habitual residence of a natural person, *see* Art. 20 PILA; for corporate bodies, *see* Art. 21 PILA CH.

1210 DFT 4P.115/2003 of 16 Oct. 2003, cons. 2.1; Arroyo-ORELLI, Art. 176 PILA CH n. 21; ZK-OETIKER, Art. 176 PILA CH n. 96; DUTOIT, Art. 176 PILA CH n. 3; CR-BUCHER, Art. 176 PILA CH n. 11; KAUFMANN-KOHLER/RIGOZZI, n. 2.28 et seqq.; AMBAUEN, n. 40 et seqq.

1211 KAUFMANN-KOHLER/RIGOZZI, n. 2.11; BSK-PFIFFNER/HOCHSTRASSER, Art. 176 PILA CH n. 19.

1212 § 1025 (1) CCP DE; S. 2 (1) EAA 1996; Art. 1504 CCP FR; § 7 FAA USA; AMBAUEN, n. 12 et seqq.

1213 Art. 1 (3) UNCITRAL ML; Digest of Case Law (2012), Art. 1 UNCITRAL ML, n. 1.

1214 Art. 1 (2) UNCITRAL ML.

1215 AMBAUEN, n. 38.

ternational standards.[1216] The UNCITRAL ML has therefore had a certain impact on the Swiss *lex arbitri*. At the time of the publication of this book (2020), the revision of the PILA CH is completed and the date of the entry into force will most likely by the 1 January 2020.[1217]

§ 2 Legal Bases

A. Overview

The PILA CH provides for assistance in arbitration on multiple levels and in various forms. At the beginning of the proceedings, court assistance might be needed with regard to the constitution of the arbitral tribunal and the appointment of the arbitrator(s) (Arts. 179 and 180 PILA CH).[1218] During the arbitral proceedings, assistance may be sought in relation to the taking of evidence (Art. 184 PILA CH), but also in respect of interim measures to preserve evidence (Art. 183 PILA CH) and other forms of court assistance (Art. 185 PILA CH). Once the arbitral award has been rendered, state courts can provide assistance regarding recognition and enforcement of the arbitral award (Art. 194 PILA CH) and the certificate of enforceability (Art. 193 PILA CH).

B. Court Assistance in Taking Evidence (Art. 184 PILA CH)

1. Jurisdiction

Regarding the taking of evidence, Art. 184 PILA CH reads as follows:

> "(1) The arbitral tribunal shall itself conduct the taking of evidence.
>
> (2) If the assistance of state judiciary authorities is necessary for the taking of evidence, the arbitral tribunal or a party with the consent of the arbitral tribunal may request the assistance of the state judge at the seat of the arbitral tribunal."

The official French version of section 2 will be amended too, as it erroneously states that the parties (plural), and not a single party can request assistance (*see* fn 1274). In addition, according to the revision, a proposed new para. (3) states:

> "(3) The state court shall apply its own law. On request, it can apply or consider different procedural forms."

1216 FCDisp PILA CH Revision (2018), 7185; Int. Arbitration in CH Study (2017), 51; EU Study (2014), 181.

1217 For an overview of the amendments, *see* FCDisp PILA CH Revision (2018), 7171 et seqq.

1218 GÖKSU, n. 293.

Art. 184 (2) PILA CH provides that the state court 'at the seat of the arbitral tribunal' is competent to render assistance (territorial jurisdiction). Subject-matter jurisdiction is determined by cantonal law, which usually falls within the competence of a regional or cantonal supreme court.[1219] In this regard, Lalive et al. argue that in addition to state courts, recourse may be had to other judicial or administrative authorities, such as the Federal Department of Justice and Police or a Swiss embassy.[1220] Although Art. 184 (2) PILA CH indeed refers to the 'assistance of state judiciary authorities', such assistance must in fact be sought from a judge. Therefore, most authors in legal doctrine argue that the competent *juge d'appui* alone is obliged to render assistance if the respective requirements are fulfilled.[1221] As a consequence, if assistance is rendered by a state judicial authority other than the state courts, this is done on a completely voluntary basis.[1222]

2. Centralised *Juge d'Appui?*

During the revision of the PILA CH, the potential establishment of a single competent authority with responsibility for handling requests for court assistance in arbitration was discussed. The few proponents of this view suggested that such a centralised, specialised authority would enhance the efficiency of arbitration.[1223] Instead of having to identify the competent *juge d'appui* in each canton, such requests would be handled by a single authority, most certainly affiliated to the SFT.[1224] As an alternative, it was proposed that each of the 26 cantons should determine a single authority, instead of multiple competent courts within each canton.[1225] Due to the few requests issued

1219 Art. 3 CCP CH; ZK-OETIKER, Art. 184 PILA CH n. 70; Art. 356 (2) (c) CCP CH; GÖKSU, n. 306; CR-BUCHER, Art. 184 PILA CH n. 14; BERGER/KELLERHALS, n. 1363; *see* e.g. for the Canton of Basle (§ 93 (1) (4) Court Organisation Act BS; Cantonal Supreme Court), Berne (Art. 8 (1) Introductory Act BE; District Court), Geneva (Art. 86 (1) Judiciary Organisation Act GE; District Court) and Zurich (§ 32 Court and Authorities Organisation Act ZH; District Court).

1220 *See also* RÜEDE/HADENFELDT, 266.

1221 Arroyo-VEIT, Art. 184 PILA CH n. 73; ZK-OETIKER, Art. 184 PILA CH n. 72; BSK-SCHNEIDER/SCHERER, Art. 184 n. 59 et seq.; BERGER/KELLERHALS, n. 1364; STACHER, n. 338; GÖKSU, n. 307; SCHNEIDER, 67 et seq.; WALTER et al., 162 et seq.

1222 SCHNEIDER, 67; BSK-SCHNEIDER/SCHERER, Art. 184 n. 60.

1223 Expl. Rep. Revision PILA CH (2017), 15.

1224 *See* e.g. Opinions Revision PILA CH (2017), ICC CH (3).

1225 *Ibid.*: Bar Association of the Canton of Fribourg (132), SCAI (189), University of St. Gallen (278 et seqq.). Prof. Sester of the University of St. Gallen even proposed that common 'judiciary administrative activities' in relation with the formation of the arbitral tribunal and the appointment of arbitrators should be governed by one single authority, while assistance in relation with interim measures and the taking of evidence should be left to Cantonal Courts.

for court assistance in the taking of evidence, the federalist structure of Switzerland and the questionable feasibility of such an authority, this idea of a centralised *juge d'appui* was rejected at the outset of the debate.[1226] Indeed, given how few such requests are issued, it would seem disproportionate to establish such an authority at this point in time.[1227] However, it remains to be seen whether this situation will change significantly in the future, since the Swiss legislature intends to open up the possibility for foreign arbitral tribunals to seek court assistance directly in Switzerland.[1228] If this happens, it would make sense to establish an additional chamber in the SFT to handle requests for court assistance.

This idea of a centralised *juge d'appui* does not seem to have been discussed in relation to the previously examined *leges arbitri*. This might be due to the different geographical sizes of these countries; in fact, a central authority might further complicate the process rather than simplifying it.

3. Restricted Assistance for Foreign Arbitral Tribunals

As previously discussed, court assistance under Art. 184 (2) PILA CH is rendered only if the seat of arbitration is located in Switzerland and if at least one of the parties does not have its domicile, its registered office or its habitual residence in Switzerland.[1229] From the perspective of an arbitration practitioner, this implies that an arbitral tribunal with its seat in a foreign country will seek court assistance only in very limited situations, which is far from satisfactory. Understandably, the delay this would cause to the respective proceedings and the costs of initiating a request for court assistance through a state court at the seat of arbitration, which would then transfer it to the Swiss court, would be most unwelcome.[1230] As seen under the previously examined *leges arbitri*, the need for assistance of foreign arbitral tribunals is considered self-evident. It is thus time to scrutinise the situation more closely.

a. Situation *de lege lata*

Hitherto, it was not considered possible for foreign arbitral tribunals to obtain court assistance in the taking of evidence, due to the clear wording of Art. 176 (1) read with Art. 184 (2) PILA CH. However, in situations where it is not

1226 *Ibid.*, ASA (7), Prof. Bucher (86), Swiss Bar Association (183), University of Lucerne (273); Int. Arbitration in CH Study (2017), 41; Expl. Rep. Revision PILA CH (2017), 15; FCDisp PILA CH Revison (2018), 7178 et seq.

1227 ZK-OETIKER, Art. 176 PILA CH n. 119.

1228 FCDisp PILA CH Revison (2018), 7198 et seq.

1229 *See* p. 222 *supra;* Art. 176 (1) PILA CH; Arroyo-VEIT, Art 184 PILA CH n. 74.

1230 *Ibid.*

possible to obtain court assistance in the foreign country, Art. 3 PILA CH provides for so-called 'emergency jurisdiction':

> "If this Code does not provide for jurisdiction in Switzerland and if proceedings abroad are impossible or cannot reasonably be required to be brought, the Swiss judicial or administrative authorities at the place with which the facts of the case are sufficiently connected shall have jurisdiction."

This article embodies an 'absolute subsidiary' rule of jurisdiction, aimed at avoiding a denial of justice. Because of its exceptional nature, it applies only under strict conditions.[1231] First, the PILA CH must offer no other jurisdiction in Switzerland, whether based on the PILA CH itself or on any international treaty.[1232] Second, there must be a sufficient connection to Switzerland–for example, because a witness is domiciled or documents are located in Switzerland. Third, proceedings abroad must be 'impossible or cannot reasonably be required to be brought'. Given that most countries provide for court assistance in the taking of evidence,[1233] situations in which it is in fact impossible to establish jurisdiction are thus very rare; this will be the case only if there is in fact a denial of justice.

The emergency jurisdiction under Art. 3 PILA CH has seldom been discussed and, as far as can be seen, there are no reported cases in which this article has been invoked to justify jurisdiction in Switzerland to support a foreign arbitration directly. Nonetheless, inspired by a decision of the Paris Court of First Instance, in which emergency jurisdiction was established in France as regards the appointment of an arbitrator, Arfazadeh has suggested that in theory, Art. 3 PILA CH could also be used in aid of arbitration in Switzerland.[1234]

One might further ask whether this is also possible with regard to the taking of evidence. Indeed, Steinbrück proposes that in order to ensure effective access to justice, the Swiss courts can use Art. 3 PILA CH to directly support foreign arbitral tribunals.[1235] As an example, he mentions the examination of a witness based in Switzerland whose testimony is crucial to an arbitration held abroad.[1236] In such a scenario, it is clear that the PILA CH offers

1231 DFT 4C_379/2006 of 22. May 2007, cons. 3.4; BSK-BERTI/DROESE, Art. 3 PILA CH n. 2a, 7; ZK-MÜLLER-CHEN, Art. 3 PILA CH n. 3.

1232 Art. 1 (2) PILA CH; OTHENIN-GIRARD, 261.

1233 *See* e.g. S. 43 and 44 EAA 1996; § 1050 CCP DE; Art. 1449 and 1469 CCP FR.

1234 ARFAZADEH, 328; *see also* FOUCHARD, note on Paris High Court, 11 May 1987, in: Rev. Arb. 1988, 699 et seqq.; BERGER/KELLERHALS, n. 820.

1235 STEINBRÜCK, 131 et seqq.

1236 *Ibid.*, 132.

no jurisdiction in Switzerland (first requirement); and because the witness is located in Switzerland, there is a sufficient connection (second requirement).[1237] Quite obviously, the problem lies in the third requirement–that is, that proceedings abroad are impossible or cannot reasonably be required to be brought. As seen in the comparative analysis, most countries provide for court assistance in the taking of evidence. Therefore, court assistance will usually be possible, except in rare cases of a denial of justice.

It is questionable whether the lengthy and cumbersome process of obtaining court assistance from the respective Swiss court via a foreign state court would in fact fall within the 'cannot reasonably be required to be brought' standard. With regard to court assistance in the taking of evidence in arbitration, this question has not been asked or answered in Swiss legal doctrine or case law. In general, however, in the case of overly long proceedings or corrupt justice systems, Art. 3 PILA CH provides for emergency jurisdiction.[1238] In conclusion, it is conceivable that the Swiss courts may support foreign arbitral tribunals in the taking of evidence based on Art. 3 PILA CH in case of a denial of justice or if the potential duration of the procedure abroad would be unreasonable. The potential application of Art. 3 PILA CH must therefore be decided on a case-by-case basis and lies within the discretion of the respective state court judge.[1239] While this discussion is interesting from a theoretical point of view, it seems superfluous in light of the current developments regarding the ongoing revision of the PILA CH.

b. Situation *de lege ferenda*

Since its establishment in 1987, Art. 184 (2) PILA CH has gone mostly unnoticed and has had little significance in practice.[1240] Most likely, this is because foreign arbitral tribunals cannot approach the Swiss courts directly to seek court assistance in the taking of evidence.[1241] Thus, parties have seldom opted for a cumbersome detour, via the state courts at the place of the seat of arbitration, to the jurisdiction in which the evidence is located. This dilemma has

1237 Art. 176 (1) i.c.w. 184 (2) PILA CH; BSK-BERTI/DROESE, Art. 3 PILA CH n. 10; ZK-MÜLLER-CHEN, Art. 3 PILA CH n. 6, 24.

1238 ZK-MÜLLER-CHEN, Art. 3 PILA CH n. 21; *see* e.g. the recent data about the length of proceedings within the EU: 2019 EU Justice Scoreboard, 12 et seqq.; for a more global view, *see* the Swiss country index on judicial assistance.

1239 BSK-BERTI/DROESE, Art. 3 PILA CH n. 8.

1240 BSK-SCHNEIDER/SCHERER, Art. 184 PILA CH n. 56.

1241 Art. 176 (1) i.c.w. Art. 184 (2) PILA CH. As discussed previously, Art. 3 PILA CH could serve to provide an emergency jurisdiction in exceptional cases *(see p. 225 et seqq. supra)*.

been criticised in legal doctrine and came up for discussion in relation to the revision of the PILA CH.[1242] Subsequently–and as under German, French and English law–the new Art. 185a (2) PILA CH provides for the direct provision of court assistance in the taking of evidence to foreign arbitral tribunals:[1243]

> "An arbitral tribunal with its seat abroad or a party of a foreign arbitral proceeding can, with the consent of the arbitral tribunal, request the assistance of the state court at the place where the taking of evidence will take place. Art. 184 (2) and (3) apply by analogy."

As a result, it is clear that the Swiss legislature intends to allow foreign arbitral tribunals to seek court assistance in the taking of evidence directly from the respective competent Swiss court.[1244] Furthermore, it is intended that this will also apply to court assistance regarding interim measures.[1245] At this point in time, the consequences of this amendment are not fully apparent. However, it is clear that this should make the PILA CH more user friendly and should be warmly welcomed by international arbitration practitioners. This modification is also in line with the position taken under German, French, English and US law. In future, if evidence is located in Switzerland, a foreign arbitral tribunal will thus be more likely to agree to seek court assistance in the taking of evidence. It remains to be seen whether a dramatic increase in the number of requests submitted to the Swiss courts will lead to discussions on the potential establishment of a centralised authority to handle such requests.[1246]

C. Interim Measures (Art. 183 PILA CH)

1. In General

The distinction between the taking of evidence and interim measures for the preservation of evidence is not always clear.[1247] In general, it is possible to distinguish between taking evidence (i.e. establishing facts) and interim

1242 ZK-OETIKER, Art. 184 PILA CH n. 87; BERGER/KELLERHALS, n. 1370; WIRTH/HOFMANN-NOWOTNY, 71; Rep. Consultation Procedure PILA CH (2018), 11; *see also* Opinions Revision PILA CH (2017): ASA (19 et seq.), ICC CH (165), University of Lausanne (242).

1243 § 1025 (2) CCP DE; S. 2 (3) EAA 1996; Art. 1504 CCP FR.

1244 FCDisp PILA CH Revision (2018), 7199.

1245 Art. 185a (1) PILA CH.

1246 *See* p. 224 et seq. *supra*.

1247 BOOG, n. 30; *see also* Art. 374 CCP CH, which applies to Swiss domestic arbitration. Unlike in Art. 183 PILA CH, measures to protect evidence fall explicitly under interim measures (BSK-HABEGGER, Art. 374 CCP CH n. 12).

measures aimed at temporarily protecting the parties' rights from possible harm during an arbitration. As previously discussed (*see* p. 87 *supra*), measures for the preservation of evidence can be considered as falling somewhere between measures for the taking of evidence and interim measures: they help to establish the facts of the case, but only for a limited period.[1248] Arts. 183 (1) and (2) PILA CH state as follows:

> "(1) Unless the parties have otherwise agreed, the arbitral tribunal may, on motion of one party, order provisional or conservatory measures.
> (2) If the party concerned does not voluntarily comply with these measures, the arbitral tribunal may request the assistance of the state court; it shall apply its own law."

It is undisputed that the arbitral tribunal and state courts have parallel competence to order interim measures.[1249] The state courts are usually approached either where the arbitral tribunal has not yet been constituted and there is no emergency arbitrator, or where a party does not comply voluntarily with an interim measure ordered by the arbitral tribunal. Alternatively, state courts will assist where the parties have excluded the arbitral tribunal's competence to order interim measures.[1250] Prior to the revision of the PILA CH, foreign arbitral tribunals could not directly seek court assistance from Swiss courts. As with the taking of evidence (Art. 184 PILA CH), the new Art. 185a (1) PILA CH would introduce a welcome change in this respect:

> "An arbitral tribunal with its seat abroad or a party of a foreign arbitral proceeding can, with the consent of the arbitral tribunal, request the assistance of the state court at the place where the provisional or conservatory measure ought to be executed. Art. 183 (2) and (3) apply by analogy."

The local jurisdiction is determined by cantonal law, which usually provides for the competence of a regional or cantonal supreme court.[1251]

1248 BERGER/KELLERHALS, n. 1247; LALIVE et al., Art. 183 PILA CH n. 6; RÜEDE/HADENFELDT, 253; *contra* WALTER et al., 135 et seq.

1249 ZK-OETIKER, Art. 183 PILA CH n. 4; BSK-MABILLARD, Art. 183 PILA CH n. 5; *see also* p. 87 *supra*.

1250 BSK-MABILLARD, Art. 183 PILA CH n. 5; CHK-FURRER et al., Art. 182-186 PILA CH n. 12.

1251 Art. 3 CCP CH; *see* e.g. for the Canton of Basle (§ 93 (1) (4) Court Organisation Act BS; Cantonal Supreme Court), Berne (Art. 8 (1) Introductory Act BE; District Court), Geneva (Art. 86 (1) Judiciary Organisation Act GE; District Court) and Zurich (§ 32 Court and Authorities Organisation Act ZH; District Court).

2. Precautionary Taking of Evidence (Art. 158 CCP CH)

The precautionary taking of evidence and its importance to arbitration must also be considered in this regard. This is a special procedure under Swiss law, as it allows for evidence to be taken even before the arbitral proceedings have started. Art. 158 CCP CH reads as follows:

> "(1) The court shall take evidence at any time if: (a) the law grants the right to do so; (b) the applicant shows credibly that the evidence is at risk or that it has a legitimate interest.
> (2) The provisions regarding interim measures apply."

In addition to the enforcement of a legal right, Art. 158 CCP CH has two main goals: to protect evidence which is likely to be lost or destroyed, or to help the parties to weigh their chances of success in future court proceedings.[1252] It is therefore quite similar to the independent evidentiary proceeding under German law, under which evidence that might be lost or destroyed may be gathered.[1253]

Measures to preserve evidence lie somewhere between interim measures (i.e. measures to protect a party's rights for a limited period) on the one hand and measures for the taking of evidence (i.e. establishing the facts of a case) on the other.[1254] This is illustrated by Art. 158 CCP CH: while it refers to the taking of evidence, the 'provisions regarding interim measures' apply simultaneously. Consequently, the provisions on summary proceedings (Arts. 248 et seqq. CCP CH) and those on interim measures (Arts. 261 et seqq. CCP CH) apply simultaneously.

In addition, in Swiss domestic arbitration, Art. 374 (1) CCP CH explicitly includes measures for the protection of evidence under the title of interim measures.[1255] Unsurprisingly, the prevailing view in Swiss legal doctrine is that measures for the protection of evidence fall within the scope of interim measures in the sense of Art. 183 PILA CH.[1256] Nevertheless, it remains doubt-

1252 DFT 138 III 76, cons. 2.4.2; Sutter-Somm et al.-FELLMANN, Art. 158 CCP CH n. 17.

1253 *See* p. 139 et seq. *supra*.

1254 *See* p. 87 *supra*.

1255 BSK-HABEGGER, Art. 374 CCP CH n. 12. HABEGGER argues, without further explanation, that the precautionary taking of evidence is excluded from interim measures, at least in Swiss domestic arbitration.

1256 Arroyo-BOOG, Art. 183 PILA CH n. 10; ZK-OETIKER, Art. 184 PILA CH n. 35; BERGER/KELLERHALS, n. 1247; DUTOIT, Art. 183 PILA CH n. 5; LALIVE et al., Art. 183 PILA CH n. 6; RÜEDE/HADENFELDT, 253; *contra* BOOG, n. 30; WALTER et al., 135; for Swiss domestic arbitration *see* BSK-HABEGGER, Art. 374 CCP CH n. 12.

ful whether Art. 158 CCP CH could be used to assess one's chances of success in advance of arbitration, where evidence is not in danger and in need of protection and preservation.[1257] This question has been subject to limited discussion in Swiss legal doctrine.[1258]

WYSS considers the precautionary taking of evidence as an extension of the measures available under Art. 183 PILA CH.[1259] He argues that since the state courts and the arbitral tribunal have parallel competence to order interim measures, the possibility to weigh one's chances of success under Art. 158 CCP CH should also be available in the case of international arbitration. He therefore argues for an extensive interpretation of Art. 183 PILA CH, emphasising that international arbitral tribunals are not limited to interim measures according to the CCP CH, and that the power to assess evidence rests with the arbitral tribunal alone.[1260]

On the other hand, as Schweizer rightly points out, the precautionary taking of evidence to weigh the chances of success in future proceedings goes beyond the mere protection and preservation of evidence; thus, Art. 158 CCP CH is not captured within the parameters of Art. 183 PILA CH.[1261] As the arbitral tribunal is the competent authority to take evidence, the possibility to use Art. 158 CCP CH to obtain interim measures pursuant to Art. 183 PILA CH would undermine the arbitral tribunal's competence to take evidence.[1262]

Indeed, a clear distinction must be drawn between the goals and intentions of the precautionary taking of evidence (Art. 158 CCP CH), interim measures and the taking of evidence in international arbitration (Arts. 183 and 184 PILA CH). As previously discussed, Art. 183 PILA CH provides for the possibility to protect and preserve evidence (*see* p. 228 *supra*). In this sense, protecting evidence under Art. 158 CCP CH is congruent with Art. 183 PILA CH. This does not apply to that part of Art. 158 CCP CH mentioning 'a legitimate interest', which hints at the possibility to assess one's chances of success in future proceedings. The precautionary taking of evidence in this sense clearly falls within the competence of the arbitral tribunal alone (Art. 184 (1) PILA CH). The possibility to assess one's chances in future proceedings under Art. 158 CCP CH should therefore be excluded in the case of both domestic and international arbitration.

1257 WYSS, 201.

1258 *Ibid.*; SCHWEIZER, 23.

1259 WYSS, 202.

1260 *Ibid.*

1261 SCHWEIZER, 24; *see also* BSK-HABEGGER, Art. 374 CCP CH n. 12.

1262 SCHWEIZER, 24.

As a result, requests submitted to state courts under Art. 158 CCP CH with the sole goal of assessing one's chances of success in a future arbitration, where no evidence is in danger, should be denied; and the parties' decision to settle their dispute through arbitration rather than before state courts should be respected and maintained.[1263]

D. Other Court Assistance (Art. 185 PILA CH)

For the sake of completeness, Art. 185 PILA CH is noteworthy as it serves as a catch-all provision, ensuring the smooth progress of the arbitration through the availability of comprehensive assistance throughout the proceedings in cases where the arbitral tribunal's powers are insufficient:[1264]

> "Where further judicial assistance is necessary, the judge at the arbitral tribunal's seat shall have jurisdiction."

These may include situations where a state court whose assistance is sought under Art. 185 PILA CH reminds the arbitral tribunal to render its award in the manner agreed by the parties (Art. 189 PILA CH), or where a party makes a complaint because of a denial of justice by the arbitral tribunal.[1265] With regard to the taking of evidence, Art. 185 PILA CH applies only if Arts. 183 and 184 PILA CH are less suitable to the situation. Since these two articles mainly cover assistance in the taking of evidence, there is little scope for Art. 185 PILA CH to apply; it thus plays a subordinate role, as mentioned in the examples above. Unlike the two other provisions governing court assistance, Art. 185 PILA CH is available only for arbitration seated in Switzerland and the Art. 185a PILA CH introduces no improvements in this regard. Finally, according to cantonal law, the competent courts to handle requests pursuant to Art. 185 PILA CH are either regional or cantonal supreme courts.[1266]

1263 SCHWEIZER, 24; *contra* BSK-SCHNEIDER/SCHERER, Art. 184 PILA CH n. 56; CR-BUCHER, Art. 184 PILA CH n. 22; WYSS, 202; *see also* Cantonal Commercial Court of Zurich, HE180200-O of 9 Aug. 2018, cons. 4.3 et seqq., in: ZR 2018, 230 et seqq.; Cantonal Supreme Court of Zurich, LB120081 of 31 Oct. 2012, cons. 3.3, in: ZR 2013, 149 et seqq.

1264 Arroyo-KNOLL, Art. 185 PILA CH n. 1; DUTOIT, Art. 185 PILA CH n. 1; BSK-MABILLARD, Art. 185 PILA CH n. 1; CR-BUCHER, Art. 185 PILA CH n. 1; WALTER et al., 170. For the respective provision in Swiss domestic arbitration, *see* Art. 375 (2) CCP CH.

1265 Arroyo-KNOLL, Art. 185 PILA CH n. 19 et seq.; ZK-OETIKER, Art. 185 PILA CH n. 4; BSK-MABILLARD, Art. 185 PILA CH n. 7 et seqq.; CR-BUCHER, Art. 185 PILA CH n. 8 et seqq.; WALTER et al., 171 et seqq.; LALIVE et al., Art. 185 PILA CH n. 5.

1266 Canton of Basle (§ 93 (1) (4) Court Organisation Act BS; Cantonal Supreme Court), Berne (Art. 8 (1) Introductory Act BE; District Court), Geneva (Art. 86 (1) Judiciary Organisation Act GE; District Court) and Zurich (§ 32 Court and Authorities Organisation Act ZH; District Court).

§ 3 Applicable Procedural Law

Before the revision of the PILA CH, there was some doubt about the applicable procedural law in cases where state courts provide assistance to arbitral tribunals.[1267] However, according to the prevailing view in Swiss legal doctrine, summary proceedings pursuant to Arts. 248 et seqq. CCP CH apply.[1268] According to the new Art. 251a (c) CCP CH, these proceedings are explicitly applicable to the taking of evidence pursuant to Art. 184 (2) PILA CH.[1269] Consequently, an application under Art. 184 (2) PILA CH must take the form of a signed application; in simple or urgent cases, it may even be filed orally on record.[1270] In most cases, the respective state court will not hold a hearing, but will rather decide on the basis of the case files.[1271] Unless the request does not seem obviously inadmissible or unfounded, the opposing party (i.e. the target of evidence) has the opportunity to comment on the application orally or in writing.[1272]

§ 4 Competence to Seek Court Assistance

A. Primacy of the Arbitral Tribunal

Unsurprisingly, and as under most other examined *leges arbitri*, the approval of the arbitral tribunal must first be obtained before seeking the assistance of the Swiss courts.[1273] The request can be made either by the arbitral tribunal itself or by a party with the consent of the arbitral tribunal.[1274] However, a request based on an agreement between the parties alone, as under English

1267 Before the enactment of the PILA CH in 1989, Art. 45 of the Intercantonal Arbitration Convention CH of 1969 expressly referred to the summary proceedings as regards the constitution of the arbitral tribunal; GÖKSU, n. 313.

1268 *Ibid.*; THORENS-ALADJEM, 531; BSK-WEBER-STECHER, Art. 356 CCP CH n. 5.

1269 FCDisp PILA CH Revision (2018), 7206.

1270 Art. 252 i.c.w. Art. 130 CCP CH.

1271 Art. 256 (1) CCP CH.

1272 Art. 253 CCP CH.

1273 *See* e.g. Art. 27 UNCITRAL ML; § 1050 (1) CCP DE; Art. 1469 i.c.w. Art. 1506 CCP FR; Art. 184 (2) PILA CH; Arroyo-VEIT, Art. 184 PILA CH n. 70.

1274 ZK-OETIKER, Art. 184 PILA CH n. 73; GÖKSU, n. 330. The official French version of Art. 184 (2) PILA CH is misleading, since it allows only *both* parties (*les parties*) to seek court assistance. The prevailing view therefore suggests that the official German and Italian versions mentioning only 'a party' deserve priority and thus no agreement between the parties is necessary (BERGER/KELLERHALS, n. 1361 fn 89; BSK-SCHNEIDER/SCHERER, Art. 184 PILA CH n. 58; CR-BUCHER, Art. 184 PILA CH n. 12; SCHNEIDER, 57; LALIVE et al., Art. 184 PILA CH n. 8).

law, is not possible.[1275] Since the arbitral tribunal itself is competent to seek court assistance on its own motion, it should also be entitled to participate in the taking of evidence.[1276] Although this option is expressly stated in Swiss domestic arbitration law, there is no urgent need to amend Art. 184 (2) PILA CH. As previously explained *(see* p. 223 *supra),* this follows from the fact that Art. 184 (2) PILA CH expressly entitles the arbitral tribunal itself to seek court assistance.[1277] As a result, and to ensure the parties' right to be heard, the arbitral tribunal should be allowed to be present during the taking of evidence. In addition, if one party alone is seeking court assistance, state courts will most likely demand that a written order be presented in order to verify the respective arbitral tribunal's consent.[1278]

As previously discussed *(see* p. 27 et seqq. *supra),* the arbitral tribunal is vested with significant discretion to determine whether court assistance is in fact necessary or whether the relevant facts of the case have already been proven. From the perspective of the arbitral tribunal, a request for court assistance is therefore a right rather than a duty.[1279] In several cases, a party claimed that the arbitral tribunal had violated its right to be heard by denying a request to seek court assistance. In this respect, the SFT made it clear that this right had not been violated simply because the arbitral tribunal had not requested court assistance on its own initiative without being invited to do so by one of the parties. Rather, this would be the case only if the request were denied without valid reason (e.g. where the possible evidence would be relevant to the outcome of the respective case).[1280] More recently, in a case in which the arbitral tribunal refused to hear a witness, the SFT confirmed its previous case law stating that the refusal to hear a certain witness does not violate the right to be heard if the tribunal considers the testimony improper to demonstrate the relevant facts or insufficient to change its opinion.[1281]

SCHNEIDER/SCHERER argue that where an arbitral tribunal refuses a request for court assistance without sufficient reason (and violates the right to be heard), a party can nonetheless challenge this violation before a state

1275 *See* p. 169 *supra.*

1276 BSK-SCHNEIDER/SCHERER, Art. 184 PILA CH n. 62.

1277 *Contra Ibid.* with reference to Art. 375 (3) CCP CH; *see also* the nearly identical provision in § 1050 (3) CCP DE.

1278 WALTER et al., 165; SCHNEIDER, 56 et seq.

1279 *See* e.g. the case cited in ASA Bull. 2005, 469 et seqq.; BERGER/KELLERHALS, n. 1362; Arroyo-VEIT, Art. 184 PILA CH n. 70.

1280 DFT 4P.217/1992 of 15 Mar. 1993, cons. 7b, in: ASA Bull. 1993, 408.

1281 DFT 4A_335/2012 of 30 Jan. 2013, cons. 2 with reference to DFT 134 I 140, cons. 5.3; DFT 131 I 153, cons. 3.

court.[1282] However, as the two authors acknowledge, since state courts will not examine the relevance, usefulness or appropriateness of the evidence requested, a state court is unlikely to grant court assistance where the arbitral tribunal has not approved such request.[1283] Even if it does so, the arbitral tribunal will have total liberty to decide whether to introduce the evidence into the arbitral proceedings.[1284]

B. Exclusion of Court Assistance in Taking Evidence

1. Current Opinions in Legal Doctrine

Thus far, because court assistance in the taking of evidence in arbitrations held in Switzerland (Art. 184 PILA CH) has seldom been sought, its exclusion has not been discussed extensively in Swiss legal doctrine.[1285] By contrast, the topic has been the subject of vigorous debate under German and, less extensively, English law.[1286] As regards the PILA CH, AMBAUEN argues that because the parties have a right to participate in the taking of evidence (as part of the right to be heard), the advance exclusion of this right is not possible.[1287] Or, to put it differently, parties cannot deprive themselves of the possibility to play an active role in the taking of evidence. In contrast, AMBAUEN does not mention the possibility of excluding court assistance during the arbitral proceedings. However, the following discussion will show that under certain circumstances, this is possible–both prior to and during the arbitral proceedings.

2. Right of Minimum Legal Protection

To begin, one must be aware that the freedom of the parties to tailor the applicable procedural rules at their (almost) full discretion (Art. 182 (1) PILA CH)

1282 BSK-SCHNEIDER/SCHERER, Art. 184 PILA CH n. 58; *contra* SCHNEIDER, 57.

1283 BSK-SCHNEIDER/SCHERER, Art. 184 PILA CH n. 58; BERGER/KELLERHALS, n. 1365; ZK-OETIKER, Art. 184 PILA CH n. 71; Arroyo-VEIT, Art. 184 PILA CH n. 71; BUCHER, n. 217; RÜEDE/HADENFELDT, 266; WALTER et al., 166.

1284 CR-BUCHER, Art. 184 PILA CH n. 22.

1285 Regarding Art. 185 PILA CH (other court assistance), MABILLARD argues, without further explanation, that the parties cannot renounce this sort of court assistance–*see* BSK-MABILLARD, Art. 185 PILA CH n. 21; for the exclusion of interim measures ordered by state courts (Art. 183 (2) PILA CH), *see also* HAAS, 347 et seqq.; KAUFMANN-KOHLER/RIGOZZI, n. 6.105 et seqq.; WALTER et al., 146.

1286 *See* p. 137 et seqq. *and* p. 170 et seq. *supra*.

1287 AMBAUEN, n. 284 and 244 with reference to DFT 124 I 241, cons. 2; DFT 4A_528/2011 of 23 Jan. 2012, cons. 2.1; RÜEDE/HADENFELDT, 263; ZK-OETIKER, Art. 182 PILA CH n. 47 et seqq.

is limited by Art. 182 (3) PILA CH, which states that the arbitral tribunal must ensure the equal treatment of the parties and their right to be heard. As previously discussed (*see* p. 106 et seqq. *supra*), these procedural guarantees must be considered within the context of their constitutional background, enshrined in Art. 29 (2) Const. CH. Therefore, parties cannot completely waive their right to legal protection, even if they wish to do so. By contrast, by tailoring the arbitral proceedings at their discretion, they can exclude certain types of evidence. One option is to agree to apply the IBA Rules or, more specifically, to resolve the dispute based on documentary evidence only.[1288] The parties can also agree to exclude expert opinions or to exclude admissions made in settlement discussions.[1289] But does the fact that different types of evidence may be excluded automatically lead to a conclusion that this also applies to court assistance in the taking of evidence? Or to put it another way, can the parties agree to exclude court assistance in the taking of evidence by not waiving their right to minimum legal protection completely? Although there is no clear indication either in the PILA CH itself or in legal doctrine, there are several arguments in favour of such an exclusion.

3. Reasons in Favour of an Exclusion of Art. 184 (2) PILA CH

First of all, if the issue is considered within the context of the main objective of arbitration–that is, to allow parties with comparable negotiating power to voluntarily decide to settle their disputes in large part without the help or interference of state courts–there are good reasons to believe that the parties can completely waive assistance under Art. 184 PILA CH. However, in some situations, the party will not have voluntarily entered into the arbitration agreement. For example, many sportspeople and athletes have no option–short of stopping playing their sport–but to agree to the dispute settlement mechanisms of their respective organisation if a dispute arises.[1290] While it makes sense to have a single forum in such situations, it is important to ask whether this provides a similar level of minimum legal protection–in terms of both equivalence and effectiveness–compared to the state courts.[1291]

1288 Art. 42 (1) (c) Swiss Rules; BSK-SCHNEIDER/SCHERER, Art. 184 PILA CH n. 14, 34.

1289 Arroyo-VEIT, Art. 184 PILA CH n. 14; BERGER/KELLERHALS, n. 1318; RÜEDE/HADENFELDT, 262 et seq.

1290 *See* e.g. Art. 37 (3) CAS Code: 'In agreeing to submit any dispute subject to the ordinary arbitration procedure or to the appeal arbitration procedure to these Procedural Rules, the parties expressly waive their rights to request any such measures from state authorities or tribunals. …'; HAAS, 358; KAUFMANN-KOHLER/RIGOZZI, n. 6.106 et seqq.; BSK-PATOCCHI/JERMINI, Art. 192 PILA CH n. 3b; DFT 133 III 235, cons. 4.3.2.2.

1291 HAAS, 359.

Quite obviously, the answer to this question must be determined on a case-by-case basis. The issue is even more delicate prior to constitution of the arbitral tribunal. If there is no emergency arbitrator competent to take evidence, the right to minimum legal protection will certainly be violated;[1292] but just because the respective arbitration institution provides for an emergency arbitrator (equivalence), this will not necessarily be as effective as a state court (effectiveness). Here, other elements–such as the types of evidence sought and the speed of the proceeding–come into play.[1293] Regarding the former issue, the possible measures available to emergency arbitrators and/or arbitral tribunals tend to be even broader than those available to state courts (as long as the parties have not excluded certain types of evidence). In addition, given the speed with which emergency arbitrators operate and the expedited procedures available under the rules of many arbitration institutions, there is no disadvantage in choosing arbitration in this regard.[1294] Furthermore, arbitral tribunals lack coercive power to enforce their orders–for instance, where a recalcitrant witness refuses to appear for examination; but HAAS argues that the impact of state court orders is often similarly limited, especially in international cases.[1295]

To summarise, given both the similarities and differences between the taking of evidence by arbitral tribunals and state courts respectively, one may conclude that–depending on the respective case–arbitral tribunals and emergency arbitrators alone can provide a similar level of minimum legal protection in terms of equivalence and effectiveness. As a result, the parties can only partially waive their right to minimum legal protection by excluding the possibility of court assistance in the taking of evidence under Art. 184 (2) PILA CH.

Second, if there is only a very loose connection to Switzerland–that is, if none of the parties has its domicile, habitual residence or business establishment in Switzerland–the possibility to make such an exclusion should be even greater. One may argue by analogy that if the parties, by virtue of Art. 192 (1) PILA CH, can almost fully waive the action for annulment or limit the grounds to challenge an arbitral award, the exclusion of Art. 184 (2) PILA CH–which

1292 KAUFMANN-KOHLER/RIGOZZI, n. 6.108; HAAS, 360; *see* e.g. Art. 29 ICC Rules; Art. 9B LCIA Rules; Art. 6 ICDR Rules; Rule 30 SIAC Rules; Art. 43 Swiss Rules.

1293 HAAS, 362.

1294 For emergency arbitrator and expedited proceedings, *see* e.g. Appendix V and VI ICC Rules.

1295 HAAS, 363; BOOG, n. 106 et seqq.

merely concerns a procedural question—should also be possible.[1296] Art. 192 (1) PILA CH aims to make arbitration more efficient, providing that if the arbitration has no real connection to Switzerland, the parties can waive the possibility of judicial review.[1297] In addition, Swiss courts should not be preoccupied by dilatory actions with no real connection to Switzerland.[1298] The SFT has held that in the interests of efficiency and to respect the autonomy of the parties, such an exclusion does not violate any public interest.[1299] By and large, the ECtHR has confirmed the SFT's position and stated that as long as such an exclusion is 'free, permissible and unambiguous', there is no violation of Art. 6 (1) ECHR.[1300] This reasoning may also be applied to the exclusion of court assistance in the taking of evidence. In sum, parties with only a loose connection to Switzerland should be able to exclude court assistance in the taking of evidence by applying Art. 192 (1) PILA CH by analogy. This can benefit the arbitration in terms of both equivalence and effectiveness.

Finally, it should be remembered that this exclusion is only temporary. If the parties subsequently wish to resort to state courts, they can easily change their minds by entering into a separate agreement during the arbitration regarding the possibility to seek assistance from state courts in the taking of evidence.[1301] Consequently, their waiver of legal minimum protection is likewise partial. Of course, the situation is different if one party refuses to conclude a separate agreement contrary to the first one. In such circumstances, the parties' prior agreement to voluntarily exclude the assistance of state courts must be respected.

4. Conclusion

In summary, it is clear that the question of whether the parties can exclude Art. 184 (2) PILA CH must be answered individually for each and every case. If the parties have entered into arbitration voluntarily, the exclusion should be considered valid in order to respect the parties' choice. By contrast, if one of the parties was *de facto* forced to settle the dispute through arbitration, one must consider whether the arbitral tribunal (or the emergency arbitrator)

1296 Art. 192 (1) PILA CH. However, the parties cannot exclude so-called 'revision', which aims to correct an arbitral award in cases of newly discovered significant facts or decisive evidence, or if the decision was influenced to the detriment of a party concerned by a felony or misdemeanour (FCDisp PILA CH Revision (2018), 7201 et seq.).

1297 ZK-OETIKER, Art. 192 PILA CH n. 1; Arroyo-BAIZEAU, Art. 192 PILA CH n. 2.

1298 BSK-PATOCCHI/JERMINI, Art. 192 PILA CH n. 1.

1299 DFT 4A_238/2011 of 4 January 2012, cons. 3.2.

1300 *Nourredine Tabbane v. Switzerland*, ECtHR, App no. 41069/12, n. 26 et seq., 1 Mar. 2016.

1301 STEINBRÜCK, 412.

can provide an equivalent level of legal protection to state courts. If so, there is only a partial waiver of minimum legal protection and thus the exclusion of Art. 184 (2) PILA CH is valid. As sports-related arbitral proceedings remain a minority in the sphere of international commercial arbitration, it is expected that in most cases, the parties will be free to exclude court assistance pursuant to Art. 184 (2) PILA CH. In addition, where the parties have only a loose connection to Switzerland, the exclusion of court assistance in the taking of evidence is even more justified, provided that the arbitration is also voluntary. Finally, the waiver of minimum legal protection is mostly partial, since the parties can include this assistance in a subsequent separate agreement.

§ 5 Spectrum of Evidence and its Target

A. Evidence According to a Party Agreement

The discretion of the parties to tailor the arbitral proceedings is a key hallmark of international arbitration.[1302] In the absence of such a choice, the arbitral tribunal will determine the procedure to be followed by the parties.[1303] Regardless of which procedural rules are chosen, the arbitral tribunal must ensure the equal treatment of the parties and their right to be heard.[1304] The parties are therefore at liberty to exclude certain types of evidence, such as witness testimony, and to agree to settle their dispute solely based on documentary evidence. This agreement binds not only the parties themselves, but also the arbitrators.[1305] In contrast to the other examined *leges arbitri*, the fact that an arbitral tribunal takes evidence contrary to an explicit agreement between the parties does not serve as grounds to annul the arbitral award under the PILA CH.[1306] Nonetheless, the arbitral award may be annulled if a party can show that the arbitral tribunal somehow violated the right to equal treatment, the right to be heard or even public policy.[1307]

1302 Art. 182 (1) PILA CH; Arroyo-KNOLL, Art. 182 PILA CH n. 1; BSK-SCHNEIDER/SCHERER, Art. 182 PILA CH n. 1.

1303 Art. 182 (2) PILA CH.

1304 Art. 182 (3) PILA CH.

1305 BSK-SCHNEIDER/SCHERER, Art. 182 PILA CH n. 10.

1306 § 1059 (2) (1.) (d) CCP DE; Art. 1520 (3) CCP FR; S. 68 (2) (c) EAA 1996; S. 10 (a) (4) FAA USA; DFT 4P.23/2006 of 27 Mar. 2006, cons. 4.2; DFT 117 II 346, cons. 1a; BSK-PFISTERER, Art. 190 PILA CH n. 61.

1307 Art. 190 (2) (d and e) PILA CH; *see also* p. 266 et seqq. *infra*.

B. Evidence According to the PILA CH

Art. 184 (2) PILA CH remains silent on the different types of evidence, stating only that 'the judge shall apply his own law'. It follows, therefore, that the respective court will take evidence according to the CCP CH.[1308] In addition, by virtue of Art. 11a PILA CH, the respective state court may take into account foreign procedures *(see* p. 242 et seqq. *infra)* or take evidence in accordance with international treaties.[1309] In most cases, however, evidence will be taken according to the CCP CH. Art. 168 (1) CCP CH designates the following evidence as admissible: testimony (lit. a), physical records (lit. b), inspections (lit. c), expert opinions (lit. d), written statements (lit. e) and questioning and statements of the parties (lit. f). In order to ensure a fair procedure and legal certainty, this list is exhaustive.[1310] Unlike under French law, for example, neither the PILA CH nor the CCP CH distinguishes between the evidence which can be sought prior to or after constitution of the arbitral tribunal.[1311]

Prior to the taking of evidence, in order to uphold the parties' right to be heard, they should be informed of the time and place of the hearing.[1312] This allows them to participate and experience the proceedings first hand.[1313] In addition, by analogy from Art. 375 (3) CCP CH, the parties should be allowed to ask questions during the taking of evidence.[1314] This also applies to the arbitral tribunal, which has the right (but not the duty) to take an active part in the taking of evidence, especially in cases where the arbitral tribunal has an interest in hearing the (chief) witnesses' examination first hand.[1315]

Hitherto, Art. 184 (2) PILA CH has primarily been invoked in order to force a recalcitrant witness to give testimony. However, such cases remain rare. In a recent case from 2015, albeit on a purely domestic level, two wit-

1308 ZK-OETIKER, Art. 184 PILA CH n. 75; BSK-SCHNEIDER/SCHERER, Art. 184 PILA CH n. 61; SCHNEIDER, 60 et seqq.; CR-BUCHER, Art. 184 PILA CH n. 15; GÖKSU, n. 308.

1309 BSK-SCHNEIDER/SCHERER, Art. 184 PILA CH n. 64; CR-BUCHER, Art. 184 PILA CH n. 20; ZK-OETIKER, Art. 184 PILA CH n. 83. In this respect, *see* e.g. the European Convention on Information on Foreign Law (1968) (entered into force in Switzerland in 1970).

1310 FCDisp CCP CH (2006), 7320; DFT 141 III 433, cons. 2.5.1.

1311 *See* p. 151 et seqq. *supra*.

1312 Art. 182 (3) PILA CH; BERGER/KELLERHALS, n. 1369; Arroyo-VEIT, Art. 184 PILA CH n. 79; WALTER et al., 168; SCHNEIDER, 65.

1313 CR-BUCHER, Art. 184 PILA CH n. 16; RÜEDE/HADENFELDT, 264; BUCHER, n. 218.

1314 GÖKSU, n. 321, 1554; SCHNEIDER, 65.

1315 *Ibid.*, n. 340; ZK-OETIKER, Art. 184 PILA CH n. 84; RÜEDE/HADENFELDT, 267; SCHNEIDER, 65 et seq.; ZK-OETIKER, Art. 184 PILA CH n. 84; SCHNEIDER, 66; RÜEDE/HADENFELDT, 267.

nesses were obliged to appear directly before the respective arbitral tribunal in Geneva to give testimony.[1316] Not only was the request answered within less than a week, but the witnesses were also ordered to appear directly before the arbitral tribunal.[1317] In this regard, Art. 184 (2) PILA CH does not express itself on the technical details of the taking of evidence (i.e. how exactly this should take place). While SCHNEIDER/SCHERER, LALIVE et al. and RÜEDE/HADENFELDT suggest that the evidence will always be taken before the requested state court, BERGER/KELLERHALS, OETIKER and GÖKSU suggest that, depending on the situation, the evidence may be taken before either the arbitral tribunal or the respective state court.[1318]

This opinion deserves approval. If the arbitral proceedings are being conducted in Switzerland, the taking of evidence directly before the arbitral tribunal is the most convenient option, since the arbitrators are already familiar with the respective case and in particular with the applicable procedural rules.[1319] In addition, this saves the respective state court judge from having to take evidence in a way to which he or she is not normally accustomed.[1320] Moreover, the translation costs can also be significantly reduced.[1321]

However, in an international arbitration with its seat outside Switzerland, evidence will most likely be taken before a state court. In this case, it would be disproportionate to relocate the arbitration to Switzerland for the taking of evidence. If the evidence is taken by a state court, the results will be forwarded to the arbitral tribunal and the parties (at best in the form of the minutes from the witness examination or site inspection).[1322] From a comparative point of view, the place where the evidence is taken is of no importance under German law, since § 1050 (3) CCP DE explicitly states that arbitrators can participate in the taking of evidence. The same seems to apply under French, English and US law, although this is not explicit.[1323]

1316 THORENS-ALADJEM, 547 et seq.; VITTOZ, 921 et seqq.

1317 *See also* S. 43 (1) EAA 1996: A party to arbitral proceedings may use the same court procedures as are available in relation to legal proceedings to secure the attendance *before the tribunal* of a witness in order to give oral testimony or to produce documents or other material evidence (emphasis added).

1318 BSK-SCHNEIDER/SCHERER, Art. 184 PILA CH n. 62; LALIVE et al., Art. 184 PILA CH n. 7; RÜEDE/HADENFELDT, 267; *contra* BERGER/KELLERHALS, n. 1367; ZK-OETIKER, Art. 184 PILA CH n. 78 et seq.; GÖKSU, n. 321.

1319 This seems to be a constant practice in Geneva; *see* ASA Bull. 1990, 283 et seqq.

1320 SCHMIDT-AHRENDTS/DE JONG, 286.

1321 *Ibid.*

1322 BERGER/KELLERHALS, n. 1369; BSK-SCHNEIDER/SCHERER, Art. 184 PILA CH n. 62; SCHNEIDER, 66; WALTER et al., 169.

1323 Arts. 1449 and 1469 CCP FR; Ss. 43 and 44 EAA 1996; § 1782.

C. Foreign Types of Evidence

The possibilities for the parties to tailor the taking of evidence according to their discretion are limited when state courts come into play. Faced with a request for court assistance in the taking of evidence pursuant to Art. 184 (2) PILA CH, the respective state court will normally apply its own law, irrespective of what the parties have agreed in the arbitration agreement.[1324] In Switzerland, therefore, it follows that foreign types of evidence such as affidavits and cross-examination will usually be excluded.[1325] Still, one may consider Arts. 11a (2) and (3) PILA CH:

> "(2) Upon petition of the requesting authority, foreign legal procedures may also be observed or taken into account, if necessary, for the enforcement of a claim abroad unless there are important reasons pertaining to the affected party not to do so.
> (3) The Swiss judicial or administrative authorities may issue documents or take an affidavit from an applicant in accordance with a form of foreign law if the Swiss form is not recognized abroad and if a claim meriting protection could not be asserted there."

The prevailing view in Swiss legal doctrine suggests that this provision may be applied to international arbitration by analogy.[1326] It therefore allows a Swiss court to recognise foreign forms of evidence (e.g. from the place of enforcement of the arbitral award).[1327] More recently, the Swiss legislature considered this fact in the drafting process of the revised PILA CH by proposing explicitly that a state court will usually apply its own law but, on request, will take into account foreign procedures (Art. 184 (3) PILA CH).[1328] This represents a certain harmonisation with US law, explicitly allowing for evidence to be taken according to foreign law.[1329] However, this is not the case as regards German, French and English law.[1330]

1324 Arroyo-VEIT, Art. 184 PILA CH n. 77.

1325 *See* e.g. a recent unpublished decision of the District Court of Zurich, FR160295-L/U of 27. May 2016, cited in BSK-HABEGGER, Art. 375 PILA CH n. 76a.

1326 ZK-OETIKER, Art. 184 PILA CH n. 77; BSK-SCHNEIDER/SCHERER, Art. 184 PILA CH n. 61; BERGER/KELLERHALS, 1366; CR-BUCHER, Art. 184 PILA CH n. 15; GÖKSU, n. 308; DUTOIT, Art. 184 PILA CH n. 3; LALIVE et al., Art. 184 PILA CH n. 7; BUCHER, n. 218; WALTER et al., 167; SCHNEIDER, 62 et seq.

1327 Arroyo-VEIT, Art. 184 PILA CH n. 77.

1328 FCDisp PILA CH Revision (2018), 7198.

1329 *See* p. 207 et seq. *supra*.

1330 *See* p. 140 et seqq., p. 159 *and* p. 174 et seq. *supra*.

For instance, if cross-examination of a witness is requested, the examination must be recorded on video or the witness must be sworn in in a certain manner, the respective state court has broad discretion to grant such a request.[1331] Nevertheless, Arts. 11a (2) and (3) apply only where there is no international treaty such as the HEC and the scope of application is not broader than that under such treaties.[1332] In such case, as regards the taking of evidence, the Hague Convention on Civil Procedure (HCP) must be considered at all times.[1333] However, since the HEC deals specifically with the taking of evidence and replaces the HCP's respective provisions, the HCP's scope of application has become increasingly limited.[1334]

Besides the petition of the requesting authority (either a foreign state court or a foreign arbitral tribunal (Art. 185a PILA CH), the consideration of a foreign procedure may be necessary to enforce a claim abroad. For instance, this applies to situations where the evidence must be taken in a specific form in order to have full evidentiary force abroad (e.g. a witness examination under oath).[1335] Lastly, a state court will consider foreign types of evidence only if there are no important reasons not to do so, such as personal privacy or the right to refuse testimony.[1336]

Because the consideration of foreign types of evidence is fully in the hands of the respective state court, there is no right thereto.[1337] There have been few reported cases in this regard and the Swiss courts tend to be reluctant to consider foreign types of evidence in aid of arbitration.[1338] Regarding the new possibility foreseen in Art. 185a PILA CH to directly approach a Swiss court for assistance in the taking of evidence in in arbitration, it remains to be seen whether requests to consider foreign types of evidence will be made more frequently.

1331 ZK-RODRIGUEZ/VOLKEN, Art. 11a PILA CH n. 9, 12, 15 et seqq.; CR-BUCHER, Art. 11-11a PILA CH n. 21; BSK-BERTI/DROESE, Art. 11a PILA CH n. 6.

1332 Art. 9 HEC; Art. 14 (2) HCP; ZK-RODRIGUEZ/VOLKEN, Art. 11a PILA CH n. 10; CR-BUCHER, Art. 11-11a PILA CH n. 22.

1333 Art. 11a (4) PILA CH; Guideline Judicial Assistance in Civil Matters CH (2013), 33.

1334 Art. 29 HEC; ZK-RODRIGUEZ/VOLKEN, Art. 11a PILA CH n. 22; DUTOIT, Art. 11a PILA CH n. 8; DFT 132 III 291, cons. 2.

1335 ZK-RODRIGUEZ/VOLKEN, Art. 11a PILA CH n. 11.

1336 *Ibid.*; *see also* Art. 11 HEC; Guideline Judicial Assistance in Civil Matters CH (2013), 25 et seq.

1337 DUTOIT, Art. 11a PILA CH n. 3; GAUTHEY/MARKUS, n. 427.

1338 *See* e.g. an unpublished decision of the District Court of Zurich, FR160295-L/U of 27. May 2016, cited in BSK-HABEGGER, Art. 375 PILA CH n. 76a.

D. Availability of Pre-trial Discovery of Documents?

While it is undoubtedly hard to predict the degree to which the Swiss courts will consider foreign types of evidence, it seems clear that there are some reservations regarding US-style pre-trial discovery. However, because it is foreseen that foreign arbitral tribunals will be able to approach the Swiss courts directly (Art. 185a (2) PILA CH), such requests may be made more frequently in the future. If they concern US-style pre-trial discovery, the respective state court will most likely orient itself according to the practice under Art. 23 HEC. Accordingly, a Member State of the HEC may declare that it will not execute 'letters of request for the purpose of obtaining pre-trial discovery of documents as known in Common Law countries'.[1339] Switzerland made use of this possibility in the form of a partial reservation:[1340]

> "6. In accordance with Article 23, Switzerland declares that Letters of Request issued for the purpose of obtaining pre-trial discovery of documents will not be executed if:
>
> a) the request has no direct and necessary link with the proceedings in question; or
>
> b) a person is required to indicate what documents relating to the case are or were in his/her possession or keeping or at his/her disposal; or
>
> c) a person is required to produce documents other than those mentioned in the request for legal assistance, which are probably in his/her possession or keeping or at his/her disposal; or
>
> d) interests worthy of protection of the concerned persons are endangered."

Generally speaking, the aim of this reservation is to avoid 'fishing expeditions'.[1341] Therefore, any requests regarding documents with no connection to the case or non-specified classes of documents over an unlimited timeframe will be denied.[1342] These include, for instance, requests to a Swiss bank to provide evidence of all connections (e.g. foundations, trusts, corporations) with correspondence and records of a certain person (directly or

1339 This article was initiated by England and many Member States made use of their right (*see* the various reservations); GAUTHEY/MARKUS, n. 696; MüKo-PABST, Art. 23 HEC n. 4.

1340 No. 6 of Switzerland's reservation.

1341 Guideline Judicial Assistance in Civil Matters CH (2013), 27; DFT 132 III 291, cons. 2.1; GAUTHEY/MARKUS, n. 696; KLAUS, 308.

1342 *Ibid.*

indirectly, and with no regard to the exact reason) held with that bank.[1343] Since Art. 23 HEC speaks only of 'documents', witness examination may not be requested, except where it relates to the existence, power of disposition or extent of the requested document(s).[1344] Regarding witnesses, the respective provisions on privilege and the right to refuse testimony apply according to the law of the state of execution, the state of origin of the request or even another state, by virtue of a separate declaration.[1345]

Lit. a-c impose no new requirements as regards the relevance of document production in Swiss civil procedure, but merely repeat that 'evidence is required to prove facts that are legally relevant and disputed' (Art. 150 (1) CCP CH).[1346] These limitations seem to be in line with the reservations of numerous other Member States.[1347] Thus, as the Cantonal Court of Zurich has held, it does not matter whether a specific request actually originated from a common law country (Art. 23 HEC).[1348] Only lit. d represents a Swiss speciality and serves as a general clause which does not refer to the Swiss *ordre public*, but instead aims to protect the interests of the relevant person.[1349] This applies, for instance, to the protection of commercial and technical confidentiality.[1350]

In sum, the Swiss courts will be rather hesitant when faced with requests for pre-trial discovery of documents. However, Switzerland has only partially excluded the possibility of granting requests for pre-trial discovery. In this respect, requesting parties would be well advised to consider the grounds listed in No. 6 (a-d) of Switzerland's reservation to Art. 23 HEC. In a case in which a US court requested a Swiss bank to produce certain documents from one of its clients, the SFT granted the request and reasoned that a direct and

1343 Cantonal Supreme Court of Zurich, RU160027-O/U of 6 Dec. 2016, cons. 5.4.

1344 FCDisp HEC CH (1993), 1301; Geimer/Schütze-KNÖFEL, Art. 23 HEC n. 10; MüKo-PABST, Art. 23 HEC n. 7.

1345 Art. 11 HEC; for the parties' and third parties' right to refuse to give testimony in Switzerland, *see* Arts. 156 and 163 et seqq. CCP CH.

1346 DFT 132 III 291, cons. 2.1; KLAUS, 308.

1347 *See* fn 1339 *supra;* DFT 4A_315/2017 of 17 Jan. 2018, cons. 5.3.1; FCDisp HEC CH (1993), 1301.

1348 *Ibid.*; Cantonal Supreme Court of Zurich, RU160027-O/U of 6 Dec. 2016, cons. 5.3; *see also* Cantonal Supreme Court of Zurich, decree of 23 Oct. 2001, cons. 4, in: ZR 2002, 262 et seqq.; *contra* Geimer/Schütze-KNÖFEL, Art. 23 HEC, n. 11.

1349 DFT 4A_315/2017 of 17 Jan. 2018, cons. 5.3.1; DFT 4A_399/2007 of 4 Dec. 2007, cons. 5.3; DFT 132 III 291, cons. 2.1; FCDisp HEC CH (1993), 1301.

1350 Guideline Judicial Assistance in Civil Matters CH (2013), 27; in this respect, *see also* Art. 56 CCP CH: The court shall take appropriate measures to ensure that taking evidence does not infringe the legitimate interests of any parties or third party, such as business secrets; BSK-GUYAN, Art. 156 CCP CH n. 2.

necessary link with the proceedings in question had been shown (lit. a).[1351] Moreover, it argued that lit. d does not prevent a Swiss court from forcing a Swiss bank to deny banking secrecy to a certain client, as long as the various interests of the concerned person are considered sufficiently protected.[1352]

E. International Judicial Assistance in Taking Evidence

In cases where evidence is not located in Switzerland, the Swiss courts may themselves be requested to seek international court assistance (e.g. by means of the HEC or other international treaties such as the European Convention on Information on Foreign Law).[1353] As the previous comparative analysis of several *leges arbitri* has shown, arbitral tribunals can often directly approach state courts at the place where the evidence is located. This strongly suggests that in order to save time and costs, the Swiss courts will most likely not be approached to initiate a request to a foreign state court at the place where the evidence is located.

F. Target of Evidence

1. Parties to the Arbitration

The classic distinction between the parties to the arbitration and third parties must also be drawn here. While state courts can force recalcitrant third parties to give testimony, this is not possible in the case of the parties to the arbitration. This is made clear by the first *Intel* factor, which suggests that requests for evidence from a party to the arbitration, over which the respective arbitral tribunal already has jurisdiction, will be denied.[1354] Thus, the prevailing view in Switzerland is that the arbitral tribunal should consider the behaviour of a non-compliant party when assessing the evidence.[1355] This could involve drawing an adverse inference under the conditions previously

1351 DFT 4A_399/2007 of 4 Dec. 2007, cons. 5.2.

1352 *Ibid.*, cons. 5.3.

1353 ZK-OETIKER, Art. 184 PILA CH n. 76; DUTOIT, Art. 184 PILA CH n. 4; BSK-SCHNEIDER/SCHERER, Art. 184 PILA CH n. 63; BERGER/KELLERHALS, n. 1368; GÖKSU, n. 322; LALIVE et al., Art. 184 PILA CH n. 6; BUCHER, n. 219; for mutual assistance between Swiss Courts *see* Arts. 194-196 CCP CH.

1354 *See* p. 196 *supra*.

1355 ZK-OETIKER, Art. 184 PILA CH n. 80; BERGER/KELLERHALS, n. 1367; BSK-SCHNEIDER/SCHERER, Art. 184 PILA CH n. 62; SCHNEIDER, 53; RÜEDE/HADENFELDT, 265; BUCHER, n. 216; *contra* LALIVE et al., Art. 184 PILA CH n. 6; WALTER et al., 164. The last two groups of authors suggest that besides third parties, Art. 184 (2) PILA CH serves to force recalcitrant parties to give testimony or produce documents too.

discussed (*see* p. 56 et seqq. *supra*). In this regard, the French approach is somewhat different, as it expressly empowers the arbitral tribunal to impose an *astreinte* in case of non-compliance.[1356]

In an arbitration in the Canton of Ticino in 1998, a party refused to allow the inspection of a machine in its possession.[1357] Consequently, the arbitral tribunal sought court assistance in order to force that party to allow the inspection, under threat of criminal sanctions according to Art. 292 SCC CH. The Supreme Cantonal Court of Ticino stated that there is no legal basis to force a recalcitrant party to comply with an evidentiary order. Rather, this fact should be considered by the arbitral tribunal in assessing the evidence.[1358] In another (ad hoc) arbitration in Geneva, an attempt to force a party to give testimony was halted by the arbitral tribunal.[1359] As the relevant party had refused to testify before the arbitral tribunal, the adverse party requested the arbitral tribunal to send a letter rogatory to a Spanish state court at the place where the recalcitrant party was domiciled. However, the arbitral tribunal denied the request, stating that a state court cannot force a party to testify based on either cantonal or federal law.[1360]

The situation is similar in state court proceedings. Based on Art. 160 (1) CCP CH, the parties have a duty to cooperate in the taking of evidence–that is, to give testimony, produce documentary evidence (except legal correspondence with lawyers) and allow expert examinations of their person or property. The right to refuse to cooperate in the taking of evidence is limited to cases in which the disclosure of a secret would breach professional confidentiality (Art. 321 SCC CH), or where the taking of evidence would expose a close associate to criminal prosecution or civil liability (Art. 165 CCP CH).[1361] However, according to Art. 164 CCP CH, 'if a party refuses to cooperate without valid reasons, the court shall take this into account when appraising the evidence'. For instance, if a party refuses to reveal a document in its possession, the court may assume that the document's contents are as claimed by the adverse party.[1362] That said, however, the respective state court will assess the evidence freely (Art. 157 CCP CH), and the mere refusal of a party to produce evidence will not automatically lead to a reversal of the burden of

1356 Art. 1467 (3) CCP FR; *see also* p. 73 *supra*.

1357 KNOEPFLER, 599 et seqq.

1358 *Ibid.*, 600.

1359 ASA Bull. 2005, 469 et seqq.

1360 *Ibid.*, 473.

1361 Art. 163 CCP CH;

1362 BSK-SCHMID, Art. 164 CCP CH n. 2; BK-RÜETSCHI, Art. 164 CCP CH n. 5.

proof.[1363] This will apply only in case of an abuse of rights, where a recalcitrant party refers to the lack of evidence of the adverse party (for which it in fact is responsible).[1364]

2. Third Parties

In contrast to the parties to the arbitration, third parties have a comprehensive right to refuse to cooperate in the taking of evidence. This holds true not only under Swiss law, but also under the other examined *lex arbitri*.[1365] Although third parties have a certain duty to cooperate in the taking of evidence, there are many possible conflicts, such as within families or professions.[1366] In Switzerland, third parties have both an absolute right to refuse and a limited right to refuse.[1367] In the former case, the third party may refuse to cooperate altogether; this is not the case in the latter. According to Art. 165 CCP CH, individuals with a close relationship to a party (e.g. through marriage, cohabitation, shared parenthood, fostering or a parental or sibling relationship) can completely refuse to cooperate. In order to protect family and partnership, the Swiss legislature allows such individuals to avoid a severe conflict of loyalty.[1368]

In contrast, Art. 166 CCP CH lists certain cases in which a third party must demonstrate the existence of a moral conflict in order to justify a refusal to cooperate. These include situations where the taking of evidence would expose that individual or a close associate to criminal prosecution or civil liability (lit. a), or would cause a breach of professional confidentiality (lit. b).[1369] Unlike under Art. 165 CCP CH, where the third party need show only the fulfilment of one of the conditions listed in this article, without further explanation, Art. 166 CCP CH is stricter in terms of substantiation.[1370] Thus, the third party must 'show credibly' why one of the grounds listed in this article applies. It is only natural that elaborations in this respect are rather vague, since the respective third party wishes to prevent disclosure of the fact in question.[1371]

1363 DFT 140 III 264, cons. 2.3; BK-RÜETSCHI, Art. 164 CCP CH n. 7; Sutter-Somm et al.-HASENBÖHLER, Art. 164 CCP CH n. 5 et seq.; BSK-SCHMID, Art. 164 CCP CH n. 2.

1364 BK-RÜETSCHI, Art. 164 CCP CH n. 7.

1365 *See* p. 142 et seq., p. 160 et seq., p. 175 et seq. *supra and* p. 209 et seq. *supra*.

1366 Sutter-Somm et al.-HASENBÖHLER, Vorbemerkungen Arts. 165-167 CCP CH n. 10.

1367 Arts. 165 and 166 CCP CH.

1368 DFT 2A.599/2006 of 5 Apr. 2007, cons. 4.2; Sutter-Somm et al.-HASENBÖHLER, Vorbemerkungen zu den Arts. 165-167 CCP CH n. 4; BK-RÜETSCHI, Art. 165 CCP CH n. 2.

1369 This applies, for instance, to lawyers, notaries, doctors, dentists etc. (Art. 321 (1) SCC CH); *see also* BSK-SCHMID, Art. 166 CCP CH n. 5 et seqq.

1370 Sutter-Somm et al.-HASENBÖHLER, Art. 165 CCP CH n. 23.

1371 BK-RÜETSCHI, Art. 166 CCP CH n. 3.

Because third parties *per se* are not part of the ongoing arbitration, the usual measures that may be taken against recalcitrant parties that refuse to cooperate in the assessment of evidence are useless.[1372] The CCP CH thus sets out a broad spectrum of measures that may be implemented against a recalcitrant third party.[1373] However, if the respective refusal is justified based on grounds foreseen in Arts. 165 and 166 CCP CH, the state courts cannot consider a certain alleged fact as proven (Art. 162 CCP CH). This article thus limits the principle of free assessment of evidence according to Art. 157 CCP CH.[1374] Otherwise, the right of third parties to refuse to cooperate would be pointless.[1375] In contrast, if the refusal is indeed unjustified, the respective state court can impose one or more of the following sanctions (Art. 167 CCP CH):

"(1) If a third party refuses to cooperate without justification, the court may:
 a. impose a disciplinary fine up to 1,000 Swiss francs;
 b. threaten sanctions under Article 292 SCC;
 c. order the use of compulsory measures;
 d. charge the third party the costs caused by the refusal.
(2) The default of a third party has the same consequences as refusing to cooperate without a valid reason.
(3) The third party may challenge the court's order by way of objection."

In sanctioning a party, the respective state court must consider the principle of proportionality.[1376] Therefore, depending on the case, a state court will usually begin by imposing indirect coercive measures (lit. a and b)–for example, the threat to impose a disciplinary fine–and will enforce it only if the third party continues to refuse to comply.[1377] The same applies with regard to the threat of sanctions under Art. 292 SCC CH ('contempt of official orders'), according to which a penal sanction in the form of a fine of up to CHF 10,000 may be imposed.[1378] In terms of proportionality, a state court should first test whether a disciplinary fine (lit. a) is effective enough before making a criminal complaint and handing the matter over to the criminal authorities.[1379]

1372 Sutter-Somm et al.-HASENBÖHLER, Art. 167 CCP CH n. 9.

1373 Art. 167 CCP CH; *see also* the two cases cited in THORENS-ALADJEM, 546 et seq.

1374 BK-RÜETSCHI, Art. 162 CCP CH n. 1.

1375 BSK-SCHMID, Art. 162 CCP CH n. 2; Sutter-Somm et al.-HASENBÖHLER, Art. 162 CCP CH n. 4.

1376 *Ibid.*, Art. 167 CCP CH n. 23; in case of a default of a party and its consequences, *see* Sutter-Somm et al.-HASENBÖHLER, Art. 167 CCP CH n. 25b et seq.

1377 DIKE-HIGI, Art. 167 CCP CH n. 11; BSK-SCHMID, Art. 162 CCP CH n. 3a; BK-RÜETSCHI, Art. 162 CCP CH n. 5.

1378 Art. 292 i.c.w. 106 (1) SCC CH; Sutter-Somm et al.-HASENBÖHLER, Art. 167 CCP CH n. 14.

1379 BK-RÜETSCHI, Art. 167 CCP CH n. 8; Sutter-Somm et al.-HASENBÖHLER, Art. 167 CCP CH n. 17.

Moreover, according to lit. c, a state court order can be enforced by means of a direct coercive measure. For instance, third parties can be forced to reveal specific documents in their possession, although 'fishing expeditions' are prohibited.[1380] Regarding the inspection of property, assistance from the police may become necessary to enforce a court order. With regard to witnesses, practice shows that in most situations it does not make sense to enforce their appearance through police assistance, since the value of their evidence will be questionable at best.[1381] The mere threat that a recalcitrant third party may be charged with any costs ensuing from its refusal (lit. c) may be more effective in increasing the pressure to appear.[1382] The costs-by-cause principle applies, for instance, in circumstances where a court hearing or inspection must be rescheduled due to the non-appearance of the respective third party.[1383]

Finally, Art. 167 (3) CCP CH states that the third party may challenge the court's order by way of objection. While this holds true for Swiss civil proceedings in general, it seems questionable whether this also applies to court assistance in the taking of evidence under Art. 184 (2) PILA CH. This question is examined in further detail below.[1384]

§ 6 Competence of the *Juge d'Appui*

A. Scope of Discretion

Although Art. 184 (2) PILA CH is not formulated as a facultative provision (*Kann-Vorschrift*), the state courts still have a wide discretion in deciding whether and how to grant court assistance in the taking of evidence. The admissibility of the request will therefore be examined in various ways.[1385] The same applies under French, English and US law.[1386] In this regard, the English approach–with its 'appropriateness threshold' set out in S. 2 (3) EAA 1996–and the *Intel* factors under US law should be emphasised. However, the discretion under Swiss law appears to be broader than that under German law, where assistance must be granted if the requirements of § 1050 CCP DE

1380 *Ibid.*; BK-RÜETSCHI, Art. 167 CCP CH n. 12.

1381 *Ibid.*

1382 Sutter-Somm et al.-HASENBÖHLER, Art. 167 CCP CH n. 19.

1383 *Ibid.*

1384 *See* p. 259 et seqq. *infra*.

1385 *See* e.g. Art. 27 UNCITRAL ML ('... The court *may* execute the request ...' (emphasis added)); § 1782 (a) ('The district court ... *may* order him to give his testimony ... '(emphasis added)).

1386 *See* p. 161, p. 177 et seqq. *and* p. 211 *supra*.

are met.[1387] Accordingly, Swiss state courts will analyse procedural requirements such as a legitimate interest; the jurisdiction of the court; the capacity to be a party and to take legal action; that the case is not subject to proceedings elsewhere or the subject of a legally binding decision; and that the advance and security for costs have been paid.[1388] In addition to the state court's jurisdiction and the admissibility of the evidence request itself, the principle of subsidiarity and the examination of the arbitration agreement deserve a closer look.

First, with regard to the respective territorial and subject-matter jurisdiction, it has previously been shown *(see* p. 224 *supra)* that, depending on the cantonal law, the 'state court at the seat of the arbitral tribunal' is in most cases a district court (first instance) or cantonal supreme court (second instance).[1389] This also applies to the alternative jurisdiction based on the new Art. 185a (2) PILA CH–that is, where a foreign arbitral tribunal directly seeks court assistance at the place where the evidence will be taken. If the relevant state court considers itself competent, it will examine the evidence request more specifically.

In this second step, the court will consider whether the evidence request complies with the procedural rules determined by the parties.[1390] For instance, if the parties have agreed to settle their dispute based on documentary evidence only, a request to examine a witness should be denied in order to respect the parties' choice.[1391] Likewise, faced with a request involving a foreign type of evidence, the respective judge cannot deviate from this, as long as it is compatible with Swiss law.[1392] Consequently, if the examination of a witness has been requested, a state court cannot order the witness to make a written statement only.[1393] The same applies to a witness examination under oath: the state court cannot skip administration of the oath on the grounds that it already considers the witness's testimony to be credible.[1394] Finally, the taking of evidence itself is a separate process from the assessment of evidence.

1387 *See* p. 143 *supra*.

1388 Art. 59 CCP CH; ZK-OETIKER, Art. 184 PILA CH n. 71; SCHNEIDER, 60.

1389 Art. 3 CCP CH; ZK-OETIKER, Art. 184 PILA CH n. 70; BERGER/KELLERHALS, n. 1365: *see* e.g. for the Canton of Basle (§ 93 (1) (4) Court Organisation Act BS; Cantonal Supreme Court), Berne (Art. 8 (1) Introductory Act BE; District Court), Geneva (Art. 86 (1) Judiciary Organisation Act GE; District Court) and Zurich (§ 32 Court and Authorities Organisation Act ZH; District Court).

1390 Art. 182 PILA CH; Arroyo-VEIT, Art. 184 PILA CH n. 76; WALTER et al., 165.

1391 *See* e.g. the standard Swiss Rules arbitration clause.

1392 CR-BUCHER, Art. 184 PILA CH n. 15; *see also* the new possibility to consider foreign forms of evidence (Art. 184 (3) PILA CH); p. 242 *supra*.

1393 Art. 190 (2) CCP CH; GÖKSU, n. 339.

1394 SCHNEIDER, 60, 65; WALTER et al., 168.

State courts therefore should not examine the admissibility, relevance, materiality and weight of evidence, which falls within the exclusive competence of the arbitral tribunal.[1395]

B. Principle of Subsidiarity

As a basic principle of civil procedure, court assistance will be granted only if the party that submits the request has a legitimate interest.[1396] Thus, in addition to considering jurisdictional matters and the taking of evidence itself, the respective state court must examine whether court assistance is indeed 'necessary'.[1397] Although the mere fact that an arbitral tribunal (or a party with the arbitral tribunal's consent) has requested court assistance in the taking of evidence seems to indicate that assistance is indeed necessary, the respective state court must nonetheless examine this requirement. It seems clear that state courts cannot be approached merely because the arbitral tribunal considers that the taking of evidence would be inconvenient and burdensome for it.[1398]

By contrast, it remains doubtful whether court assistance in the taking of evidence will be considered 'necessary' if the arbitral tribunal could take the evidence itself, but only with disproportionately high effort. On the one hand, there is no similar provision to S. 44 (5) EAA 1996, describing scenarios in which the arbitral tribunal 'has no power or is unable for the time being to act effectively'.[1399] On the other hand, no statute or case law expressly mentions an 'exhaustion requirement', such as that set out in *Malev Hungarian Airlines*.[1400] In some situations where a witness or expert witness is located in a foreign jurisdiction, it may seem unlikely from the outset that this person will testify. In order to be certain, the arbitral tribunal must at least attempt to summon the witness. In Swiss legal doctrine, this issue is not undisputed. WALTER et al. and GÖKSU argue that as long as it is 'legally' possible to take evidence, the arbitral tribunal cannot resort to state courts for assistance.[1401]

1395 Art. 9 (1) IBA Rules; Arroyo-VEIT, Art. 184 PILA CH n. 71; GÖKSU, n. 337; VITTOZ, 921 et seq.; WALTER et al., 166; *see also* p. 107 *supra*.

1396 Art. 59 (2) (a) CCP CH.

1397 'If the assistance of state judiciary authorities is *necessary* for the taking of evidence ...' (emphasis added) (Art. 184 (2) PILA CH).

1398 GÖKSU, n. 298.

1399 *See* p. 178 et seq. *supra*.

1400 *Malev Hungarian Airlines*, 964 F.2d 97, 100 (2d Cir. 1992).

1401 WALTER et al., 161. They are arguing nonetheless for a 'reasonable interpretation', admitting that seeking court assistance is already justified if the arbitral tribunal 'might fail' to take the evidence; *see also* GÖKSU, 298 et seq.

Consequently, if there is a way for the arbitral tribunal to obtain the evidence itself, court assistance must be denied. By contrast, the majority of authors take the view that significant hurdles in the taking of evidence will justify a request for the assistance of state courts.[1402] This view deserves approval, for the following reasons.

Put simply, the overall aim of Art. 184 (2) PILA CH is to assist in the taking of evidence in arbitration.[1403] This has been reinforced by the new Art. 185a PILA CH, which aims to assist even foreign arbitral tribunals in this regard. Therefore, one may conclude that the threshold for such assistance should not be set too high. In particular, as already seen under US law, there is no strict 'exhaustion requirement'; it is merely at the discretion of the respective state court to grant or deny assistance.[1404] However, this does not preclude the respective state court from examining whether the arbitral tribunal could not otherwise gather the evidence in question. This applies in particular prior to constitution of the arbitral tribunal, when the emergency arbitrator may be unable to provide sufficient support in gathering evidence.[1405] In addition, in order to prove that court assistance in the taking of evidence is in fact necessary, the request should include an explanation of why the assistance is sought and what the arbitral tribunal has already done in an attempt to gather it.[1406] In doing so, court assistance under Art. 184 (2) PILA CH is limited to cases in which this is indeed necessary.

C. Examination of the Arbitration Agreement

Since Art. 184 (2) PILA CH serves only to assist in the taking of evidence in arbitration, one might ask whether the state courts must examine the validity of the arbitration agreement. In this regard, WALTER et al. suggest that the arbitration agreement should be examined in order to avoid inadvertently supporting an 'unlawful arbitral proceeding'.[1407] This should take place through a summary examination, irrespective how hard or time consuming

1402 BSK-SCHNEIDER/SCHERER, Art. 184 PILA CH n. 57; Arroyo-VEIT, Art. 184 PILA CH n. 72; VITTOZ, 922; SCHNEIDER, 53, 56; RÜEDE/HADENFELDT, 265.

1403 *See also* the state court's assistance regarding interim measures (Art. 183 (2) PILA CH) and other assistance (Art. 185 PILA CH).

1404 *Malev Hungarian Airlines*, 964 F.3d 97, 100 (2d Cir. 1992).

1405 *See* e.g. Art. 29 ICC Rules; Art. 43 Swiss Rules; Rule 30 SIAC Rules.

1406 *See also* the suggestion for Swiss domestic arbitration of DIKE-BRUNNER/STEININGER, Art. 375 CCP CH n. 7.

1407 WALTER et al., 165.

this might be.[1408] By contrast, the prevailing view in Swiss legal doctrine is that when assisting in arbitration in accordance with Art. 184 (2) PILA CH, the state court should not examine the arbitration agreement.[1409] Art. 179 (3) PILA CH provides that a state court presented with a request to appoint an arbitrator must proceed as requested, 'unless a summary examination shows that no arbitration agreement exists between the parties'.[1410]

The prevailing opinion deserves thus approval. As regards proceedings in which the *juge d'appui* comes into play, Art. 179 (3) PILA CH is the only provision that expressly states that the arbitration agreement can be examined on a prima facie basis. As under German, French and English law, this provision emphasises the so-called 'competence-competence' principle, according to which the arbitral tribunal shall itself decide on its jurisdiction.[1411] Since the respective *juge d'appui* examines the arbitration agreement on a purely prima facie basis–that is, without expressing any opinion on the validity or consequence of the arbitration agreement–Art. 179 (3) PILA CH serves to prevent a party from engaging in arbitration only if there is not even the slightest suggestion of the existence of an arbitration agreement.[1412] Consequently, if the Swiss legislature had wanted to equip the *juge d'appui* with the same powers as regards court assistance in the taking of evidence (Art. 184 (2) PILA CH), it would have done so expressly.

Finally, one cannot speak of 'unlawful arbitral proceedings' if court assistance has been requested with the consent of the arbitral tribunal and there has been no plea of lack of jurisdiction.[1413] The situation is different regarding § 1782, which arguably may not apply to international arbitration at all.[1414] Special scrutiny will therefore be paid to the second *Intel* factor, taking into account the nature of the foreign tribunal as a first-instance decision maker whose decisions are subject to review.[1415]

1408 *Ibid.*

1409 BERGER/KELLERHALS, n. 1365; Arroyo-VEIT, Art. 184 PILA CH n. 71; ZK-Oetiker, Art. 184 PILA CH n. 71; BSK-SCHNEIDER/SCHERER, Art. 184 PILA CH n. 62; CR-BUCHER, Art. 184 PILA CH n. 13; GIRSBERGER/VOSER, n. 1045; GÖKSU, n. 336; RÜEDE/HADENFELDT, 266; BUCHER, n. 217; SCHNEIDER, 59.

1410 Art. 173 (3) PILA CH; BERGER/KELLERHALS, n. 1365; ZK-OETIKER, Art. 186 PILA CH n. 116 et seq.

1411 Art. 186 (1) PILA CH; ZK-OETIKER, Art. 179 PILA CH n. 71; for the German, French and English approach *see also* p. 145 et seq., 162 et seq. *and* 179 et seq. *supra*.

1412 DFT 118 Ia 20, cons. 5b; ZK-OETIKER, Art. 179 PILA CH n. 71.

1413 Art. 184 (2) and 186 (2) PILA CH; SCHNEIDER, 59; *contra* WALTER et al., 165.

1414 *See* p. 209 *supra*.

1415 *See* p. 196 *supra*.

In sum, a state court whose assistance is sought under Art. 184 (2) PILA CH should not examine the arbitration agreement. This examination forms part of a separate procedure, in which a party can raise a plea of lack of jurisdiction prior to any defence on the merits.[1416] A detailed examination can also be conducted at the recognition and enforcement stage.[1417]

D. Decision on Costs

According to the CCP CH, procedural costs include the court costs and the parties' costs.[1418] Court costs include the expenses of taking evidence; while the parties' costs cover legal representation.[1419] Procedural costs are determined by the cantons, which set the tariffs.[1420] As a general rule, the court will decide on the procedural costs in the final decision; the costs are normally charged to the unsuccessful party. However, the CCP CH remains silent on the issue of the costs of court assistance in the taking of evidence, where neither party is successful or unsuccessful.

It therefore seems appropriate that the Swiss courts will charge the requesting party with the costs of taking evidence. This will either be the arbitral tribunal itself or a party to the arbitration. In the former case, the arbitral tribunal will pay the costs and can allocate them accordingly in the arbitral proceedings.[1421] In the latter case, the parties will most likely be charged with the costs subject to the definitive decision of the costs by the arbitral tribunal.[1422]

The PILA CH includes no provisions on an advance on costs, as in domestic arbitration pursuant to Art. 378 CCP CH. Nevertheless, the arbitral tribunal commonly orders an advance on the presumed costs of the arbitration and, for instance, assistance proceedings before state courts.[1423] Even in the absence of any institutional arbitration rule in this respect,[1424] the arbitral tribunal has the authority to order an advance on costs based on its right to

1416 Art. 186 (2) PILA CH; ZK-OETIKER, Art. 186 PILA CH n. 55 et seqq.; BSK-SCHOTT/COURVOISIER, Art. 186 PILA CH n. 88 et seqq.

1417 *See* p. 276 et seq. *infra*.

1418 Art. 95 (1) CCP CH.

1419 Arts. 95 (2) (c) and (3) (b) CCP CH.

1420 Art. 96 CCP CH.

1421 BSK-MABILLARD, Art. 185 PILA CH n. 18; GÖKSU, n. 325; BSK-HABEGGER, Art. 375 CCP CH n. 81; BK-BOOG/STARK-TRABER, Art. 375 CCP CH n. 133.

1422 BSK-HABEGGER, Art. 375 CCP CH n. 81 with reference to an unpublished decision of the District Court of Zurich, FR160295-L/U of 27. May 2016.

1423 BERGER/KELLERHALS, 1564; BSK-HABEGGER, Art. 378 CCP CH n. 2.

1424 *See* e.g. Art. 43 UNCITRAL Rules; Art. 41 Swiss Rules; Art. 37 ICC Rules.

determine the arbitral procedure (Art. 182 (2) PILA CH), or more generally from the legal relationship between the parties and the arbitral tribunal.[1425] If the advance is not paid, it may be appropriate to suspend the proceedings and, upon informing the parties of the consequences of non-payment, order their termination.[1426]

§ 7 Appellate Remedies, Recognition and Enforcement

A. Introduction

With regard to whether the parties to arbitration and third parties can appeal a decision to grant or deny a request pursuant to Art. 184 (2) PILA CH, a clear distinction must be drawn between the state court proceeding according to Art. 184 (2) PILA (i.e. the taking of evidence itself) and the challenge to the arbitral award. First off, the issue should be treated by examining the appellate remedies against a state court order. Both the parties and concerned third parties (and even the arbitral tribunal itself) may have an interest in directly appealing this order. This might happen if a third party invokes a privilege and the respective state court either allows or denies it.

Second, one might ask whether the parties could also challenge a state court order indirectly by challenging the arbitral award–for instance, based on alleged violation of procedural rules during court assistance in the taking of evidence.[1427] Finally, it remains to be seen whether this can be addressed during the recognition and enforcement stage.

B. Challenge of the Decision of the *Juge d'Appui*

In both Swiss domestic and international arbitration, it remains questionable whether decisions concerning court assistance in the taking of evidence may be appealed.[1428] This question has been answered differently in different countries. Although the CCP DE provides that a remedy cannot be sought

1425 BERGER/KELLERHALS, n. 1565.

1426 *See* e.g. Art. 43 (4) UNCITRAL Rules; BERGER/KELLERHALS, 1569 et seqq.

1427 Regarding the situation where parties claim a violation of the right to be heard because the arbitral tribunal has refused to seek court assistance in the taking of evidence, *see* DFT 4P.217/1992 of 15 Mar. 1993, cons. 7b, in: ASA Bull. 1993, 408.

1428 For an overview regarding the situation in Swiss domestic arbitration, *see* BK-PFISTERER, Art. 356 CCP CH n. 19 et seqq.

against an order pursuant to § 1050 CCP DE, this nevertheless appears to be possible if a request is denied.[1429] The same applies under French law: depending on the proceeding and the point at which an evidence request is granted, remedies are possible either against a decision denying an evidence request only or against a decision granting or denying such request.[1430] By comparison, according to S. 44 EAA 1996, the leave of the court is required to appeal any order under S. 44 and (most certainly) S. 43 EAA 1996. This provision, which is unique in international arbitration, aims to ensure a high degree of finality and sets strict boundaries to any intervention by state courts.[1431]

Under Swiss law, however, it is doubtful whether possible appellate remedies may be sought. Although it has been shown that a state court whose assistance is sought under Art. 184 (2) PILA CH will proceed according to the CCP CH, the CCP CH does not apply with regard to appellate procedures. This is because the decision to grant or deny court assistance in the taking of evidence is rendered by a sole (cantonal) instance, by either a district court (first instance) or a cantonal supreme court (second instance).[1432] As a result, its decision is not subject to review by a higher cantonal instance. However, one might ask whether the parties can appeal to the SFT under the Federal Supreme Court Act (FSCA CH).[1433] In such case the objection would have to be filed within 30 days of notification of the state court's decision.[1434] Subject to a different ruling of the instructing judge, an objection in civil matters has no suspensive effect.[1435] Moreover, as there is no specific statutory basis for this, the minimum threshold of CHF 30,000 as the value in dispute does not apply to arbitration; otherwise, the parties could be deprived of their right to challenge an arbitral award in cases where this threshold is not reached.[1436]

1429 *See* p. 146 et seqq. *supra*.

1430 *See* p. 163 et seq. *supra*.

1431 *See* p. 180 et seq. *supra*.

1432 Art. 356 (2) (c) CCP CH; FCDisp CCP CH (2006), 7377; BSK-WEBER/STECHER, Art. 356 CCP CH n. 13; GÖKSU, n. 306; CR-BUCHER, Art. 184 PILA CH n. 14; BERGER/KELLERHALS, n. 1363; Arroyo-VEIT, Art. 184 PILA CH n. 73; *see* e.g. for the Canton of Basle (§ 93 (1) (4) Court Organisation Act BS; Cantonal Supreme Court), Berne (Art. 8 (1) Introductory Act BE; District Court), Geneva (Art. 86 (1) Judiciary Organisation Act GE; District Court) and Zurich (§ 32 Court and Authorities Organisation Act ZH; District Court).

1433 GÖKSU, n. 316.

1434 Art. 100 (1) FSCA CH; for the formal requirements *see* Art. 42 FSCA CH; KAUFMANN-KOHLER/RIGOZZI, n. 8.35.

1435 Art. 103 (1) and (3) FSCA CH; but *see* as regards third parties p. 260 *infra*; BRACHER, n. 529.

1436 Left open by the SFT in DFT 142 III 521, cons. 2.3.5; DFT 4A_576/2012 of 28 Feb. 2013, cons. 2; DFT 4A_110/2012 of 9 Oct. 2012, cons. 1; but *see* the new Art. 77(1) FSCA CH; FCDisp PILA CH Revision (2018), 7204; ZK-OETIKER, Art. 190 PILA CH n. 10; CR-BUCHER, Art. 191 PILA CH n. 17; KAUFMANN-KOHLER/RIGOZZI, n. 8.44.

As far as can be seen, however, this question has not been answered clearly in Swiss statutory law, in case law or in legal doctrine.[1437] Although the *juge d'appui* can support the arbitral proceedings in various ways, only Art. 180 (3) PILA CH refers to the finality of a decision to challenge an arbitrator. Accordingly, the *juge d'appui* can make a final decision as long as the parties have not made provisions for this challenge procedure.[1438] The SFT has reasoned that the finality of this provision can be explained by the fact that the Swiss legislature limited the possibility to make such a challenge, to ensure the effectiveness of arbitration.[1439] Similarly, regarding the appointment of an arbitrator, the SFT held that if a state court refuses to appoint an arbitrator, the parties can object directly to the SFT, because the decision is final and *de facto* makes arbitration impossible.[1440] However, if an arbitrator has been appointed, no objection is possible. The SFT justified this by stating that there is limited opportunity to appeal in arbitration, to ensure its independence and effectiveness.[1441] Rather, the parties can challenge the arbitrator's jurisdiction in the subsequent arbitration.

Apart from that, no provision of the PILA CH provides further guidance about a possible appeal. However, since Art. 184 (2) PILA CH states that the state court shall 'apply its own law'–that is, the CCP CH–the respective provisions of the CCP CH regarding domestic arbitration can (largely) be applied by analogy.[1442]

As regards the taking of evidence, an unpublished decision of the SFT in Swiss domestic arbitration provides some insight on the finality of state court decisions.[1443] In this case, a party to the arbitration requested the production of certain documents held by a third party, the Federal Roads Office. The

1437 But *see* MARKUS, 504 et seqq; DIKE-STACHER, Art. 356 CCP CH n. 14; BSK-PFISTERER, Art. 356 CCP CH n. 21.

1438 DFT 138 III 270, cons. 2.2.1.

1439 *Ibid.*; DFT 128 III 330, cons. 2.2; MARKUS, 514. However, in cases of a violation of equal treatment or the right to be heard as well as if there is a denial of access to justice, OETIKER suggests allowing an objection in civil matters to the SFT (Arts. 72 et seqq. FSCA CH; ZK-OETIKER, Art. 180 PILA CH n. 41; *see* also BERGER/KELLERHALS, n. 915; BSK-PETER/BRUNNER, Art. 180 PILA CH n. 35; GIRSBERGER/VOSER, n. 775).

1440 DFT 4A_215/2008 of 23 Sept. 2008, cons. 1.1; DFT 121 I 81, cons. 1; DFT 118 Ia 20, cons. 2; *see also* for domestic arbitration DFT 141 III 444, cons. 2.3; HURNI, 299 et seqq.

1441 DFT 115 II 294, cons. 2 et seq.; *contra* MARKUS, 506 et seqq.; for domestic arbitration, *see also* DFT 142 III 230, cons. 1.4.4. This decision states that an objection against the appointment of an arbitrator by a state court is possible only where a state court decides at the same time about the appointment of the arbitrator and the request to challenge it (with reference to DFT 5P.362/2005 of 19 May 2006, cons. 1).

1442 This is expressly stated in Art. 179 (2) PILA CH.

1443 DFT 4A_214/2012 of 10 Jan. 2013; ASA Bull. 2017, 616 et seq.

Federal Roads Office refused the request, based on professional confidentiality; so the arbitral tribunal requested court assistance in the taking of evidence. The Cantonal Supreme Court of Ticino granted the arbitral tribunal's request and ordered the production of the documents. After the Federal Roads Office appealed, the SFT stated that since the Cantonal Supreme Court of Ticino has decided as the sole instance, its decision was final and binding, and an objection in civil matters to the SFT thus was not possible. In its very short reasoning, the SFT did not elaborate further on why it refused the objection; however, this may be because the Federal Roads Office is only part of a federal department, with no independent right to object.[1444] In any case, this decision has various implications–first and foremost for third parties, but also for the parties to arbitration.

1. Third Parties

Unsurprisingly, the decision was criticised soon after it was rendered.[1445] In particular, its critics pointed out that it deprived third parties of the right to object based only on the fact that the request arose from arbitral proceedings and not state court proceedings. In contrast, the following discussion will show that in theory, there is nothing to prevent a third party from resorting directly to the SFT by means of an objection in civil matters against a state court order forcing it to assist an arbitral tribunal in the taking of evidence.[1446]

a. Legitimate Interest

First, the third party must show that it is particularly affected by the state court order and that there is a legitimate interest to amend or quash it. As previously discussed (*see* p. 250 *supra*), Art. 167 (3) CCP CH provides for the possibility to challenge a court order forcing a third party to cooperate in the taking of evidence by way of objection. This immediate objection is justified by the fact that the sanctions provided in Art. 167 (1) CCP CH to force a third party to reveal evidence are a strong intrusion into its legal status.[1447] This is even more so the case since the third party *per se* does not participate in the ongoing proceedings between the parties to the arbitration, and an objection in civil matters is its only possibility to object. In order to avoid any delay to

1444 Art. 76 (2) FSCA CH *e contrario*; DFT 142 II 324, cons. 1.3.1.

1445 BEYELER, note on DFT 4A_214/2012 of 10 Jan. 2013; GÖKSU, note on DFT 4A_214/2012 of 10 Jan. 2013, 376.

1446 Arts. 72 FSCA CH et seqq.

1447 BK-RÜETSCHI, Art. 167 CCP CH n. 20.

the proceedings, a third party can object only to the sanctions imposed on it and not merely to an order to assist in the taking of evidence without the threat of sanctions pursuant to Art. 167 (1) CCP CH.[1448]

As previously discussed, an objection in civil matters has no suspensive effect, unless the instructing judge rules otherwise.[1449] In this particular context, it seems that such suspensive effect should be affirmed; otherwise, the third party's right to refuse to cooperate would be undermined.[1450]

More generally, the legitimate interest to object also follows from Art. 29a Const. CH, according to which every person has the right to have their case determined by a judicial authority, subject only to certain exceptions set out in federal or cantonal law. As discussed below, there seems to be no exception regarding third parties. Thus, if the conditions for making an objection in civil matters to the SFT are met, the possibility to object should also be allowed, against the background of the right of access to justice.[1451] If the parties to the arbitration have expressly excluded any intervention by state courts, this can nonetheless be ignored, since third parties are not bound by any agreement between the parties.

b. Objection Against an Interim Decision

Second, an objection in civil matters is possible only against certain kinds of decisions. As regards arbitral proceedings, this objection can usually be made only directly against the arbitral award, based on the very limited grounds set out in Arts. 190-192 PILA CH.[1452] Since a state court decision on assistance in the taking of evidence is not an arbitral award, it cannot be challenged based on Art. 77 (1) (a) FSCA CH. Thus, the question arises as to whether this could be qualified as a final or interim decision. The distinction is important, since interim decisions are usually challenged only along with the final decision.[1453] According to the SFT's broad interpretation of final decisions, it is sufficient that a proceeding has come to an end in a purely formal way, irrespective if this has happened for procedural or material reasons.[1454] One might think that this might apply to the situation in question, where assistance is sought in

1448 *Ibid.*, 21; BRACHER, n. 468.

1449 *See* p. 257 *supra;* Art. 103 (1) and (3) FSCA CH; BRACHER, n. 529.

1450 *Ibid.*

1451 GÖKSU, note on DFT 4A_214/2012 of 10 Jan. 2013, 376.

1452 Art. 77 (1) (a) FSCA CH.

1453 BSK-UHLMANN, Art. 90 FSCA CH n. 1.

1454 DFT 141 III 395, cons. 2.2; DFT 133 III 629, cons. 2.2.

a separate (state court) proceeding.[1455] However, because court assistance in the taking of evidence is merely one procedural stage of the arbitration, the state court decision may be qualified as an interim decision.[1456] Accordingly, such decisions can be challenged only along with the final decision, except where the interim decision has been independently notified.[1457] If so, it can be challenged if, for instance, 'it threatens to cause irreparable harm'.[1458] This would be the case, for example, if someone were ordered to reveal documents which are protected by professional confidentiality.[1459]

c. Requirement of the Lower Court

Third, a closer look at the cantonal instance that assisted in the taking of evidence (i.e. the lower court) is required. According to Art. 75 (2) FSCA CH, an objection in civil matters is possible only against decisions of higher cantonal courts, which decide as appeal authorities, except in cases where a federal act appoints a single cantonal instance (lit. a). As a consequence, it remains questionable whether decisions of lower cantonal courts can also be challenged before the SFT when those courts act as the sole cantonal instance.[1460] Indeed, in most of Switzerland's 26 cantons, cantonal law appoints lower cantonal courts to act as the sole instance to assist in the taking of evidence.[1461] In DFT 141 III 444, this question was answered in the affirmative.[1462] Therefore, at least with regard to a third party's right to object, one may conclude that this should also apply to court assistance in the taking of evidence in international arbitration which is ordered by a sole lower cantonal court.[1463] This is even more so the case because the intention behind Art. 75 (2) FSCA CH could not have been to allow objections to be made to the SFT only within the ten cantons in which higher cantonal courts assist in the taking of evidence.[1464]

1455 BSK-KLETT/LEEMANN, Art. 77 FSCA CH n. 1c; *contra* MARKUS, 517.

1456 DFT 5A_171/2009 of 15 Oct. 2009, cons. 1.5; BRACHER, n. 526; BSK-KLETT/LEEMANN, Art. 77 FSCA CH n. 1c.

1457 Art. 93 (1) FSCA CH.

1458 Art. 93 (1) (a) FSCA CH.

1459 DFT 4A_64/2011 of 1 Sept. 2011, cons. 3.1; DFT 129 II 183, cons. 3.2.2.

1460 DFT 141 III 444, cons. 2.2.5.

1461 DFT 141 III 444, cons. 2.2.4.1.

1462 *Ibid.*, cons. 2.3.

1463 GÖKSU, note on DFT 4A_214/2012 of 10 Jan. 2013, 376.

1464 For an overview of the competent authorities *see* BSK-WEBER-STECHER, Art. 356 CCP CH n. 21; *see also* the database of Swiss localities and courts. In this respect, it is noteworthy that the vast majority only appoints the competent court to assist in the taking of evidence within domestic arbitration. Against this background, there is no distinction made between domestic and international arbitration (GÖKSU, n. 306).

d. Result

To sum up, there is no reason why third parties faced with an order to assist in arbitral proceedings cannot make an objection in civil matters to the SFT.[1465] If there is a legitimate reason and a threat of irreparable harm can be shown, an objection can be initiated even if the order was rendered by a (sole) lower cantonal instance. However, in light of the previous discussion, it remains highly doubtful whether this would also be the case in international arbitration.[1466] Thus far, the question has not been confirmed in either domestic arbitration or international arbitration. There are good reasons to believe that the SFT's decision will have little influence in practice, as it is unpublished (i.e. it is not considered a decision of 'fundamental importance').[1467] It is therefore hoped that the SFT will change its mind and allow objections in civil matters in this context. In this regard, a glimmer of hope may be seen in a recent decision of the District Court of Zurich, in which explicit reference was made to the possibility to make an objection in civil matters to the SFT.[1468] However, it is still doubtful whether the SFT would consider such objections admissible.

2. Parties

The situation is different as regards the parties to the arbitration and whether they can object to a state court order. They might seek to do so if the respective state court refuses to take evidence because privilege applies or if there was a violation of the agreed procedural rules during the taking of evidence (e.g. if a state court allowed cross-examination where this was excluded by the parties).

As previously discussed (*see* p. 261 *supra*), the fact that court assistance might be granted by a lower cantonal court (Art. 75 (2) FSCA CH) is not problematic. One might therefore ask whether the foregoing discussion in relation to third parties may also apply to the parties themselves. In this regard, the case law of the SFT and other conditions, such as the existence of a legitimate interest and the conditions to object to interim decisions, are of particular interest.

a. Case Law of the SFT

First, it is worth examining whether the case law of the SFT provides further guidance. In this regard, the aforementioned decision of the SFT regarding

1465 *Contra* BSK-KLETT/LEEMANN, Art. 77 FSCA CH n. 1b.

1466 DFT 4A_214/2012 of 10 Jan. 2013.

1467 The fact that the decision is formulated in the form of 'that'-sentences (*Dass-Entscheid*) strenghtens this assumption; Art. 58 (1) Federal Supreme Court Regulations.

1468 Unpublished decision of the District Court of Zurich, FR160295-L/U of 27. May 2016, cited in BSK-HABEGGER, Art. 375 PILA CH n. 76a.

the Canton of Ticino states only that it is final and that an objection to the SFT is therefore excluded.[1469] Unfortunately, the SFT has not further examined the party's authorisation to appeal.[1470] With regard to the appointment and challenge of arbitrators, it has further been shown that the SFT usually allows an objection only if the state court has refused the respective request.[1471] Otherwise, this would undermine the parties' original choice to settle their dispute through arbitration rather than through state court litigation.

At this point, one might ask whether the case law regarding the appointment and challenge of arbitrators could be applied to court assistance in the taking of evidence. This seems to be questionable at best. The SFT allows objections to be made only in circumstances where the parties would otherwise have been forced to settle their dispute through state court litigation. In contrast, the taking of evidence is a procedural part of arbitration; if a state court refuses to assist, the arbitration continues and the arbitral tribunal can nonetheless render an arbitral award. As this is an interim result, the case law of the SFT would suggest that the parties cannot challenge a decision of the *juge d'appui* regarding the taking of evidence.[1472]

b. Legitimate Interest

Second, the question arises as to whether the parties even have a legitimate interest (Art. 76 (1) FSCA CH) in directly objecting to the state court's decision. According to Art. 76 (1) (b) FSCA CH, a party must show that it is particularly affected by a decision and that there is a legitimate interest to amend or quash it. In this regard, it is obvious that the parties cannot have a legitimate interest if court assistance in the taking of evidence is granted as requested.

Admittedly, a party seeking to challenge a state court decision to deny assistance in the taking of evidence may be particularly affected because, for instance, that evidence may be crucial to substantiate its claims in the arbitration. As a result, this party would be disproportionately affected by the refusal.[1473] However, the crux concerns whether this constitutes a legitimate interest.

There are two conceivable situations in which there is a legitimate interest to amend or quash a state court decision to deny court assistance in the taking of evidence: where the arbitral tribunal either gives its consent to the

1469 DFT 4A_214/2012 of 10 Jan. 2013.

1470 *See also* THORENS-ALADJEM, 536.

1471 *See* p. 258 *supra*.

1472 *See also* BSK-KLETT/LEEMANN, Art. 77 FSCA CH n. 1c *in fine* as regards Swiss domestic arbitration.

1473 BSK-KLETT, Art. 76 FSCA CH n. 4a.

objection or denies it without a valid reason. In the former case, one must bear in mind that the arbitral tribunal is in charge of the arbitral proceedings in general and the taking of evidence in particular. This is evident from the fact that the arbitral tribunal's prior consent must be obtained in order to seek court assistance in the taking of evidence.[1474] The arbitral tribunal has full discretion to assess the importance of a piece of evidence. As a consequence, a party that wishes to challenge a state court decision regarding the taking of evidence must obtain the arbitral tribunal's consent before doing so. Otherwise, there is no legitimate interest to object. In most cases, due to procedural economy and because the arbitral tribunal can render an arbitral award without the evidence in question, the request to object will be denied. However, if the evidence is crucial to the case at hand, the arbitral tribunal may allow an objection to be made against the state court's refusal to grant assistance in the taking of evidence. In this way, the overall intention of the SFT to limit the possibility to appeal in (domestic and international) arbitration and the principle of procedural economy may be sustained.[1475]

With regard to an unjustified denial of consent to object against a state court decision, the case law of the SFT merits a closer look. According to the PILA CH, the grounds to challenge an arbitral award are very limited (e.g. a violation of equal treatment or the right to be heard).[1476] The SFT has held that the right to be heard will be violated if, for instance, the arbitral tribunal denies a request to seek court assistance without a valid reason–for example, where the evidence in question is relevant to the outcome of the case.[1477] As a result, this could be applied by analogy to the question of whether parties can challenge a state court decision denying court assistance in the taking of evidence. Consequently, the SFT should allow parties to object where the importance of the evidence justifies this course of action and the arbitral tribunal's denial of consent to object is unjustified. This is also appropriate in the interests of procedural economy. It would thus seem better to try to gather crucial evidence in the arbitral proceedings themselves, rather than by subsequently challenging the arbitral award based on a violation of the right to be heard because the arbitral tribunal refused to gather that evidence itself.[1478]

1474 Art. 184 (2) PILA CH; *see also* p. 233 *supra*.

1475 DFT 142 III 230, cons. 1.4.2.

1476 Art. 190 (2) (d) PILA CH.

1477 DFT 4P.217/1992 of 15 Mar. 1993, cons. 7b, in: ASA Bull. 1993, 408.

1478 *See* p. 270 et seqq. *infra*.

c. Objection Against an Interim Decision

Third, reference may be made to what has previously been discussed with regard to third parties (*see* p. 260 et seq. *supra*). Accordingly, one must demonstrate the existence of a threat of irreparable harm in order to object against an interim decision (Art. 93 (1) (a) FSCA CH). Apart from this, the possibility for a party to object against an interim decision ordering a third party to produce evidence has thus far been discussed only in state court proceedings. While under Art. 167 (3) CCP CH the right of third parties to object is expressly stated, nothing is said about the parties to the arbitration. BRACHER, RÜETSCHI and HASENBÖHLER therefore argue that in general, the parties do not have an independent right to appeal a state court order on third-party cooperation in the taking of evidence.[1479] As an exception, an objection may be possible if there is a threat of irreparable harm.[1480] This might apply, for instance, where the court refuses to examine a terminally ill witness because of alleged privilege or where a decisive piece of evidence might be lost or destroyed.[1481] There is no reason why this practice could not also be applied to an objection in civil matters before the SFT in arbitration.

d. Result

By analysing the case law of the SFT regarding other proceedings in which the decision of the *juge d'appui* can be challenged, the foregoing examination has shown that there seem to be no similarities that would justify this possibility in the case of court assistance in the taking of evidence. With regard to the legitimate interest to object, the parties either need the consent of the arbitral tribunal or must show that such consent was refused without a valid reason. Finally, in exceptional cases, an objection in civil matters may be initiated by showing a threat of irreparable harm if the objection were denied.

All told, it may be concluded that the SFT will usually have plausible reasons to reject an objection in civil matters against a state court decision on the taking of evidence. However, this is not always the case. Accordingly, since the SFT seems to be rather strict in this respect, the respective party–with the consent of the arbitral tribunal–must sufficiently substantiate why it considers such an objection appropriate.

1479 BRACHER, n. 469; BK-RÜETSCHI, Art. 167 CCP CH n. 22; Sutter-Somm et al.-HASENBÖHLER, Art. 167 CCP CH n. 33.

1480 For state court proceedings *see* Art. 319 (b) (2.) CCP CH.

1481 DFT 4P.335/2006 of 27 Feb. 2007, cons. 1.2.4; FCDisp CCP CH (2006), 7377; BK-RÜETSCHI, Art. 167 CCP CH n. 22.

C. Challenge of the Arbitral Award

The parties may also consider challenging a court order on assistance in the taking of evidence indirectly, by challenging the arbitral award. This might be based on the fact that either the arbitral tribunal refused to allow such assistance to be sought or that the procedural rules agreed by the parties were violated during this process. Such matters may be categorised as either unequal treatment or violation of the right to be heard, which is a central pillar of international arbitration.[1482] The following thus examines how parties can challenge this assessment by challenging the arbitral award.

In general, violations of due process must be addressed immediately–if possible, during the arbitral proceedings.[1483] It would be against good faith to challenge a violation of procedural rules only in the proceeding to set aside an arbitral award if this had been possible at an earlier stage.[1484] In particular, as regards an alleged violation of the right to be heard, it is considered abusive to invoke this only where the party is about to lose the case.[1485] For instance, the SFT rejected a party's claim that the right to be heard had been violated based on the fact that it had been unable to cross-examine a key witness.[1486] The SFT stated that the claim had not been brought up during the arbitral proceedings and the party had not tried to seek court assistance.[1487] In the ongoing revision of the PILA CH's 12th chapter, 'immediate recourse' is recognised in a new proposed para. 4 to Art. 182. Accordingly, a party which continues the arbitral proceedings without claiming a recognised violation of the procedural rules cannot invoke that violation at a later date–for example, by trying to set aside the arbitral award.[1488]

1. Conditions According to the FSCA CH

To promote the efficiency and effectiveness of arbitration in Switzerland, the Swiss legislature significantly limited the grounds for appeal.[1489] Only arbitral

1482 DFT 4A_214/2013 of 5 Aug. 2013, cons. 4.1; DFT 4A_538/2012 of 17 Jan. 2013, cons. 5.1; BERGER/KELLERHALS, n. 1356.

1483 Arroyo-ARROYO, Art. 190 PILA CH n. 75; KAUFMANN-KOHLER/RIGOZZI, n. 8.170.

1484 DFT 135 III 334, cons. 2.2; DFT 119 II 386, cons. 1a; CR-BUCHER, Art. 182 PILA CH n. 40; BSK-SCHNEIDER/SCHERER, Art. 182 PILA CH n. 70.

1485 DFT 4A_438/2018 of 17 Jan. 2019, cons. 4.3; DFT 143 III 578, cons. 3.1.2; DFT 136 III 605, cons. 3.2.2.

1486 DFT 4A_12/2017 of 19 Sept. 2019, cons. 4.2.2 (= DFT 143 III 578).

1487 *Ibid.*

1488 FCDisp PILA CH Revision (2018), 7197; *see also* Art. 373 (6) CCP CH.

1489 ZK-OETIKER, Art. 190 PILA CH n. 1; BSK-PFISTERER, Art. 190 PILA CH n. 2a; KAUFMANN-KOHLER/RIGOZZI, n. 8.01.

awards rendered by an arbitral tribunal seated in Switzerland may be challenged according to Art. 190 PILA CH.[1490] In general, the arbitral award is final upon notification and enjoys full legal force, and there is no need for a separate enforcement procedure.[1491] Accordingly, court intervention by the SFT is kept to an absolute minimum and the opportunity to examine the facts of the respective case is strictly curtailed.[1492] In addition, the parties cannot claim a direct violation of the Const. CH, the ECHR or other international treaties, but may refer only to the grounds set out in Art. 190 (2) PILA.[1493] Consequently, instead of the content of the arbitral award, the examination focuses on how it was rendered.[1494] Thus, the parties may not resort to the SFT on the grounds of a violation of the right to be heard in a bid to have the content of the arbitral award re-examined.[1495]

An objection in civil matters to the SFT must be filed within 30 days of notification of the arbitral award.[1496] In the absence of any clear statutory basis, there is no minimum threshold for the value in dispute; otherwise, the parties would be deprived of their right to challenge an arbitral award in arbitrations involving small claims.[1497]

The restrictive approach to appeal is evident in the SFT's status as the sole appellate court and the limited grounds on which the arbitral award can be challenged, as foreseen in the PILA CH.[1498] In this respect, Arts. 190 (2) (d and e) PILA CH deserve a closer look:

"(2) The award may only be challenged:

(d) if the principle of equal treatment of the parties or the right of the parties to be heard was violated;

(e) if the award is incompatible with public policy."

1490 BERGER/KELLERHALS, n. 1674; GÖKSU, n. 1983; regarding the types of decisions (final-, partial- and interim decisions) *see* ZK-OETIKER, Art. 190 PILA CH n. 20 et seqq.; Arroyo-ARROYO, Art. 190 PILA CH n. 234 et seqq.; BSK-PFISTERER, Art. 190 PILA CH n. 21.

1491 Art. 190 (1) PILA CH; Arts. III and V (1) (e) NYC: BSK-PFISTERER, Art. 190 PILA CH n. 7 et seqq.; ZK-OETIKER, Art. 190 PILA CH n. 5 and 10 et seqq.; GÖKSU, n. 1979.

1492 Art. 99 (1) FSCA CH; Arroyo-ARROYO, Art. 190 PILA CH n. 4.

1493 DFT 4A_178/2014 of 11 Jun. 2014, cons. 2.4; DFT 4A_198/2012 of 14 Dec. 2012, cons. 3.1.

1494 KAUFMANN-KOHLER/RIGOZZI, n. 8.01.

1495 DFT 4A_520/2015 of 16 Dec. 2015, cons. 3.3.1; DFT 142 III 360, cons. 4.1.2.

1496 Art. 100 (1) FSCA CH; KAUFMANN-KOHLER/RIGOZZI, n. 8.35 et seqq.

1497 Art. 174 and 190 PILA CH *e contrario*; ZK-OETIKER, Art. 190 PILA CH n. 10; CR-BUCHER, Art. 191 PILA CH n. 17; left open by the SFT in DFT 142 III 521, cons. 2.3.5; DFT 4A_576/2012 of 28 Feb. 2013, cons. 2; DFT 4A_110/2012 of 9 Oct. 2012, cons. 1.

1498 Art. 191 PILA CH.

Lit. d represents the counterpart to what has already been discussed concerning the discretion of the parties and the arbitral tribunal to tailor the arbitral proceedings.[1499] As a consequence, regardless of what procedure is chosen, the arbitral tribunal must ensure equal treatment and the right to be heard; it follows that these two procedural guarantees may be subject to examination in an appeal. Thus, a party seeking to challenge an arbitral award must show that a violation of the right to be heard or equal treatment influenced the award.[1500]

According to recently published data, international arbitral awards rendered in Switzerland were set aside in only approximately 7-10% of cases in 2016 and 2017.[1501] Concerning the grounds listed in Arts. 190 (2) (d and e) PILA CH, only 5.5% (twelve out of 208 arbitral awards) of all challenges claiming a violation of equal treatment or the right to be heard were upheld.[1502] As regards an alleged violation of the *ordre public*, only two out of 194 arbitral awards were set aside–representing a mere 1% chance of success.[1503]

2. Equal Treatment of the Parties

The right to equal treatment requires that parties be treated equally in comparable situations–that is, in respect of all procedural matters, such as the examination of witnesses and the parties' submissions.[1504] Accordingly, the arbitral proceedings must be tailored in such a way that each party has the same opportunity to participate and present its case.[1505] Therefore, the arbitral tribunal cannot deny to one party what has been granted to the other and vice versa.[1506]

The right to equal treatment is largely considered to be congruent with the right to be heard.[1507] However, it can still be invoked separately–for

1499 *See* p. 235 *supra;* Art. 182 (3) PILA CH; ZK-OETIKER, Art. 190 PILA CH n. 81; KAUFMANN-KOHLER/RIGOZZI, n. 8.167.

1500 DFT 142 III 360, cons. 4.1.1.

1501 DASSER/WÓJTOWICZ, 280; these numbers apply to decisions on the merits of non-sports-realted arbitration (2017: setting aside of 23 out of 321 cases (7.37%), 2016: setting aside of 10 out of 103 cases (9.71%).

1502 *Ibid.*, 281.

1503 *Ibid.*

1504 ZK-OETIKER, Art. 182 PILA CH n. 35; Arroyo-ARROYO, Art. 190 PILA CH n. 83.

1505 DFT 4A_424/2011 of 2 Nov. 2011, cons. 2.2.

1506 DFT 4A_236/2017 of 24 Nov. 2017, cons. 4.1; DUTOIT, Art. 182 PILA CH n. 6; BSK-SCHNEIDER/SCHERER, Art. 182 PILA CH n. 65; Arroyo-ARROYO, Art. 190 PILA CH n. 84.

1507 DFT 4A_672/2012 of 23 Apr. 2013, cons. 4.1.1; DFT 4P.208/2004 of 14 Dec. 2004, cons. 5.1; DFT 133 III 139, cons. 6.1; Arroyo-ARROYO, Art. 190 PILA CH n. 86.

instance, alongside claims regarding the assessment of evidence by the arbitral tribunal, which would fall under the right to be heard.[1508] This follows from the fact that the duty to treat the parties equally begins with the constitution of the arbitral tribunal and ends with the conclusion of the arbitral proceedings. However, it excludes the subsequent consultation process, during which the arbitral tribunal renders its verdict.[1509] Accordingly, the assessment of evidence or the application of law cannot be challenged under the title of equal treatment, even where this is obviously untenable.[1510]

As a consequence, the same action of an arbitral tribunal can lead to a violation of both the right to be heard and equal treatment. This might apply where the arbitral tribunal grants one party consent to seek court assistance in the taking of evidence while denying the same to the adverse party without a valid reason. The following discussion will show that, with regard to the assessment of evidence, it is difficult to prove a violation of the right to be heard. However, if a party can show that the arbitral tribunal treated the parties unequally in comparable situations, the SFT might set aside the arbitral award based on Art. 190 (2) (d) PILA CH.[1511]

Nonetheless, it is important to note that the right of equal treatment is not absolute–a certain degree of inequality must be accepted.[1512] Consequently, the parties have no right to expect the extension of identical timeframes to both parties, for example.[1513] Likewise, the SFT has stated that the parties cannot expect to have exactly the same amount of time to examine witnesses at the hearing.[1514] Finally, the SFT has made it clear that non-consideration of a rule or a crucial allegation of fact does not constitute unequal treatment.[1515] Rather, by drafting Art. 190 (2) (d) PILA CH narrowly, the Swiss legislature avoided the scope for objections against arbitrary conduct.[1516]

1508 DFT 4A_672/2012 of 23 Apr. 2013, cons. 4.1.2; DFT 4A_360/2011 of 31 Jan. 2012, cons. 4.1.

1509 *Ibid.*

1510 *Ibid.*

1511 DFT 4A_672/2012 of 23. Apr. 2013, cons. 4.2.1.

1512 ZK-OETIKER, Art. 182 PILA CH n. 35; CR-BUCHER, Art. 182 PILA CH n. 51; KAUFMANN-KOHLER/RIGOZZI, n. 8.173.

1513 DFT 4A_450/2017 of 12 Mar. 2018, cons. 3.2.1; DFT 4A_405/2016 of 2 Mar. 2017, cons. 3.3; DFT 4A_539/2008 of 19 Feb. 2008, cons. 4; BSK-SCHNEIDER/SCHERER, Art. 182 PILA CH n 66; DUTOIT, Art. 182 PILA CH n. 6; Arroyo-ARROYO, Art. 190 PILA CH n. 88 et seqq.

1514 In DFT 4A_407/2012 of 20 Feb. 2013, cons. 3.4., the SFT stated that equal treatment is not violated even if one party had 14 hours to examine their witnesses while the adverse party had 23 hours.

1515 DFT 4A_236/2017 of 24 Nov. 2017, cons. 4.2.2; DFT 4A_360/2011 of 31 Jan. 2012, cons. 4.1.

1516 *Ibid.*

3. Right to be heard

Looking at the second part of Art. 190 (2) (d) PILA CH, a few comparative remarks are necessary in order to assess the Swiss approach to setting aside arbitral awards based on a violation of the right to be heard. With regard to evidence, the tension between the parties' right to present evidence on the one hand and the free assessment of evidence by the arbitral tribunal on the other must be considered when examining whether the right to be heard has been violated.

a. Comparative Aspects

The comparative analysis in the previous chapter has shown that although the grounds to challenge an arbitral award may vary under the examined *leges arbitri*, the basic approach always aims to limit this possibility. For instance, under German and English law, the arbitral award may be challenged if the arbitral tribunal failed to conduct the proceedings in accordance with the procedure agreed by the parties and this had an influence on the arbitral award.[1517] In this regard, S. 68 (1) EAA 1996 is illustrative: it refers to the possibility to challenge an arbitral award, but only if there is a serious irregularity which affected the arbitral tribunal, the proceedings or the award. While it may be easy to prove an irregularity, it will be much more difficult to show that this was 'serious' and also to demonstrate its influence.[1518] Similarly, the UNCITRAL ML states that an arbitral award may be set aside if the arbitral proceedings were not in accordance with the agreement of the parties or if the arbitral award conflicts with public policy (i.e. the *ordre public*).[1519] Finally, under French and US law, the parties can challenge the arbitral award on the grounds that the arbitral tribunal violated the right to be heard or exceeded its powers.[1520] The rationale behind this common approach is that the arbitral tribunal acts not as a mere first instance, but rather as the sole instance; the grounds for challenging the arbitral award are thus restricted.[1521]

As a consequence, although these *leges arbitri* may vary in their scope and in the grounds on which an arbitral award may be set aside, the aim in all cases is to examine procedural aspects such as the invalidity of the arbitration

1517 § 1059 (2) (1.) (d) CCP DE; S. 68 (1) (c) EAA 1996. Regarding recognition and enforcement of arbitral awards *see* Art. V (1) (d) NYC.

1518 MERKIN/FLANNERY, 305.

1519 Arts. 34 (2) (a) (iv) and (2) (b) (i) UNCITRAL ML.

1520 Arts. 1520 (3) and (4) CCP FR; § 10 (a) (4) FAA USA.

1521 UNCITRAL, Case Law (2012), Art. 34 UNCITRAL ML, n. 3 with reference to OLG Karlsruhe, 14 Sept. 2007, 10 Sch 01/07, cons. 2a.

agreement or the composition of the arbitral tribunal, rather than reviewing the merits of the dispute.[1522] As regards court assistance in the taking of evidence, the respective appellate court should not examine whether and how the arbitral tribunal assessed the evidence or applied the correct law.[1523]

b. Free Assessment of Evidence

As previously discussed *(see* p. 266 *supra)*, the possibility to set aside an arbitral award is similarly restrictive in Switzerland–in some ways, even more restrictive. For example, while German and English law and the UNCITRAL ML all allow for the arbitral award to be challenged on the grounds that the arbitral tribunal failed to conduct the arbitral proceedings according to the procedure agreed by the parties, there is no comparable provision under Swiss law.[1524] Rather, because the only procedural guarantees that bind the arbitral tribunal are equal treatment and the right to be heard, it follows that non-compliance with other procedural rules agreed by the parties (e.g. institutional arbitration rules) cannot be subject to challenge according to Art. 190 (2) (d) PILA CH.[1525] Still, one might ask whether the assessment of evidence of the arbitral tribunal may be challenged under a violation of the right to be heard.

This right is of a formal nature, so in case of a violation, the arbitral award must be set aside irrespective of why the violation arose.[1526] This is why the SFT will examine this issue first. In addition, the duty to substantiate the influence that such a violation had on the arbitral award is reduced to a certain degree. However, the party must show that the arbitral tribunal did not consider certain elements of the case at hand, certain pieces of evidence or certain legal opinions of the parties, and that this could have influenced

---

1522 Mistelis et al.-BREKOULAKIS et al., Art. 34 UNCITRAL ML, 1; MüKo-MÜNCH, § 1059 CCP DE n. 29; HARRIS et al., S. 68 EAA 1996 n. 68B.

1523 Mistelis et al.-BREKOULAKIS et al., Art. 34 UNCITRAL ML, 1; SHEPPARD, S. 68 n. 2 EAA 1996; HARRIS et al., S. 68 EAA 1996 n. 68I with reference to *World Trade Corporation v. C. Czarnikow Sugar Ltd* [2004] EWHC 2332 (Comm.) and *Schwebel v. Schwebel* [2010] EWHC 3280 (TCC).

1524 § 1059 (2) (1.) (d) CCP DE; S. 68 (1) (c) EAA 1996; Art. 34 (2) (a) (iv) and (2) (b) (i) UNCITRAL ML.

1525 DFT 117 II 346, cons. 1a; DFT 4P.23/2006 of 27 Mar. 2006, cons. 4.2; ZK-OETIKER, Art. 190 PILA CH n. 81; BSK-PFISTERER, Art. 190 PILA CH n. 61; GÖKSU, n. 2069: but *see* Art. V (1) (d) NYC.

1526 DFT 142 III 284, cons. 4.1; DFT 142 III 360, cons. 4.1.4; DFT 4A_532/2016 of 30 May 2017, cons. 4.1 with further references; ZK-OETIKER, Art. 190 PILA CH n. 87; CR-BUCHER, Art. 190 PILA CH n. 83; KAUFMANN-KOHLER/RIGOZZI, n. 8.167; BSK-PFISTERER, Art. 190 PILA CH n. 70; but *see also* the most recent case law, suggesting that if a violation of the right to be heard had no influence on the arbitral award, it does not necessarily has to be set aside (DFT 4A_424/2018 of 29 Jan. 2019, cons. 5.2.2; DFT 143 IV 380, cons. 1.4.1).

the arbitral award.[1527] In addition, with regard to court assistance in the taking of evidence, the SFT has stated that the right to be heard is violated if the arbitral tribunal refuses to seek court assistance without a valid reason where the evidence in question is crucial to the case.[1528] Otherwise, this would lead to a denial of justice.[1529] As a result, the arbitral tribunal enjoys wide discretion when it comes to the taking of evidence and the SFT will examine whether the right to be heard has been violated only under strict conditions.

c. Anticipated Assessment of Evidence

In this regard, the case law of the SFT merits closer scrutiny. It has repeatedly held that the right to be heard corresponds in large part to the constitutional right enshrined in Art. 29 (2) Const. CH. Regarding its content, reference can be made to what has previously been discussed in this regard.[1530] The right to be heard is substantiated through the right to evidence, which entitles each party to have the court accept suitable evidence that is presented to it.[1531]

In contrast to the right to evidence, the SFT has several times referred to the right of the arbitral tribunal to freely assess the evidence without violating the right to be heard or the right to evidence, respectively.[1532] In this regard, mention is made of the so-called 'anticipated assessment of evidence', which forms part of the free assessment of evidence.[1533]

According to this concept, which has been developed in Swiss case law, the arbitral tribunal is at liberty to assess the importance of evidence even before it has been taken; this might apply, for example, where a selection must be made from multiple similar pieces of evidence or where sufficient evidence has already been gathered.[1534] It therefore facilitates the efficient and expedient conduct of the proceedings.[1535] This also applies where the

1527 DFT 4A_592/2017 of 5 Dec. 2017, cons. 4.1.2 with further references.

1528 DFT 4P.217/1992 of 15 Mar. 1993, cons. 7b, in: ASA Bull. 1993, 408; *see also* DFT 142 III 360, cons. 4.1.1; DFT 133 III 235, cons. 5.2.

1529 Arroyo-ARROYO, Art. 190 PILA CH n. 119.

1530 *See* p. 106 et seqq. *supra;* DFT 142 III 360, cons. 4.1.1; ZK-OETIKER, Art. 190 PILA CH n. 86.

1531 Art. 152 CCP CH; FCDisp CCP CH (2006), 7312; DFT 4A_427/2017 of 22 Jan. 2018, cons. 5.1.1; DFT 133 III 295, cons. 7.1; DFT 114 II 289, cons. 2a.

1532 DFT 143 III 297, cons. 9.3.2.

1533 Art. 157 CCP CH; FCDisp CCP CH (2006), 7312; Arroyo-KNOLL, Art. 182 PILA CH n. 45; Arroyo-ARROYO, Art. 190 PILA CH n. 137; ZK-OETIKER, Art. 182 PILA CH n. 47 et seqq.; BERGER/KELLERHALS, n. 1357; for a critical assessment of this concept, *see* HASENBÖHLER, 5.77 et seqq.; Sutter-Somm et al.-HASENBÖHLER, Art. 157 CCP CH n. 38 et seqq.

1534 Sutter-Somm et al.-HASENBÖHLER, Art. 157 CCP CH n. 32; BK-RÜETSCHI, Art. 152 CCP CH n. 57; HASENBÖHLER, n. 5.71 et seqq.

1535 BK-RÜETSCHI, Art. 152 CCP CH n. 58.

arbitral tribunal refuses to examine evidence any further because the facts have already been established or because the evidence to be presented will not suffice to persuade it to change its findings (e.g. if the arbitral tribunal refuses to examine a witness since there is already sufficient documentary evidence).[1536] Thus, the arbitral tribunal can establish the facts based on the evidence which it considers suitable and substantial.[1537] Moreover, the SFT has stated that as long as the right to be heard is not simply ignored and a denial of justice therefore ensues, even an incorrect assessment of evidence cannot be challenged.[1538] This underlines the common approach to avoid undue court intervention in the sphere of arbitration and ensure merely that important procedural guarantees have been respected. Therefore, the SFT has stated that the anticipated assessment of evidence can be examined only from the limited angle of a violation of the *ordre public* (i.e. public policy).[1539]

As an intermediate result, it may be concluded that under the right to be heard, the SFT will allow a challenge against the arbitral award only if the arbitral tribunal refused to seek court assistance without a valid reason where the evidence in question was crucial to the case. Apart from that, there is little scope to challenge an arbitral award based on a violation of the right to be heard, because of the arbitral tribunal's broad discretion in terms of the anticipated assessment of evidence. Since this may be examined only on the grounds of a violation of the *ordre public*, the following will examine the extent to which this is in fact possible.

4. Violation of Public Policy

The statistical data shows that challenges to an arbitral award based on a violation of public policy fail in 99% of cases.[1540] Although such challenges seem to be popular, the SFT has set aside just two awards based on a violation of

1536 FCDisp CCP CH (2006), 7312; DFT 4A_427/2017 of 22 Jan. 2018, cons. 5.1.1; DFT 4A_277/2017 of 28 Aug. 2017, cons. 3.1; DFT 4A_342/2015 of 26 Apr. 2016, cons. 4.1.1; DFT 4A_246/2014 of 15 Jul. 2015, cons. 6.1; DFT 4A_386/2010 of 3 Jan. 2011, cons. 7.2; DFT 134 I 140, cons. 5.3; DFT 131 I 153, cons. 3; DFT 130 II 425, cons. 2.1 with further references; HABERBECK, 1422 et seq.

1537 DFT 4A_427/2017 of 22 Jan. 2018, cons. 5.1.1; DFT 4A_178/2014 of 11 Jun. 2014, cons. 5.1; DFT 119 II 386, cons. 1b; DFT 116 II 639, cons. 4c; HASENBÖHLER, n. 5.75.

1538 DFT 127 III 576, cons. 2e and 2f; DFT 121 III 331, cons. 3a.

1539 Art. 190 (2) (e) PILA CH; DFT 142 III 360, cons. 4.1.1; DFT 4A_544/2014 of 24 Feb. 2015, cons. 3.2.1; DFT 4A_178/2014 of 11 Jun. 2014, cons. 5.1; DFT 4P.23/2006 of 27 Mar. 2006, cons. 4.2; HABERBECK, 1423; KAUFMANN-KOHLER/RIGOZZI, n. 8.175; *contra* GÖKSU, n. 2087.

1540 DASSER/WÓJTOWICZ, 280.

public policy so far.[1541] The bar is thus set significantly high. While lit. a-d relate to procedural questions, Art. 190 (2) (e) PILA CH provides the only means to review the merits of the case.[1542] According to the SFT, the grounds listed in lit. a-d take precedence over any violation of public policy pursuant to lit. e, which therefore serves as a last resort.[1543] Public policy can be divided into substantive and procedural public policy.[1544]

With regard to the former, the SFT has adopted the following definition: 'An award is incompatible with public policy if it disregards the essential and broadly acknowledged values which, according to prevailing views in Switzerland, should constitute the basis of any legal order.'[1545] Such values include the sanctity of contracts, compliance with the rules of good faith, and the prohibition of abuse of rights and discriminatory measures.[1546] The SFT has deliberately kept open the interpretation of substantive public policy, since it considers it a delicate–even dangerous–task to create an exhaustive list.[1547] Hitherto, the SFT has set aside a single arbitral award based on a violation of substantive public policy.[1548] The case concerned the threat of a lifelong ban from football if the respective player did not pay damages arising from a breach of contract.[1549] As this would have excessively restricted the player's personal freedom, the SFT considered this *de facto* lifelong ban to be a violation of substantive public policy.[1550] In no other case has the high hurdle of a violation of substantive public policy been met. This has especially been the case regarding evidence-based matters, such as the burden and standard of proof[1551] or the (obviously erroneous) establishment of facts.[1552]

1541 *Ibid.*

1542 Arroyo-ARROYO, Art. 190 PIL A CH n. 160; BSK-PFISTERER, Art. 190 PILA CH n. 72.

1543 DFT 4A_682/2011 of 31 May 2012, cons. 4.3 with further references; ZK-OETIKER, Art. 190 PILA CH n. 93; BKS-PFISTERER, Art. 190 PILA CH n. 72.

1544 DFT 141 III 229, cons. 3.2.1; DFT 138 III 322, cons. 4.1.

1545 DFT 144 III 120, cons. 5.1; DFT 4A_312/2017 of 27 Nov. 2017, cons. 3.1; DFT 4A_304/2013 of 3 Mar. 2014, cons. 5.1.1; DFT 132 III 389, cons. 2.2.3.

1546 DFT 144 III 120, cons. 5.1; DFT 4A_532/2016 of 30 May 2017, cons. 3.1 et seqq.; DFT 4A_304/2013 of 3 Mar. 2014, cons. 5.1.1; ZK-OETIKER, Art. 190 PILA CH n. 102 et seqq.

1547 *See* e.g. DFT 4A_32/2016 of 20 Dec. 2016, cons. 4.1; ZK-OETIKER, Art. 190 PILA CH n. 103; Arroyo-ARROYO, Art. 190 PILA CH n. 173 et seqq.

1548 *Ibid.*, n. 219 et seqq.; ZK-OETIKER, Art. 190 PILA CH 109 et seq.

1549 DFT 138 III 322; *see also* DFT 4A_320/2009 of 2 Jun. 2010, cons. 4.4; DFT 4A_508/2017 of 29 Jan. 2018, cons. 4.3.

1550 *Ibid.*, cons. 4.3.5.

1551 DFT 4A_32/2016 pf 20 Dec. 2016, cons. 4.1; DFT 4A_312/2017 of 27 Nov. 2017, cons. 3.1.

1552 DFT 127 III 576, cons. 2b; DFT 121 III 331, cons. 3a.

It has also proved very difficult to prove a violation of procedural public policy. According to the SFT's case law, an arbitral award violates procedural public policy if 'it infringes fundamental and generally recognized principles of procedure, the disregard of which is intolerably contrary to the sense of justice so that the award seems to be absolutely incompatible with the legal system and values applying in a state of law'.[1553] This includes, for instance, the principles of res judicata and ne bis in indem,[1554] as well as the right to a fair proceeding[1555] and the fundamental procedural guarantees of the ECHR, but only as a means of ascertainment.[1556] The only case thus far in which the SFT has found a violation of procedural public policy was another sports-related arbitration, in which the arbitral tribunal disregarded the final and binding force (res judicata) of a previous decision.[1557] As regards the assessment of evidence, the SFT has held that since procedural public policy has a mere 'defense function', it cannot serve to establish a 'procedural arbitration code' with which the arbitral proceedings must comply.[1558] As a consequence, even the erroneous or arbitrary application of the agreed procedural rules does not serve as grounds to invoke a violation of procedural public policy.[1559]

On the whole, it is clear that although the parties can try to challenge an arbitral award based on a violation of (substantive or procedural) public policy, the SFT will almost certainly deny it. The parties will succeed only by demonstrating that either 'essential and broadly acknowledged values' or 'fundamental and generally recognized principles of procedure' have been violated.

5. Result

The previous discussion endeavoured to outline how parties can address matters regarding court assistance in the taking of evidence by trying to challenge the arbitral award. It was shown that in the case of alleged violations of both Arts. 190 (2) (d and e) PILA CH, such claims must be presented as early as possible during the arbitral proceedings. Even if a violation of equal treatment or

1553 DFT 4A_236/2017 of 24 Nov. 2017, cons. 5.1; DFT 141 III 229, cons. 3.2.1; DFT 140 III 278, cons. 3.1; DFT 136 III 345, cons. 2.1; DFT 128 III 191, cons. 4a.

1554 DFT 4A_386/2010 of 3 Jan. 2011, cons. 9.3.1.

1555 DFT 4P.143/2001 of 18 Sept. 2001, cons. 3a.aa; ZK-OETIKER, Art. 190 PILA CH n.

1556 ZK-OETIKER, Art. 190 PILA CH n. 116 et seqq.; Arroyo-ARROYO, Art. 190 PILA CH n. 173 et seqq.; BSK-PFISTERER, Art. 190 PILA CH n. 81 et seqq.; BERGER/KELLERHALS, n. 1780 et seqq.; GÖKSU, n. 2140 et seqq.

1557 DFT 136 III 345; Arroyo-ARROYO, Art. 190 PILA CH n. 167 and 209 et seqq.

1558 DFT 126 III 249, cons. 3b; Arroyo-ARROYO, Art. 190 PILA CH n. 174.

1559 DFT 4A_438/2018 of 17 Jan. 2019, cons. 5.2.2; DFT 4A_308/2018 of 23. Nov. 2018, cons. 5.3.1; DFT 4A_392/2015 of 10 Dec. 2015, cons. 4.2; DFT 129 III 445, cons. 4.2.1.

the right to be heard is invoked, the SFT requires that the violation be sufficiently severe before it will consider setting aside an award. Unlike under other *leges arbitri*, under which an arbitral award may be challenged on the grounds that the arbitral tribunal failed to conduct the proceedings in compliance with the procedure agreed by the parties, there is no comparable provision under Swiss law. However, if a party can show that a failure of the arbitral tribunal to seek court assistance in the taking of evidence resulted in a denial of justice, the arbitral award may be set aside.

In most cases, the question of how and whether to gather evidence touches on the arbitral tribunal's discretion to assess the evidence. In this regard, it has been shown that the right to be heard is not violated if the evidence is taken in accordance with the concept of the anticipated assessment of evidence. This central pillar of international arbitration will be subject to examination only if there is a violation of substantive or procedural public policy. In this regard, the SFT's case law has demonstrated a broad reluctance to find such a violation, at least thus far. It may therefore be concluded that, in the absence of a denial of justice, indirectly attacking court assistance in the taking of evidence through challenging the arbitral award will in most cases fail.

D. Recognition and Enforcement

Finally, parties might seek to challenge the arbitral award pursuant to Art. V (1) (d) NYC, which reads as follows:

> "Recognition and enforcement of the award may be refused at the request of the party against whom it is invoked, only if that party furnishes to the competent authority where the recognition and enforcement is sought, proof that:
> (d) ... the arbitral procedure was not in accordance with the agreement of the parties, or, failing such agreement, was not in accordance with the law of the country where the arbitration took place."

As is evident from the comparative analysis conducted in this book, this provision is mirrored in many *leges arbitri*.[1560] It is widely accepted that Art. V NYC always requires a certain causality–that is, that the violation of this article could have influenced the arbitral award.[1561] Otherwise, recognition and enforcement of an arbitral award would be denied too easily and a new arbitration would most likely lead to the same result.[1562]

1560 *See* p. 146 et seqq., p. 163 et seq., p. 180 et seq. *and* p. 212 et seq. *supra*.

1561 Kronke et al.-NACIMIENTO, Art. V (1) (d) NYC, 298 et seq.

1562 *Ibid*.

As an overall approach, the bar to deny recognition and enforcement under the NYC is set high and state courts enjoy wide discretion in this regard.[1563] At this point too, it must again be mentioned that in general, violations of due process must be addressed immediately (i.e. during the arbitral proceedings).[1564] They cannot be invoked afterwards if this would have been possible at an earlier stage.[1565]

Although Art. V (1) (d) NYC is designed to protect party autonomy, the state courts generally take a very pro-arbitration stance by applying this article only rarely and thus upholding the arbitral tribunal's discretion to tailor the arbitral proceedings.[1566] As a consequence, recognition and enforcement will not usually be denied where the arbitral tribunal was at liberty to govern evidentiary matters such as whether to hold an oral hearing or whether to allow a certain witness to testify.[1567]

The same applies regarding court assistance in the taking of evidence. It therefore follows that as long as the arbitral tribunal did not act directly against an explicit agreement between the parties–for instance, to allow only document production and therefore exclude witness testimony–the arbitral award will most likely be upheld under the NYC. The situation is different if the parties excluded court assistance in the taking of evidence, but the arbitral tribunal nonetheless allowed this or sought such assistance itself. Although unheard-of in practice, this should constitute a reason to deny recognition and enforcement pursuant to the NYC.

E. Summary

The foregoing examination aimed to provide an overview of possible appellate remedies, either directly against the decision of the *juge d'appui* or indirectly against the arbitral award. In the former case, the topic was considered from the perspective of third parties as well as the parties to the arbitration. With regard to the former, it was demonstrated that despite the recent SFT decision, they can still meet the requirements to make an objection in civil matters to the SFT.

1563 Balthasar-SOLOMON, n. 173; PAULSSON M., 158; Mistelis et al.-MISTELIS/DI PIETRO, Art. V NYC 24.

1564 *See* p. 266 *supra*.

1565 *See* e.g. DFT 4A_124/2010 of 4 Oct. 2010, cons. 6.3.3.1; OLG München, 15 Mar. 2006, 34 Sch06/05; UNCITRAL NYC Guide, Art. V (1) (d) n. 51 et seqq.

1566 PAULSSON M., 191 et seq.; Kronke et al.-NACIMIENTO, Art. V (1) (d) NYC, 282 et seq.

1567 *See* e.g. OLG Köln, 6 Jul. 2012, 19 Sch 8/11, n. 41; *Stati v. Republic of Kazakhstan*, 302 F. Supp. 3d 187, 207 (D.C.C. 2018).

This stands in stark contrast to the position of the parties to the arbitration. Unfortunately, decisions in other cases in which the *juge d'appui* comes into play cannot be applied by analogy to court assistance in the taking of evidence in arbitration. In addition, with regard to the existence of a legitimate interest, the previous discussion demonstrated that this can be demonstrated only if the arbitral tribunal gives its consent to the objection or denies its consent without a valid reason. Special attention should be paid to this condition if there is crucial evidence to be gathered with the assistance of state courts. Often, however, the arbitral tribunal will find a way to avoid seeking court assistance–for example, by drawing an adverse inference.[1568] Finally, since the decision of the *juge d'appui* is an interim decision, it can be challenged only if the party can prove the existence of a threat of irreparable harm, which is rarely the case.

It was further examined whether matters relating to court assistance in the taking of evidence can be addressed by trying to set aside the arbitral award according to Arts. 190 (2) (d and e) PILA CH. Besides the fact that alleged violations of procedural rules and/or due process, as well as public policy, must be invoked immediately during the arbitral proceedings, it is also very difficult to set aside an arbitral award based on the PILA CH. Unlike other *leges arbitri*, under which parties can seek to have an arbitral award set aside if the procedural rules on which they agreed were not complied with, Swiss law does not include a comparable provision. Thus, the SFT's case law shows that in the absence of a denial of justice, arbitral tribunals enjoy wide discretion in conducting the arbitral proceedings, especially with regard to the assessment of evidence, and an arbitral award will not be set aside merely because this assessment was incorrect. This is especially true with regard to an alleged violation of public policy, which is very hard to prove and has been upheld only twice thus far.

The outcome as regards the NYC has been similar. Although recognition and enforcement can be denied based on the fact that the arbitral proceedings were not in accordance with the agreement of the parties, state courts will tend to uphold the arbitral award as far as possible, except where there has been a clear violation of the arbitration agreement.

1568 *See* p. 56 et seqq. *supra*.

§ 8 Conclusion

From the foregoing analysis of the Swiss status quo, it is clear that the *lex arbitri* lays the foundations for effective and efficient domestic and international arbitration in Switzerland. In particular, the PILA CH–with its few and concise articles–provides a framework conducive to arbitration; as a result of the proposed revisions to this statute, the popularity of Switzerland as a forum for arbitration is expected to increase even further. This is evident from the following five factors.

First, as regards court assistance in the taking of evidence, under the new Art. 185a (2) PILA CH, assistance will also be granted directly to foreign arbitral tribunals. Although this is theoretically possible under Art. 3 PILA CH (emergency jurisdiction), it does not seem to have occurred with regard to court assistance in the taking of evidence. While it is too early to assess the importance and consequences of this amendment, it aligns Swiss law with the German, French and English *leges arbitri*, as previously discussed.[1569] While in all three of these jurisdictions court assistance can be granted directly to foreign arbitral tribunals, the French approach is by far the most liberal, imposing almost no requirements for the provision of court assistance other than the 'internationality' of the respective dispute.[1570] The stance taken under Swiss law does not go so far; but–quite similar to that under German and English law–it specifically provides for foreign arbitral tribunals to obtain direct assistance in the taking of evidence. It remains to be seen whether this will result in an increase in the number of evidence requests submitted to Swiss courts and thus whether a centralised *juge d'appui*, as suggested during the revision of the PILA CH, may become necessary. Finally, the debate on the applicability of § 1782 under US law continues–although it seems that by applying the *Intel* factors, a possible misuse of § 1782 can be significantly minimised.[1571]

Second, the prior consent of the arbitral tribunal to seek the assistance of state courts comes as no surprise and the PILA CH's revision has brought no changes in this regard. Thus, as under German and French law, the arbitral tribunal has full control and decides whether the assistance of state courts is in fact necessary. It follows that the arbitral tribunal can either seek assistance itself, be persuaded by one or both of the parties to do so or refuse to follow this path. In contrast, under the EAA 1996, if both parties agree to

1569 *See* p. 135, p. 154 *and* p. 169 *supra.*

1570 *See* p. 154 *supra.*

1571 *See* p. 185 et seqq. *supra.*

seek court assistance in the taking of evidence, the consent of the arbitral tribunal is irrelevant. The situation under US law is even more complicated: in addition to the arbitral tribunal, 'any interested person' can seek court assistance. Understandably, this has caused several authors to suggest that the third *Intel* factor–that is, the receptivity of the respective arbitral tribunal–should always be taken into consideration.[1572]

Furthermore, the possibility to exclude Art. 184 (2) PILA CH has been discussed. In this regard, a distinction must be made between arbitration that has been chosen voluntarily and that which has been imposed on a party, such as sports-related arbitration. In the latter case, special attention must be paid to the degree to which the respective arbitral tribunal can guarantee a similar level of legal protection to state courts.

Third, under the CCP CH, a broad range of evidence may be sought from the Swiss courts. Since Art. 11a PILA CH allows foreign types of evidence to be taken into consideration, a third para. will be added to Art. 184 PILA CH, expressly stating that the arbitral tribunal can consider 'different' (i.e. foreign) procedural types of evidence. Compared to the other examined *leges arbitri*, under which evidence must generally be taken in accordance with the respective civil procedural rules, the Swiss approach is very liberal. The US approach alone is similar, taking into consideration the 'practice and procedure, which may be in whole or part the practice and procedure of the foreign country or the international tribunal'.[1573] Although it is hard to predict how far the Swiss courts will go in this regard, one may conclude with certainty that, for instance, requests for US-style pre-trial discovery will be denied.

With regard to the target of evidence, a distinction between the parties to arbitration and third parties must be drawn here too. While a party's failure to produce evidence without a valid reason will be considered when assessing the evidence, this does not apply to third parties. Although third parties can be forced to give evidence, possible rights to refuse to do so based on the CCP CH must be respected. In comparison with the other examined *leges arbitri*, these rights seem to be rather comprehensive under Swiss law.

Fourth, as became apparent in the sixth chapter of this book, state courts are generally not forced to assist arbitral tribunals under either constitutional or international public law. Nonetheless, the Swiss courts will not only exercise their own discretion, but also consider any agreement between the parties in this regard (e.g. to allow document production only). With regard to the principle of subsidiarity and the examination of the arbitration

1572 *See* p. 203 et seq. *supra*.

1573 *See* § 1782 (a) (3rd. para.).

agreement, it has been shown that the Swiss approach is in line with German, France, English and US law. Therefore, there is no strict exhaustion principle, allowing state courts to assist only if the respective arbitral tribunal has absolutely no possibility to take the respective evidence itself. The same applies to the examination of the arbitration agreement, which should take place in a separate proceeding and not under Art. 184 PILA CH.

Finally, in the last part of this chapter, the possibility to appeal directly against the decision of the *juge d'appui* was analysed from the perspective of both the parties to the arbitration and third parties. Third parties should have the right to object to a decision of the *juge d'appui* if they can show a threat of irreparable harm. By contrast, the parties to the arbitration can do so only if the arbitral tribunal gives its consent to object (as under English law), or if it denies such consent without a valid reason.

Furthermore, as regards the challenge of the arbitral award based on a violation of procedural rules during court assistance in the taking of evidence, the parties could claim a violation of either the right to be heard or public policy. In the former case, a party would have to show that the arbitral tribunal refused to seek court assistance without a valid reason even though the evidence was crucial to the dispute. By contrast, in the latter case, violations of public policy–although frequently claimed–have so far been admitted by the SFT in just two cases. Finally, the NYC imposes strict standards to deny recognition and enforcement of an arbitral award. Accordingly, unless the arbitral tribunal acted against an explicit agreement between the parties, the arbitral award will most likely be upheld. To sum up, as confirmed under the other *leges arbitri*, it is very difficult to have an arbitral award set aside based on what happened (or did not happen) during court assistance in the taking of evidence.

These five factors demonstrate that the Swiss approach to court assistance in the taking of evidence is becoming increasingly arbitration friendly. First and foremost, this is evident in the amendments to the PILA CH to assist foreign arbitral tribunals directly and to consider foreign types of evidence. As compared to the other *leges arbitri* analysed in this book, the openness towards foreign types of evidence in particular is remarkable; it remains to be seen whether the assistance of Swiss courts will be sought more frequently as a result.

Concluding Remarks

§ 1 Introduction

As stated in the introductory remarks, this book aims to provide a comprehensive analysis of court assistance in the taking of evidence, focusing on whether, when and how this can take place.[1574] It began with a discussion of the taking of evidence in international arbitration in general, before taking a closer look at the powers of the arbitral tribunal in this regard. Because these powers are limited in various ways, the focus then shifted to the main topic, examining it first from the perspective of constitutional and international public law. In a second step, the different approaches taken in the *leges arbitri* of various countries were scrutinised, in order to assist in assessing the current situation in Switzerland. The most important findings and possible future developments are summarised below.

§ 2 Results

A. Complex Legal Framework

Although the legal cultures of common and civil law increasingly tend to overlap, a few crucial distinctions may still be observed. While civil procedure in common law systems is far more party led and thus accusatorial in nature, its counterpart in civil law systems is largely inquisitorial (i.e. judge-led).[1575] In terms of the taking of evidence, the issue becomes more complex in international arbitration, where parties from different legal cultures meet and try to strike a balance through the respective *leges arbitri*, the arbitration agreement and arbitration rules.

Most *leges arbitri* provide only a general procedural framework and evidence is only briefly mentioned.[1576] Thus, another option is to agree on evidentiary issues in the arbitration agreement–either directly or, as in most

1574 *See* p. 3 *supra*.

1575 *See* p. 10 et seqq. *supra*.

1576 *See* p. 17 et seqq. *supra*.

cases, by reference to a set of ad hoc or institutional arbitration rules.[1577] To some extent, institutional arbitration rules reflect the conventions of the legal culture within which they have been developed–for example, by appointing the arbitral tribunal as an active case manager and therefore reflecting an inquisitorial civil law approach.[1578] In this regard, the IBA Rules elegantly combine common and civil law elements in order to provide a fair process for the taking of evidence in international arbitration.[1579] The parties therefore enjoy unique freedom in tailoring the arbitral proceedings to their respective needs.

B. Sanctions Available to the Arbitral Tribunal

When recalcitrant parties prove unwilling to produce evidence, the arbitral tribunal is not completely helpless and has the power to impose certain sanctions. In international arbitration, adverse inference is the most effective sanction in this regard. In drawing an adverse inference where a party refuses to produce a certain piece of evidence without sufficient reason, the arbitral tribunal will consider the relevant fact as proven despite the absence of the evidence. Although some institutional rules and the IBA Rules empower arbitral tribunals to draw an adverse inference, they do not provide them with guidelines on how to do so.[1580] In this regard, the conditions of the Iran-United States Claims Tribunal can provide further guidance.[1581] However, an adverse inference is not an automatic result where a party fails to produce evidence; it rather lies within the discretion of the arbitral tribunal to decide whether to draw an adverse inference.[1582] As a result, the parties have no right to an adverse inference and the arbitral tribunal's failure to do so will not result in a violation of the right to be heard.

In addition to this main sanction, several institutional arbitration rules as well as the IBA Rules provide that the parties' conduct during the arbitral proceedings can be considered in allocating the costs.[1583] Instead of merely letting the costs follow the event, the winning party may be sanctioned too if, for example, it unnecessarily delayed or manipulated the arbitral proceed-

1577 *See* p. 23 et seqq. *and* p. 26 et seqq. *supra.*

1578 *See* p. 46 et seq. *supra.*

1579 *See* p. 31 et seqq. *supra.*

1580 *See* p. 58 et seqq. *supra.*

1581 *See* p. 60 et seqq. *supra.*

1582 *See* p. 63 et seq. *supra.*

1583 *See* p. 66 et seqq. *supra.*

ings. The possibility to punish party representatives was also discussed. Although this topic has gained some attention in recent years, mainly as a result of the IBA and LCIA Guidelines from 2013 and 2014 respectively, the international arbitration community has rejected this idea almost unanimously, due to the potential risk to the arbitral tribunal's impartiality.[1584] Thus, sanctioning party representatives should rather be left to national bar councils or even a global arbitration ethics council, as suggested by the ASA.[1585]

Finally, the French concept of *astreintes* was considered. Although French arbitral tribunals are competent to impose such penalties, this is not the case in Switzerland, under either statute law or the implicit consent theory.[1586] However, the situation is different if the parties have explicitly empowered the arbitral tribunal to impose such a monetary penalty.

C. Limited Power of the Arbitral Tribunal

Despite the arbitral tribunal's powers to sanction non-compliant parties, there are several limits when it comes to the taking of evidence. First, arbitral tribunals must be constituted before they can act and thus are not always 'on duty'.[1587] Emergency arbitrators–which are now available under the rules of almost all arbitration institutions–help to bridge this jurisdictional gap, so this limitation is increasingly becoming a minor issue.[1588] Second, private arbitral tribunals obviously lack coercive power–that is, they cannot enforce their orders and awards, so compliance depends exclusively on the willingness of the parties to the arbitration.[1589] Third, the most significant limitation as regards the taking of evidence is the arbitral tribunal's lack of power over third parties.[1590] While the arbitral tribunal can impose sanctions on the parties to the arbitration, this does not apply to third parties which are not participants in the arbitral proceedings. If evidence is in the possession of third parties that do not voluntarily hand it over, the only way to obtain such evidence is to resort to state courts–the main topic of this book.

1584 *See* p. 68 et seqq. *supra*.

1585 *See* p. 73 *supra*.

1586 *See* p. 74 et seqq. *supra*.

1587 *See* p. 79 et seqq. *supra*.

1588 *See* p. 80 *supra*.

1589 *See* p. 81 et seq. *supra*.

1590 *See* p. 82 et seq. *supra*.

D. Court Assistance versus Court Intervention

While state courts can provide a wide range of assistance, the main focus for the purposes of this book is on interim measures granting temporary protection of the parties' rights from possible damage during the arbitration and measures for the taking of evidence that help to establish the facts of the case.[1591] Although court assistance in the taking of evidence is provided for in the IBA Rules, among others, the question arises as to whether court assistance is in the interests of the parties to the arbitration, given that they have specifically chosen arbitration instead of state court litigation.[1592] In this regard, it has been shown that in most cases, resorting to state courts does not circumvent the arbitration agreement, but rather strengthens it. If the parties have not explicitly excluded court assistance, seeking such assistance is in the interest of the smooth functioning of the arbitral proceedings.[1593] This especially applies where non-compliant parties are not acting in good faith. If drawing an adverse inference is insufficient, court assistance actually helps to reinforce the role of the arbitral tribunal as the authority in charge of the arbitral proceedings.[1594] Furthermore, since state courts usually require the respective arbitral tribunal's consent before taking action, this should not be regarded as a disturbing intervention in the arbitration, but rather as helpful assistance that equips the arbitral tribunal with more information to render a fairer, more considered verdict.[1595]

E. (No) Obligation to Assist in the Taking of Evidence

In a further step, the question of whether state courts are obliged to grant assistance based on Swiss constitutional or international public law was considered.[1596] Although Switzerland is one of the most arbitration-friendly countries in the world, no such obligation may be derived from either the Swiss Constitution or the case law of the SFT.[1597] This was confirmed by an analysis of international public law, which revealed that no obligation to provide court assistance may be derived from the ECHR, the NYC, the HEC or

1591 *See* p. 85 et seqq. *supra*.

1592 *See* p. 91 et seqq. *supra*.

1593 *See* p. 100 *supra*.

1594 *See* p. 101 *supra*.

1595 *See* p. 102 *supra*.

1596 *See* p. 103 et seqq. *supra*.

1597 *See* p. 104 et seqq. *supra*.

European law.[1598] The ECHR does not apply directly to arbitral proceedings and therefore serves only as a source of inspiration to interpret minimum procedural guarantees according to Art. 190 (2) PILA CH.[1599] In contrast, the NYC's main aim is to uphold arbitration agreements and facilitate the recognition and enforcement of arbitral awards.[1600] As a consequence, it says very little about the arbitral proceedings themselves. The same applies to European law, under which court assistance is foreseen, but nothing more is said, especially as regards any obligation to provide assistance.[1601]

It has been suggested that the HEC could also be applied to arbitral proceedings.[1602] However, according to the prevailing view in legal doctrine, this convention does not apply directly to arbitral proceedings, but only indirectly (i.e. via state courts). Nevertheless, as previously discussed, the HEC could contribute significantly to the effectiveness of international arbitration. Still, this could be done only by amending the HEC as a whole or on a purely national level by amending the respective reservations of Member States.[1603] It remains to be seen whether they will choose to do so in the near future. The same also applies to the EER on a purely European level.[1604]

F. Inconsistency Among Different Leges Arbitri

Since there is no obligation to assist arbitral tribunals in the taking of evidence, each country deals differently with the issue. To assist in assessing the Swiss status quo, the *leges arbitri* of four jurisdictions were analysed; the findings are discussed below.

1. Germany: Rising Popularity

Although Germany is not yet among the leading forums for international arbitration, its importance cannot be underestimated.[1605] In order to facilitate international arbitration, the German courts can be approached directly in order to obtain court assistance in the taking of evidence. This simple procedure could even induce parties to comply voluntarily with evidentiary

1598 *See* p. 109 et seqq. *supra*.

1599 *See* p. 112 et seq. *supra*.

1600 *See* p. 114 et seqq. *supra*.

1601 *See* p. 126 et seqq. *supra*.

1602 *See* p. 118 et seqq. *supra*.

1603 *See* p. 122 *supra*.

1604 *See* p. 128 et seqq. *supra*.

1605 *See* p. 134 et seqq. *supra*.

orders of the tribunal; hence, it is likely that Germany will gain in importance as a forum for arbitration. Although German law takes a liberal approach in providing access to the courts to assist in the taking of evidence, it limits this by allowing evidence to be taken only according to the CCP DE.[1606] In this regard, it is hard to predict the extent to which the German courts will nonetheless consider foreign types of evidence. Given the general pro-arbitration stance in Germany, it is at least conceivable that a request could be adapted until it is in line with the CCP DE.[1607]

2. France: Ongoing Success

Mainly due to the presence of the ICC headquarters in Paris, France enjoys a long and successful tradition as a forum for arbitration.[1608] What distinguishes French law from other *leges arbitri* is first and foremost the fact that the CCP FR applies based on economic reasons only–that is, if international trade interests are at stake.[1609] As a consequence, arbitral tribunals can resort to the French courts based solely on the fact that evidence is located in France, which makes it much easier for foreign arbitral tribunals to gather evidence. It is also noteworthy that the CCP FR expressly provides for *ex parte* applications as a measure of surprise prior to constitution of the arbitral tribunal.[1610]

However, two limitations regarding the taking of evidence are worth mentioning. First, once the arbitral tribunal has been constituted, only document production can be sought, which stands in stark contrast to the situation prior to constitution of the arbitral tribunal.[1611] Second, only evidence that accords with French law can be taken, so it does not seem possible to consider foreign types of evidence.[1612]

3. England: Keep Calm and Carry on Arbitrating in London

Recent statistics seem to indicate that England will retain its popularity as a forum for arbitration.[1613] Its stable legal framework and pro-arbitration case law should prevail even while the Brexit discussions are ongoing. Or, to put it

1606 *See* p. 140 et seqq. *supra.*

1607 *See* p. 141 et seq. *supra.*

1608 *See* p. 150 *supra.*

1609 *See* p. 154 *supra.*

1610 *See* p. 157 et seqq. *supra.*

1611 *See* p. 158 et seq. *supra.*

1612 *See* p. 159 *supra.*

1613 *See* p. 166 *supra.*

in the words of one of the members of the LCIA Board: 'Keep calm and carry on arbitrating in London!'[1614] Irrespective of the location of the arbitral tribunal's seat, the English courts will assist in the taking of evidence. With regard to securing the attendance of witnesses, it is not possible to exclude this possibility even by agreement between the parties.[1615] What is more, the EAA 1996 offers a wide range of 'powers exercisable in support of arbitral proceedings', such as witness examination, preservation of evidence and inspections.[1616] As regards foreign types of evidence, the English courts tend to take evidence based solely on their own law or even deny assistance because it would fall under the 'inappropriate rule' of S. 2 (3) EAA 1996.[1617] This broad discretion thus cannot be underestimated.

Finally, the English approach to appellate remedies against the *juge d'appui* is unique.[1618] In order to limit the role of the court and ensure a high degree of finality, leave of the court to appeal is always required, except in case of a lack of jurisdiction or denial of justice.

4. USA: Lasting Confusion

Court assistance in the taking of evidence in the US has become a major issue since the powerful discovery weapon of § 1782 became partially available in international arbitration.[1619] The 2004 *Intel* decision caused a considerable stir–not only among the international arbitration community, but also among several district and circuit courts.[1620] Because whether § 1782 can be invoked in arbitral proceedings varies from state to state, a Supreme Court decision in this regard–or even an amendment of § 1782–is long overdue.[1621] In the meantime, however, the *Intel* factors leave US courts well equipped to assess whether an arbitral tribunal should in fact be assisted.[1622] By applying these factors, the risk of a potential misuse of § 1782 can be dramatically reduced. Therefore, from the point of the practitioner, it is crucial to understand which state courts are receptive to granting § 1782 requests in aid of arbitration.

1614 LCIA's response to Brexit.

1615 *See* p. 170 *supra*.

1616 *See* p. 173 et seq. *supra*.

1617 *See* p. 175 *and* p. 177 et seqq. *supra*.

1618 *See* p. 180 et seq. *supra*.

1619 *See* p. 185 et seqq. *supra*.

1620 *See* p. 190 et seqq. *supra*.

1621 *See* p. 197 et seqq. *supra*.

1622 *See* p. 194 et seqq. *supra*.

G. Switzerland's Way Forward

Nothing suggests that the popularity of Switzerland as a forum for arbitration will wane in the near future–in fact, quite the opposite. Switzerland's neutrality and political stability, together with its pro-arbitration case law and modern legal framework, contribute to its ongoing success.[1623] More than 30 years after its enactment, the PILA CH still represents a short and concise *lex arbitri*, and the revisions to the statute are only enhancing its appeal, as is evident from the following two amendments.

First, the Swiss legislature recently decided to facilitate the taking of evidence in aid of foreign arbitration and thus aims to allow such assistance to be granted directly to foreign arbitral tribunals.[1624] Hitherto, the Swiss courts have provided assistance only to other state courts, and not directly to arbitral tribunals. This change in approach brings the Swiss *lex arbitri* into line with German, French, English and US law. Second, as a result of another amendment, Swiss courts, when assisting in arbitration, will be expressly allowed to consider foreign types of evidence, such as cross-examination.[1625] While the CCP CH already offered a broad range of evidence, the types of evidence that may be considered under the revised law are therefore even more diverse.[1626] Although it is too soon to assess the consequences of these amendments, they should certainly enhance the attractiveness of Switzerland as a forum for arbitration.

Furthermore, the appellate remedies available in Switzerland–whether directly against the decision of the *juge d'appui* or indirectly through a challenge to the arbitral award–were also subject to careful scrutiny.[1627] Regarding the former, it was demonstrated that third parties must demonstrate a threat of irreparable harm in order to appeal such a decision; while the parties to the arbitration–in order to avoid jeopardising the effectiveness of the arbitral proceedings–require the consent of the arbitral tribunal to appeal.[1628] Regarding the latter, the reluctance of the SFT to set aside arbitral awards and therefore its commitment to respecting the discretion of the arbitral tribunal were discussed. It is thus difficult to have an arbitral award set aside based on what happened during court assistance in the taking of evidence. This is

1623 *See* p. 219 et seqq. *supra*.

1624 *See* p. 227 et seq. *supra*.

1625 *See* p. 223 *and* p. 242 *supra*.

1626 *See* p. 240 et seqq. *supra*.

1627 *See* p. 256 et seqq. *supra*.

1628 *See* p. 259 et seqq. *supra*.

completely in line with the other *leges arbitri* analysed in this book, and the tendency to uphold arbitral awards represents one of the key hallmarks of arbitration.

§ 3 Outlook

From the examination of the present topic, one thing has become clear: court assistance in the taking of evidence is above all a matter of legal policy and thus varies from jurisdiction to jurisdiction. However, as the comparative section and the chapter on the Swiss status quo have shown, there seems to be a clear tendency among state courts to voluntarily assist arbitral tribunals. If this liberal approach were also adopted in other jurisdictions, this would take us significantly closer to reaching an international consensus on how court assistance in the taking of evidence should be provided. As a next step, it could even be enshrined in an international convention such as the HEC.[1629]

Until such a consensus is reached, it remains crucial that practitioners understand the different mechanisms for obtaining court assistance in the various jurisdictions in which evidence is located. One way or another, it is to be expected that court assistance in the taking of evidence will become a more important procedural issue in international arbitration. As pointed out in the introduction to this book, concern seems to be growing over the arbitral tribunal's lack of power over third parties.[1630] This book therefore aims to provide in-depth analysis of how this obstacle may be overcome. It has not only demonstrated how this works in practice in several of the most popular forums for arbitration, but also provided tactical insights which will hopefully be of great value in future arbitrations.

1629 *See* p. 118 et seqq. *supra*.

1630 *See* p. 3 *supra;* Queen Mary Survey (2018), 8.

Table of Cases

The numbers in bold letters refer to the respective page number.

I. Arbitral Tribunals

ICC

ICSID

IUSCT

II. European Court of Human Rights

III. Countries

Canada

England and Wales

Court of Appeal of England and Wales

France

Paris Court of Appeal

Courts of Cassation

Court of First Instance

Germany

Hong Kong

Singapore

Switzerland

Swiss Federal Tribunal (published decisions)

Table of Legislation

I. Conventions

ECHR – Convention for the Protection of Human Rights and Fundamental Freedoms (1950), as amended in 2013.
ECICA – European Convention on International Commercial Arbitration (1961).
European Convention on Information on Foreign Law – European Convention on Information on Foreign Law (1968).
HEC – Convention of 18 March 1970 on the Taking of Evidence Abroad in Civil or Commercial Matters (1970).
HCP – Convention of 1 March 1954 on civil procedure (1954).
ICSID Convention – Convention on the Settlement of Investment Disputes Between States and Nationals of Other States (1966), as amended on 10 April 2006.
NYC – United Nations Convention on the Recognition and Enforcement of Foreign Arbitral Awards (1958).
Panama Convention – Inter-American Convention on International commercial arbitration (1975).
Treaty of Friendship, Commerce and Navigation between USA and Germany – Treaty of Friendship, Commerce and Navigation between USA and Germany (1956).

II. European Law

EER – Council Regulation (EC) No 1206/2001 of 28 May 2001 on cooperation between the courts of the Member States in the taking of evidence in civil or commercial matters (2001).
Paris Agreement – Agreement relating to Application of the European Convention on International Commercial Arbitration (1962).

III. Countries

Austria

CCP AU – Code of Civil Procedure (1895), as amended in 2018.

Belgium

JC BE – Belgian Judicial Code (2013), as amended in 2019.

Colombia

Const. CO Constitution of Colombia (1991), as amended in 2015.

Costa Rica

Const. CR Constitution of Costa Rica (1949), as amended in 2015.

El Salvador

Const. SV Constitution of El Salvador (1983), as amended in 2014.

England, Wales and Northern Ireland

Civil Evidence Act 1995 – Civil Evidence Act (1995), as amended of 5 October 2015.

CPR 1998 The Civil Procedure Rules (1998), as amended in 2019.

CPR 1998 Practice Directions – Practice Direction to the Civil Procedure Rules (1998).

EAA 1996 English Arbitration Act (1996), as amended of 20 February 2020.

EAA 1950 English Arbitration Act (1950).

High Court and County Courts Order 1996 – The High Court and County Courts (Allocation of Arbitration Proceedings) Order (1996).

France

CCP FR Code of Civil Procedure (1973), as amended on 1 January 2019.

Const. FR (1791) Constitution of France (1791).

Germany

CCA DE Courts Constitutions Act Germany (1975), as amended on 12 December 2019.

CCP DE Code of Civil Procedure (1950), as amended on 12 December 219.

Netherlands

CCP NL Code of Civil Procedure of the Netherlands (1986), as amended on 1 January 2019.

Panama

Const. PA Constitution of Panama (1972), as amended in 2004.

Paraguay

Const. PY Constitution of Paraguay (1992), as amended in 2011.

Peru

Const. PE — Constitution of Peru (1993), as amended in 2009.

Singapore

IAA SG — International Arbitration Act (1994), as amended on 21 November 2019.

Sweden

SAA SE — Swedish Arbitration Act (1999), as amended on 1 March 2019.

Switzerland

CCP CH — Swiss Civil Procedure Code (2008), as amended on 1 January 2020, SR 272.

Const. CH — Federal Constitution of the Swiss Confederation (1999), as amended on 1 January 2020, SR 101.

Federal Supreme Court Regulations – Federal Supreme Court Regulations (2006), SR. 173.110.131, as amended on 1 February 2018.

FSCA CH — Federal Supreme Court Act (2005), as amended on 1 January 2019, SR 173.110.

Intercantonal Arbitration Convention CH — Intercantonal Arbitration Convention (1969), SR 220.300.

PILA CH — Federal Act on Private International Law (1987), as amended on 1 January 2020, SR 291.

SCC CH — Swiss Criminal Code (1937), as amended on 3 March 2020, SR 311.0.

Cantonal Legislation

Court and Authorities Organisation Act ZH – Court and Authorities Organisation Act in Civil and Criminal Procedure of the Canton of Zurich (2010), as amended on 26 February 2019.

Court Organisation Act BS – Court Organisation Act of the Canton of Basle City (2015), as amended on 23 December 2019.

Introductory Act BE – Introductory Act to Civil Procedure Code, Swiss Criminal Procedure Code and Swiss Juvenile Criminal Procedure Law of the Canton of Berne (2009), as amended on 1 June 2013.

Judiciary Organisation Act GE – Judiciary Organisation Act of the Canton of Geneva (2011), as amended on 14 May 2019.

United States of America

FAA USA — Federal Arbitration Act (1925), Title 9 USC, as amended in 2018.

FRAP USA	Federal Rules of Appellate Procedure (1967), as amended on 1 December 2019.
FRCP USA	Federal Rules of Civil Procedure (1938), as amended on 1 December 2018.
USC	The Code of Laws of the United States of America (1994), as amended in 2018.

Uruguay

Const. UY	Constitution of Uruguay (1985), as amended in 2004.

Venezuela

Const. VE	Const. of Venezuela (1999), as amended in 2009.

Legislative Materials

I. Bibliography of United Nations Documents

UNCITRAL, A/CN.9/669 (2009)
UNCITRAL, General Assembly, Report of Working Group II (Arbitration and Conciliation) on the work of its fiftieth session, A/CN.9/669, 9 March 2009.

UNCITRAL, A/CN.9/WG.II/WP.108 (2000)
UNCITRAL, General Assembly, 32nd session, Settlement of Commercial Disputes, A/CN.9/WG.II/WP.108, 14 January 2000.

UNCITRAL, A/40/17 (1985)
UNCITRAL, General Assembly, Report of the United Nations Commission on International Trade Law on the work of its eighteenth session, 3-21 June 1985, A/40/17.

UNCITRAL, Summary Records of the 325th meeting (1985)
UNCITRAL, Summary Records of the United Nations Commission on International Trade Law for meetings devoted for the preparation of the UNCITRAL Model Law on International Commercial Arbitration, 309th Meeting, Article 25; Article 26, Article 27, 17 June 1985.

UNCITRAL, Summary Records of the 309th meeting (1985)
UNCITRAL, Summary Records of the United Nations Commission on International Trade Law for meetings devoted for the preparation of the UNCITRAL Model Law on International Commercial Arbitration, 309th Meeting, Article 5; Article 6, 5 June 1985.

UNCITRAL, A/CN.9/264 (1985)
UNCITRAL, 18th session, 25 March 1985, A/CN.9/264, Analytical Commentary on Draft Text of a Model Law on International Commercial Arbitration.

UNCITRAL, A/CN.9/263 (1985)
UNCITRAL, 18th session, Vienna, 19 March 1985, A/CN.9/263, Analytical compilation of comments by Governments and international organizations on the draft text of a model law on international commercial arbitration: Report of the Secretary-General.

UNCITRAL, A/CN.9/246 (1984)
UNCITRAL, General Assembly, Report of the Working Group on International Contract Practices on the Work of its seventh session, 6 March 1984, A/CN.9/246.

UNCITRAL, A/CN.9/245 (1983)
UNCITRAL, General Assembly, Report of the Working Group on International Contract Practices on the Work of its sixth session, 22 September 1983, A/CN.9/245.

UNCITRAL, A./CN.9/WG.II/WP.44 (1983)
UNCITRAL, Working Group, 6th session, 29 August-9 September 1983.

II. Bibliography of the Hague Convention on International Private Law

HEC Questionnaire (2014)
Hague Conference on Private International Law, Synopsis of Responses to the Questionnaire of November 2013 Relating the Hague Convention of 18 March 1970 on the Taking of Evidence Abroad in Civil or Commercial Matters (Evidence Convention), Revised Version (2014).

HEC Questionnaire (2009)
Hague Conference on Private International Law, Synopsis of Responses to the Questionnaire of May 2008 Relating the Hague Convention of 18 March 1970 on the Taking of Evidence Abroad in Civil or Commercial Matters (Evidence Convention).

HEC Questionnaire (2004)
Hague Conference on Private International Law, Synopsis of the Replies to the Questionnaire Relating to the Hague Convention of 18 March 1970 on the Taking of Evidence Abroad in Civil or Commercial Matters (Prel. Doc. No 4).

HEC Recommendations (2003)
Hague Conference on Private International Law, Conclusions and Recommendations Adopted by the Special Commission on the Practical Operation of the Hague Apostille, Evidence and Service Conventions (2003).

HEC Special Commission (1985)
Hague Conference on Private International Law: Report of the Special Commission on the Operation of the Hague Convention on the Taking of Evidence Abroad in Civil or Commercial Matters (1985), 24 International Legal Materials 1668 (1985).

III. European Law

ECtHR Annual Report (2018)
ECtHR Annual Report (2018).
EER Impact Assessment (2018)
European Commission, Impact Assessment, Proposal for Regulation of the European Parliament and the Council amending Council Regulation (EC) No 1206/2001 of 28 May 2001 on cooperation between the courts of the Member States in the taking of evidence in civil or commercial matters.
EU Study (2014)
Legal Instruments and Practice of Arbitration in the EU, Directorate-General for Internal Policies (2014).
EER Study (2007)
European Commission, Study on the Application of Council Regulation (EC) No 1206/2001, on Cooperation Between the Courts o the Member States in The Taking of Evidence in Civil or Commercial Matter (2007).
EER Report (2007)
Report from the Commission to the Council, the European Parliament and the European Economic and Social Committee on the application of the Council Regulation (EC) 1206/2001 of 28 May 2001 on cooperation between the courts of the Member States in the taking of evidence in civil or commercial matters (2007).

IV. Countries

England, Wales and Northern Ireland

EAA Supplementary Report (1997)
1997 Supplementary Report on the Arbitration Act 1996, Departemental Advisory Committee on Arbitration Law, January 1997.
EAA Report (1996)
1996 Report on the Arbitration Bill, Departmental Advisory Committee on Arbitration Law, February 1996.

France

Rapport to the Premier Minister (2011)
Rapport au Premier Ministre relatif au décret 2011-48 du 13 Janvier 2011 portant réforme de l'arbitrage, in: L'arbitrage: principes et pratiques 32, Les cahiers du Conseil National des Barreaux (Conseil National des Barreaux 2011).

Germany

Parliamentary Documentation 13/5274 (1996)
Deutscher Bundestag, Drucksache 13/5274 (1996).

Switzerland

FCDisp PILA CH Revision (2018)
Federal Council Dispatch About the Amendments of the PILA CH, 12th ch.: International Arbitration, 24 October 2018, Federal Law Gazette 2018, 7163 et seqq.

Rep. Consultation Procedure PILA CH (2018)
Revision of the PILA CH (International Arbtiration), Report of the Result of the Consultation Procedure, 8 August 2018.

Int. Arbitration in CH Study (2017) Internationale Schiedsgerichtsbarkeit in der Schweiz: Eine Markt- und Regulierungskostenanalyse: Schlussbericht, School of Management and Law (2017).

Expl. Rep. Revision PILA CH (2017)
Explanatory Report of the Revision of the PILA CH (International Arbitration), 11 January 2017.

Opinions Revision PILA CH (2017) Opinions of several Swiss organizations about the Revision of the PILA CH (2017).

Guideline Judicial Assistance in Civil Matters CH (2013)
Federal Office of Justice, International Judicial Assistance in Civil Matters: Guidelines, 3rd ed., January 2013.

FCDisp CCP CH (2006)
Federal Council Dispatch about the Federal Code of Civil Procedure, 28 June 2006, Federal Law Gazette 2006, 7221 et seqq.

FCDisp HEC CH (1993)
Federal Council Dispatch about the Approval of Four Conventions in the Field of International Judicial Assistance in Civil- and Commercial Matters, 8 September 1993, Federal Law Gazette 1993 III, 1261 et seqq.

United States of America

Advisory Committee FRCP USA (1970)
Notes of Advisory Committee on Rules–1970 Amendment.

Sen. Rep. 1580, 88th Cong. 2nd Sess. (1964)
Senate Report No. 1580, 88th Congress, 2nd Session (1964).

H.R. Rep. 1052, 88th Cong. 1st Sess. (1963)
House of Representatives Report No. 1052, 88th Congress, 1st Session. (1963).

Permissions

All chapters in this book were first published in CATEIA, by Sui Generis Verlag by Lorenz Raess; hereby published with permission under the Creative Commons Attribution License or equivalent. Every chapter published in this book has been scrutinized by our experts. Their significance has been extensively debated. The topics covered herein carry significant information for a comprehensive understanding. They may even be implemented as practical applications or may be referred to as a beginning point for further studies.

We would like to thank the editorial team for lending their expertise to make the book truly unique. They have played a crucial role in the development of this book. Without their invaluable contributions this book wouldn't have been possible. They have made vital efforts to compile up to date information on the varied aspects of this subject to make this book a valuable addition to the collection of many professionals and students.

This book was conceptualized with the vision of imparting up-to-date and integrated information in this field. To ensure the same, a matchless editorial board was set up. Every individual on the board went through rigorous rounds of assessment to prove their worth. After which they invested a large part of their time researching and compiling the most relevant data for our readers.

The editorial board has been involved in producing this book since its inception. They have spent rigorous hours researching and exploring the diverse topics which have resulted in the successful publishing of this book. They have passed on their knowledge of decades through this book. To expedite this challenging task, the publisher supported the team at every step. A small team of assistant editors was also appointed to further simplify the editing procedure and attain best results for the readers.

Apart from the editorial board, the designing team has also invested a significant amount of their time in understanding the subject and creating the most relevant covers. They scrutinized every image to scout for the most suitable representation of the subject and create an appropriate cover for the book.

The publishing team has been an ardent support to the editorial, designing and production team. Their endless efforts to recruit the best for this project, has resulted in the accomplishment of this book. They are a veteran in the field of academics and their pool of knowledge is as vast as their experience in printing. Their expertise and guidance has proved useful at every step. Their uncompromising quality standards have made this book an exceptional effort. Their encouragement from time to time has been an inspiration for everyone.

The publisher and the editorial board hope that this book will prove to be a valuable piece of knowledge for students, practitioners and scholars across the globe.

Index

www.ingramcontent.com/pod-product-compliance
Lightning Source LLC
LaVergne TN
LVHW080642210926
848485LV00003B/308